Windows 95 Administration

Wave Technologies International, Inc.
MNT4-COR2-8041A
Release 2

Contents

Introduction

COURSE PURPOSE

This book is designed for network managers, network administrators, MIS, and support personnel who are planning to implement and support Windows 95. It is also targeted to any persons wanting a better understanding of Windows 95. The course covers the objectives for the Microsoft Certified Professional and Microsoft Certified Systems Engineer exams for Implementing and Supporting Microsoft Windows 95, 70-064.

During this course, you will have the opportunity to work with several phases of Windows 95 use, management, and support. You will install and configure Windows 95 to meet specified criteria based on common operational requirements. You will also support and use Windows 95 as a stand-alone system, as a member of a peer-to-peer workgroup, and as a local area network (LAN) client. Both Windows NT Server domain and Novell NetWare network client set up and management are discussed.

In addition to being exposed to the Windows 95 operating system, users of Windows 95 must also understand issues such as implementation guidelines, installation procedures, upgrade concerns, hardware management, memory management, software management, and integration of Windows 95 into existing networks. You will learn of potential pitfalls and possible shortcuts for implementing and administering Windows 95 within your organization while gaining hands-on experience using the product.

This course also covers day-to-day use issues including application management, printer management, and mobile computing support. You will have the opportunity to test selected Windows and MS-DOS applications for performance and compatibility. The course will also discuss remote access and connections to the Internet.

Make as many notes in this manual as necessary to reinforce your learning during the course. This training manual is intended to supplement your Windows 95 documentation and hands-on experience to assist you as you implement and administer the Windows 95 operating system within your enterprise.

NOTICE:

The exercises in this self-study product are designed to be used on a system that is designated for training purposes *only.* Practicing the exercises on a LAN or workstation that is used for other purposes may cause configuration problems, which could require a reinstallation and/or restoration from a tape backup of the original configuration. Please keep this in mind when working through the exercises.

COURSE GOALS

This self-study course will provide you with the information you need to complete the following:

- Installation planning and requirements
- Installation of Windows 95 as an upgrade to MS-DOS
- Installation of Windows 95 as an upgrade to Windows 3.x
- Installation of Windows NT on a Windows 95 machine
- Installation of Windows 95 as a dual-boot operating system
- Automated installations of Windows 95
- Uninstalling Windows 95
- Troubleshooting installation and startup failures
- Navigation of the Windows 95 user interface
- Customization of the Windows 95 user interface
- Using Control Panel utilities to configure Windows 95
- Creation of multiple hardware configurations
- Partioning hard disk devices for optimal performance
- Using built-in tools and utilities to manage system hardware
- Troubleshooting file system problems
- Using Windows Explorer and My Computer for file management
- Managing virtual memory in the Windows 95 environment
- Win16 API and MS-DOS application support
- Understanding the role of the Registry
- Installation of network components such as clients, protocols, adapters, and services

- Discussion of the various network protocols
- Discussion of TCP/IP and IP addressing
- Managing shared resources, passwords, profiles, and policies in a peer-to-peer network
- Managing shared resources, passwords, profiles, and policies in a mixed environment of Windows 95 and Windows NT
- Managing shared resources, passwords, profiles, and policies in a mixed environment of Windows 95 and Novell NetWare
- Printer management
- Installation and configuration of a modem
- Configuring remote access clients and servers for Dial-Up Networking
- Remote administration using Windows 95 system tools
- Performance monitoring using built-in tools

Hands-on exercises for many of these areas are presented in corresponding chapters throughout the book.

EXERCISES

The exercises in this manual are designed to give you hands-on practice working with Windows 95 in both stand-alone and network environments. It is suggested that you complete the exercises when referenced. However, this may not always be convenient. If you need to skip an exercise, you should plan on completing the exercise later, when time and circumstances allow.

You may find that there are some exercises that you are unable to complete due to hardware or software requirements. Do not let this stop you from completing the other exercises in this manual.

SIMULATIONS

Throughout the course, you will see icons asking you to practice the concepts you have learned in that chapter using NEXTSim. NEXTSim is an interactive simulation product that provides you with scenario-based training and hands-on experience in a *safe* environment. This tool should be used strictly as a supplement to the course, and not to replace the course content.

WORKSTATION REQUIREMENTS

The system requirements for this manual are as follows:

- 80386 (or above)
- 8 MB RAM (or above)
- Mouse or other pointing device
- VGA Monitor
- 200 MB hard disk
- Network adapter card

You will also need Windows 95 installation media. Most exercises can be run from either diskette or CD-ROM installation media, but the CD-ROM version is strongly suggested.

NETWORK REQUIREMENTS

You will need access to a Novell NetWare and a Windows NT Server network to complete some of the exercises in this manual. Most of the exercises at the beginning of the course can be completed without access to a network server.

WARNING!
> *It is suggested that a training network be set up for completing the exercises in this manual. Some of the exercises do require network configurations to change. Therefore, you should speak with your network administrator before running ANY exercises on a working network.*

Remember, there is always help available online. Please refer to the Support pages in Getting Started for further information regarding online support.

CHAPTER 1

Introducing Windows 95

MAJOR TOPICS

OBJECTIVES

At the completion of this chapter, you will be able to:

- Describe the new features of Windows 95.

- List the benefits of Windows 95 compared with Windows 3.x.

- Briefly discuss guidelines for implementing Windows 95.

PRE-TEST QUESTIONS

The answers to these questions are in Appendix A at the end of this manual.

1. What is meant by a Document-Centric environment?

    ....

    ....

2. Windows 95 provides approximately _____ of free conventional memory to MS-DOS sessions.

    ....

    ....

3. Windows 95 ships with 32-bit network clients for what popular network operating systems?

    ....

    ....

4. What is the best Windows-family operating system selection for RISC-based machines?

    ....

    ....

INTRODUCTION

The Windows family of products has progressed through many incarnations in ten years of releases. A common theme during this transition is an increased trend towards Windows performing as a true operating system combined with ease of use. Windows 95 continues this trend with plenty of new features and benefits compared with the products that it intends to replace, Windows 3.x and Windows for Workgroups.

Many users that are content with the Windows 3.x and Windows for Workgroups 3.x operating environments will find that the transition to Windows 95 will be less painful than they might believe. Microsoft has taken steps to ensure that the transition to Windows 95 will not be traumatic to users, and will continue to support Windows 3.x products into the future.

The chapter will take a look at the new features included with the release of Windows 95 and see how Windows 95 compares to Windows 3.x and Windows NT. A chronology of Windows-family development will also be presented. This will give us the necessary background to move on to installing and customizing Windows 95.

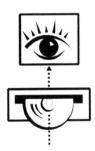

Stop now and view the following video presentation on the Interactive Learning CD-ROM:

Windows 95 Administration

Overview

EVOLUTION OF WINDOWS

This section will present a brief history and summary of Microsoft Windows products. It will also include a brief summary of Windows 98, Microsoft's newest PC operating system. The following topics are discussed within this section:

- Windows-Family Development: A Chronology

- A Comparison of Windows 95 and Windows 98

Familiarity with these products will provide you with an understanding of the benefits of the ever-changing progress of Windows products.

Windows-Family Development: A Chronology

Throughout the last ten years, Microsoft has sought to improve their Windows family of Graphical User Interface (GUI) products.

Windows 1.0x (1985)

- First version of Windows

- GUI

- 16-bit real mode

- Allowed non-preemptive multitasking

- Similar to the GEO environment on Commodore 64 computers

Windows 2.x (1987)

- Allowed overlapping windows

- Introduced DDE (Dynamic Data Exchange)

Windows/386 2.10 (1988)

- Supported multiple virtual machines

- Allowed preemptive multitasking of MS-DOS based applications

Windows 3.0 (1990)

- Supported Standard and 386 Enhanced modes

- Debut of the Program Manager/File Manager interface

Windows 3.1 (1992)

- Support for Multimedia was featured

- Real mode was discontinued

Windows for Workgroups 3.1 (1992)

- Introduced Microsoft Mail
- Supported Network DDE
- Allowed peer-to-peer networking

Windows for Workgroups 3.11 (1993)

- Featured 32-bit networking and 32-bit file system
- Introduced the Microsoft At Work fax

Windows NT 3.x (1993)

- Full 32-bit operating system with fully preemptive multitasking
- Designed to make full use of 32-bit processors
- Integrated networking
- C2 level security

Windows NT 4.x (1996)

- New user interface
- PPTP (point-to-point tunneling protocol)
- Internet Information Server (IIS)
- WINS/DNS integration

A COMPARISON OF WINDOWS 95 AND WINDOWS 98

Windows 98, like Windows 95, is a full operating system and is not dependent on MS-DOS. This new operating system is based on the Windows 95 environment, but integrates Microsoft's Internet Explorer 4.0, as well as other enhancements. This integration allows users to have their desktop appear as a Web browser, known as an Active Desktop. Users can choose between the Standard Desktop and this new Active Desktop.

Microsoft has enhanced the current Windows 95 desktop environment by incorporating an Internet look and feel for users. The basic desktop environment remains the same with a few additions and enhancements. For example, the **Start** menu includes a few new selections such as **Favorites** and the ability for the user to log off without shutting down. Users are also able to access desktop properties and other applications through icons located on the taskbar.

Perhaps the most exciting feature of Windows 98 is the Active Desktop. This new feature allows users to work with a *live* desktop environment. Active Desktop allows the user to view their favorite Web pages from the desktop. Users can access links, sounds, animations, and all other resources available on a Web page. The functionality of Active Desktop is similar to that you would find in using Internet Explorer.

Internet Explorer 4.0

Windows 98 ships with Internet Explorer 4.0. Some of the features of IE 4.0 are:

- AutoComplete

   Users can type in Web addresses quickly with the aid of the AutoComplete feature. As a user types in a Web address, IE will offer the remainder of the address which the user can either accept or reject.

- SmartFavorites

   This feature allows users to know when their favorite Web sites have been updated.

- Full screen view

   Users can work at full screen to optimize the viewing area of a Web site.

- Video conferencing

   Internet Explorer 4.0 allows users to set up video conferencing and broadcasting, as well as publishing Web pages.

- Access to the file system

    Users can browse My Computer resources directly in Internet Explorer.

Windows 98 Advantages

Some of the advantages of the new Windows 98 operating system are:

- Win32 driver model

    Windows 98 implements a Win32 driver model. This model has also been designed for use in the upcoming product, Windows NT 5.0. The Win32 driver model will allow new devices to have one single driver across both operating systems.

- FAT32

    Instead of the traditional FAT file system, Windows 98 allows disks over 2 GB to be formatted as a single drive. This is known as FAT32. FAT32 support for Windows 95 can be downloaded from Microsoft's Web site. If you are running the OSR2 release of Windows 95, FAT32 support is included.

- Multiple displays

    Windows 98 also enables users to support multiple displays on a single PC. This type of feature can be especially useful when working on large projects requiring several intensive software packages.

- Active Desktop

    Windows 98 integrates the look and feel of a Web browser environment. Since the Internet has become such an integral part of most users' lives, Microsoft has decided to customize the new Windows 98 product accordingly. Many options and features of the product have much similarity to a Web browser.

- Dial-Up Networking

    Windows 98 has also improved the Dial-Up Networking capability. Users are now able to combine dial-up lines to access higher speeds. For example, users who have two modems may combine them to connect at a higher baud rate.

- Internet System Update

    Windows 98 also has a new Internet System Update. This service will scan your system, check the Internet for any updated drivers, and download the appropriate selections for your system.

- Disk Defragmenter

    The Disk Defragmenter Optimization Wizard will monitor a user's most frequently used programs. Once it creates a log file containing this information, the Wizard will store files associated with these frequently used programs.

On the whole, Microsoft has taken the success of the Windows 95 user environment and integrated Internet components wherever possible. In response to current technology's reliance on Internet connectivity, Windows 98 provides the end user with an open Internet environment.

INTRODUCING WINDOWS 95

This section will present the features and benefits of Windows 95. The following are topics discussed within this section:

- New Features of Windows 95
- Benefits of Windows 95
- End User Benefits
- User Management Benefits
- OSR2

This information will show you the benefits that Windows 95 has to offer over its predecessors. Use this information to determine where Windows 95 provides the most appropriate solution to your operating system requirements.

Windows 95 Features

Windows 95 is a completely different operating system than its predecessors in the Windows family. Windows 95 provides:

- A complete, integrated 32-bit operating system that does not require MS-DOS.

- Some 16-bit components to ensure backwards compatibility.

- The ability to run MS-DOS and Windows 3.1 applications.

- Preemptive multitasking and multiple threads of execution for 32-bit applications.

- A more intuitive user interface.

- Integrated networking support with higher performance.

- Integrated messaging and dial-up network access services.

- Long filenames (to 255 characters) support.

- Increased user efficiency through Windows Explorer.

- Plug and Play architecture.

- Context-sensitive menus for all objects.

- Document-Centric interface through OLE (OLE2).

- Enhanced multimedia support with full screen and full motion video without special hardware assistance.

Benefits of Windows 95

If you are currently using Windows 3.x, Windows 95 will provide you with many important benefits, both from the end user's point of view and in terms of user management. Let's look at each of these. The section will then describe the differences between the standard release of Windows 95 and the OSR2 release.

- User Benefits
- User Management
- OSR2

The architecture of Windows 95 allows the end user to be more productive through a new, more intuitive interface and improved performance. Users will see an increase in reliability even when running 16-bit Windows and MS-DOS based applications.

Management of Windows 95 users is simplified as well, due to reduced support time required and through built-in support for networking, plug and play, and mobile computing.

End User Benefits

Windows 95 contains many improvements over Windows 3.x. At the top of the list of improvements asked of Microsoft was an easier way to work with the PC. As a result, a new user interface was designed in Windows 95 that attempts to make computing easier for both less experienced users and experienced users who want greater efficiency and flexibility.

The items below illustrate the benefits of the Windows 95 operating system:

- Preemptive multitasking

    Windows 95 can perform multitasking smoothly and responsively for 32-bit applications.

- Scaleable performance

    The performance improvements that Windows 95 provides over Windows 3.1 increase as the amount of RAM increases, due to the high-performance 32-bit architecture of Windows 95.

- Support for 32-bit applications

    Windows 95 supports the Win32 API, which means users can look forward to a new generation of easier, faster, and more reliable applications.

- Increased reliability

    Windows 95 increases protection for running existing MS-DOS and Windows-based applications and provides the highest level of protection for 32-bit applications for Windows. As a result, an errant application will be much less likely to disable other applications or the system.

    For example, MS-DOS applications running under Windows 3.x can make a prohibited call to a null pointer. This would cause a GPF, and frequently, a system crash. With Windows 95, the operating system intercepts invalid instructions and terminates the offending application without crashing the system.

- Faster printing

    Windows 95 features a new 32-bit printing subsystem that reduces the time spent waiting for print jobs to finish and improves system response when jobs are printing in the background.

- Better multimedia support

    Just as Windows 3.1 made sound a part of the system, Windows 95 now includes support for video playback. The video system and CD-ROM file system will provide high-quality output for multimedia applications.

- More memory for MS-DOS-based applications

    Windows 95's use of protected-mode drivers means users will have more than 600 KB free conventional memory in each MS-DOS session. This even includes support for mouse operations, network connections, CD-ROM drives, and so forth.

- Microsoft Exchange client

    Windows 95 includes the Microsoft Exchange client, a universal client that retrieves messages into one universal inbox from many kinds of mail systems. This includes support for Microsoft Mail, Microsoft Fax, Internet Mail, The Microsoft Network, CompuServe Mail, Universal BBS clients, and so on.

User Management Benefits

Enterprises may want to move to Windows 95 because it will help reduce their PC support burden, help increase their control over the desktop, and help increase the productivity of their end users. Windows 95 includes numerous features designed to reduce the costs of managing and supporting PCs and PC users, including the following:

- Simpler, more intuitive user interface

    The user interface can reduce training requirements for novice users and enable experienced users to learn new tasks with less help.

- Built-in networking support

    Network support is easy to set up and configure. Support for popular network clients using a variety of protocols and drivers is integrated.

    Windows 95 includes 32-bit clients for both NetWare and Microsoft networks. These require no conventional memory.

    A Windows 95-based PC can have multiple network clients and transport protocols running simultaneously for connecting heterogeneous systems.

- Plug and Play device installation

    This automates the process of adding devices to a PC. Plug and play also enables innovative new system designs that support such capabilities as hot docking and undocking.

- System policies that enable an administrator to control a desktop configuration

    Windows 95 supports policies, which are settings an administrator configures to define the operations users can access on their PCs and the appearance of the desktop.

- Support for roving users

    Windows 95 can present different configurations, depending on who has logged into the PC. This option allows users to log on to different machines on the network and see their personal configurations.

    Windows 95 also includes the Briefcase that allows users to keep various copies of files updated on mobile and desktop systems.

- Built-in agents for automating backup of desktop systems

    Windows 95 includes the software required to back up a desktop system using a server-based backup system. The backup agents included with Windows 95 work with the most popular server-based systems.

OSR2

Windows 95 OEM Service, Release 2 (OSR2) is slightly different than the retail version of Windows 95. OSR2 often ships preinstalled on new PCs. It is not available *off-the-shelf*, but key features of OSR2 have been made available as a retail upgrade.

To identify which version of Windows 95 is installed, right-click on My Computer on the desktop. Then, run **Properties**. OSR2 is either version 4.0.950 A or 4.0.950 B. The original retail version is 4.0.950. The information available on this Properties dialog can also be viewed in the System utility. This control panel utility will be discussed later in the course.

Key features of OSR2 include:

- FAT32
- TCP/IP multihoming
- Internet Explorer 3.0
- NetMeeting
- Infrared device drivers
- 32-bit DLC drivers

SUMMARY

During this chapter you were introduced to basic Windows 95 features and benefits including:

- New features included in Windows 95
- Benefits of Windows 95
- Advantages of managing users

In the next chapter, you will see how to install and implement Windows 95.

POST-TEST QUESTIONS

The answers to these questions are in Appendix A at the end of this manual.

1. What Windows-family product introduced the 386 Enhanced Mode and the Program Manager/File Manager interface?

    ....

    ....

2. What Windows-family product was the first real operating system?

    ....

    ....

3. Windows 95 supports long filenames. How long can these filenames be?

    ....

    ....

4. Which Windows 95 utilities replace the former Program Manager and File Manager?

    ....

    ....

5. List six features of Windows 95 that will assist you in managing users within an enterprise.

    ....

    ....

CHAPTER 2

Installing Windows 95

MAJOR TOPICS

OBJECTIVES

At the completion of this chapter, you will be able to:

- Plan for Windows 95 implementation.
- Determine minimum hardware and software requirements for Windows 95.
- Discuss various installation options.
- List the steps of the Windows 95 Setup Wizard.
- Install Windows 95 as an upgrade to Windows 3.x.
- Install Windows 95 as an upgrade to Windows for Workgroups 3.11.
- Install Windows NT on a Windows 95 machine.
- Install Windows 95 over DR DOS or OS/2.
- Describe the installation options supported.
- Discuss the various procedures for an automated installation.
- Discuss considerations for Windows 95 as a dual-boot operating system.
- Uninstall Windows 95.
- Resolve installation failures.

PRE-TEST QUESTIONS

The answers to these questions are in Appendix A at the end of this manual.

1. What is the minimum processor required for Windows 95 installation?

   ....

   ....

2. Windows 95 can be installed as an upgrade to what operating systems?

   ....

   ....

3. Assuming you are upgrading an existing Windows 3.x station that was originally installed in the default directory, where does Windows 95 store updated utilities such as XCOPY.EXE and SORT.EXE?

    ....

    ....

4. During startup, how do you force the Windows 95 startup menu to display?

    ....

    ....

5. Once you have upgraded your Windows v3.x system to Windows 95, how can you uninstall the new operating system?

    ....

    ....

INTRODUCTION

In this chapter, you will perform an installation of Windows 95 for the very first time, as well as an upgrade to several different Windows products and other operating systems. You will note that there are improvements in the installation and setup of Windows 95 over Windows 3.x or Windows for Workgroups. The Windows Setup Wizard will guide you through all the necessary steps, with little input required.

This chapter begins with a discussion of the steps necessary to plan for a Windows 95 implementation. The minimum workstation requirements for Windows 95 will be listed. You will also examine the various options for installation. Finally, you will see how to upgrade various systems to Windows 95.

The steps involved with the installation of Windows 95 follow a logical sequence. The Setup Wizard searches for and detects existing hardware, asks the user configuration questions, and copies files to the hard disk with minimal intervention.

By the end of this chapter, you will have a Windows 95 client installed and configured correctly. This will enable you to move forward to explore and customize the Windows 95 User Interface in the next chapter.

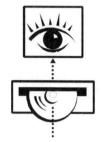

Stop now and view the following video presentation on the Interactive Learning CD-ROM:

Windows 95 Administration

Installation

PREPARING FOR WINDOWS 95 INSTALLATION

This section will present points to consider prior to installing Windows 95. These key issues may determine whether you are able to install Windows 95 on selected machines. The following topics are discussed within this section:

- Planning for Implementation
- Supported Hardware
- System Hardware Requirements
- Optional Hardware
- Hard Disk Requirements
- Operating System Requirements

These guidelines will prepare you for installing Windows 95 for the very first time. Hardware configuration issues and system settings will also be noted.

Planning for Implementation

To have a successful enterprise-wide implementation of Windows 95, you must have a complete plan. This plan should address the following areas:

- Review the Windows 95 operating system.

   Take the time to learn the operating system and how it will affect your users.

- Inventory client hardware and software configurations.

   Identify a sample of client hardware and software configurations to test Windows 95 installations before you implement them enterprise-wide.

- Determine and test the optimal network client configuration.

   Use enhanced mode NDIS 3.1 compatible drivers, if available. These drivers take up no real-mode conventional memory and are loaded dynamically.

- Evaluate the features of Windows 95 to decide whether you should enable them at client workstations.

   Evaluate features such as System Policies, User Profiles, Peer Sharing, Remote Administration, Dial-up Networking, and Microsoft Exchange to determine their value to your enterprise.

- Determine your security issues and security requirements.

   Share-level and pass-through user-level security schemes for Windows NT domains, standalone Windows NT servers or workstations, and Novell NetWare file servers are supported. You must define user accounts and permissions for network resources.

- Select a preferred installation method.

   Windows 95 setup supports various installation methods, including shared installation, automated installation, and network installation.

- Determine whether you want a dual-boot system.

   Windows 95 allows you to install it as a dual-boot operating system with Windows 3.x, DOS, OS/2, or Windows NT. The advantage of a dual-boot system is that it allows you to retain an operating system that might be needed to run certain software. You can set up Windows 95 as a dual-boot system after it has been installed. However, you will need to install Windows 95 in a separate directory.

- Provide training for end users.

  End user training is essential for a successful implementation of Windows 95. Use the Windows Tour and Help utilities to start the formal training.

Supported Hardware

Although the Windows 95 development team attempted to support all legacy or non-plug and play hardware currently in use, certain hardware does not work well with Windows 95. A list of problematic hardware is located in the HARDWARE.TXT file on the Windows 95 installation media. This file is placed in the \Windows directory during installation.

To view the HARDWARE.TXT file before installing Windows 95, follow these steps:

From floppy diskettes:

1. Insert Disk 1 into drive A.

2. At the MS-DOS command prompt, type the following and press *ENTER*:

   ```
   a:extract.exe /a /l c:\windows win95_03.cab hardware.txt
   ```

3. At the MS-DOS prompt, change to the \Windows directory.

4. At the command prompt, type the following and press *ENTER*:

   ```
   edit hardware.txt
   ```

From a CD-ROM:

1. Insert the CD into your CD-ROM drive.

2. At the MS-DOS command prompt, change to the \Win95 directory on your CD-ROM drive.

3. Type the following and press *ENTER*:

   ```
   extract.exe /a /l c:\windows win95_02.cab hardware.txt
   ```

4. Change to the Windows directory on your C: drive.

5. At the command prompt, type the following and press *ENTER*:

   ```
   edit hardware.txt
   ```

You will find fixes and workarounds for problematic hardware within the HARDWARE.TXT file. You can download a more current hardware compatibility list from Microsoft's Web site on the Internet:

www.microsoft.com

System Hardware Requirements

Your system must meet the minimum installation requirements before you can install Windows 95. These are:

Component	Minimum	Suggested
Microprocessor	80386DX or above	80386DX/33 or above
RAM	4 MB or more	8 MB or more
Monitor/Adapter	VGA or better	Super VGA or better

You will also need the following:

- Mouse or other pointing device
- High-density floppy diskette drive

A hard disk drive is not required, but is strongly suggested. If you do not have a local hard disk, you will have to install Windows 95 so that it accesses a shared copy of Windows 95 on a network server. The hard disk space required for installation depends on the operating system from which you are upgrading.

Current Operating System	Space Requirement
MS-DOS 3.2 or above	30 - 60 MB
Windows 3.1	20 - 30 MB
Windows 3.11	10 - 20 MB

This does not include disk space for applications or data files.

Windows 95 will not install on an 80386-based computer that has a B1-stepping processor. A B1-stepping chip is any Intel 386 microprocessor dated before April 1987. These chips are known to introduce random math errors when performing 32-bit operations. These chips frequently bear the label "For 16-bit Operations Only."

Because Windows 95 is an operating system designed for computers that use Intel processors, it cannot be installed on systems that have RISC-based processors. Also, Windows 95 does not have Symmetric Multiple Processor (SMP) support and, therefore, cannot take advantage of multiple processor machines. Windows NT is the product of choice for RISC and SMP support.

Optional Hardware

The following optional hardware is also suggested:

- Modem

    A modem will let you use Dial-up Networking, access the Microsoft Network, and access the Internet.

- Network adapter

    This is required for LAN access.

- CD-ROM

    Either a directly connected CD-ROM or network access to a CD-ROM is strongly suggested. Most software manufacturers are using CD-ROMs as their preferred method of distribution.

- Sound card

    Many commercial applications include a sound component.

Hard Disk Requirements

Windows 95 Setup must install the Windows 95 Operating System on a File Allocation Table (FAT) partition located on the hard disk. It cannot install Windows 95 on a computer that has only HPFS which is used in OS/2 or NTFS (Windows NT) partitions. Windows 95 cannot read any information stored on partitions other than FAT. Although Windows 95 Setup reads most partitioning schemes and writes the appropriate information to the master boot record (MBR), certain third-party disk configuration utilities may cause problems. If this occurs, close all programs except Program Manager and disable 32-bit disk access then run **Setup**.

The amount of disk space required for Windows 95 setup varies. It will depend on your hardware configuration and the device drivers you require. A new installation of Windows 95 (no existing Windows versions present) can take anywhere between 30 to 60 MB of hard disk space. An upgrade from Windows 3.1 can take anywhere between 20 to 30 MB of additional disk space, and an upgrade from Windows for Workgroups 3.11 can take an additional 10 to 20 MB of space.

In addition to the space required for system files, you will also need extra disk space for a swap file. A good rule of thumb is that Windows 95 requires 14 MB of memory. This can be any combination of RAM and virtual memory. For example, if you have 8 MB of RAM, you would need 6 MB of free disk space for a swap file.

The Windows 95 swap file is dynamic. This means that the swap file changes size during use. The Windows 95 virtual memory scheme is discussed later in this course.

Operating System Requirements

Windows 95 installed as an upgrade over an existing operating system, such as MS-DOS, Novell DOS (DR DOS), Windows 3.x, and Windows for Workgroups 3.1x. Windows 95 can also be installed as a dual-boot operating system with Windows NT, Windows for Workgroups, Windows 3.1, OS/2, or MS-DOS.

The minimum operating system software required to install Windows 95 is any one of the following:

- MS-DOS 3.2 or higher, or an equivalent OEM version that supports disk partitions greater than 32 MB
- Windows 3.x
- Windows for Workgroups 3.1x

Because of several variations of MS-DOS 3.2, Microsoft recommends that you have MS-DOS 5.0 or higher for a Windows 95 upgrade.

NOTE: *Windows 95 Setup needs at least 417 KB of free conventional memory to run.*

NEW INSTALLATIONS OF WINDOWS 95

This section will present steps for installation. The Installation Wizard will prompt you to select choices ranging from system and hardware configurations to components necessary for Windows 95 to work efficiently within your environment. You will also be introduced to the Safe Mode feature of Windows 95. The following are topics discussed in this section:

- Installation Procedures
- Installation Methods
- Push Installation
- Starting Setup
- Windows 95 Setup Wizard Options
- Steps in Windows 95 Setup
- Hardware Detection Phase
- Configuration Options
- First Time Run
- Windows 95 Safe Mode Operations
- MS-DOS Files Changed By Windows 95 Setup

The Installation Wizard provides you with an automated and easy to follow installation process. By understanding each component within the Wizard, you will be able to make the most appropriate selections for your system. This will help ensure that your system will run efficiently.

Installation Procedures

Windows 95 supports the following upgrade options:

- Windows 95 upgrade from Windows 3.1x or Window for Workgroups 3.1x

    Most new Windows 95 users will upgrade from Windows 3.1. The upgrade process for Windows 3.1x and Windows for Workgroups 3.1x is the same.

    It is recommended that Windows 3.0 users run **Setup** from MS-DOS rather than from the Windows GUI.

- Windows 95 upgrade from MS-DOS

    After beginning setup, MS-DOS upgrades are essentially the same as Windows upgrades. Setup begins a "mini" Windows session and installation proceeds from there.

Installations of Windows 95 as an upgrade will be discussed later in the chapter.

You also have a choice for installation sources and methods. These include:

- Shared installation to a file server.

    Installation of Windows 95 to a network server allows you to set up Windows 95 on diskless workstations that share Windows 95 system files.

- Automated installations.

    You can automate installation by using a login script to run setup from a batch script, allowing automatic installation to remote workstations.

- Customized installations.

    Using custom setup scripts, Windows 95 Setup can use predefined settings for all options, including hardware detection and the addition of new software.

- Upgrade or maintenance installations.

    After a successful Windows 95 installation, you can run **Setup** to verify and repair the existing installation.

Installation Methods

Windows 95 supports the following installation sources:

- Floppy Disks
- CD-ROM
- Network

Select a source appropriate to your needs and available resources.

Push Installation

As an administrator of a network with many workstations, it would be a time consuming task to physically go from one workstation to another to install Windows 95. A push installation uses Windows 95 Setup with a setup script, plus login scripts and user accounts on a network, to create an automated installation process. Once the scripts are in place, you may install Windows 95 remotely using one of the following methods:

- Create a network login script that runs the setup script automatically when each user logs on.

- Use an electronic mail message to allow a user to start Windows 95 Setup by clicking on a setup object.

- Use Microsoft Systems Management Server (SMS) to make Windows 95 Setup a mandatory job.

- Use network management software provided by other vendors to automate the setup process.

Starting Setup

To start Setup, run SETUP.EXE from your installation source.

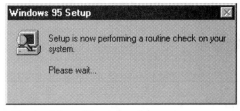

The Setup procedure will take 30 to 60 minutes.

After the system check, the Windows 95 Setup Wizard is initiated.

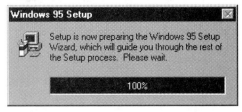

The Setup Wizard will guide you through the remaining Setup steps.

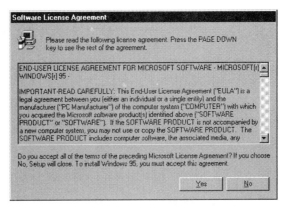

The Setup Wizard next presents the licensing agreement which you must either accept or decline. If you decline the licensing agreement, Setup will terminate. If you accept the licensing agreement, Setup will continue. You should close all Windows applications before running the Setup Wizard. If you do not, this dialog will appear:

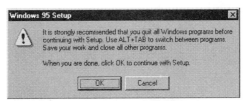

During the system check, the Setup Wizard tries to detect any potential problems. If any problems are found, you will receive an informational dialog box, as indicated in the following example:

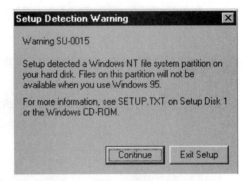

Windows 95 Setup Wizard Options

After a Setup option is selected, you will have the option of selecting the destination directory for Windows 95 files.

If you choose to install a directory other than C:\WINDOWS, your settings from your previous version of Windows will not be migrated. However, you will be able to dual boot to your previous version of Windows. Dual-boot configurations are discussed later in the chapter.

After the directory has been selected, the Setup Wizard will prepare the directory, checking for necessary disk space and installed components. The Setup Wizard then provides four options to complete an installation:

- Typical
- Portable

- Compact
- Custom

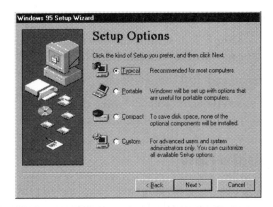

Most users will select the typical option to perform a *normal* Windows 95 installation. The portable option installs the components of Windows 95 that are most useful for portable or mobile computer users. The compact option performs a minimal installation of Windows 95, installing the fewest files needed for the operating system. The custom option provides full customization of the Windows 95 setup process, allowing users complete control to install all or selected components.

Steps in Windows 95 Setup

Setup in Windows 95 is more automated than Windows 3.1 Setup and is divided into the following steps:

- Setup information and PC hardware detection

  Setup will compile system information and attempt to detect installed hardware.

- Configuration questions

    Setup will ask the user questions about some of the hardware devices the system contains.

- Copying component files

    Setup will determine the files that are required for your configuration and copy them to your hard disk.

- Restart and final configuration

    Setup restarts your PC using the Windows 95 operating system and performs final configuration tasks.

Hardware Detection Phase

During the hardware detection phase, Setup analyzes installed system components. Setup then searches for installed hardware devices and detects any connected peripherals. During this phase of Setup, Windows 95 analyzes the system to identify any hardware resources that are available.

For legacy or non-Plug and Play PCs, Windows 95 maintains a database of known hardware devices. It also performs a manual detection to check I/O ports and specific memory addresses to identify whether they are being used by any known devices. Windows 95 also checks for Plug and Play peripherals connected to legacy PCs. For PCs that contain a Plug and Play BIOS, Windows 95 queries the PC for installed components and the configuration used by these components.

Windows 95 prompts the user during the detection process to indicate whether certain devices are present, including:

- Sound Cards
- SCSI Devices
- Network Adapters
- Proprietary CD-ROMs

If the user indicates that one or more of these devices are present, Windows 95 Setup attempts to identify the hardware through more aggressive methods. This may cause the system to crash. If this occurs, restart Setup. On the next attempt, Windows 95 Setup will avoid the method of detection that caused the system crash.

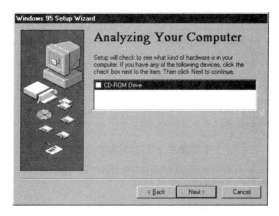

The detection process uses *safe* detection methods for most hardware. This involves searching the PC for any software that could indicate the presence of a specific device. For example, if fax software is present, the INI file for the software could contain references to the modem type and COM port settings. The automatic detection process may take several minutes. Windows 95 displays a progress indicator during this phase.

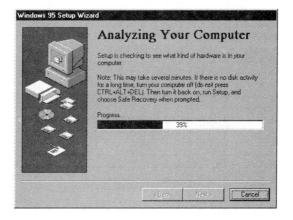

Configuration Options

When the hardware detection phase is complete, a dialog box gives users the option to review the detected hardware devices and the system components that Windows 95 will install.

Windows 95 will allow you to select the software components you wish to install.

If you choose to select the components that Windows 95 will install, it will present a list from which to select.

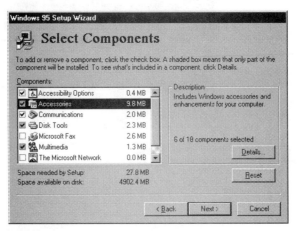

A custom installation takes you directly to this dialog.

If you plan to use a network, Windows 95 needs information to identify your system.

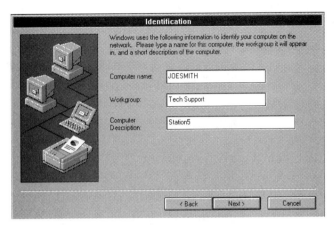

Creating a Startup Disk is highly recommended. This disk contains utilities that will allow you to boot your system from a floppy in case of operating system failure.

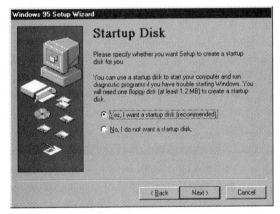

Windows 95 Setup will format the diskette and transfer operating system startup files as the initial step prior to copying files.

Windows 95 now takes the information that it has gathered through interrogation of the system and user input, and determines which files need to be copied to the PC.

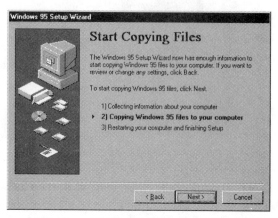

If you choose to create a Windows 95 Startup Disk, it is created before the operating system files are copied to the hard disk. Windows 95 only copies the files required for the specific PC's current hardware configuration. If you add or remove hardware later, you will need to update the startup disk.

As you add or remove hardware devices, Windows 95 remembers the location of the Setup files and whether you performed an installation with a CD-ROM, floppy disks, or a Workstation installation from a network.

During this phase, Windows 95 Setup modifies the boot record and replaces the CONFIG.SYS and AUTOEXEC.BAT files before restarting the PC with the Windows 95 operating system. The boot record is untouched until this portion of Setup. This allows you to recover from system crashes that may occur earlier in the Setup process.

New IO.SYS and MSDOS.SYS files are copied at this time. The boot record points to the new IO.SYS file. Windows 95 Setup now renames the existing MS-DOS boot files.

The CONFIG.SYS and AUTOEXEC.BAT files are not needed, except in very special cases. Windows 95 passes all pertinent startup information directly to COMMAND.COM.

Exercise 2-1: Installation

During this exercise, you will upgrade your system to Windows 95. You must read the prerequisites listed in the Introduction before attempting this exercise. You will also need a blank, formatted diskette to complete this exercise.

This exercise assumes that you are installing Windows 95 using a CD-ROM as your installation source. If you are using a different source, or if your system varies from the suggested hardware list, you may receive prompts in addition to those described here. If you receive an unfamiliar prompt, take the default selections for now. You will not be able to start your original Windows after running this exercise.

If you have a printer attached, it should be turned off while you are running this exercise.

At the beginning of this exercise, your system should be running Windows 3.1 or Windows for Workgroups 3.11.

1. Select **Run** from the **File** menu.
2. Click on **Browse**.
3. Locate the installation source directory and double-click on SETUP.EXE. If installing from CD-ROM, the setup file is located in the \Win95 directory.
4. Click on **OK**.
5. At the Run dialog, click on **OK**.
6. When prompted with the opening dialog, click on **Continue**. There will be a delay while Windows 95 Setup copies files.

7. When the Software License Agreement dialog displays, click on **Yes**.

    NOTE: *If your system has an NTFS file partition, you will be warned at this time.
    Click on* **Continue** *to continue your installation.*

8. When the first screen of the Setup Wizard displays, click on **Next**.

9. When prompted, select C:\WINDOWS and click on **Next**. Setup will check for
    installed components.

10. When prompted to save system files, verify that Yes is selected and click on **Next**.
    There will be a delay while your system files are backed up. If prompted for a
    location for the uninstall files, accept the default by clicking on **OK**.

11. When prompted to select your installation method, select **Custom** and click on
    Next.

12. When prompted for your User Information, type your name in the Name field
    and any text string in the Company field.

13. Click on **Next**.

14. When prompted for your CD Key, enter the value from your CD-ROM package.

15. Click on **Next**.

16. When prompted to look for all hardware devices, verify that Yes is selected and
    click on **Next**.

17. From the Analyzing Your Computer dialog, click on any appropriate selections
    (such as CD-ROM drive) and click on **Next**. There will be a delay while
    Windows 95 Setup analyzes your computer.

18. At the Get Connected dialog, do not select any options and click on **Next**.

19. On each of the grayed option box selections, **Accessories**, **Communications**, **Disk
    Tools**, and **Multimedia**, click once to remove the check, and then click a second
    time to select with a clear checkbox. This means that all components available for
    that selection will be installed.

20. Verify that the following are selected:

    ```
    Accessibility Options

    Accessories

    Communications

    Disk Tools

    Multimedia
    ```
    Click on **Next**.

21. If the Network Configuration dialog displays, leave all settings at default and click on **Next**.

22. If prompted for Identification, type the following in the prompt fields:

    Name   SSTUDY

    Workgroup   WAVESS

    Computer Description Self Study

    NOTE: *If attaching to an existing network, check with your network administrator before using the WAVESS workgroup name.*

23. Verify that your computer settings are correct and click on **Next**.

24. When prompted, select to create a startup diskette and click on **Next**.

25. When prompted to start copying files, click on **Next**.

26. When prompted, insert your blank diskette into the diskette drive and click on **OK**.

27. After Setup has finished creating your startup diskette, remove the diskette and click on **OK**. There will be a delay while the operating files copy.

28. When prompted, click on **Finish**. The system will restart and prepare to launch Windows 95 for the first time.

29. After the system restarts, it will complete the installation and configuration process. If you are prompted to configure a printer, click on **Cancel**.

30. When prompted, type in Student as your name and wave as your password.

31. Click on **OK**.

32. When prompted to confirm your password, type wave as your password and click on **OK**.

    NOTE: *If connecting to an existing network, contact your network supervisor for the username and password to use.*

33. Click to select the appropriate time zone on the map graphic, or select your time zone from the drop down menu. Click on **Apply**, then on **OK**.

34. If prompted, click on **OK** to restart your system.

35. When prompted, log on using your username and password as in step 30 and press *ENTER*.

36. If you wish, go through the Windows Tour at this time. Otherwise, click on **Close**.

First Time Run

Final configuration takes place after you start Windows 95 for the first time.

- You enter an initial password which creates the password list.

- The **Start** menu is configured and any existing Windows 3.1 program groups are converted to folders.

- Windows 95 sets up plug and play printers.

- Time zone information is entered.

- The Windows 95 Tour is enabled, and you are asked if you would like to take the tour.

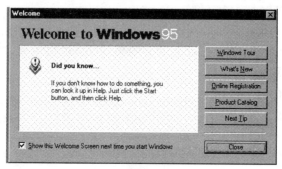

Upon completion, the Windows 95 Setup process has ended and you have successfully installed Windows 95 on your PC.

You should always shut down your system normally before exiting or restarting. To shut down, run **Start/Shut Down** and select your shut down option. Then click on **Yes**. This will flush the contents of the file cache to disk, close all program sessions, and save a copy of the current Registry.

Safe Recovery

If Windows 95 Setup crashes during installation, the next time you start Setup, you will be given the opportunity to recover Setup safely. The following dialog allows you to either continue using Safe Recovery or without Safe Recovery. Using Safe Recovery will enable Setup to work around the problems that caused the crash. If you choose not to use Safe Recovery, there is no guarantee that Setup will not encounter the same problems again.

Windows 95 Safe Mode Operations

Once Setup has been completed, Windows 95 has a special diagnostic mode, Safe Mode, that allows you to fix problems that keep you from starting Windows properly. Frequently, incorrect network or hardware settings cause these types of problems.

If Windows 95 has problems booting, it will display the following menu on restart.

```
Microsoft Windows 95 Startup Menu

==============================

1.  Normal

2.  Logged (\BOOTLOG.TXT)

3.  Safe mode

4.  Safe mode with network support

5.  Step-by-step confirmation

6.  Command prompt only

7.  Safe mode command prompt only

Enter a choice:

F5=Safe mode     Shift+F5=Command Prompt

Shift+F8=Step-by-step confirmation [N]
```

You may access the Windows 95 startup menu during bootup by pressing the *F8* key when **Starting Windows 95...** appears on the screen.

After you enter Safe Mode, make sure that all settings are correct in the Control Panel and try starting Windows 95. While in Safe Mode, Windows 95 uses these default settings:

- VGA Monitor
- No Network (unless in Safe Mode with network support)
- Microsoft Mouse Driver
- Minimum Device Drivers

You will not have access to CD-ROM drives, printers, PCMCIA cards, or other devices while in Safe Mode.

MS-DOS Files Changed by Windows 95 Setup

If your Windows 95 installation was an upgrade from an existing version of Windows, MS-DOS files are deleted from the \DOS directory. These files are known to be incompatible with Windows 95 because they do not support the use of long filenames. Windows 95 stores the updated command line utilities in the \Windows\Command directory.

The updated files include:

EXTRACT.EXE	FORMAT.COM	EDIT.SYS	MEM.EXE
SCANDISK.INI	ATTRIB.EXE	SYS.COM	SORT.EXE
MSCDEX.EXE	EDIT.HLP	CHOICE.COM	DOSKEY.COM
MODE.COM	MORE.COM	DISKCOPY.COM	CHKDSK.EXE
XCOPY.EXE	NCOPY32.EXE	ANSI.SYS	COUNTY.SYS
KEYBOARD.SYS	KEYBRD2.SYS	EGA.CPI	DRVSPACE.BIN
SCANDISK.EXE	FDISK.EXE	KEYB.COM	DEBUG.EXE
SUBST.EXE	DISPLAY.SYS	DRVSPACE.SYS	

NOTE: If the previous MS-DOS version is preserved, the files in the DOS directory remain unchanged.

Exercise 2-2:
Start up and Shut Down

During this section, you will practice start up and shut down. You should be logged on to your system at the beginning of this exercise.

1. Click on the **Start** button.

2. Click on **Shut Down** on the **Start** menu.

3. When prompted with your Shut Down options, verify that **Shut down the computer?** is selected and click on **Yes**. There will be a delay while your system prepares to shut down. You should always shut a system down before powering off to protect system integrity.

4. When prompted that it is safe to turn off your computer, press *CONTROL+ALT+DELETE* to restart.

5. Log on if prompted.

6. When the Welcome to Windows dialog appears, click to remove the check next to **Show this Welcome Screen next time you start Windows**.

7. Click on **Close**.

8. Run **Shut Down** from the **Start** menu. Select **Restart the computer?** and click on **Yes**.

9. The system will shut down then restart automatically. Watch closely during restart and press *F8* when **Starting Windows 95...** appears on the screen.

10. Type *3* and press *ENTER* to start your system in Safe Mode. This is commonly used when troubleshooting configuration or other system errors.

11. The system will restart and display Safe Mode graphics in the corners as a reminder that it is in the Safe Mode.

12. When the desktop appears displaying Safe Mode messages, click on **OK**.

13. Using the procedures discussed in this exercise, shut down your system and allow it to restart automatically.

UPGRADE INSTALLATIONS

This section will present guidelines for upgrading previous Windows products, as well as other operating systems, to Windows 95. The following are topics discussed in this section:

- Upgrade From Windows 3.x
- Upgrading from Windows for Workgroups 3.11
- Upgrading a Windows 95 Installation
- Installing Windows NT 4.0 on a Windows 95 Machine
- Installation Over DR DOS
- Installation Over OS/2

Upgrade from Windows 3.x

The preferred method for running Windows 95 Setup is from within Windows 3.1 or Windows for Workgroups 3.11. If MS-DOS, OS/2, Windows NT 3.x, Windows NT 4.x, or Windows 3.0 is installed, it is recommended that you run Setup from MS-DOS.

By default, Windows 95 Setup installs program files in the existing \Windows directory. This upgrades the existing version of Windows and migrates Windows 3.x Program Manager groups to folders within the **Programs** menu in the **Start** menu. Settings within Windows 3.x SYSTEM.INI, WIN.INI, and PROTOCOL.INI files migrate to the new environment as well.

> *NOTE:* *During Setup, Windows renames the COMMAND.COM, CONFIG.SYS, and AUTOEXEC.BAT files to COMMAND.DOS, CONFIG.DOS, and AUTOEXEC.DOS, respectively.*

Before upgrading a PC to Windows 95, collect the following information:

- Default user name
- Workstation name for network users
- Workgroup name for network users
- Domain name for Windows NT Server domain members
- Preferred server name for Novell NetWare environments

Windows 95 can detect most of the other settings on your PC automatically. You have the option of providing these settings manually, if you wish.

Upgrading a Windows 95 Installation

If you run **Windows 95 Setup** after the operating system installs successfully, you have the option to verify the existing installation. You can use this option to verify or repair the Windows 95 operating system files.

Windows 95 also provides a variety of maintenance applications for adding, removing, and configuring Windows 95 components. These include the **Add/Remove Programs** and **Add New Hardware** options accessible through the Control Panel. By selecting the **Add/Remove Programs** option, you can add or remove Windows 95 components by selecting the **Windows Setup** tab.

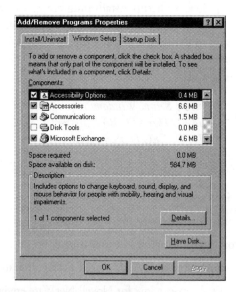

Installing Windows NT 4.0 on a Windows 95 Machine

To install Windows NT 4.0 on a machine with Windows 95 installed:

1. Verify that the devices currently in your computer are supported by Windows NT 4.0. Start Windows 95.

2. Run **Start/Run**.

3. Type the following:

   ```
   sourcepath:\winnt /w
   ```

   NOTE: The /w switch allows Windows NT Setup to be run from Windows 95. When it is used, Windows NT Setup will not detect the CPU or restart the system.

4. Install Windows NT into a different folder than Windows 95. If you want Windows NT files to be protected by the enhanced security offered by NTFS, you will need to install it on an NTFS partition.

5. Reinstall any programs you plan to use under Windows NT. This will update the Program Groups in the **Start** menu and make any necessary changes to the registry. You should install the programs into their original folders; i.e., the same ones used for Windows 95 *except* if you have a program that has both a Windows 95 version and a Windows NT version. In that case, you should install the NT version to a new folder, leaving the Windows 95 version folder intact so that it can be used when you are running Windows 95.

6. Restart your computer. You should be prompted to choose the operating system you would like to use.

NOTE: *The information about dual-booting is stored in the BOOT.INI file at the root of the C drive. This file is used by NTLDR to determine which operating system to boot. An operating system can be configured as the default from the Startup/Shutdown property page of the System control panel under Windows NT 4.0.*

Installation Over DR DOS

DR DOS is an operating system provided by Novell. It cannot be used as a dual-boot operating system with Windows 95. Your only option is to install Windows 95 over DR DOS.

There are several DR DOS utilities that cause conflicts with Windows 95. Windows 95 locates the command lines for these utilities in the configuration files, and converts them to comments.

If DR DOS password protection is used, Windows 95 setup cannot use the protected volume. This protection must be removed before Windows 95 Setup can continue.

Installation Over OS/2

OS/2 can optionally use High Performance File System (HPFS) instead of the traditional File Allocation Table (FAT) for its directory structure. Windows 95 cannot be installed over HPFS. If, however, the OS/2 system being converted has a FAT partition available, Windows 95 can be installed. When installing Windows 95 on a computer running OS/2, the following notes apply:

- You must install Windows 95 in a different directory.

- Desktop or other settings used in OS/2 cannot be migrated to Windows 95.

- Windows-based applications may have to be reinstalled to run under Windows 95.

Windows 95 Setup cannot be started from within OS/2 or OS/2 for Windows. If you have a dual-boot system with OS/2 and MS-DOS, boot MS-DOS and then run **Windows 95 Setup.** If you have just an OS/2 system, install MS-DOS and then run **Windows 95 Setup.**

Windows 95 Setup will disable the OS/2 Boot Manager by removing its partition information during installation. This is necessary because there is no way to determine which operating system or configuration Boot Manager will use to restart the system. Removing Boot Manager ensures that Windows 95 starts during the installation process.

Although you must disable the OS/2 Boot Manager during installation, it is still possible to dual boot with OS/2 and Windows 95. After you have installed Windows 95, enable the OS/2 Boot Manager by running OS/2 **FDISK** from the OS/2 boot disk. Any HPFS partitions will be accessible under OS/2, but not under Windows 95.

> *NOTE:*   *You must have an MS-DOS partition to install Windows 95.*

AUTOMATED INSTALLATIONS

This section will describe procedures for performing automated installations of Windows 95. Automated installations benefit administrators by allowing them to perform installation unsupervised. The following are topics discussed within this section:

- Push Installation Upgrade from MS-DOS or Windows 3.1
- Upgrading From Windows for Workgroups 3.11
- Automated Batch Installation Using Script Files
- Using Login scripts For a Push Installation
- Windows 95 Setup Options
- Shared Installation
- NetWare Network Login Script
- Creating a MACHINES.TXT file

Most times, administrators are stretched far and thin with various duties and responsibilities that they must perform. Automated installations provide an easy way to perform installations without having to be physically available.

Windows 95 Setup Options

As stated previously, Windows 95 supports various setup options, including shared installation to a file server, automated installations, and customized installations.

Setup allows the use of various option switches:

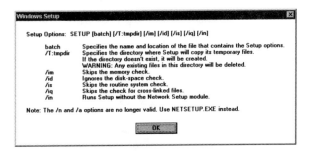

For example:

```
SETUP E:\admin\win95\setup E:\admin\win95\mybatch.inf /is / id
```

This command starts **Setup** in the specified directory using the information in the MYBATCH.INF file, skipping the routine system and the space checks.

Automated Batch Installation Using Script Files

Windows 95 allows you to complete network installation automatically using batch installation. By running BATCH.EXE and answering as many or as few questions as desired, an administrator can automate user setup.

NOTE: *It is recommended that you run Batch Setup from the Windows 95 compact disc from the \Admin\Nettools\Netsetup directory.*

Batch

The Batch utility creates an INF file that is used for network installation. When you open this utility, you will see a screen like the following:

Network configuration options include:

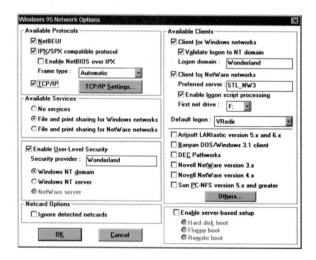

Installation options include:

The optional component selections include:

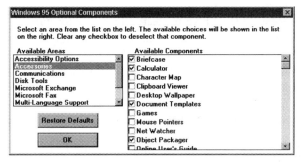

A sample INF file is contained in Appendix B.

After running this program, the INF file created can be used by Windows 95 Setup. Note that the .INF file does not run Windows 95 Setup. It only stores the preferences to allow an unattended installation. An example of the syntax to run Setup with the INF file would be:

```
E:\win95\setup C:\windows\bsetup.inf
```

Using BATCH.EXE

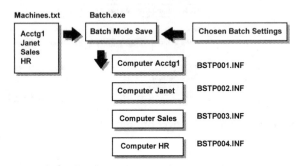

Batch Mode Save

In order for BATCH.EXE to create an INF file for different computers, you will need to supply at least one computer name for each machine so that it will be unique on the network. If you want to include an IP address for a given computer, put a single comma after the computer name and then type the IP address. These settings can be kept in a text file and supplied to batch when you save.

Following are some of the basics to creating a batch text file:

- A single blank line signifies the end of the machine name file.

- No error checking of these values is performed by the batch-mode save process.

- If incorrect information is entered using batch-mode save, Windows 95 Setup might stop and prompt the user to enter correct the information.

The following shows an example of a text file for batch-mode save:

```
Acctg1, 128.2.3.4
Janet
Sales, 128.3.4.5
HR
Shuma
```

Notice that you can include an IP address for any particular computer without having to include addresses for all computers. In the example, Acctg1 and Sales will be set up with previously defined IP addresses.

After you select the machine name file, Batch Setup reads and saves all names and addresses. A message announces how many names were read in.

You must then select a directory where all of the .INF files are to be saved. In the Select A Target Directory dialog box, find the directory you want to use. The directory must already exist. The name of the file is not important.

After the target directory has been selected, click on the **Save** button. Batch Setup will create one INF file per name, containing all the settings currently defined. To do so, it will use a series of files named BSTP0001.INF through BSTP9999.INF, written in the order in which the names are listed in the machine name file. The only unique information in each file will be the Computer Name and any IP address provided. Using the previous example, the file BSTP0001.INF will contain the setup information for the computer named Acctg1 and file BSTP0006.INF will contain the setup information for the computer named Shuma.

Click on the **Close** button to dismiss the Batch Save dialog box.

Push Installation Upgrade from MS-DOS or Windows 3.1

For a computer running MS-DOS or Windows 3.1 with a real-mode network client, the login script should be as follows:

```
Net start full

Net use drive_letter: \\server\share

drive_letter: setup drive_letter:msbatch.inf
```

The **Net start full** command is only required if you are logging on to a LAN Manager or a Windows for Workgroups network. If you are logging on to a Windows NT network, you should not use the command. If you are logging on to a Windows for Workgroups network with a real-mode client, you will also need to include the statement **lmlogon=1** under the [Network] heading in SYSTEM.INI.

Upgrading from Windows for Workgroups 3.11

If you are installing over Windows for Workgroups 3.11 from a Windows NT server using a protected-mode network client, you will need to create a special startup group to launch Windows 95 setup as a Windows application.

> *NOTE:* *If you are using a real-mode networking client, creating a startup group will not be necessary.*

To create a Startup group under Windows for Workgroups:

1. Launch Program Manager.
2. Open the Startup group and run **File\New**. Create an Upgrade icon with the following command:

   ```
   source_drive:setup [scriptpath]
   ```

   The *scriptpath* argument is optional, provided you are using a script named MSBATCH.INF that is located in the Windows directory at the same path as SETUP.EXE.

3. Copy the file STARTUP.GRP to the directory that contains your shared installation of Windows 95.

> *NOTE:* *Make sure to delete the startup group from the computer where you are working.*

4. Add the following statements to your Setup script (MSBATCH.INF by default):

```
[install]

renfiles=replace.startup.grp


[replace.startup.grp]

startup.grp, startup.sav


[destinationdirs]

replace.startup.grp=10
```

This will ensure that existing startup groups are restored after Windows 95 has been installed.

Once you have created a Startup group, you will need to write a login script to initiate the push installation. The syntax of the login script should be as follows:

```
net use driveletter \\server\sharename

rename .\startup.grp *.sav

copy \winnt\system32\repl\import\scripts\startup.grp
    .\startup.grp

exit
```

The *server**sharename* is the universal naming convention path to the shared setup files.

When the user logs on to Windows for Workgroups, the login script will run. It will log on to the network share, save the user's current Startup group with a .SAV extension, copy the new startup group from the Windows NT server, then exit. The new Startup group will run and launch SETUP.EXE. After Setup completes, the user's Startup group will be restored.

Using Login Scripts For a Push Installation

If you need to upgrade a number of computers to Windows 95, you can use a push installation that is initiated through a login script, provided the computers are running MS-DOS or Windows 3.x with one of the following network clients.

- Microsoft Workgroup Add-on for MS-DOS

- LAN Manager 2.x real-mode network client

- Novell NetWare real-mode network client (NETX or VLM)

- Any Windows for Workgroups real-mode or protected-mode network client

You can either modify each user account to use the login script that launches Setup or create a special login account that users are instructed to use when they are ready to upgrade to Windows 95. Each of these approaches has its advantages and disadvantages. Modifying each user account is more work. However, if user profiles are stored on the network, it will allow users to migrate their application settings. Another disadvantage to this approach is that it will cause Windows 95 Setup to be run when the user logs in after installation unless precautions are taken. To prevent this, modify the batch file to check for the version of MS-DOS before running Setup. After Windows 95 has been installed, the version of DOS will be Windows 95 [4.00.950].

Using a special login for upgrade simplifies this process. However, user settings that are tied to their username will not be migrated.

NetWare Network Login Script

If you are planning to perform the push installation from a NetWare network, your login script will have the following syntax:

```
attach nwserver\sharename:
map driveletter:nwserver\sharename
driveletter:setup driveletter:msbatch.inf
```

Shared Installation

Windows 95 provides you with a tool, NetSetup, that allows administrators to install Windows 95 source files on a network server. This allows you to support shared, automated, and custom installations.

NOTE: It is recommended that you run NetSetup from the Windows 95 compact disc from the \Admin\Nettools\Netsetup directory.

Netsetup

NetSetup provides you with a step-by-step process to complete a shared installation. After you launch NetSetup, the following screen appears:

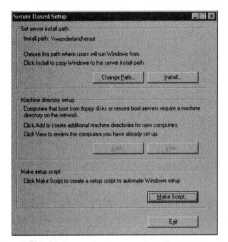

NetSetup walks the administrator through each step, prompting for information as necessary, as shown in the following example:

NetSetup creates a shared installation where the Windows 95 program files reside on the server instead of the workstation. Windows 95 Setup copies the files that are relevant to the user's computer and desktop preferences to the user's personal Windows directory. This directory can be located on the server.

The shared installation is used to install local or shared copies of Windows 95 on the client workstations. After the conclusion of NetSetup, the administrator may create customized setup scripts to automate Windows 95 Setup, as described earlier in the chapter.

DUAL-BOOT INSTALLATIONS

This section will discuss considerations for installing Windows 95 as a dual-boot operating system with Windows NT. The following topics are discussed within this section:

- Upgrade From MS-DOS and Dual-Booting
- Considerations When Dual Booting Between Windows 95 and Windows NT
- Installing Windows 95 on a Windows NT Machine

These topics will help you understand factors you must consider when installing Windows 95 as a dual-boot operating system.

Upgrade From MS-DOS and Dual-Booting

As stated previously, Windows 95 Setup can be started from MS-DOS. After beginning Setup, MS-DOS upgrades are essentially the same as Windows upgrades. Setup begins a *mini* Windows session, and installation proceeds from there.

To allow dual boot between MS-DOS or Windows 3.x and Windows 95, you must specify a directory that does not have a previous version of Windows installed during installation. Windows 95 Setup will install the Windows 95 system files without altering the MS-DOS and existing Windows settings. After installation, you must place the following entry in the MSDOS.SYS file. This file resides at the root directory of the boot drive.

```
BootMulti=1
```

During bootup you can start the previous version of MS-DOS that was loaded on this computer by pressing *F4*. This option is only available if BootMulti=1 in MSDOS.SYS.

Upon starting MS-DOS, the COMMAND.DOS, CONFIG.DOS, and AUTOEXEC.DOS files are renamed back to COMMAND.COM, CONFIG.SYS, and AUTOEXEC.BAT, respectively. The Windows 95 versions of these files are renamed with a W40 extension.

Considerations When Dual-Booting Between Windows 95 and Windows NT

Dual-boot operating systems allow users and administrators to start their systems in a different operating environment as needed. Installing Windows 95 and Windows NT as dual-boot operating systems can provide easy transition from one system to the other. However, prior to installing Windows NT on a Windows 95 machine, you must take a few considerations into account. These relate to migration of program groups, installation destination, and supported file systems.

- Program Settings

   For MS-DOS 6.x, Windows 3.x, or Windows for Workgroups 3.x, Windows NT could be installed into the same folder that contained the system files for these operating systems such as C:\Windows. Program groups and device information was migrated and preserved, allowing you to dual boot between both operating systems and access the same programs. This is not true with Windows 95. You cannot upgrade to Windows NT from Windows 95. You must install Windows NT and then re-install all of your programs so that the Windows NT registry contains the necessary information for them to run, such as the location of necessary dynamic-link libraries. You can install your programs in the same folders where they are installed under Windows 95, allowing you to preserve hard disk space. However, if you have one version of an application strictly for Windows 95 and another version strictly for Windows NT, you must install these into separate directories.

- Installation destination

   You need to ensure that Windows NT 4.0 is installed into a different folder than Windows 95 for the following reasons:

   Registry structure

      The registry structure between Windows 95 and Windows NT is different, making it impossible for the Windows NT setup program to transfer the settings from the Windows 95 registry.

   Hardware devices

      Windows 95 supports more devices than Windows NT. It is possible that you may have devices installed that are supported by Windows 95, but not by Windows NT.

- File Systems

    Windows 95 supports only FAT partitions. It does not support the NTFS file system, which is often used with Windows NT. If you have any NTFS partitions, they will not be available while the computer is running Windows 95. They will be available only when you boot to Windows NT.

    A side effect of this is that your drive letters may be different when you are running Windows NT than when you are running Windows 95. Consider a computer with the following partitions under Windows NT:

C:	FAT
D:	NTFS
E:	CD-ROM

    When you boot to Windows 95, the CD-ROM will be drive D.

Installing Windows 95 on a Windows NT Machine

It is recommended that you create a Windows NT Emergency Repair Diskette and back up any important data before you begin installing Windows 95. If you do not have MS-DOS installed, creating the Emergency Repair Diskette is not optional. You will need it after Windows 95 installation to enable dual boot. An Emergency Repair Diskette is created by running the Windows NT RDISK utility or you may create one during installation.

You cannot run the Windows 95 setup program from within Windows NT. You must start your system with MS-DOS. This can be accomplished in one of two ways, depending on whether the system is configured to dual-boot between Windows NT and MS-DOS:

- Dual boot

    If the system is already configured for dual-boot, simply choose MS-DOS from the **Startup** menu.

- No dual-boot

    If you do not have MS-DOS available, you will need to boot from an MS-DOS diskette. If you must boot from a floppy to install Windows 95, be aware that you will not be able to start Windows NT after installing Windows 95. You will need to enable your ability to multi-boot by starting your computer with the Windows NT startup diskettes and choosing **Repair** during the installation routine. It will prompt you to insert your Emergency Repair Diskette.

After you have booted to MS-DOS, run the Windows 95 setup program as usual, making sure that you install Windows 95 in a separate folder from Windows NT. Be aware that if your Windows NT computer has any NTFS file system partitions, they will not be available from within Windows 95.

After Windows 95 is installed, and you have run **Repair** if necessary, the Startup menu will allow you to choose between Windows NT and MS-DOS. Choosing MS-DOS will launch Windows 95.

If you want to triple-boot (Windows NT, Windows 95, and MS-DOS), you will need to edit the MSDOS.SYS file in the root directory of your boot-up drive. By default, this file's attributes are read-only and hidden, so you will need to change them before it can be edited. Edit the file with any standard text editor. Change the line

```
BootMulti=0
```

   to read

```
BootMulti=1
```

Save the file and exit. Now when you want to start MS-DOS, choose MS-DOS from the selection menu when the **Startup** menu appears on your screen. This will start loading Windows 95. When you see **Starting Windows 95...** on the screen, press *F8* and choose **Load Previous Version of DOS**. This will start MS-DOS.

UNINSTALL

If you install Windows 95 over Windows 3.1 or Windows for Workgroups 3.11, you will be given the option of saving the files necessary to uninstall Windows 95 and revert to your previous operating system. If you choose to back up your previous version of Windows, Setup will compress and store the following hidden files on your local hard drive:

W95UNDO.DAT	This file is a compressed backup of the Windows 3.x folder.
W95UNDO.INI	This file contains a list of the contents of the W95UNDO.DAT file.
SUHDLOG.DAT	This file contains a snapshot of the master boot record and each partition boot record both before and after Windows 95 was installed.

The path to these files will be listed in the MSDOS.SYS file as follows:

```
UnInstallDir = path
```

In order to be able to uninstall Windows 95, you will need to select the option to save the necessary files during the installation of Windows 95. In addition, you must have installed:

- Over MS-DOS 5.0 or higher.
- In the same directory as your Windows 3.1 or Windows for Workgroups 3.11 installation.

To uninstall Windows 95 and revert back to your prior version of Windows:

1. Run **Start/Settings** and launch the Control Panel.
2. Launch the Add/Remove Programs utility.
3. Select **Windows 95** from the **Install/Uninstall** tab.
4. Click on **Remove**.
5. Verify that long filename support can be removed.
6. Verify that the disk should be scanned.
7. Verify that Windows 95 should be shut down.

Windows 95 will be shut down and uninstalled. If uninstalling Windows 95 in this manner fails, restart the system to a command prompt and type the following:

```
UNINSTAL
```

You can also uninstall Windows 95 by booting from your Windows 95 Startup diskette and running UNINSTAL.EXE.

INSTALLATION FAILURES

This section will present troubleshooting concepts for a failed Windows 95 installation. The following topics are discussed within this section:

- Failed Windows 95 Installations

- Crash During Hardware Detection

- Startup Problems in Windows 95

- Startup Problems During Your First Restart After Installation

- MSDOS.SYS

- Bad or Missing Files

- Device Driver Problems

Even though Windows 95 Setup was designed to install easily and without problems, crashes may occur. You will see how Windows 95 Setup works through an installation crash.

Failed Windows 95 Installation

If Setup hangs during installation, run Windows 95 Setup again and the Safe Recovery option in Setup automatically skips detected problems. This allows Setup to complete the installation process.

Windows 95 Setup creates four hidden files in the root directory of the installation drive containing information about setup and startup processes. These are:

- BOOTLOG.TXT

    This file contains information about the boot process. Problems that occur during Windows 95 startup are recorded in this file.

- SETUPLOG.TXT

    This file contains information that allows Setup to recover if failure occurs before hardware detection. Setup reads this file to determine what processes to redo, and what to omit.

- DETCRASH.LOG

  This file contains information that allows Setup to recover if failure occurs during hardware detection. This file can only be read by Windows 95 Setup, but this information can be accessed by reading the DETLOG.TXT file. This file cannot be viewed with a text editor.

- DETLOG.TXT

  This file is the equivalent of the DETCRASH.LOG but is created whether or not the installation is successful. Any edits made to this file are not passed to the DETCRASH.LOG file.

Crash During Hardware Detection

Windows 95 Setup uses the DETCRASH.LOG file to recover from a crash during the hardware detection phase of installation. The following graphic demonstrates the process of recovery.

Failed Install Recovery

Startup Problems in Windows 95

Windows 95 was designed to install easily. Assuming that all of your hardware is compatible with Windows 95 and your hardware is configured correctly, most setups should be troublefree. To check the compatibility of your hardware with Windows 95, check the Hardware Compatibility List Help files which are HCL95.HLP and HCL95.RTF.

Startup Problems During Your First Restart After Installation

If you encounter a startup problem during installation, it is likely to be caused by one of the following:

- Legacy Hardware

    The primary reason for problems during your first restart is incorrectly configured legacy hardware. If your system contains legacy equipment and you are having difficulty during the first restart, simply remove the entries related to legacy hardware from your CONFIG.SYS and AUTOEXEC.BAT files. If you are using SCSI devices that require termination, make sure that they are correctly terminated.

- ISA Enumerator

  Another reason why you might have difficulty on first startup has to do with the ISA enumerator for I/O processes. The ISA enumerator is software that detects a plug and play adapter. Occasionally it will try to perform I/O processes on ports that are used by some other device. If a conflict occurs, you will need to disable the ISA enumerator. To do this, simply remove the following line from the [386Enh] section of SYSTEM.INI:

  ```
  device = isapnp.386
  ```

- BIOS Problems

  In order for Windows 95 to setup and start correctly, it needs to be able to write to your boot sector. Some ROM BIOS settings prevent this from happening. Usually this is associated with a boot sector anti-virus program that is set in your computer's CMOS. If this is enabled, Windows 95 may stall during setup or may stall while starting. Symptoms of this problem during setup may include:

  Setup hangs.

  You are prompted to overwrite your boot record.

  The image is distorted.

  When you reboot the system you will receive the message, "Windows Setup was unable to update your system files."

  You will need to consult your hardware documentation to turn off the anti-virus software.

MSDOS.SYS

MSDOS.SYS is a hidden, read-only system file located at the root of the Windows 95 boot drive. Windows 95 uses this file to locate other Windows 95 files. The MSDOS.SYS file contains two sections. The [Options] section can be used to customize the startup process. The [Paths] section is used by Windows 95 to locate important files such as the Registry.

The following is a sample of an MSDOS.SYS file.

```
[Paths]
WinDir=C:\WINDOWS
WinBootDir=C:\WINDOWS
HostWinBootDrv=C
[Options]
BootMulti1
BootGUI=1
Network=1
;
;The following lines are required for compatibility with other
    programs.
;Do not remove them (MSDOS.SYS needs to be >1024 bytes).
```

The BootMulti=1 statement allows the user to start a previous version of MS-DOS (installed in a separate directory) by pressing the *F8* key during startup. The default is 0.

The BootGUI=1 statement enables startup to launch the Windows 95 graphical user interface. If the 0 value is used, startup will launch the command prompt instead of the graphical interface. The default is 1.

The Network=1 statement enables the **Safe Mode With Networking** menu option.

The BootMenu=1 statement causes the **Startup** menu to display by default. Otherwise, you have to use the *F8* key to display the **Startup** menu.

Bad or Missing Files

You may receive a message that there is a bad or missing file. If this is the case, ensure that the entry in the CONFIG.SYS file (or other startup file referenced by the error message, SYSTEM.INI) has the correct syntax. Also, check to ensure that the file is indeed on your system, in the correct location, is the right version, and is not corrupt.

If the file refers to a device driver that Windows 95 needs to start up (for example, a device that lets Windows 95 access a drive), edit the CONFIG.SYS file to ensure that the device is being loaded first.

If there are core files like VMM32.VXD that are damaged or missing, you might need to run the Windows 95 Setup program again. Windows 95 counts on certain files being present during startup. If any of these core files are missing or corrupt, this may be your only option. If this file is intact and a particular VxD file is missing, Windows 95 will alert you to this fact. You can copy the referenced VxD file to the C:\Windows\System directory manually and attempt a restart. If, however, one of the missing VxDs is critical to Windows 95 startup, you will need to run **Setup** again and select Verify or Safe Recovery to replace the missing VxD.

Windows 95 has two important registry files that it needs to load: SYSTEM.DAT and USER.DAT. Normally these are backed up as a precaution to SYSTEM.DA0 and USER.DA0. If, during startup, Windows 95 recognizes that one of these files is missing or corrupt, it automatically starts in Safe Mode and prompts you to restore the registry file in question. However, if both of these are missing, then Windows 95 cannot be restored. You will have to reinstall.

Device Driver Problems

If you install a third-party Windows 3.x version of a device driver in Windows 95 through the manufacturer's installation program, Windows 95 might not recognize it. It may cause Windows 95 not to start up properly. If this is the case, restart in Safe Mode, remove all entries in SYSTEM.INI that were added by this installation, delete the device in Device Manager, shut down and restart Windows 95. Try using the Add New Hardware Wizard to reinstall the device.

SCENARIOS

Scenario 1

You are planning to upgrade several OS/2 computers to Windows 95. Each has a single HPFS partition. They do not have MS-DOS installed. You want to preserve the data. How can you accomplish this?

....

....

Scenario 2

You are upgrading your computer from Windows for Workgroups 3.11 to Windows 95. You want to ensure that all of your Program Group settings are migrated to Windows 95. What is the best way to install Windows 95 to accomplish this?

....

....

Scenario 3

Your company has decided to run two shifts in order to meet escalating demand without buying new equipment. The people on the day shift use an OS/2 application and they have been storing data on a single HPFS partition for several years. The long term goal of the company is to migrate everyone to Windows 95, but there is not time to retrain the first shift now. However, the employees for the second shift are new hires, so they are not familiar with the OS/2 application. You would like them to run Windows 95. How can you configure the systems to use both OS/2 and Windows 95?

....

....

Scenario 4

You are testing a data processing application before deploying it company wide. Some users will need to use it under Windows 95 and some will need the NTFS security offered by Windows NT Workstation. You have configured a computer to dual boot between Windows NT Workstation 4.0 and Windows 95. You have installed and tested the application under Windows 95 and booted to Windows NT Workstation to begin testing. Since the application is not on your **Start** menu, you locate it on the hard drive and launch it. You receive an error that it cannot find a dynamic-link library. What is most likely the problem?

....

....

Scenario 5

You are configuring a system that will be used by multiple users. Managers will boot the system to Windows NT. Temporary employees will boot the computers to Windows 95. Managers will need to store sensitive information. How can you configure a private location that only managers can access?

....

....

Scenario 6

You need to upgrade 150 computers from Windows for Workgroups 3.11 to Windows 95. The users have various levels of technical expertise, but most of them are novice users. You are running on a NetWare network. What is the most efficient way to accomplish this task?

....

....

Scenario 7

Several months ago you upgraded your boss's computer from Windows 3.1 to Windows 95. When you did, you selected to back up the system files because you suspected that he might want to revert to his old operating system. Now he wants to revert to Windows 3.1. You try to run **Uninstal** from Add/Remove Programs and from a command prompt, but it fails. What is most likely the problem? How can you be sure?

....

....

Scenario 8

One of your users is used to working in MS-DOS. Most of the applications he runs are MS-DOS applications. He would like to launch the Windows 95 interface only when he needs to run Windows applications. How can you configure his computer to do this?

....

....

Scenario 9

One of the employees at your company has called, complaining that Windows 95 will not start. He does not even get the option of going into Safe Mode. When questioned about the changes he might have made to his system, he said that he had deleted some data files to recover disk space. You asked him which files and he replied that he deleted all files with a .DAT extension and all files with a .DA0 extension. How can you recover Windows 95?

....

....

SUMMARY

During this chapter, you looked at how to install Windows 95, as well deployment concerns. These included:

- Planning for a Windows 95 implementation

- Minimum hardware and software requirements for Windows 95

- Installation options

- Installation of Windows 95 as an upgrade to Windows 3.x and Windows for Workgroups

- Installation of Windows 95 over DR DOS

- Installation of Windows 95 over OS/2

- Command line utilities changed by Windows 95

- Use of the NetSetup utility

- Windows 95 maintenance installations

- Windows 95 Safe Mode operations

- Push Installations
- Use of the Batch utility to create customized .INF files
- Dual-booting between Windows 95 and MS-DOS/Windows 3.x
- Recovery from failed Windows 95 installations

In the next chapter, you will see how to customize the desktop using Control Panel utilities, as well as other methods. You will also be introduced to profiles and policies.

Stop now and complete the Chapter 2 NEXTSim simulation exercise on the Interactive Learning CD-ROM.

POST-TEST QUESTIONS

The answers to these questions are in Appendix A at the end of this manual.

1. Briefly describe the minimum hardware and software requirements of Windows 95, for the following:

     MS-DOS version

     Processor

     Memory

     ....

     ....

2. After installation, where would you find a list of potential problematic hardware?

     ....

     ....

3. List hard disk requirements for Windows 95 installation for each of the following:

   Windows 3.1 upgrade

   Windows for Workgroups 3.11 upgrade

   MS-DOS upgrade

   ....

   ....

4. What are the four steps in the Windows 95 Setup process?

   ....

   ....

5. In Windows 95 usage, what is a legacy PC?

   ....

   ....

6. How would you set up a Windows 95 installation to dual-boot with the previous MS-DOS installation? What is an advantage of a dual-boot system?

   ....

   ....

7. What is the purpose of the NetSetup utility?

   ....

   ....

8.   How can you switch Windows 95 into Safe Mode during startup?

     ....

     ....

9.   What file is used by Windows 95 Setup to recover a crash during the hardware
     detection phase of installation?

     ....

     ....

User Interface Tour

OBJECTIVES

- Discuss Windows 95 Startup.
- Describe Windows 95 Logon.
- Describe the Windows 95 user interface.
- Use the Windows Explorer to view files and folders.
- List common desktop objects and their purposes.
- Describe the troubleshooters available through the Help utility.
- List other troubleshooting resources available for Windows 95 administrators and users.

PRE-TEST QUESTIONS

The answers to these questions are in Appendix A at the end of the manual.

1. What is the name of the first file to load when the system is booted?

   ....

   ....

2. How does Windows 95 know which application to launch when a user double-clicks on a document file on the Desktop?

   ....

   ....

3. How do you delete a file without moving it to the Recycle Bin?

   ....

   ....

INTRODUCTION

The most obvious difference with Windows 95 is the improved User Interface (UI). The UI can be customized in various ways. The interface contains many new tools and some very familiar ones. There are many significant improvements over Windows 3.x in this respect. This chapter will highlight several of them.

The chapter continues with a discussion of the **Start** menu and Taskbar. These additions to the UI provide easy access to the primary activities of the Windows 95 PC and help keep active applications organized. It is easy to customize the **Start** menu and Taskbar. You will see how it can be done.

WINDOWS 95 USER INTERFACE TOUR

This section will concentrate on the physical aspects of the Windows 95 user interface (UI). Each feature will be described in detail. Many of these features have been designed to allow the user easier access to information, files, and objects. The following are topics discussed within this section:

- System Startup
- System Logon
- The Windows 95 UI
- The Pointing Device
- New Appearances
- Windows Explorer Basics
- Windows Explorer Features
- The Start Menu
- The Taskbar and Task Switching
- Common Desktop Objects
- Finding Computers, Files, and Folders
- Recycling Files and Folders
- The Briefcase
- Quick View
- Getting Help
- Troubleshooters

Many of these features are the basic changes within Windows 95. As many of these features will be new to users, it will be important for you to understand each of them as an Administrator. Microsoft has also implemented a very similar user interface in Windows NT 4.0 Workstation and Server. This interface has also been carried over to the new Windows 98 environment with a few visual enhancements.

System Startup

As you start up Windows 95, the following steps occur:

- Bootstrap starts the system with the system BIOS in control.

  For legacy computers, BIOS enables all devices on the ISA bus.

  With a plug and play BIOS, non-volatile RAM tracks Plug and Play device I/O addresses, IRQs, and other settings. Through these stored settings, BIOS programs the cards that should be enabled at startup with their specific device settings. BIOS also configures all devices on the motherboard at this time.

- MS-DOS drivers and TSRs load for compatibility.

  The operating system attempts to determine the current hardware configuration. Support for multiple hardware configurations is discussed later in this course.

  CONFIG.SYS and AUTOEXEC.BAT are processed if present. Drivers and TSRs contained within these files load in real mode.

- Virtual Device Drivers are initiated in real mode.

  Common static VxDs, such as dynapage, vcache, and reboot load as part of VMM32.VXD. VMM32.VXD also includes the real-mode loader and the executable Virtual Machine Manager.

  WIN.COM and SYSTEM.INI are loaded.

- The protected-mode operating system takes control and loads the remaining VxDs.

  VMM32.VXD switches the processor to protected mode.

  Protected-mode VxDs are loaded.

- The final system components are loaded.

  KERNEL32.DLL provides Windows 95 components.

  KRNL386.EXE loads device drivers.

  GDI.EXE and GDI32.EXE provide code for the GUI.

  USER.EXE and USER32.EXE provide code for the user interface.

  WIN.INI values are checked.

  The Windows 95 shell and desktop are loaded.

  The logon prompt is displayed.

System Logon

As Windows 95 boots up, you are transferred to the Windows 95 user interface. Before beginning your session, a dialog box appears asking for a username and password. These usernames and passwords are tracked and can be used by an administrator to enforce policies and profiles. User profiles and system policies are discussed later in the course.

Windows 95 offers a consistent user interface for logging on to and validating access to network resources. The first time the user logs on to Windows 95, logon dialog boxes appear for each network client on that computer and for Windows 95. If the user sets identical passwords for each network and for Windows 95, the user will be able to take advantage of the Unified System Logon offered by Windows 95.

Unified logon allows the user to log on to Windows 95 and the primary logon server from a single dialog box. Different passwords for other networks are stored in a password cache after their first use. This allows the user to log on to these other networks without typing the additional password. The password cache for a user can only be unlocked by the user's Windows 95 password. By using this logon scheme, users benefit by a single logon dialog box, and administrators benefit from the use of existing user accounts to validate access to the network.

NOTE: *It is fairly easy for an unauthorized user to gain access to the .PWL file. An encrypted version is available on Microsoft's Web site.*

The Windows 95 UI

The Windows 95 user interface (UI) contains many changes and enhancements from the Windows 3.x interface. One of the most apparent changes is the replacement of the Program Manager, File Manager, and Print Manager with the Windows Explorer.

Another improvement is the usability of the UI. The Windows 95 UI looks and behaves much like the Macintosh UI. To copy or move files, drag their icons from one folder to another. To delete files, drag their icons to the Recycle Bin. Windows 95 supports long filenames. In addition, the desktop and **Start** menu are easy to customize

Navigating the UI

The Windows 95 UI has several new features, which you will learn to use in the next few pages. These are:

- Using the pointing device
- New appearance for applications running under Windows 95
- Using the Windows Explorer
- Using the Taskbar
- Switching active tasks

The Pointing Device

The mouse or other pointing device has additional capabilities within Windows 95. The primary button (the left button on a right-handed mouse) and the secondary button (the right button on a right-handed mouse) perform different tasks. To display a menu for an object, point at the object and click the secondary button. The menu displayed will be specific to the type of object selected. It will nearly always include the *Properties* selection. This menu is sometimes called a context menu or pop-up menu. The primary and secondary mouse buttons are also called mouse button 1 and mouse button 2.

The primary mouse button continues to perform its traditional function of clicking and dragging, but clicking and dragging with the secondary mouse button produces a menu of possible choices when the object is dropped. These normally include:

- Move Here
- Copy Here
- Create Shortcut Here

You can also move or copy several objects by clicking the primary mouse button near, but not on the first object desired, and holding the button while dragging across the additional objects to be manipulated. This action will be familiar to Apple Macintosh users. You can also click on the first object with the primary mouse button, hold down the *SHIFT* key, and click on the last object in the list to be moved or copied.

The mechanism of pointing and clicking has undergone some additional refinements. While browsing a menu, you can release the primary mouse button after the menu appears and still move left and right to view other menus. Also, a double-click is not required in Windows 95, but may be used as a shortcut to open items. It is possible to navigate the entire Windows 95 interface without ever double-clicking.

Exercise 3-1:
Pointing Device

During this exercise, you will work with the pointing device (mouse). During this and all remaining exercises, the terms *Click* and *Left-Click* refer to the primary mouse button, and the term *Right-Click* refers to the secondary mouse button.

You should be logged on at your system at the beginning of this exercise.

1. Right-click on an empty area of the desktop.

2. Hold the pointer over the **New** selection until the nested menu appears.

3. Left-click to select **Text Document**.

4. Overwrite the name with the following and press *ENTER*:

   ```
   My new text document is here
   ```

5. If you receive a filename extension warning, click on **Yes**.

6. Right-click on the new text document icon on the desktop and select **Properties** from the menu.

7. Click on the checkbox next to **Read-only** to set the attribute for this object.

8. Click on **OK** to save your changes and close the properties dialog.

9. Place the pointer on the text document. Press and hold the secondary mouse button while dragging the document to another area of the desktop. Release the mouse button.

10. Click to select **Copy Here** from the menu. A copy of the object appears in that location. This is true only if you do not have **Auto Arrange** enabled for the arrangement of icons on the desktop.

11. Click in the upper-left corner of the screen and drag downwards to select all of the objects along the left of your screen.

12. Release the mouse button. Click on any object with the left mouse button, drag right, and release. All selected objects move as a group.

13. Click on any object, move the objects back to their original position, and release.

14. Run **Start/Programs/Windows Explorer.**

15. Click on **File** in the menu bar. Move the pointer right and the other menus will open. It is not necessary to open each menu separately.

16. Close Windows Explorer by clicking on the close button (the "X") in the upper right corner of the window.

NOTE: *If you were not running any programs before the start of this exercise, then Windows Explorer should be the only program active at your system.*

Application Appearance

Windows 3.x applications have a different appearance within Windows 95. The minimize, maximize, and close buttons now appear together on the upper right of the title bar, and the application menu continues to reside on the upper left.

Minimize Button   Maximize Button   Close Program

Menus also have undergone a slight visual change, as the following graphic illustrates with Word 6 menus under Windows 3.1, compared to Word 6 menus under Windows 95:

Word 6 under Win 3.1   Word 6 under Win 95

Windows 95 uses this graphical scheme throughout the user interface.

Windows 95 also has many visual cues for users, as is illustrated in the following graphics:

- If you decide to change your screen saver, a sample will appear in the monitor:

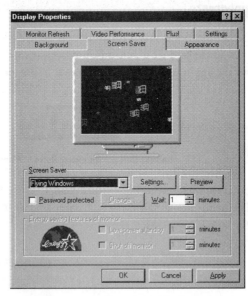

- If you change time zones, a graphical map helps you orient yourself:

Throughout Windows 95, users will find more graphical cues and pointers to assist them in configuration and customization tasks.

Windows Explorer Basics

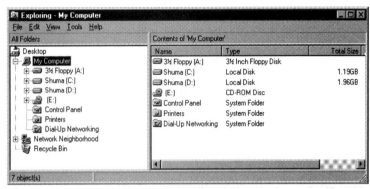

At first look, Windows Explorer appears to be somewhat similar to the Windows 3.x File Manager. Although the functionality of File Manager remains, there are additional features. Often, you will hear Windows Explorer referred to as "Explorer."

As you explore the contents of a selected resource, you can point to an object and click with your right mouse button to display a context-sensitive menu. This menu varies according to the object to which you are pointing. You may have options such as **Open**, **Send To**, **Cut**, **Copy**, **Paste**, **Create Shortcut**, **Delete** and **Rename**. These are among the most common options. Depending on the application you use, there may be additional options available.

Because of the document-centric nature of Windows 95, you only need to locate the file you wish to view, and Windows will open up the associated application for you.

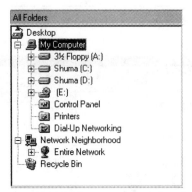

A significant improvement over the Windows 3.x File Manager is the ability to view all mapped network drives, CD-ROM drives, and additional local drives on the left side of the Explorer. This allows you to easily explore all resources without opening and closing multiple windows.

File Associations

As mentioned previously, Windows 95 provides a document-centric environment. When a user double-clicks on a file in Windows Explorer, the file is opened in its associated application. Many files are automatically associated to applications given their file extensions. However, there are times when it is necessary for a user to manually define the association between a file and an application. The user may either know that the file does not have an association of any kind, or the user finds out when trying to open the file.

Creating an Association

If the user right-clicks on an unassociated file, the pop-up menu offers the following menu options:

If the user selects **Open With**, the following dialog opens, allowing the user to select an application to associate with the file:

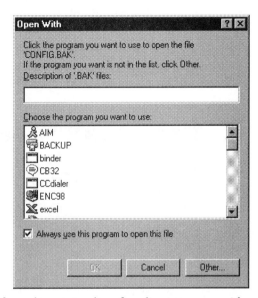

The user can select from the existing list of applications to provide an association to the file. If the user cannot find the appropriate application in the list, click on **Other** to browse for a different application which is not listed. Then, click on **OK**. The application will then open, displaying the contents of your file or running the file if it is a type of program. The other menu options available in the pop-up menu displayed above will be discussed during the file management portion of the course.

NOTE: *The dialog displayed may be different depending on the version of Windows 95 you are running.*

Creating a New File Type

Users can also create new file types, edit existing file types, or remove file types entirely from the system. As you install software applications on your computer, Windows 95 retains the file types associated with the new applications in a list. Given a file's extension, Windows 95 can determine which application to launch when a user opens a given file. To view the list of existing file types on your system, open **View/Options** from the Windows Explorer or **My Computer** menu. Select the **File Types** tab. The following dialog is displayed:

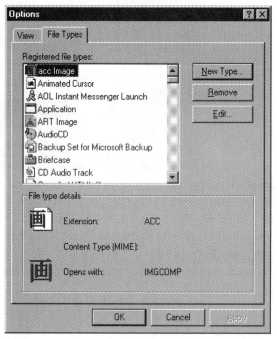

This dialog displays detailed information about a selected file type at the bottom of the dialog. For example, the dialog shows "acc Image" selected. At the bottom of the dialog, you can view information about the extension associated with this file type, any content type information, and the application that is used to open any files with the listed file extension. Users can also create a new file type, remove an existing file type, or edit an existing file type simply by clicking on the appropriate option. Click on **New Type** to display the following dialog:

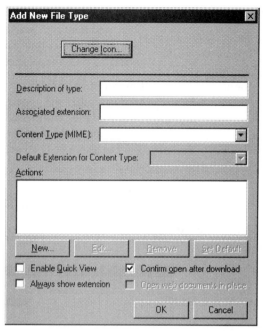

The Add New File Type dialog allows the user to configure many different options for a file type.

Description of type   Enter a description for the file type that you are creating. This description is what is listed in the View/Options dialog.

Associated extension   This option lets you assign the extension you wish to use for the new file type.

Content Type (MIME)
    This option lets you select the content type of the file as application, audio, image, text, or video. There are detailed entries for each of these content types.

Default Extension for Content Type

Once a content type is selected, you can select the default extension as either that you created or the file type associated with the selected content type.

Actions

Entering an action allows you to specify the name of the command that will appear on the popup menu for the associated file. Normally, **Open** or **Print** are the common action names, although you can specify whatever you like. You can also specify an accelerator such as **&** for the action.

The Application used to perform action option specifies what will happen when the command (Action) is chosen.

You can also select the new action to use dynamic data exchange.

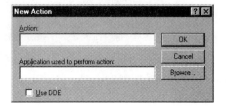

Editing an Existing File Type

Users can also edit existing file types by clicking on **Edit** from the View\Options dialog. The icon for the file type can be changed by clicking on Change Icon. The user can then browse existing icons to select a new icon.

As you can see, the description of the file type can be changed. Content Type and the Default Extension for Content Type can be reconfigured as well. Actions are listed for the selected file type. Note that this file type has three actions available: **New**, **Open**, and **Print**. As we mentioned previously, **Open** and **Print** are the most common selections used. You can have any number of actions. However, it is suggested that you set a default action by selecting the action and clicking on **Set Default**. You can create a **New** action, **Edit** an existing action, or **Remove** an action.

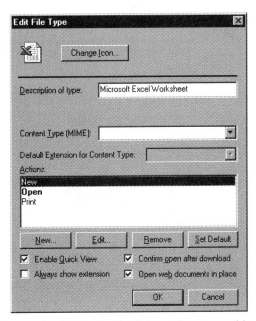

Four additional options are available on this dialog. You can enable **Quick View** for the file type. This allows you to view the contents of a file using popular Windows-based programs. You can also enable the **Always show extension** option to view the extension of the file always.

Two additional options are available for files that you may download off of the Internet: **Confirm open after download** and **Open web documents in place**. These, of course, apply to the selected file type only if enabled.

Editing an Action

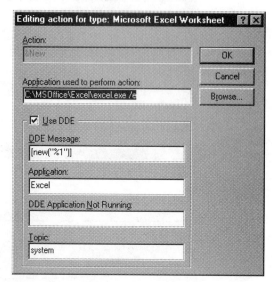

Actions can be edited for a selected file type's action. You can select a different application to perform the selected action. If you do not know the exact path to the application, you can click on **Browse**. You can enable dynamic data exchange. You can change the name of the Application associated with this action. If necessary, you can also set a DDE application to not run, if you have enabled dynamic data exchange. The **Topic** setting allows you to set the topic string that should be used to initiate a conversation between the DDE application and the program.

Removing a File Type

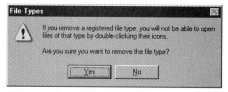

Before removing a file type, you should be aware that you will not be able to open files of that type any longer.

Windows Explorer Features

The Windows Explorer toolbar contains several icons to assist the user. By pointing the mouse pointer at a menu button, a description of the selected icon appears. Icons on the toolbar include:

- Up One Level
- Map Network Drive
- Discount Network Drive
- Cut
- Copy
- Paste
- Undo
- Delete
- Properties
- Large Icons
- Small Icons
- List
- Details

You can view the Options dialog for Explorer by running **View/Options**:

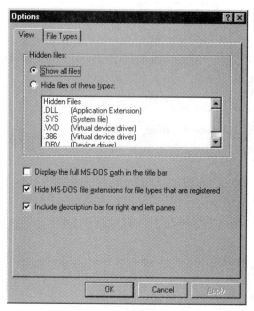

Through use of Explorer options, the user configures the way the Explorer displays files and folders.

The user selects from four different views when using the Explorer. These include Large Icons, Small Icons, List, and Details. Viewing the items within a selected container while in Details mode allows the user to quickly sort the items. To accomplish this, simply click on either Name, Size, Type, or Modified columns. The Explorer sorts the list by the header selected. To reverse the sort order, click on the selected column header again.

A valuable feature of the Explorer is Undo. To undo a file copy, deletion, or move, run **Edit/Undo**. The file returns to its original location.

Exercise 3-2:
Explorer

During this exercise, you will use the Windows Explorer to browse drive resources. You will also work with Explorer options.

1. Launch Windows Explorer using **Start/Programs/Windows Explorer**.

2. Run **View/Large Icons**. The files in the Contents window are now displayed as large icons.

3. Run **View/Details**. The files are now displayed with their file details including name, size, type, and modified information.

4. Maximize Explorer by clicking on the maximize button in the upper right-hand corner of the Explorer window. It is between the Close and Minimize buttons.

5. Click on **View** from the **Explorer** menu. Display the **Arrange Icons** menu item choices. Then, click on **by Date**. The folders and files are now sorted by modification date.

6. Click on **View** from the **Explorer** menu. Display the **Arrange Icons** menu item choices. Then, click on **by Size**. The folders and files are now sorted in ascending order according to size.

7. Click on the heading Name listed in the Contents pane. Files and folders are sorted in ascending alphabetical order by name. Folders are listed first, and then files.

    Click on the maximize button to return the Explorer window to its original size.

9. Run **View/List** from the Explorer menu to return to the original view.

10. Run **View/Options** from the Explorer menu. Using the primary mouse button, clear the check mark from the box next to **Hide MS-DOS file extensions for file types that are registered**.

11. Click on **OK** to save the change and close the Options dialog.

12. Click on the **Windows** folder in the All Folders section in the left portion of the Explorer window.

13. Locate and select the PROGMAN.EXE file in the Contents section of the Explorer window.

14. Right-click on the icon from PROGMAN.EXE and select **Open** from the menu or double-click on PROGRMAN.EXE. The Windows 3.x Program Manager launches.

15. Minimize the Program Manager by clicking on the minimize button.

16. From the Content section of Explorer, right-click on **SOL.EXE**.

17. Click to select **Copy**.

18. Right-click on an empty area of the desktop and select **Paste** from the context-sensitive menu.

19. Click on the copy of SOL.EXE. Wait a moment and click on the object name again. A highlight will appear surrounding the object name.

20. Overwrite the name as the following as press *ENTER*:

```
Time Waster.EXE
```

21. Double-click to launch Time Waster.

22. Close all programs and windows running on your system.

The Start Menu

Clicking on the **Start** button at the bottom left of the desktop reveals the **Start** menu.

The **Start** menu displays a list for accessing the primary applications and features of the Windows 95 PC. These include:

- Programs

  This selection allows you to access programs much in the same way as the Windows 3.x Program Manager. You also can organize program folders within folders, creating a *nested* menu.

- Documents

  This option lists the most recently-used document files, regardless of type. This is similar to the most recently used file list in Microsoft Word.

- Settings

    This selection contains the Control Panel, Printers folder, and configuration dialog for the Taskbar and **Start** menu. You will have a chance to customize the **Start** menu later in the course.

- Find

    This option allows you to locate files, folders, or computers either locally or across a network.

- Help

    This option allows you to access the robust Windows 95 help utility.

- Run

    This item allows you to run a DOS- or Windows-based program by entering the program's path and filename.

- Shut Down

    This option allows you to shut down the computer, restart the computer, restart the computer in MS-DOS mode, or close all programs and log on as a different user.

Press *CONTROL+ESC* at any time to display the **Start** menu.

The Taskbar and Task Switching

Windows 95 places all active applications on the Taskbar, rather than displaying minimized active applications as icons.

The Taskbar allows you to quickly access all active objects by clicking on the appropriate icon on the Taskbar. If a window becomes hidden behind other windows, clicking on its icon in the Taskbar will call it to the foreground. This prevents you from losing minimized icons behind other active windows, as was frequently the case in Windows 3.x. Customizing your Taskbar will be discussed later in the course.

Windows 95 also allows you to quickly switch between tasks using the familiar *ALT+TAB* keystroke. However, Windows 95 provides a more informative display.

All active tasks are displayed with a description and the appropriate application icon. This alleviates the problem of skipping past the task while hitting *ALT+TAB* repeatedly. To select a task immediately to the left of the active task, use the *SHIFT+ALT+TAB* combination.

Exercise 3-3:
Taskbar

The purpose of this exercise is to have you work with the Taskbar and program objects. You should be logged on to your system at the beginning of this exercise.

1. Run **Start/Programs/Accessories/Calculator**. This will launch the Calculator application.

2. Repeat the procedures in step 1 to launch Paint and Wordpad.

3. Launch the MS-DOS Prompt by running **Start/Programs**.

4. Press and hold the *ALT* key.

5. While continuing to hold the *ALT* key, press and release the *TAB* key.

6. While continuing to hold the *ALT* key, press and release the *TAB* key several times. This allows you to cycle through the active programs. If you release the *ALT* key after selecting a particular icon, its corresponding window will move to the foreground.

7. Use the *ALT+TAB* key combination to bring the Calculator to the foreground.

8. Right-click on an empty portion of the Taskbar. Select **Minimize All Windows**. It may be necessary to drag the edge of the Taskbar up to provide more open space. To drag, move the pointer to the top edge of the Taskbar until the pointer becomes a two-headed arrow. Then, click and move the pointer upwards or downwards, depending on whether you want to increase or decrease the space in the taskbar. Release the pointer once you have the desired amount of space.

9. Click on the **Calculator** button from the Taskbar. The Calculator application will be restored to the desktop.

10. Launch Windows Explorer by running **Start/Programs**.

11. Select the Windows directory.

12. Select EXPLORER.EXE.

13. Right-click and drag EXPLORER.EXE to the desktop. You may have to resize the window manually or use the maximize button to view both Explorer and the desktop.

14. When prompted, select **Copy Here**.

15. Click and drag the Explorer to the **Start** button and release.

16. Click on **Start**. You should see EXPLORER.EXE listed as the top object in the menu.

17. Click on a clear area of the desktop to close the Start menu or click on the **Start** button.

18. Close all open programs on your desktop.

Common Desktop Objects

Depending on the Windows 95 components installed, you will see several objects on the desktop. These include:

- My Computer

The My Computer object contains all the resources and information associated with your computer. Opening this object presents you with icons representing all disk drives, and folders for Control Panel, Printers, and Dial-Up Networking. My Computer can be renamed like any other object.

- Network Neighborhood

Opening this object displays all members of your workgroup, and accessible network resources. You can explore the resources displayed, as long as you have appropriate network permissions to the resource. Networking components will be examined closely later in the course.

- The Microsoft Network (MSN)

The Microsoft Network is an online service tailored to the Windows 95 user. To set up MSN for first time use, double-click on the desktop icon to launch the Setup Wizard.

- Recycle Bin

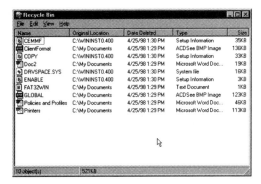

The Recycle Bin contains all recently deleted files, folders, and objects. Files are permanently deleted as the bin becomes full on a first in, first out basis. You can view the items in the Recycle Bin by opening the Recycle Bin object.

You may recover deleted items from the Recycle Bin by dragging the items out and placing them in a folder or directly on to the desktop. The Recycle Bin will be discussed in greater detail later in this chapter.

- Microsoft Exchange

Opening this object will allow the user to set up the Microsoft Exchange client.

- My Briefcase

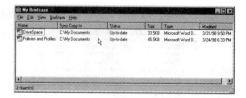

The Briefcase allows the user to keep files synchronized between two or more computers. This is useful if a user has a portable and a desktop system, or if several people edit a large document. The Briefcase will be discussed later in the chapter.

Finding Computers, Files, and Folders

The **Find** option on the **Start** menu allows you to search for files or other computers on a network. The **Find** option supports searching by filenames, by modification date, text strings, file size, or any combination of these variables.

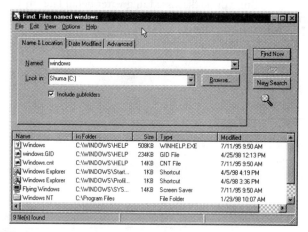

A new tool for Windows users is the text string search. This allows you to find a file with specific text even if you have no idea of the type of file or its location. UNIX users will recognize this as being similar to the GREP utility.

In addition, you can specify several MS-DOS filename extensions with wildcards to find files. For example, you may search for *.DOC and *.TXT to find all Word documents and all text files. You can also use the wildcard within a file name such as Letter*Document, where * might represent a number. Find can also be used to search the MSN (Microsoft Network) in the same fashion.

Recycling Files and Folders

The Recycle Bin contains recently deleted files, folders, and objects. When you delete a file or folder, it goes into the Recycle Bin, but it still takes up space on the hard disk. Files are permanently deleted from the hard disk as the bin becomes full on a first in, first out basis.

You can view the items in the Recycle Bin by opening the Recycle Bin object. To do so, double-click on the Recycle bin icon on the desktop. You can also view the contents of the Recycle Bin through Windows Explorer. The Recycle Bin is listed in the All Folders section of the Explorer at the root of the drive that contains the Windows 95 system files. You can recover a deleted item from the Recycle Bin by dragging it out and placing it in a folder or on the desktop.

To avoid moving items to the Recycle Bin, press *SHIFT* as you delete the item. To empty the Recycle Bin, right-click on the Recycle Bin icon and select **Empty Recycle Bin**. You can set aside a percentage of your hard drive space for the Recycle Bin through its **Properties** dialog. This option is available in the context-sensitive menu for the Recycle Bin.

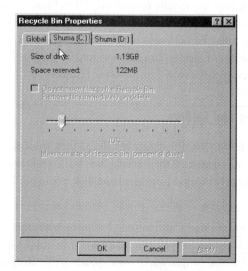

If you have multiple local hard drives, the Recycle Bin properties can be set globally, or independently for each drive. If you want deleted items to be removed from the Recycle Bin immediately, mark the **Do not move files to the Recycle Bin. Remove files immediately on delete** option on the property sheet.

The Briefcase

The Briefcase allows the mobile user to keep various copies of files updated between two computers.

To use the Briefcase, drag files from a shared directory on the desktop computer to the Briefcase on the mobile computer.

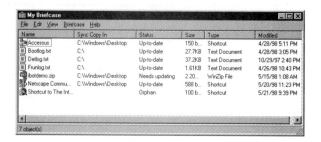

After you have finished editing files on the mobile computer, connect to the desktop computer via a network or direct cable connection and run **Briefcase/Update All** from the menu. The files on your desktop computer are automatically updated without moving any files from the Briefcase.

Quick View

Quick viewers allow you to view files that are in specific formats without opening the application that generated the file. To Quick View a file, click on the object with the secondary mouse button, and select **Quick View**. From the Quick View window, you easily can open the file for editing, if desired.

Windows 95 contains Quick Viewers for the following file formats:

Extension	Description
.ASC	ASCII files
.BMP	Windows Bitmap Graphic files
.CDR	Corel Draw files
.DOC	Word for MS-DOS 5.x and 6.x, Word for Windows 2.x and 6.x, WordPerfect 4.2, 5.x, 6.0, and 6.1 files
.DRW	Micrographix Draw files
.EPS	Encapsulated PostScript files
.GIF	CompuServe GIF files
.INF	Windows Setup files
.INI	Windows Configuration files
.MOD	Multiplan 3.x, 4.0, and 4.1 files
.PPT	PowerPoint 4.x files
.PRE	Freelance for Windows files
.RLE	Windows Bitmap files

Extension	Description
.RTF	Rich Text Format files
.SAM	AMI and AMI PRO files
.TIF	TIFF files
.TXT	Text files
.WB1	Quattro Pro for Windows files
.WK1	Lotus 1-2-3 Release 1 and 2 files
.WK3	Lotus 1-2-3 Release 3 files
.WK4	Lotus 1-2-3 Release 4 files
.WKS	Lotus 1-2-3 and Microsoft Works 3.x files
.WMF	Windows Metafiles
.WPD	WordPerfect demo files
.WPS	Microsoft Works Word Processing files
.WQ1	Quattro Pro for MS-DOS files
.WQ2	Quattro Pro for 5.x for MS-DOS files
.WRI	Windows 3.x Write files
.XLC	Excel 4.x Chart files
.XLS	Excel 4.x spreadsheet and Excel 5.x spreadsheet and chart files

After a Quick View window is open, you can drag other files into the Quick View window to view them. The quick viewers are especially valuable when you have a file but not the associated application.

Quick View can be added during installation of Windows 95 by selecting the **Accessories** component. Then click on the **Details** button, and choose **Quick View**. To add Quick View after Windows 95 is installed, run **Start/Settings/Control Panel**. Double-click on the Add/Remove Programs utility. Display the **Windows Setup** tab by clicking on it. Then, click on the **Details** button to select **Quick View**.

Exercise 3-4:
Basic Tools

During this exercise, you will continue working on the desktop and working with basic tools. You should be logged on with no applications running at the start of this exercise.

1. Select the object Copy of My new text document is here and press the *DELETE* button on your keyboard.

2. When prompted to confirm the file delete, press *ENTER*.

3. Drag the object My new text document is here to the Recycle Bin and release.

4. Double-click on the **Recycle Bin**.

5. Locate and select My new text document is here and drag the object to the desktop.

6. Run **Empty Recycle Bin** from the **File** menu.

7. When prompted to delete the item, click on **Yes**.

8. Click on the **Close** button to close the Recycle Bin.

9. Double-click on the My Computer icon. You will see all local drives, the Control Panel, Printers, and the Dial-Up Networking folders displayed.

   NOTE: *If your system is attached to any network drives, these are also listed.*

10. Double-click on drive C:.

11. The files and directories (shown as folders) at the root directory are displayed.

12. Run **View/List** from the menu. This changes the view to list all folders as they are displayed in Windows Explorer.

13. Click on **My Computer** in the taskbar. The view has not changed in this window.

14. Close all open windows.

Getting Help

Windows 95 contains a new help engine that allows you to search for key words and topics. Run **Start/Help** to access the help utility.

The Help utility has three pages:

- Contents

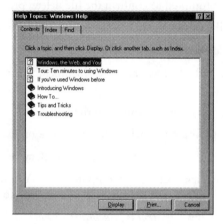

This tab allows the user to browse the contents of the Help utility. You can access the Windows 95 Tour and Troubleshooters from this tab.

- Index

This tab allows the user to search the Help index for topics.

• Find

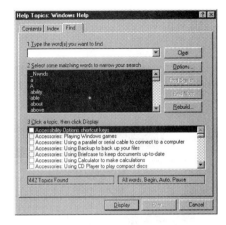

The **Find** tab allows the user to search the text of all help files for a specific item.

After you select the **Find** tab for the first time, Windows will create the word list. You have three options for the creation of the word list:

• Minimize database size

- Maximize search capabilities

- Customize search capabilities

The customize option allows the user to select the specific help files to include in the word list.

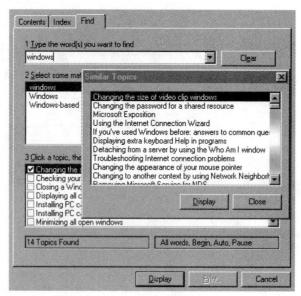

The primary source for Windows 95 documentation is the online help facility.

Troubleshooters

One of the best tools available to you is Windows 95 online help system. The Windows 95 Troubleshooters, part of the help system, provide assistance for a number of common problem areas. When you select a troubleshooter topic, you are taken into a series of questions to help you define the problem.

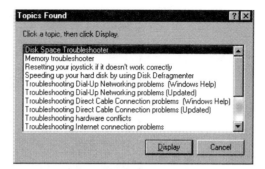

Users may access the troubleshooters by running **Start/Help** and clicking on the **Contents** tab. Troubleshooters include:

- Printing Troubleshooter

- Memory Troubleshooter

- Disk Space Troubleshooter

- Hardware Conflict Troubleshooter

- MS-DOS Application Troubleshooter

- Network Troubleshooter

- Modem Troubleshooter

- Dial-Up Networking Troubleshooter

- Direct Cable Connection Troubleshooter

- PC Card (PCMCIA) Troubleshooter

- Starting Windows Troubleshooter

After starting a troubleshooter, the user answers questions about the specific problem. As you move down through the questions, the troubleshooter will provide procedures to try, often with shortcuts to Windows 95 utilities.

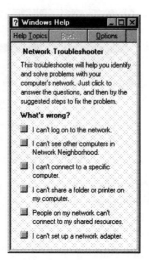

Training users to take advantage of the troubleshooters can help reduce unnecessary support calls to the system administrator.

Other Resources

When problems occur, it is important to keep in mind that there are a number of sources available for troubleshooting assistance. These include:

- Microsoft TechNet
- Microsoft Development Network
- CompuServe
- Internet resources

Let's take a brief look at each of these, with suggestions on how to best use them to supplement your troubleshooting efforts.

TechNet

TechNet is provided by Microsoft as a monthly subscription service. Each month, Microsoft sends an update which includes the latest technical information, current service kits, and updated device drivers.

TechNet provides documentation for Microsoft products, including:

- Product Facts
- Resource Kits
- Technical Notes

Each issue of TechNet also includes the complete Microsoft Knowledge Base, a database of known problems and corrections (or workarounds). TechNet lets you define bookmarks, making it easy to return to commonly used references, and annotations, so that you can add your own notes. TechNet also includes a powerful query engine. This query engine will be discussed in more detail later in the chapter.

You can print information from TechNet, giving you a hard copy of the information. Keep in mind that some sections may be lengthy.

Microsoft Developer Network

The Microsoft Developer Network (MSDN) is a quarterly subscription service provided by Microsoft. The MSDN provides three membership levels:

- MSDN Library Subscription

    This subscription levels supplies subscribers with CDs containing the Microsoft Developer Knowledge Base, technical articles, MS Press books, code samples, technical specifications, and utilities. You will receive information about Microsoft products and programming knowledge.

- MSDN Professional Subscription

    This subscription level provides those benefits of the Library level plus software for all Microsoft operating systems, Software Development Kits (SDKs), and Device Driver Kits (DDKs). Subscribers also receive product updates and pre-releases of products through the subscription time.

- MSDN Universal Subscription

  This subscription combines the Library and Professional membership levels with the addition of Microsoft's BackOffice, Visual Studio 97 (Enterprise edition), Office 97 (Developer Edition), FrontPage, Team Manager, Microsoft Project. Again, subscribers receive updates and any pre-released software packages throughout the subscription year.

Development Library

The Development Library is an extensive reference library on CD-ROM. The Development Library includes:

- Technical articles

  Included is a variety of technical articles from the Developer Network News covering a wide range of development topics.

- Sample program code

  Selected code samples are provided for Microsoft development products. These include samples from technical articles, books, periodicals, product, conferences, and seminars.

- Backgrounders and White Papers

  These include papers on applications, programming languages, and operating systems. Also provided are selected case studies showing practical applications where Microsoft products are used to solve business problems.

- Specifications documentation

  These include a wide assortment of specification documents covering both hardware and software related issues.

- Microsoft Knowledge Base

  The knowledge base contains known issues, solutions, and workarounds for Microsoft development products, SDKs, DDKs, and operating systems. Known bugs are also documented.

- Selected books and periodicals

  This section contains electronic copies of selected books, as well as many popular publications such as Dr. Dobb's Journal and selected Visual Basic Programming Journal articles.

- Development product documentation

  Full product documentation is provided for Microsoft applications, programming languages, SDKs, and DDKs.

- Product tools and utilities

  This contains selected tools and is set up to run from CD-ROM, if supported, or automatically copy the tools you wish to your hard disk.

- Unsupported tools and utilities

  These are tools that Microsoft makes available to developers by way of the Development Library. As with the product tools and utilities, these may be opened or copied to your hard disk. They are not, however, supported by Microsoft.

- TechEd Conference papers

  All of the conference papers, articles, and appropriate session materials from recent TechEd conferences are included.

As with TechNet, the Development Library supports a powerful query engine, letting you easily find the information you need. You can also print any of the information included with the Development Library.

Query

Both TechNet and Microsoft Developer Network support a powerful query engine, letting you define custom queries and search for selected information.

Query strings let you define words included and excluded from the search. Both **AND** and **OR** functions are supported. You can select to search the entire CD or selected portions only, if you have an idea where the information should be found.

When you select to run the query, the selected portion of the CD is searched and a results list returned.

You can display the contents of any of the documents in the results list. You can return to the list at any time to select a different document, or choose to fine tune and run your query again.

Internet Resources

The Internet has long been a boon to researchers and scientists, but until recently, was almost unknown outside of academia. Over the last few years, the world has *discovered* the Internet and the wealth of information available.

There are three primary information sources on the Internet:

- Newsgroups

    The newsgroups are open discussion groups on nearly every subject you can imagine. They are a way of sharing information and files across the Internet.

- FTP sites

    FTP refers to File Transfer Protocol, a means of transferring files between different platforms. FTP is part of the TCP/IP protocol suite. FTP is also used to refer to servers set up as files sources. Many manufacturers have FTP sites available from which you can download information and updated support files.

- World Wide Web

    The World Wide Web is the interactive, graphic portion of the Internet. It is well suited to both information delivery and direct marketing. A large number of organizations now have Web sites, and will often refer requests for information or updated files to their Web pages.

Much of the interest in the Internet has been fueled by the World Wide Web. The Web's graphic environment has put a *user-friendly* face on the Internet. Most commercial subscription services now also act as Internet service providers, giving their subscribers a link into the Internet. In addition, innumerable independent service providers have sprung up all over the world. Add to this total the number of companies and individuals who are directly connected, and you have an idea of the amount of information moving across the Internet.

Internet Search Tools

Key to efficient use of Internet resources are the search tools. There are several available and many Web pages contain direct links to search tools. These tools, such as AltaVista, Webcrawler, Yahoo, and Lycos are similar in function to the Microsoft's TechNet and Developer Library query engines.

You enter a search string with the keywords for which you want to search. The search engine goes through its database and returns the most likely matches. These matches act as hot links to the listed sites, so that you can select any item out of the list and jump to that site. Most commercial Web pages provide links to popular search services. The services themselves provide online help to guide you through writing and fine-tuning your queries.

Microsoft Web Page

Microsoft's home page on the Web is located at:

```
www.microsoft.com
```

It provides direct access to Microsoft services and product information. It provides a good source for both general product and product troubleshooting information.

Getting on the Internet

Microsoft has provided a suggested series of steps for getting access to the Internet. These are:

- Obtain an Internet PPP or SLIP account from an access provider.
- Obtain account information for server connection from the access provider.
- Install and configure a modem.
- Install TCP/IP.

You can connect to the service provider through Dial-Up Networking. If the Internet provider does not dynamically assign a DNS name and IP address, this information will need to be configured through Dial-Up Networking. FTP and Telnet are provided with the TCP/IP protocol suite on Windows 95. Most popular Windows-based Web browsers, such as Netscape and Microsoft Internet Explorer (which is now included with Windows 95), are compatible with Windows 95. Dial-Up Networking will be discussed later in the course.

SUMMARY

During this chapter, you looked at the changes in the User Interface for Windows 95. These included:

- Windows 95 Startup

- Windows 95 Logon

- Windows 95 user interface

- Using Windows Explorer to view files and folders

- Listing common desktop objects and their purposes

- Describing the troubleshooters available through the Help utility

- Listing other troubleshooting resources available for Windows 95 administrators and users

POST-TEST QUESTIONS

The answers to these questions are in Appendix A at the end of this manual.

1. Describe the Windows 95 Startup process.

   ....

   ....

2. List the sections that are present on the **Start** menu by default.

   ....

   ....

3. Opening My Computer reveals what objects?

....

....

4. What type of information is displayed in the Network Neighborhood icon on the desktop?

....

....

5. Explain how to recover a recently deleted file or folder.

....

....

CHAPTER 4

Customizing Windows 95

OBJECTIVES

At the completion of this chapter, you will be able to:

- Customize the Windows 95 User Interface (UI).
- Configure the Windows 95 Desktop.
- Customize the **Start** menu and Taskbar.
- Define and enable user profiles for a Windows 95 client.
- Describe the purpose of system policies.
- Configure system policies using System Policy Editor.

PRE-TEST QUESTIONS

The answers to these questions are in Appendix A at the end of this manual.

1. For what types of items can you create shortcuts?

   ....

   ....

2. How can you create a shortcut on the top portion of the **Start** menu?

   ....

   ....

3. How can you configure a manual update for a policy file?

   ....

   ....

4. What two areas can you configure for a computer policy?

   ....

   ....

INTRODUCTION

The user interface (UI) can be customized in various ways. Windows 95 contains many new tools and some of those that are familiar to you from past Windows products. The chapter begins with a discussion of customizing the **Start** menu and Taskbar. You will see the benefits that users can obtain by customizing their work environment to their own preferences and needs. Windows 95 has simplified this customization.

User Profiles and System Policies are discussed next. Through the use of User Profiles, the administrator has the ability to ensure that roving users maintain a consistent desktop environment. System Policies allow the administrator to override local registry values for user or computer settings. Using profiles and policies also allows the administrator to control a user's access to Windows 95 utilities and settings.

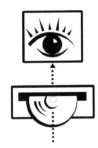

Stop now and view the following video presentation on the Interactive Learning CD-ROM:

Windows 95 Administration
    User Profiles
    System Policies

CREATING A CUSTOM ENVIRONMENT

This section will describe how to customize the user environment on a Windows 95 system. Windows 95 provides options for configuring a system to meet specific user needs or preferences. The following are topics discussed in this section:

- Customizing the UI
- Using Property Sheets
- Customizing the Desktop
- Customizing the **Start** menu and Taskbar
- Shortcuts

Each user will have different needs when it comes to accessing files, applications, and objects. To simplify the ability to access these resources, Windows 95 allows you to create shortcuts and menu items to meet your needs.

Customizing the UI

The Windows 95 UI can be customized in several ways. These include:

- Use of Property Sheets.

    Property Sheets are a notable feature of Windows 95. Every object in the UI contains properties that can be manipulated.

- Customization of the Desktop.

    As you start Windows 95, the Desktop is the initial portion of the UI presented. The Desktop provides the user with a simple starting point to navigate the UI. Through the use of properties for each object in the Windows 95 environment as well as the properties of the desktop itself, the user can design an individual environment. The Desktop can be associated with a username, providing each user with his or her own familiar interface.

- Customization of the Start menu and Taskbar.

    The **Start** menu serves as a place to get a quick start through easy access to applications, utilities, and system settings. The Taskbar organizes active tasks and allows the user to rapidly switch from one to another.

• Creating and Managing Shortcuts.

Shortcuts are powerful tools that allow the user to make a graphical *pointer* to a file or folder, similar to the aliases found in the MAC OS. Shortcuts reduce the amount of time necessary to open a file, find a folder, or launch an application.

Using Properties Sheets

You can access the Properties sheet for any object by pointing and clicking with the secondary mouse button to display the context-sensitive menu, and selecting **Properties**.

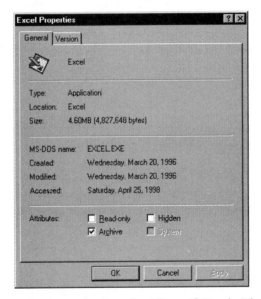

The previous graphic is the properties sheet for Microsoft Excel. The **General** tab is currently displayed. The tabs at the top of the sheet entitled **General** and **Version** are accessible by clicking on the desired tab.

A property sheet for an MS-DOS-based program has six tabs.

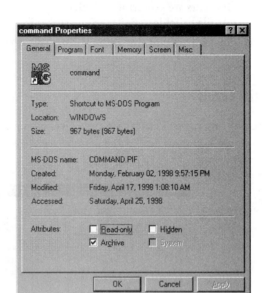

We will discuss MS-DOS application properties and support later in the course.

You will see many different property sheets. There may be buttons, fields, checkboxes, or pull-down menus present on any given property sheet. Remember that every object within Windows 95 has properties, and these properties can be viewed and edited.

Customizing the Desktop

With Windows 95, the Desktop becomes more functional than in Windows 3.x. On the Desktop, you will find shortcuts, folders, documents, and three special icons: My Computer, the Network Neighborhood, and the Recycle Bin.

The Windows 95 Desktop supports drag and drop. For example, you can use Explorer to find a file or folder that you often use and then drag and drop it to the desktop. This will allow you to access the item directly from the desktop rather than having to launch Explorer and proceed with additional steps. The objects that are placed on the desktop for quick and easy access are referred to as Shortcuts. Shortcuts will be discussed in more detail later in this chapter.

You can also create a Printer icon for your printer and drop any files that you would like to print onto the icon for processing. This will be discussed in more detail later in the course.

The \Windows\Desktop directory stores all items that you place on the desktop.

NOTE: *Through the use of user profiles, individual users can have a specific desktop configuration associated with their login name. In this case, the desktop configuration is stored in the \Windows\Profiles\username\Desktop directory. User profiles and system policies are discussed later in this chapter.*

Customizing the Start Menu and Taskbar

To customize the **Start** menu and Taskbar, you must run **Start/Settings/Taskbar** to display the properties sheet for these two selections. You may also obtain this properties sheet by clicking the secondary mouse button while pointing at a blank area of the Taskbar and running **Properties**.

To configure the Taskbar, select the **Taskbar Options** tab on the Taskbar Properties sheet.

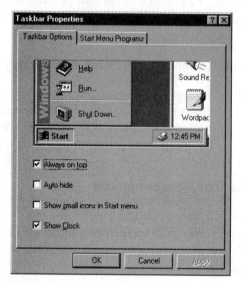

The options presented include:

- Always on top

  Checking this box causes the Taskbar to always be on top of the active application. Consider using this option in conjunction with Auto hide.

- Auto hide

  This option hides the taskbar as the mouse pointer moves away from it. The taskbar reappears as the pointer moves to the edge of the screen where the taskbar resides.

- Show small icons in Start menu

  This option shows small icons on all **Start** menu items.

- Show Clock

  This option hides or shows the clock on the Taskbar.

To relocate the Taskbar, click and drag the Taskbar to the top, bottom, left, or right of the screen and release.

You can customize your **Start** menu by adding and removing shortcuts or program items.

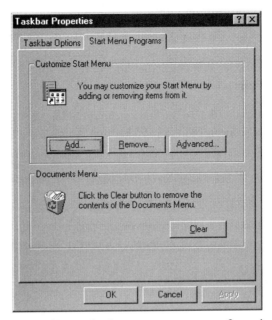

To add a new program shortcut to the **Start** menu, you must first select the **Start Menu Programs** tab. Then click on **Add** to create a new shortcut. You can either type the complete path including the filename or click on **Browse** to find the path to the application. You must choose where on the **Start** menu you would like the shortcut to appear. You may select from existing folders on the **Start** menu or click on **New Folder** to create a new folder. Finally, name the shortcut by either accepting the default or typing a new name.

To remove an application or shortcut from the **Start** menu, click on **Remove** from the **Start Menu Programs** tab. Select the item from the designated folder and click on **Remove**. Once you have removed all the unwanted items, click on **Close**.

The **Advanced** option on the **Start Menu Programs** tab displays a hierarchical structure of your applications similar to the look and feel of Windows Explorer. This view allows you to drag and drop an application or folder onto the **Start** menu. Dropping it onto the **Start** menu folder icon places the shortcut to the application or folder on the portion of the **Start** menu above the Programs listing.

Adding an application to the **Start** menu should not be confused with starting a program automatically during Windows 95 Startup. This is done by placing the application in the Startup folder within the Programs folder.

> *NOTE:*   *Start menu items are located in the \Windows\Start menu folder.*

An alternative method of adding a program or shortcut to the **Start** menu is to drag the program from its current location on the computer or on the network and drop it on the **Start** button. You can use either My Computer, Windows Explorer, or the Find utility to locate the program or shortcut. The program or shortcut will appear on the top of the **Start** menu above the Programs listing.

Shortcuts

Have you ever been involved in a project that required you to repeatedly access the same file or folder (directory)? If so, you probably found it necessary to weave your way through a maze of program groups or windows each time you had to access the file. Windows 95 shortcuts can help simplify that operation.

The Windows 95 shortcut concept allows you to create a link to a document, application, file, network resource, or any other object without having to make a physical copy of the object. Shortcuts can be placed in a convenient location, such as directly on the desktop, on the **Start** menu, or even within a folder. If the time comes when the shortcut is no longer needed, simply drag and drop it into the Recycle Bin. Keep in mind, however, that deleting the shortcut only deletes the link, not the object or its associated files.

Shortcuts appear as normal objects, but have a small *right-turn* arrow on the bottom left of the icon, as in the following examples of shortcuts to an application, a file, and a folder:

Information for a shortcut is listed in its properties sheet on the **Shortcut** tab as shown in the following example:

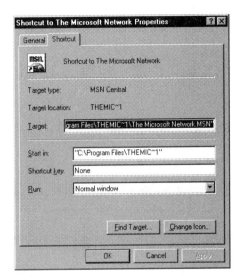

The options on the **Shortcut** tab include:

- Target

  This displays the path and filename of the object to which the shortcut points.

- Start in

  This allows you to specify an alternate location for files that the target may need to function correctly.

- Shortcut key

  This Specifies the keyboard shortcut to this object, if any.

- Run

  This specifies how the window should display when activated: Normal Window, Maximized, or Minimized.

- Find Target

    This opens the container that contains the target file or folder.

- Change Icon

    Through this, you can change the icon for the shortcut.

Shortcuts have an MS-DOS filename extension of LNK.

Exercise 4-1:
Customizing the Desktop

During this section, you will practice procedures for customizing the Desktop and system objects. You will also be introduced to the online help system.

At the start of this exercise, you should be logged onto your system.

1. Open the Windows Explorer from **Start/Programs**.

2. Select the Windows directory.

3. Scroll to locate the Notepad executable file. Right-click on Notepad (NOTEPAD.EXE) and select **Properties** from the pop-up menu.

4. The properties dialog has two tabs, initially showing General settings, including file attributes. Click on the **Version** tab. This displays information about the program. Click on the **Cancel** button.

6. Select the **DOS** directory.

7. Run **View/Options** from the menu.

8. Confirm that the checkbox next to **Hide MS-DOS file extensions for file types that are registered** is clear, and click on **OK**.

9. Right-click on QBASIC (QBASIC.EXE) and select **Properties**.

10. There are six tabs displayed for MS-DOS applications. These are covered in detail later in the course. Click on **Cancel**.

11. Minimize the Windows Explorer window.

12. Open the **My Computer** object located on the desktop.

13. Right-click on drive (C:) and select **Properties**.

14. There are three tabs for your drive object. **General** shows disk usage, **Tools** takes you to disk tools, and **Sharing** lets you share the drive to the network. Click on **Cancel**.

15. Close the My Computer window.

16. Display the Windows Explorer window by selecting the item from the taskbar.

17. Right-click on the Windows folder and select **Properties**.

18. There are two tabs, **General** and **Sharing**. **General** displays folder properties and **Sharing** is for managing resource sharing for the folder. The **Sharing** tab will be visible only if you have the File and Print Sharing service installed. This service will be discussed later in the course. Click on **Cancel**.

19. Close the Windows Explorer.

20. Open **Start/Help** from the **Start** menu.

21. Click on the **Find** tab.

22. Select to **Minimize the database** and click on **Next**.

23. Click on **Finish**.

24. Type in the following:

    ```
    drive
    ```

25. View the details of each topic selection presented.

26. Click on **Cancel**.

PROFILES

This section will present an introduction to user management. We will take a look at how user profiles can be used to maintain desktop and environment settings for multiple users at one workstation. This discussion includes user profiles and their significance in a network environment. The following topics are discussed in this section:

- User Profiles

- Understanding User Profiles on Windows 95

- Enabling User Profiles

- When User Profiles Are Not Used

- Default User Profile

Profiles allow users to customize their desktop environment and **Start** menu items even though they are not stationary users.

User Profiles

User Profiles allow users to customize their desktop settings; these settings are then stored in a profile on their computer. As the user logs on to the local machine, preferences and settings that the user has set are loaded. Users who log on to different stations can also use profiles which are stored on a network. This will be discussed later in the course. An administrator can use user profiles to provide a standard desktop with certain desktop objects or **Start** menu items not visible. We will see how this is done later in this chapter.

User Profiles provide many benefits:

- Multiple users can use a single computer and retain their personal settings.

  When user profiles are enabled locally, information about desktop settings is stored in a separate directory for each user who logs on to the computer. The directory is identified by the username.

- Windows 95 performs all the work automatically for maintaining each user's profile, regardless of the profile's location.

  Therefore, the administrator simply needs to enable User Profiles for the appropriate computers.

- Through the use of mandatory profiles, the administrator can centrally enforce a consistent desktop for all users.

  This is useful for managing desktop settings for novice users, increasing user productivity, and easing the burden of training and support for system managers. Mandatory profiles will be discussed later in this chapter.

Understanding User Profiles on Windows 95

A local user's profile is stored in the \WINDOWS\PROFILES*USERNAME* directory. Most of the configuration is stored in the USER.DAT file. This file contains user-specific information for the Windows 95 Registry. User settings are stored in the HKEY_CURRENT_USER key of the Windows 95 Registry. This key includes subkeys that store Control Panel settings, persistent network connections, and various application settings. Not all applications will write information to HKEY_CURRENT_USER. This means that some application settings will be stored with the user profile and some will not. Implementation of user profiles in a mixed network environment will be discussed later in the course.

Each user's profile consists of the following:

- A USER.DAT file

    This file contains the information that will be loaded into the HKEY_CURRENT_USER key of the registry.

- A USER.DA0 file

    This file serves as a backup for USER.DAT. When the profile is first loaded, the contents of USER.DAT and USER.DA0 are identical.

- A Desktop folder

    This folder contains shortcuts to items on the desktop, including information about mapped drives.

- A Recent folder

    This folder contains a list of the most recent documents. These are the documents that can be accessed through **Start/Documents**.

- A Start Menu folder

    This folder contains the shortcuts that appear in the user's **Start** menu. If a user installs an application and user profiles are enabled, a shortcut to the application will only appear in that user's **Start** menu. Other users who want to be able to launch the application from the **Start** menu will have to manually add the shortcut.

Enabling User Profiles

To enable User Profiles, run **Start/Settings** to launch the Control Panel. Open the
Passwords utility. Select the **User Profiles** tab.

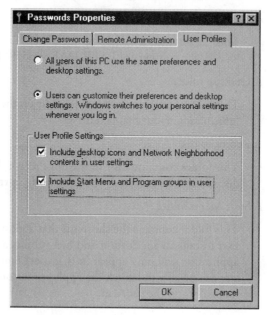

By default, the **All users of this PC...** option is enabled. To allow users to create a profile
with their customized environment settings, select the **Users can customize their
preferences...** option. To enable all User Profile properties, check both of the following
options.

- Include desktop icons and Network Neighborhood contents in user settings
- Include Start Menu and Program groups in user settings

One or both of these options may be selected, depending on the user's needs. Selecting
both options will allow users to see familiar Start Menus, Program Groups, Desktop
Icons, etc. To disable User Profiles, select the **All users of this PC...** option.

After enabling User Profiles, you will need to restart the system. A directory is created
under the \WINDOWS\PROFILES directory for the current user. Beneath this
directory and its subdirectories are the files defining the user's configuration.

When user profiles are enabled and a user logs on to the local machine, Windows 95 will check for the existence of a user profile. If no profile exists or if the user cancels from the logon dialog box, the default profile will be used. The default profile will be discussed a little later.

When User Profiles Are Not Used

If the option **All users of this PC...** is enabled, all settings governed by user profiles are shared between any new user or existing user who logs on to this computer. This is the default when Windows 95 is installed.

For example, Bob has his desktop set up like the following graphic:

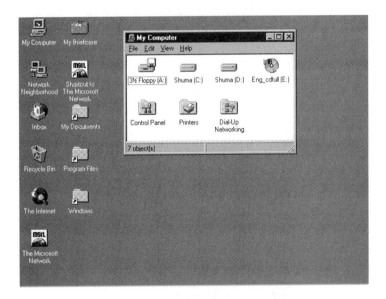

If the **All users of this PC... setting** is enabled, when Bob logs off the computer and Stacey logs on under her own name and password, her screen will look exactly like Bob's. If Stacey makes changes before she logs off, Bob's desktop will reflect those changes at his next logon. This could be confusing for users and may result in calls to technical support.

Default User Profile

When a user logs on to Windows 95 for the first time, he uses the default user profile. This profile can be specifically set so that a new user's desktop looks a particular way. This is especially important if you want to give the user easy access to installed applications. To set up a default profile:

1. Verify that the **All users of this PC use the same preferences and desktop settings** option is selected in the Passwords property dialog.

2. Make any necessary changes to the desktop, such as mapping network drives and installing applications.

3. Select the **Users can customize their preferences and desktop settings** in the Passwords property dialog.

4. Restart the system.

Exercise 4-2: Profiles

During this exercise, you will work with user profiles. You will be working with locally stored profiles only during this exercise. You should be logged on as Student (or the username you have used in previous exercises) at the beginning of this exercise. During the remaining exercises, this will be referred to as your primary user.

1. Open **Start/Settings/Control Panel**.

2. Double-click on the Passwords utility.

3. Select the **User Profiles** tab.

4. Click on the radio button to select **Users can customize their preferences and desktop settings. Windows switches to your personal settings whenever you log in.**

5. Verify that the checkbox for **Include desktop items and Network Neighborhood contents in user settings** is enabled. Also, verify that the checkbox for **Include Start Menu and Programs in user settings** is enabled. Then, click on **OK**.

6. You are prompted to restart your system. Click on **Yes** to restart.

7. Log on to the system using your user logon and password.

8. You will receive the following dialog:

   You have not logged on at this computer before. Would you like this computer to retain your individual settings for use when you log on here in the future?

   Click on **Yes**. There will be a slightly longer than normal delay as the user's settings are saved.

9. Confirm your logon password by typing it in again. Click on **OK**.

10. Run **Shut Down** from the **Start** menu and select **Close all programs and log on as a different user?**

11. Click on **Yes**.

12. At the logon dialog, type the following information and press *ENTER*:

    User name   TestUser

    Password   password

13. You will receive the following dialog:

    You have not logged on at this computer before. Would you like this computer to retain your individual settings for use when you log on here in the future? Click on **Yes**.

14. When prompted to confirm your password, type the password and click on **OK**.

15. Right-click on the desktop and select **Properties**.

16. On the **Background** tab, select **Metal Links** from the list of available wallpapers. Then, click on **Apply**.

17. Click on **OK**.

18. Right-click on the desktop and select **New**.

19. Select **Folder**.

20. Overwrite the name as Test Folder and press *ENTER*.

21. Right-click on Test Folder and select **Create Shortcut**.

22. Run **Start/Shut Down** and select **Close all programs and log on as a different user?**

23. Click on **Yes**.

24. When prompted, log on as your primary user. What happens to your desktop?

    Your desktop returns to its original settings and the objects created by TestUser are no longer there. Profiles allow you to support different settings for each user.

POLICIES

This section discusses the concept of system policies for a Windows 95 client. You will learn how to implement system and user policies using the System Policy Editor system tool. The following topics are discussed within this section:

- System Policies
- Installation
- Policies and User Profiles
- Registry Mode vs. Policy Mode
- User Policy Settings
- Computer Policy Settings
- States of a Policy
- Creating User Policies
- Creating System Policies
- Locating Policies

System Policy Editor is a safe method of making changes to the registry for the HKEY_LOCAL_MACHINE and HKEY_LOCAL_USER root keys.

System Policies

System policies allow an administrator to override local registry values for user or computer settings. Policies are defined in a policy file, usually called CONFIG.POL. When a user logs on, system policy settings override default USER.DAT and SYSTEM.DAT settings in the registry. System policies can also contain specific custom network settings as established by the network administrator. Unlike SYSTEM.DAT and USER.DAT, CONFIG.POL is not a required component of Windows 95.

System policies offer many benefits:

- The administrator can restrict what users are allowed to do from the desktop.

- The administrator can configure network settings, such as the network client configuration and the ability to install or configure File and Printer Sharing services.

- The Administrator can easily change important registry settings through the use of the system policy file.

- The Administrator can restrict access to options contained within the Control Panel.

- Group policies can be used to define a specific set of policies to be applied based on the membership of groups already defined on a Windows NT or NetWare network. Group policies will be discussed later in the course.

- The Administrator can allow only approved applications to be accessed.

The system policy file changes the registry by modifying the HKEY_CURRENT_USER key for desktop settings, and the HKEY_LOCAL_MACHINE key for network access settings.

Installation

The System Policy Editor installation files are on the Windows 95 installation CD-ROM, under the \ADMIN\APPTOOLS\POLEDIT directory. To install the policy editor:

1. #Change these to a numbered list.Launch the Control Panel.
2. Launch Add/Remove Programs.
3. Click on the **Windows Setup** tab.
4. Click on **Have Disk**.
5. Locate the POLEDIT directory and click on **OK**.

You will be prompted to install the support dynamic link library for using group policies. Group policies will be discussed later in the course.

The System Policy Editor installs to the \WINDOWS directory.

> *NOTE:*   *You will not want to install the System Policy Editor on an end user's computer. Instead, create the system policy on an administrative computer. You can do this through remote administration, which is discussed later in the course.*

The System Policy Editor is an executable named POLEDIT.EXE. After it has been installed, it can be launched from **Start/Programs/Accessories/System Tools/System Policy Editor**.

Policies and User Profiles

You must enable user profiles in order to use policies. This is done on the **User Profiles** tab of the Passwords utility. A good way to think about the distinction between user profiles and system policies is that as a general rule, user profiles influence the way the desktop looks and the options that are available. Policies determine which aspects of the desktop and operating system a user is allowed to modify.

Registry Mode vs. Policy Mode

System Policy Editor allows you to work in two different modes: Registry mode and Policy mode. Registry mode allows you to make direct changes to the Registry for the local user and the local computer. It is important to remember that any changes made here will affect any local user on the local system. Basically, the local user or local system overrides the user profile for the user logged on at that time. For example, if the Network utility is restricted in the Local User, no user logging on at that station will be able to access the Network utility. Even if the policy for that user does not restrict access to the Network utility, the local user policy takes over.

In Policy mode, there are two types of policies you can define: one for the user and one for the system. If a user is not created or specified, the System Policy Editor uses Default User and Default Computer items. To view the default user or default computer policies, run **File/New File**. This will display the icons for both default user and default computer. You can either double-click on the icons to view properties for defining a policy or you can select the user or computer and run **Edit/Properties**.

The objects displayed in the System Policy Editor relate to registry files. User objects relate to USER.DAT and computer objects relate to SYSTEM.DAT.

User Policy Settings

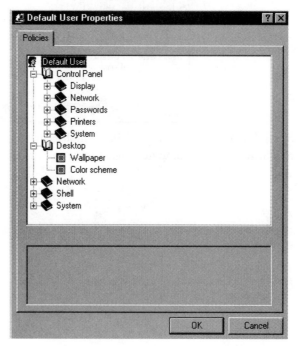

The following user policy settings can be set for specific users, the Default User, or for the Local User in Registry mode:

Control Panel

This option allows the administrator to restrict users from the following utility items: Display, Network, Passwords, Printers, and System.

For example, if you do not want users to be able to configure or change network settings, you must click the checkbox for Restrict Network utility. When the user tries to open the Network utility, he will receive an error.

Desktop

This option allows the administrator to restrict users from modifying the following Desktop settings: Wallpaper and Color Scheme. These options can be used to maintain a standard desktop color or wallpaper theme. Selecting these items does not restrict users from changing other desktop settings, such as shortcuts or desktop items.

Network

This option allows the administrator to restrict users from sharing resources the network. File and print sharing is controlled from this selection. For example, a temporary employee may need to access a network printer, but you want to ensure that this temporary employee cannot share files.

The Shell option allows the administrator to set policies for Custom Folders and Restrictions subitems. The specific settings that can be modified in Custom Folders are:

Custom Programs Folder

This option allows the administrator to customize the Programs folder. If this selection is chosen, you must provide the new path from which application items should be obtained. You may also set the path to *.LNK files which are the files for shortcut items. For example, suppose your company wants to have all users view the same Program items on every workstation. The administrator can create a customized Programs folder, and then set the path here. The default path for Programs folder items is C:\PROGRAM FILES.#Do you mean default path?

Custom Desktop Items

This option allows the administrator to customize desktop items. If this selection is chosen, you must provide the new path from which to obtain the application items. You may also set the path to *.LNK files which are the files for shortcut items.

Hide Start Menu Subfolders

If you use a custom Programs folder, this selection should be checked. If it is not checked, you will see not only your custom Programs folder in the **Start** menu, but the default Programs folder.

Custom Startup Folder

> This option allows the administrator to customize items within the Startup folder of the **Start** menu. If this selection is chosen, you must provide the new path from which to obtain the application items. You may also set the path to *.LNK files which are the files for shortcut items.

Custom Network Neighborhood

> This option allows the administrator to customize the Network Neighborhood. If this selection is chosen, you must provide the new path from which to obtain the application items. You may also set the path to *.LNK files which are the files for shortcut items. Using this option would be beneficial for restricting users from seeing network drives they are not permitted to use.

Custom Start Menu   This option allows the administrator to customize items in the **Start** menu. If this selection is chosen, you must provide the new path from which to obtain the application items. You may also set the path to *.LNK files which are the files for shortcut items.

The Restrictions option lists restrictions for standard desktop items, as well as items listed within the **Start** menu:

Remove 'Run' command

> This option removes the **Run** command from the **Start** menu.

Remove folders from 'Settings' on Start Menu

> This option restricts the user from accessing items listed in the **Settings** menu item.

Remove Taskbar from 'Settings' on Start Menu

> This option removes the **Taskbar** item from the **Settings** menu item.

Remove 'Find' command

> This option removes the **Find** option from the **Start** menu as well as from Windows Explorer.

Hide Drives in 'My Computer'

> This option hides all drives in the My Computer icon on the desktop. The user will only be able to view and access the Control Panel, Printers, and Dial-Up Networking.

Hide Network Neighborhood

> This option hides the Network Neighborhood icon on the desktop, as well as in Windows Explorer.

No 'Entire Network' in Network Neighborhood

> This option removes the Entire Network item from the Network Neighborhood.

No workgroup contents in Network Neighborhood

> This option will not display workgroup contents in the Network Neighborhood.

Hide all items on Desktop

> This option will hide all items located on the Desktop, including any shortcuts that may have existed.

Disable Shut Down command

> This option will disable the **Shut Down** command in the **Start** menu.

Don't save settings at exit

> This option will not save any setting changes that have been made to the system.

The System option allows the administrator to place restrictions for System registry tools, as well as MS-DOS applications. The following settings are available:

Disable Registry editing tools

> This option will allow users to launch the Registry Editor through the **Start/Run** command. However, once you try to launch the utility, you will receive a message stating that the administrator has restricted access to registry tools.

Only run allowed Windows applications

> This option will allow the administrator to select individual Windows applications by clicking on the **Show** button. The name of each Windows application item to which you want to allow access must be added.

Disable MS-DOS prompt

> This option will disable the MS-DOS prompt located in the **Start** menu. The MS-DOS prompt will also not be visible in C:\PROGRAMS FOLDER\PROGRAMS.

Disable single-mode MS-DOS applications

> This option will prevent the user from running MS-DOS applications in MS-DOS mode. MS-DOS mode will be discussed later in the course.

Computer Policy Settings

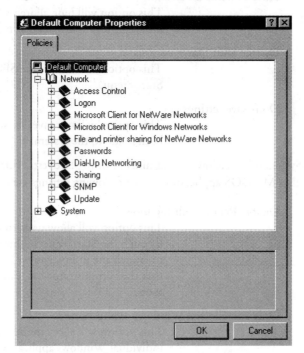

The following policy settings apply for any newly created computer policy within the System Policy Editor, as well as the Default Computer in Policy mode and Local Computer in Registry mode.

These settings apply to network issues ranging from access control, logon, clients for networks, file and print sharing, passwords, dial-up networking, sharing, SNMP, and update.

The only setting available under the Access Control item is **User Level Access Control**. This option enables user-level security for the system. If this selection is chosen, you must specify the authenticator's name, as well as the authenticator type. The authenticator name would be the server or domain name. Authenticator type would be either a Windows NT Domain, Windows NT Workstation, Windows NT Server, or NetWare 3.x or 4.x server. One reason you might want to check the **User Level Access Control** option is to enable user-level security without enabling remote administration.

The following settings are available under the Logon option:

Logon Banner   This option allows the administrator to set a caption which will display during user logon. This could be used to warn users about company-set network policies.

Require Validation by Network for Windows Access
    This option requires the system to obtain authentication for logon. The authentication must come from either a Windows NT Server or a NetWare server.

Available settings for the Microsoft Client for NetWare Networks and Microsoft Client for Microsoft Networks will be discussed later in the course.

Settings related to passwords include:

Hide share passwords with Asterisks
    This option will replace characters with asterisks when users type passwords to shared resources. This provides security to prevent users from watching another user enter a password.

Disable password caching
    This option prevents the system from saving passwords in the password list file.

Require alphanumeric Windows Password
    This option will require users to include both letters and numbers in their Windows password.

Minimum Windows password length

> This option allows you to set a minimum password length. The number can be anywhere between 1 and 8.

Dial-Up Networking

> This option prevents users from creating Dial-Up Networking connections on their systems.

Settings that affect file and printer sharing include:

File Sharing   This option disables file sharing.

Printer Sharing   This option disables printer sharing.

Settings that affect Simple Network Management Protocol (SNMP) will be covered later in the course.

Settings that affect how user policies are updated include:

Remote Update   This option allows you to enable remote updates either automatically or manually. If you select manual remote updates, you must specify the path for the computer policy file. You can also choose to view error messages. The load-balance selection enables Windows 95 to look for policy files on a server, provided it is part of a Windows NT network.

The System option allows you to set the following policies:

Enable User Profiles This option enables user profiles automatically. If you set this policy, you will not have to make the selection in the Passwords utility manually.

Network path for Windows Setup

> This option specifies the path for Windows Setup in a network environment. You must specify the UNC server path.

Network path for Windows Tour

> This option specifies the path for Windows Tour in a network environment. You must be sure to include TOUR.EXE at the end of the path.

Run   This option will allow the administrator to select specific application items to run when users log on to the system.

Run Once	This option will allow the administrator to select specific application items to run the next time a user logs on to the system.
Run Services	This option allows the administrator to have specific services start when users log on to the system.

Beneath many of the major policy headings are subitems that allow more detailed policy management.

States of a Policy

Each policy checkbox has three potential states. Click on the checkbox to toggle between these states.

- Checked

    This policy will be implemented when the user logs on. This changes the state of the policy in the user's registry.

- Cleared

    This policy will not be implemented. Registry entries, if any, for this policy will be removed when the user logs on.

- Grayed

    This is used when you do not want the user's local policy changed. Windows 95 will not process this entry when the user logs on. Since the entries are not processed, you can potentially improve startup performance.

There is a significant difference between Cleared and Grayed. Cleared will cause all references to the policy to be deleted from the registry. Grayed means that the references in the registry are not changed.

Creating Local User Policies

To enable policies on a computer that is not part of a network, you must first launch the System Policy Editor from **Start/Programs/Accessories/System Tools.** Run **File/New File** to create a new policy file in Policy mode.

To create a new user in this policy file, run **Edit/Add User** from the menu. This will prompt you to enter the name of the user for whom you are creating the policy. After typing in the name, click on **OK.**

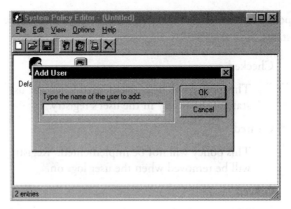

The new user now appears.

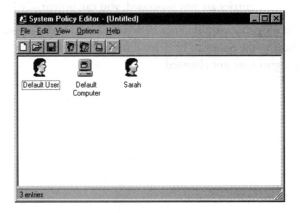

Configuration settings for this user's policy can be displayed by double-clicking on the user's icon. You can also view the Policy properties by running **Edit/Properties** once you have selected the user's icon. To set restrictions for the new user, expand the policy items and click on the appropriate checkboxes. Be sure to check at the bottom of the Properties dialog for additional settings that may need to be set for the selected policy. These will be policy-specific. Once you have completed your configurations, click on **OK** to confirm the new policy settings.

To save the new policy, run **File/Save As**. Save the policy in the \WINDOWS directory. It is suggested that you name the policy file CONFIG.POL to allow Windows 95 to locate the policy automatically. If you choose to have your own naming scheme for policy files, you will need to enable Windows 95 to locate the policy files manually. This will be discussed later in the chapter. The next time the user logs on, the restrictions defined in the policy will take effect.

You can also create a policy file for a local user simply by using the Registry mode. Once you have launched the System Policy Editor, run **File/Open Registry**. Two icons are displayed: Local User and Local Computer. Double-click on the Local User icon to display the Local User Properties dialog. Then, you can set any and all policy restrictions that you want to enable for the local user. Once you have completed the configurations, click on **OK**. Run **File/Save** to save the changes to the Registry. The next time the user logs on, the local system policy will take effect for the local user logging in. Even in situations where multiple users are logging on to the same workstation, the same local system policy will be applied to each and every user on that local workstation.

Creating System Policies

You can also create system policies for a computer. To do so, you can either open an existing policy file or create a new policy file.

To open an existing policy file, run **File/Open File**. Browse to locate the policy file in the \WINDOWS directory. The policy file is usually named CONFIG.POL. Next, run **Edit/Add Computer** to add the name of the user's computer.

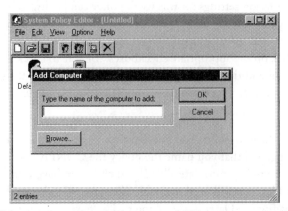

Type the name of the computer for which you would like to create a policy. To locate the name of a computer, you can click on **Browse**. Using the machine name located in the **Identification** tab of the Network utility allows Windows 95 to match the policy name with the machine.

Configuration settings for the system policy can be displayed by double-clicking on the system icon. You can also view the Policy properties by running **Edit/Properties** once you have selected the system icon.

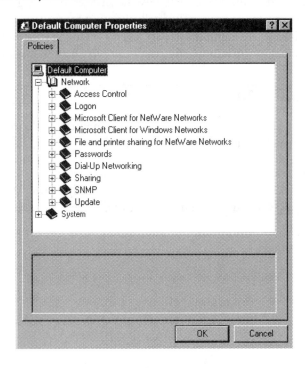

Once the properties sheet appears for the computer, set restrictions by expanding the policy items and clicking on the appropriate checkboxes. Again, check the bottom of the Properties dialog for additional settings that may need to be set for the selected policy setting. These will be policy-specific. Once you have completed your configurations, click on **OK** to confirm the new policy settings.

To save the new policy, run **File/Save As**. Save the policy in the \WINDOWS directory. You should save the policy as CONFIG.POL if you create a brand new policy file to allow Windows 95 to locate the policy automatically. You can also save the policy as its own name. This will require you to enable Windows 95 to locate the policy manually. This will be discussed later in the chapter. If you added a computer policy to an existing policy file, run **File/Save**. The next time the computer is logged onto, the restrictions defined in the policy will take effect.

Locating Policies

When a Windows 95 computer is not part of a Windows NT or NetWare network, policy files are normally stored in the C:\WINDOWS directory. If you name the policy file CONFIG.POL, it will be located automatically. Otherwise, it must be configured to update manually. Implementation of system policies in a mixed network environment will be discussed later in the course.

To configure the update manually, double-click on the computer icon to display the computer properties sheet for the policy. If there is no specific system policy established, you can use the Default Computer icon. Expand the **Network** option. Then, expand the **Update** option. Click on the checkbox for **Remote Update**. You must then change the update mode to Manual. Once you have done so, enter the path to the policy file making sure to include the policy filename. This will enable Windows 95 to check for a matching policy file. If it finds the file, it applies the appropriate settings for the user.

Exercise 4-3:
Policies

The purpose of this exercise is to work with the System Policy Editor. A network connection is not required. We will be configuring a system policy for a new user. We will not be implementing the policy in this exercise.

This exercise requires that you have CD-ROM installation source media available.

You should be logged on as your primary user at the beginning of this exercise.

1. Open **Start/Settings/Control Panel**.
2. Double-click on the Add/Remove Programs utility.
3. Click on the **Windows Setup** tab.
4. Click on **Have Disk**.
5. Click on **Browse** to locate the proper source directory on the CD-ROM installation files. The path to the files is:

   \ADMIN\APPTOOLS\POLEDIT

6. Click on **OK**.
7. Click on **OK** to install.
8. Click on the checkbox for **System Policy Editor**.
9. Click on **Install**.
10. Click on **OK** to close the Add/Remove programs dialog.
11. Close the Control Panel.
12. Run **Start/Programs/Accessories/System Tools/System Policy Editor**.
13. Run **File/New File** from the menu.
14. Run **Edit/Add User** from the menu.
15. Type the following as the username and press *ENTER*:

    TestUser

16. Double-click on the icon for TestUser to display the TestUser Properties dialog.
17. Expand **Shell/Restrictions**.
18. Click once to place a check by **Remove 'Run' command**.
19. Expand **System/Restrictions**.
20. Click to place a check by **Disable MS-DOS prompt**.

21. Click on **OK**.

22. Run **File/Exit** to exit the System Policy Editor.

23. Click on **No** to not save the changes.

SCENARIOS

Scenario 1

Jill and Tom participate in the job-sharing program at your office. Jill works Monday through Wednesday and Tom works Thursday and Friday. Last Wednesday, Jill installed Microsoft Project and mapped a network drive to a shared folder containing her project files. When she returned to work on Monday, the drive containing her project files was no longer mapped. What is the problem? How can you prevent it from happening in the future?

....

....

Scenario 2

You are setting up a computer that will be used by retail clerks who will run only the CASHREG.EXE program. The computer is not part of a network. You do not want the user to be able to do anything except run the CASHREG.EXE program and either log off or shut down. There is quite a bit of employee turnover. However, employees need to be logged on uniquely so that CASHREG.EXE can provide statistics on their sales. You are the only other person who should have access to the system. What is the best way to configure this?

....

....

Scenario 3

One of your users frequently complains that resources cannot be found. When you try to troubleshoot the problem, you notice that keys are missing from the registry. You suspect that the user is *curious* and that he may be modifying the registry by hand. How can you prevent him from using REGEDIT?

....

....

SUMMARY

During this chapter, you were introduced to the Windows 95 User Interface and basic system configuration. These included:

- Customizing the Windows 95 User Interface (UI)
- Configuring the Windows 95 Desktop
- Customizing the Start Menu and Taskbar
- Enabling user profiles
- System policies
- System Policy Editor

Later in the course you will see how to implement user profiles and policies on a network. In the next chapter, however, the focus stays local with a look at Control Panel utilities.

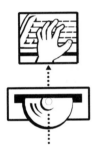

Stop now and complete the Chapter 4 NEXTSim simulation exercise on the Interactive Learning CD-ROM.

POST-TEST QUESTIONS

The answers to these questions are in Appendix A at the end of this manual.

1. A new employee has just joined your company's Sales department. You are in charge of setting up a computer system for her. You want to leave most of the default items that are located on the desktop with one exception. Her department accesses a database rather frequently. What can you do to set her computer up to access this database without having to go through the **Start** menu each time?

    ....

    ....

2. How can you display the clock on your taskbar?

    ....

    ....

3. You are the administrator for a small printing office. Because there are two shifts, the company has decided to save money by allowing users to share computers. Since each employee works on different tasks and has different responsibilities, you want to allow users to customize their desktops. What must you do to enable such customization of the user desktop environment?

    ....

    ....

4. Why should you name a policy file CONFIG.POL?

    ....

    ....

5. Where in the registry are policy settings stored for a user? How about for a system policy?

    ....

    ....

6. List five areas pertaining to users that may be set using the System Policy Editor.

....

....

7. List the three states of a policy and define each.

....

....

CHAPTER 5

System Configuration

OBJECTIVES

At the completion of this chapter, you will be able to:

- Describe the use of selected Control Panel utilities.

- Define the Plug and Play standard.

- Describe the utilization of the Plug and Play standard within Windows 95.

- Add new hardware to a computer.

- Use the Device Manager to configure hardware devices.

PRE-TEST QUESTIONS

The answers to these questions are in Appendix A at the end of this manual.

1. Which Control Panel object lets you select high-contrast screen options for visually impaired end users?

   ....

   ....

2. Which of the Control Panel utilities allows you to add a new MIDI instrument?

   ....

   ....

3. How can you view a list of network components installed on your system?

   ....

   ....

4. How can you view the Display property page without using the Control Panel?

   ....

   ....

5.   The Add New Hardware Wizard supports _____ hardware.

....

....

INTRODUCTION

This chapter begins with a topic familiar to Windows 3.x users, the Control Panel. The Windows 95 Control Panel contains many utilities to configure and customize the operating system. You will see the information and options available within each Control Panel utility. Most users never need to access the majority of these utilities. Administrators, however, must use these utilities for system configuration.

One of the most frustrating areas of managing PCs is hardware installation and configuration. The Plug and Play standard attempts to streamline this process by enabling the computer to automatically adapt to a new configuration any time the user adds, removes, or changes hardware components. The goal of this standard is to minimize the user's need to configure hardware settings. This chapter continues by taking a look at the Plug and Play specification and what it means to Windows 95 users.

This chapter finishes with a discussion of hardware administration. This includes using the Device Manager, viewing System Performance, setting up multiple Hardware Profiles, and obtaining System Information. In particular, the Device Manager provides the user with the ability to view and configure installed devices.

USER PREFERENCES

This section will present those Control Panel utilities that enable users to customize their Windows 95 system. These utilities can be used for installing and removing software applications, configuring display and other user preferences, as well as customizing Internet settings. The following topics are discussed within this section:

- The Control Panel
- Accessibility Options
- Add/Remove Programs
- Date/Time
- Display
- Internet
- Keyboard
- Sounds

These utilities will enable the user to customize certain properties for a user's
Windows 95 system. The utilities discussed in this section will relate to personal
preferences of a user, while the remaining utilities will be discussed later in this chapter.

The Control Panel

There are three methods for launching the Control Panel. These are:

- Open the My Computer object from the desktop and launch the Control Panel.
- Run **Start/Settings/Control Panel**.
- Select **Run** from the **Start** menu and type:

        CONTROL

- Launch Windows Explorer and select Control Panel from the All Folders
  section.

Control Panel

The Control Panel contains several objects. Some applications and utilities may add
objects to the Control Panel.

These icons, representing various system utilities, will display one or more property pages for system configuration and customization.

Depending on the type of installation selected (Typical, Compact, Portable, or Custom), there will be different items present in the Control Panel. Custom installation allows you to install all components.

Accessibility Options

The Accessibility Options utility allows you to customize the Windows 95 User Interface for users with physical disabilities, including visually and hearing-impaired persons. Each accessibility option has a configurable hotkey for easy access. The typical installation method configures Accessibility settings. The five different options available in this utility are displayed and discussed below.

Keyboard

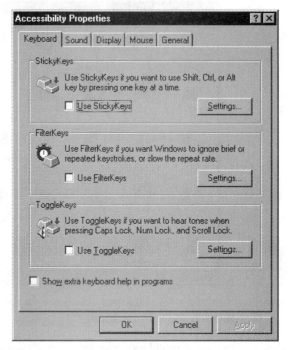

The **Keyboard** tab allows you to configure *StickyKeys, FilterKeys*, and *ToggleKeys*. These options are available for users who have physical disabilities.

- StickyKeys

    There are many times when a user must press a combination of keys to perform a function; for example, *CONTROL+S* is often used to save a file. Users who are not able to do so can enable the StickyKeys option. This allows the user to press modifier keys such as the *SHIFT, CONTROL*, or *TAB* keys one at a time as opposed to all at once. Clicking on the **Settings** button will display the following dialog providing additional configurations:

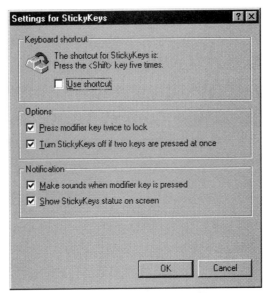

Keyboard shortcut

This option allows the user to use a shortcut to turn the use of StickyKeys on or off by pressing the *SHIFT* key five times.

Options

This option allows advanced configuration for StickyKeys such as locking a modifier key if it has been pressed twice or turning StickyKeys off if two keys are pressed at one time.

Notification

This feature allows the user to use sounds when a modifier key is pressed or to view the status of StickyKeys while they are being used.

- FilterKeys

    This option can be enabled for users whose fingers frequently press keys multiple times or hold them down too long, causing Windows to recognize one keystroke as perhaps a repeated keystroke. FilterKeys allows you to slow the repeat rate so that Windows can recognize a user's pace of keystrokes. Clicking on the **Settings** button will display the following dialog providing additional configurations:

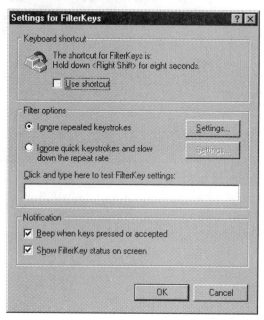

Keyboard shortcut	This option allows the user to use a shortcut to activate or deactivate the use of FilterKeys by pressing the *RIGHT SHIFT* key for eight seconds.
Filter options	This option allows the user to define additional settings for ignoring repeated keystrokes or for ignoring quick keystrokes. Default settings can be tested using the test field.
	If **Ignore repeated keystrokes** is selected, the following dialog can be displayed by clicking on the **Settings** button.

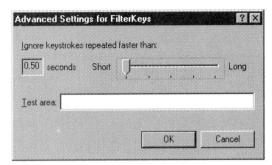

The timing for ignoring repeated keystrokes can be set from 0.50 to 2.00 seconds. The Test Area field allows the user to test the new configuration. For example, if the user holds down the *J* key, a new "j" character will appear every 0.50 seconds since the current setting is set to short or 0.50 seconds.

If **Ignore quick keystrokes and slow down the repeat rate** is selected, the **Settings** button becomes enabled. Clicking on this option will display the following dialog:

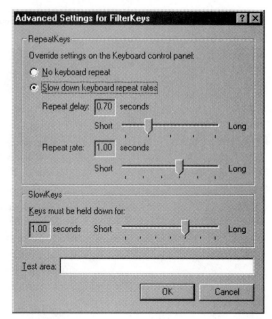

Configurations for RepeatKeys include adjustments for repeat delay and repeat rate. Repeat delays and repeat rates can be set from either 0.30 to 2.00 seconds or zero, which allows no keyboard repeat rate.

Configurations for SlowKeys allow the user to select how long a key must be held down before it is registered as a keystroke. This value can range from zero to 2.00 seconds.

The test area allows the user to test these new configurations to ensure they meet their needs.

Notification

This option causes Windows to beep when keys are pressed. Status of FilterKeys can also be displayed if the option is enabled.

- ToggleKeys

    This option allows users to hear beeps of various pitches when toggle keys such as the *CAPS LOCK, NUM LOCK*, and *SCROLL LOCK* are pressed. Clicking on the **Settings** button will display the following dialog providing additional configurations:

Keyboard shortcut

This option allows the user to use a shortcut to activate or deactivate the use of ToggleKeys by pressing the *NUM LOCK* key for 5 seconds.

Sound

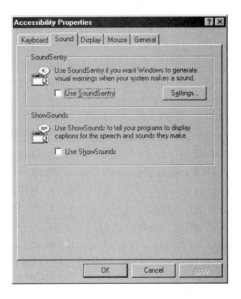

The **Sound** tab allows you to configure SoundSentry and ShowSounds. These options are helpful to those who are hearing impaired.

SoundSentry

This option forces the computer to flash part of the screen when the system makes a sound. Users can specify which part of the screen should flash by clicking on **Settings**.

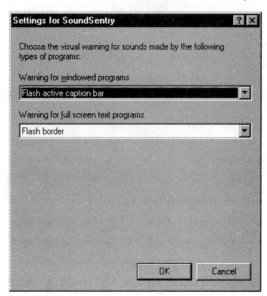

Windows can be set to display a flash for Windowed programs on the active caption bar, active window, or desktop for the SoundSentry feature. A setting for no flash is also available.

For fullscreen text programs, Windows can be set to display a flash on characters, border, or display. A setting for no flash is also available.

ShowSound

This option causes programs to display captions for the speech and sounds they make.

Display

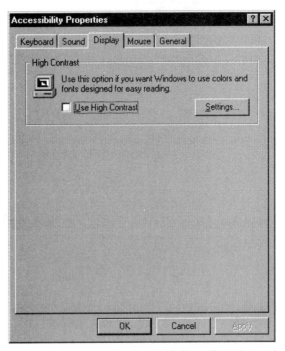

The **Display** tab allows Windows to use colors and fonts for enhanced reading capabilities. Clicking on the **Settings** button allows the user to configure additional settings:

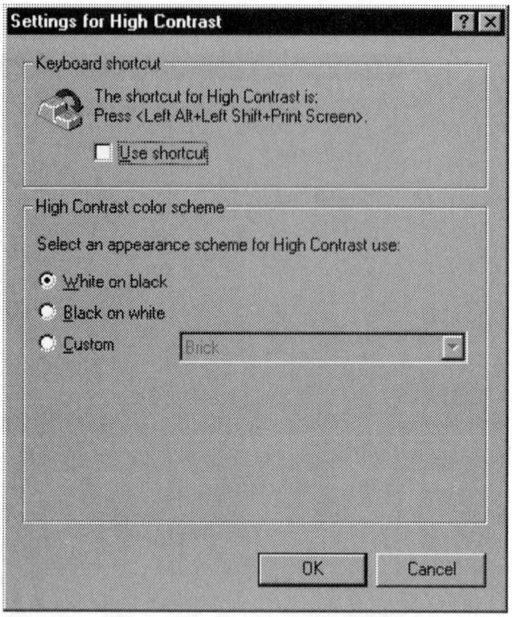

Keyboard shortcut

This option allows the user to use a shortcut to activate or deactivate the use of High Contrast by pressing *LEFT ALT+LEFT SHIFT+PRINT SCREEN*.

High Contrast color scheme

Users can select either white on black, black on white, or a custom color scheme for displaying the high-contrast reading enhancements. The custom selection offers the color schemes available in the Display utility's **Appearance** tab. The Display utility will be discussed later in this chapter.

Mouse

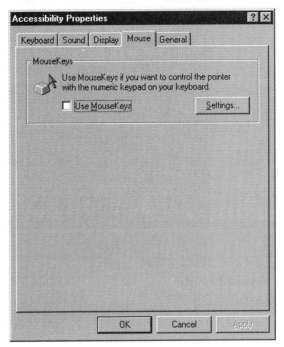

The **Mouse** tab allows users to use the numerical pad's directional keys for mouse activity. Most Windows applications allow users to navigate without a mouse. However, there are times when it is necessary to position the cursor over an area of the screen that does not have an assigned access key.

There is an option available to use MouseKeys when the NumLock is either on or off. Clicking on the **Settings** button will display the following dialog providing additional configurations.

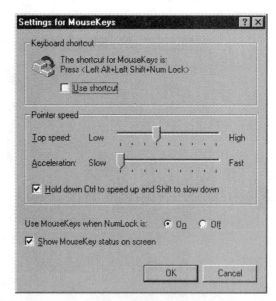

| Keyboard shortcut | This option allows the user to use a shortcut to activate or deactivate the use of MouseKeys by pressing *LEFT ALT+LEFT SHIFT+NUM LOCK*. |

Keyboard shortcut — This option allows the user to use a shortcut to activate or deactivate the use of MouseKeys by pressing *LEFT ALT+LEFT SHIFT+NUM LOCK*.

Pointer speed — The top speed selection designates the speed at which the pointer moves while holding down a MouseKey. The acceleration selection designates how fast the pointer accelerates to the top speed while holding down a MouseKey. An additional setting is available for speeding up or slowing down the movement of the pointer.

General

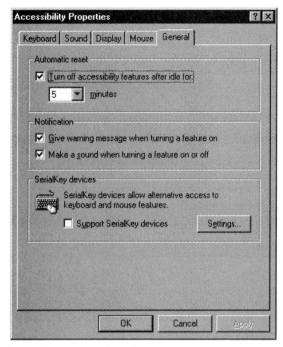

The **General** tab allows three types of configuration: Automatic reset, Notification, and SerialKey devices.

Automatic reset	This option will turn off accessibility features after the designated time. Time may be set from 5 to 30 minutes.
Notification	You can enable a warning message to be displayed when an accessibility feature is enabled. You can also enable an audio notification when an accessibility feature is turned on or off.

SerialKey devices

This option allows you to designate alternative access for SerialKey devices other than the standard keyboard and mouse. Additional settings can be configured by clicking on **Settings**.

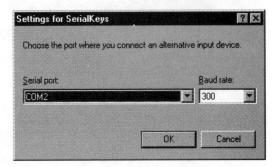

Users can select from Com1 through Com4 to connect an alternative input device. Baud rate can be specified as 300, 1200, 2400, 4800, 9600, and 19,200 bps.

Add/Remove Programs

The Add/Remove Programs utility includes three property pages:

- Install/Uninstall

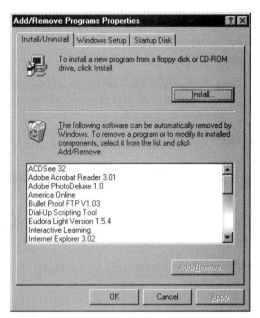

The **Install/Uninstall** tab allows the user to install new programs from floppy diskette or CD-ROM. To install a new program, click on **Install**. This will launch a wizard that will locate the setup program if a floppy disk or CD-ROM is available in the system already. If Windows is unable to locate a SETUP.EXE file, the user can browse to a location.

Windows 95 has created this utility to provide users with an easy method of installing new programs without having to use Explorer or the **Start/Run** command to launch setup programs. Programs that supply their own uninstall program can be uninstalled from this tab.

NOTE: *To use the Uninstall feature of the Add/Remove Programs utility, the software must provide its own Uninstall program. If there is no Uninstall program available, all related files to the software application must be manually deleted using Windows Explorer. Program items referring to the software application must be manually removed from the Taskbar Properties dialog. Be very careful when manually removing programs. Some programs depend on shared components such as dynamic-link libraries and ActiveX components.*

•   Windows Setup

The **Windows Setup** tab allows the user to add or remove Windows components such as Accessibility Options, Accessories, Communications, Disk Tools, Microsoft Fax, Multilanguage Support, Multimedia, The Microsoft Network, and Windows Messaging. Specific utilities within any of these components can be selected by clicking on the **Details** button. A dialog specific to the component will be displayed. In the following graphic, utilities for the Accessories component are shown.

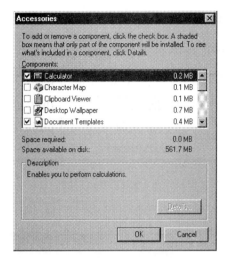

- Startup Disk

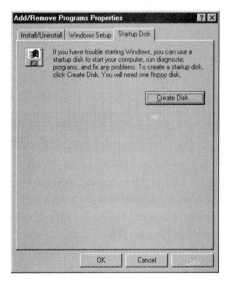

The **Startup Disk** tab allows the user to create a startup disk if one was not created during installation. The bootable startup disk contains diagnostics, tools to fix problems encountered at startup, and the following files:

DRVSPACE.BIN	COMMAND.COM	FORMAT.COM	SYS.COM
FDISK.COM	ATTRIB.EXE	EDIT.COM	REGEDIT.EXE
SCANDISK.EXE	SCANDISK.INI	DEBUG.EXE	CHKDSK.EXE
UNINSTAL.EXE	IO.SYS (hidden)	MSDOS.SYS (hidden)	EBD.SYS (hidden)

Date/Time

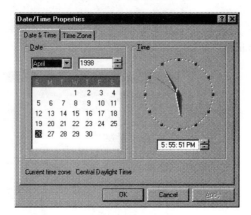

The Date/Time utility has two property pages available: **Date/Time** and **Time Zone**. The **Date/Time** tab allows the user to change the current date and system time. This property page displays a calendar and clock which can be used to change the month, date, year, and time fields. Click on **Apply** to apply the changes. You can also apply changes and exit directly by clicking on **OK**.

The **Time Zone** tab allows the user to specify which time zone the system will use for time information. Windows 95 can automatically enable Daylight Savings Time, depending on the time zone selected. International time zones are also available in the list. The time zone can be selected by either clicking on the appropriate area of the map or by clicking on the drop-down arrow next to the time zone field and selecting the time zone.

Display

The Display utility allows the user to configure display properties relating to background, screen saver, appearance, and monitor settings. Display properties can also be viewed by right-clicking on the desktop and selecting **Properties**. Let's take a closer look at each property pages available in the Display utility.

Background

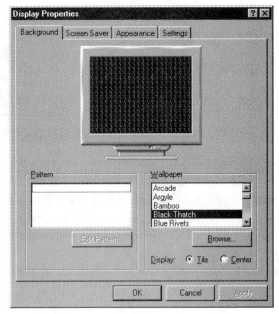

The **Background** tab allows the user to set the desktop pattern, as well as the wallpaper, if desired. The items listed are installed by Windows 95.

• Pattern

The existing patterns may be altered by clicking on **Edit Pattern**.

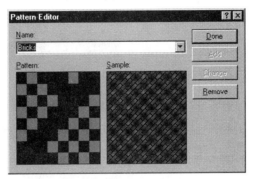

For example, if you want to change the current design or color of the Bricks pattern, just click on the desired area of the pattern. The color is determined by whatever is selected on the **Appearance** tab of the Display control panel at the time of editing. To add the new pattern to the list on the **Background** tab, click on **Add**. To remove a current pattern from the list, click on **Remove**. The **Change** button saves your edits to the pattern. Once you have finished your edits, click on **Done** to close the Pattern Editor.

• Wallpaper

Wallpapers may be displayed on the desktop as either tile or center. Tile displays the wallpaper in a repeated pattern until the entire desktop is covered. Center displays the wallpaper as an image centered on the desktop. To select a new wallpaper from a different source, click on **Browse**. The user can then browse to locate the new.bmp file to be used.

Screen Saver

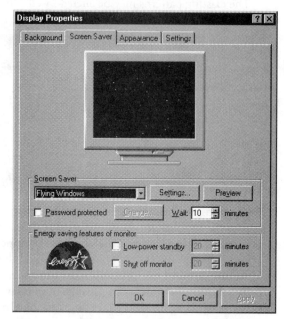

The **Screen Saver** tab allows the user to select a screen saver from the selections provided by Windows 95.

Screen Saver

Depending on the screen saver, additional settings may be configured. To configure settings specific to the chosen screen saver, click on **Settings**. Clicking on **Preview** allows you to view the new configurations for your screen saver. You also set a password for the screen saver by clicking on the **Password protected** checkbox and then clicking on **Change**. Once the screen saver activates, users must enter the password to gain access to the system. If the password is forgotten, you must reboot the system.

Change Password	? X
Change password for Windows Screen Saver	OK
New password:	Cancel
Confirm new password:	

Synchronizing the screen saver password with the logon password will be discussed later in the course. You can also set a time frame for the screen saver to activate using the time selection.

Energy saving features of monitor   This option allows the user to conserve power by allowing the monitor to switch to standby mode if the system is idle for a length of time greater than that selected for the screen saver. You can also select to shut the monitor off completely given the above time constraint. The **Shut off monitor** selection will provide a higher conservation of power.

Appearance

The **Appearance** tab allows you to select a color scheme for your desktop and application environments. You can select from standard desktop schemes installed by Windows 95. You can modify an available desktop scheme by first selecting an item from the Item or clicking on the desired item in the graphical display. Then, you may modify the Size and Color of various desktop objects. You can also modify the Font of an item (if appropriate) by selecting the scheme and then clicking on **Font, Size, Color,** and two additional selections which are **Bold** and **Italics.** You can even create new desktop schemes and change colors for desktop items.

To save the new scheme, click on **Save As.** The new scheme will then be added to the existing list. You can also delete an existing scheme. Once you have selected or created the scheme, click on **Apply** to apply the new configurations.

Settings

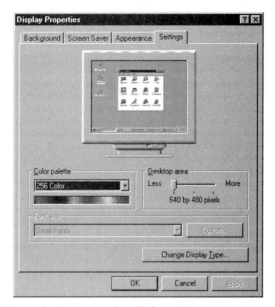

The options available on the **Settings** tab will depend on your monitor and your display adapter.

- Color palette

  This selection allows you to specify the number of colors you want to view on your monitor.

- Desktop area

  This selection allows you to specify the resolution for your monitor.

- Font size

  This selection allows you to change the system font size for the Windows environment. This selection may not be available at all resolutions. Custom font settings can be set by clicking on **Custom**.

You can also change the current display type from this tab. This selection is useful when you have a new video driver that you want to install for your monitor. Click on **Change Display Type** to display the following dialog:

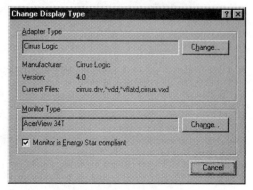

Here, you can change either the adapter type or the monitor type.

To change the adapter type, click on the **Change** button for Adapter Type:

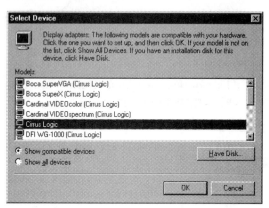

You can either **Show compatible devices** or **Show all devices**. If you have a special driver disk, you should click on **Have Disk**. The above graphic displays only compatible devices installed on the computer used. The next graphic will show the type of listing available if **Show all devices** is selected, even if you are configuring a new monitor type.

To configure a new monitor type, click on **Change** for Monitor Type.

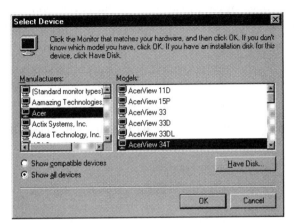

This dialog shows all the devices available from various manufacturers. Again, you can install from a supplied driver disk simply by clicking on **Have Disk**.

Exercise 5-1:
Control Panel Basics

The purpose of this exercise is to introduce you to Control Panel objects. During the exercise, you will use Control Panel objects to manage system parameters.

1. Run **Start/Settings/Control Panel** to launch the Control Panel.

2. Double-click on the Accessibility Options icon. You can also launch this utility by right-clicking on the icon and selecting **Open**.

3. Click on the **Display** tab.

4. Click on the checkbox for **Use High Contrast**.

5. Click on the **Settings** button.

6. In the Settings dialog, click on the option for **Custom.**

7. Select **High Control Black (extra large)** from the list of custom settings.

8. Click on **OK.**

9. Click on **Apply**. There will be a short delay while your desktop is reconfigured.

10. Disable the **Use High Contrast** option. Click on **Apply** to reconfigure the desktop and application environment back to its original settings.

11. Open the Display control panel. You can also open this dialog by right-clicking on the desktop and selecting **Properties**.

12. Launch the Display control panel.

13. Verify that you are on the **Background** tab. Select **Black Thatch** as your new wallpaper.

14. Select the **Screen Saver** tab.

15. Select Flying Windows as the screen saver for your system.

16. Click on **Settings**.

17. Change the warp speed to slow.

18. Change the number of windows to 35.

19. Click on **OK**.

20. Click on **Apply**.

21. Click on **OK**. Notice your new background wallpaper.

22. Close the Control Panel.

Internet

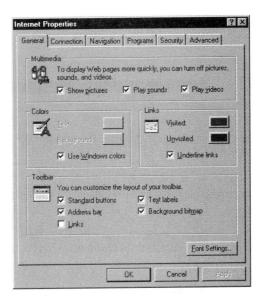

The Internet utility is related to features used in the Internet Explorer browser which ships with Windows 95. Since these options are also available in the browser, they will be discussed later in the course.

Keyboard

The Keyboard utility includes three property pages: Speed, Language, and General. Let's take a look at each of the property pages.

Speed

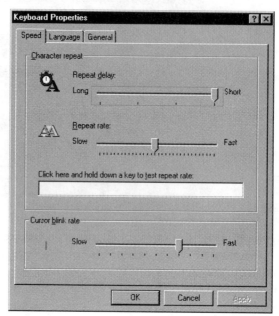

Character repeat

This option allows you to configure the repeat delay and repeat rate for keyboard activity. These features are similar to those discussed in the Accessibility Options utility. You can also test the repeat rate using the test field.

Cursor blink rate

This option allows you to select the speed at which you want your cursor to blink. To the left of the scroll bar is a blinking cursor that will change its blinking speed as you adjust the rate.

Language

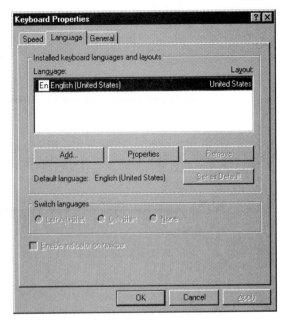

Installed keyboard languages and layouts

This option allows you to install new languages for your system. Clicking on **Add** will display the list that you may install from. These are the languages that are available with Windows 95 installation.

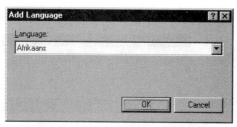

To view the properties of an installed language, click on **Properties** on the **Language** tab. You can select the layout for your keyboard based on the installed language.

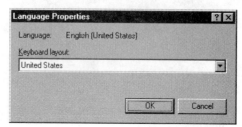

Switch languages

This option allows you to select a combination keystroke to switch between installed languages on the system.

To set the default language for your system, select a language from the list of installed languages, and click on the **Set as Default** button. You can also set a taskbar indicator by selecting the checkbox at the bottom of the **Language** tab.

General

This option allows you to change the keyboard type installed for the system. Click on **Change** to display the following dialog:

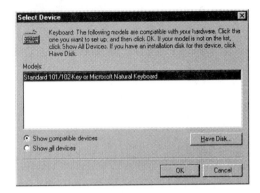

If you want to view all devices that are available for selection, click on **Show all devices**. Once you have selected the type of keyboard you wish to install, click on **OK**.

Sounds

The Sounds utility allows the user to associate sounds with system events.

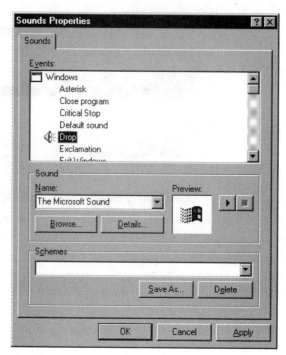

The Sounds utility displays sounds for various Windows events. These sounds can be changed by selecting an event, then making a selection from the Name drop-down list. Users may also browse to locate other sound files that may be available from sources other than Windows 95. **Details** displays information for a selected sound similar to the following:

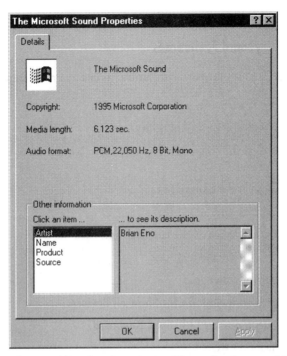

Users may click on the items listed such as Artist, Name, Product, and Source to view additional information for the selected sound. Media length describes the length of the sound wave. The audio format is also displayed.

Schemes allow the user to select the Windows-default scheme, as well as any others available. Once a scheme is chosen, all events will be assigned new sound associations. Any modifications to the scheme may be saved under a new scheme name. Schemes can also be deleted.

Exercise 5-2:
Configuring Keyboard Preferences

This exercise uses the Keyboard utility to install a new language for keyboard use.

1. Run **Start/Settings/Control Panel**.

2. Launch the Keyboard utility.

3. Change the cursor blink rate to Fast. Notice the pace of the cursor. It has increased.

4. Click on the **Language** tab.

5. Click on **Add**.

6. Select **Swedish** as the language and click on **OK**.

7. Click on the **General** tab.

8. Click on **Change**.

9. Click on the option for **Show all devices**.

10. Select **Compaq Enhanced Keyboard**.

11. Click on **OK**.

12. Click on **Change** again.

13. Verify that **Standard 101/102-Key or Microsoft Natural Keyboard** is selected and click on **OK**.

14. Click on **Close**.

15. Restart your computer when prompted.

SYSTEM MANAGEMENT

This section discusses the Control Panel utilities used to configure system settings. The following topics are discussed within this section:

- Fonts
- Mail and Fax
- Network
- Passwords
- Regional Settings
- System

Normally, administrators use the above-listed utilities to configure the system components of a computer. Some of these utilities will be discussed later in the course in more detail.

Fonts

Windows 95 provides a new method for adding, deleting, and viewing fonts.

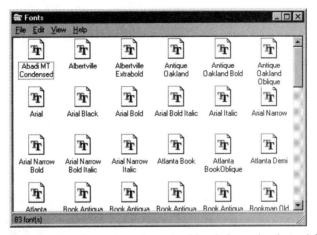

To view detailed information for a given font, double-click on the desired font. A dialog specific to the selected font will be displayed:

To install a new font, run **File/Install New Font** from the menu. You will see the following dialog displayed:

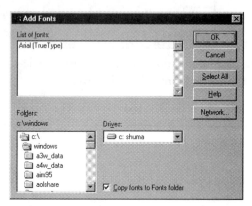

Browse to locate the new font and click on **OK**. If the font is located on a network drive, you can click on **Network** to browse to the network path. If there are multiple fonts located in the same directory, you can click on **Select All** to select all font files. Fonts will be covered in more detail later in the course.

Mail and Fax

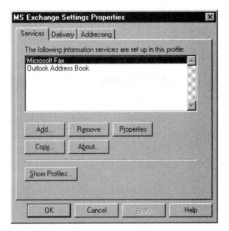

Opening the Mail and Fax object displays the MS Exchange Settings property page. Microsoft Exchange will be discussed later in the course.

Network

The Network utility is used for configuring network components such as clients, protocols, services, and adapters. This networking utility will be discussed in greater detail later in the course.

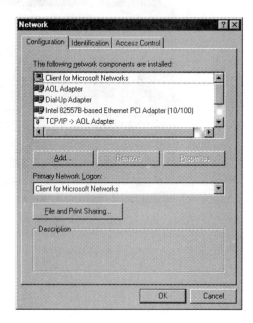

Passwords

You have already seen how the Passwords utility can be used to enable user profiles. It also allows the user to set configurations for Passwords and Remote Administration. Configuring Password and Remote Administration options will be discussed later in the course.

Regional Settings

Regional Settings properties include: Regional Settings, Number, Currency, Time, and Date. Let's take a look at each of these property pages.

Regional Settings

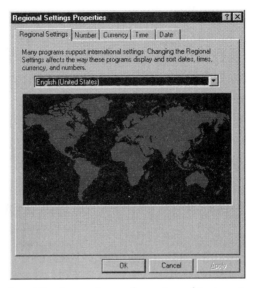

The **Regional Settings** tab sets the universal international settings for the operating system. Users can select from fifty different international schemes. Selections made on this property page will automatically affect settings for the **Number**, **Currency**, **Time**, and **Date** property pages.

Number

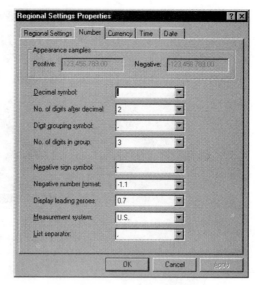

Decimal symbol
For United States English, the only available selection is a period (.). To modify the decimal symbol, type the symbol in the field and press **_ENTER._** The new symbol will appear in the list for this option.

No. of digits after decimal
The number of digits after a decimal can be set between 0 and 9.

Digit grouping symbol
For United States English, the only available selection is a comma(,). To modify the digit grouping symbol, type the symbol in the field and press **_ENTER._** The new symbol will appear in the list for this option.

No. of digits in group
The number of digits in a group can be set between 0 and 9.

Negative sign symbol
For United States English, the negative sign symbol is a hyphen (-). To modify the negative sign symbol, type the new symbol in the field and press **_ENTER._** The new symbol will appear in the list for this option.

Negative number format

> A negative number may be displayed in any of the following formats: (1.1), or -1.1, - 1.1, 1.1-, and 1.1 -.

Display leading zeros

> This option allows you to display leading zeros, if desired. For example, 0.7 has shows a leading zero whereas .7 does not.

Measurement system

> You can select the measurement system to be either Metric or U.S.

List separator

> For United States English, the list separator can be either a semi-colon or a comma. To modify the list separator, type the new separator in the field and press *ENTER*. The new symbol will appear in the list for this option.

To accept the changes you have made in settings, click on **Apply**. The changes will be displayed in the Appearance samples section of the **Number** tab.

Currency

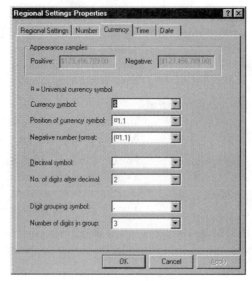

Currency symbol   For United States English, the standard currency symbol
is "$". To modify the currency symbol, type the new
symbol in the field and press *ENTER*. The new symbol
will appear in the list for this option.

Position of currency symbol
This selection allows you to designate the position of the
currency symbol within a numerical amount.

Negative number format
This selection allows you to designate the format of a
negative currency amount.

Decimal symbol   For United States English, the standard decimal symbol is
a period (.). To modify the decimal symbol, type the new
symbol in the field and press *ENTER*. The new symbol
will appear in the list for this option.

No. of digits after decimal
The number of digits after a decimal can be set between
0 and 9.

Digit grouping symbol

> For United States English, the standard digit grouping symbol is a comma (,). To modify the grouping symbol, type the new symbol in the field and press *ENTER*. The new symbol will appear in the list for this option.

Number of digits in group

> The number of digits in a group can range from 0 to 9.

To accept the changes you have made in settings, click on **Apply**. The changes will be displayed in the Appearance samples section of the **Currency** tab.

Time

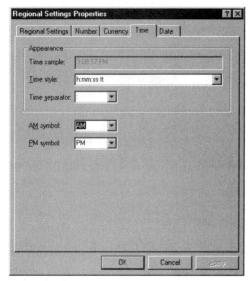

Appearance

> This option allows you to change the style of the time selection. The time separator can also be changed. Once you click on **Apply**, the changes will be displayed in the Time sample field.

The settings for AM and PM will change based on a new selection made on the **Regional Settings** tab.

Date

Short date   This option allows you to change the style of the short date display. Date separators can also be changed. Changes will be reflected in the Short date sample once you click on **Apply**.

Long date   This option allows you to change the style of the long date display. Once you click on **Apply**, changes will be displayed in the Long date sample field.

System

One of the most important objects in the Control Panel is the System object. The System utility contains information pertaining to hardware profiles, device configuration, and performance.

There are four tabs on System Properties.

General

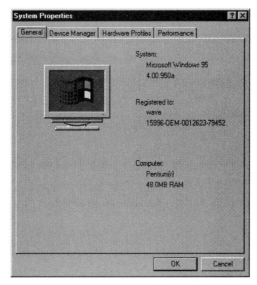

The **General** tab displays system, registration, and computer information. System information consists of the operating system and its version number. Registration information usually includes the user's name, as well as the product registration number. Computer information includes the processor type, as well as the current amount of RAM installed. No properties can be modified on this property page.

Device Manager

The **Device Manager** tab displays a tree structure listing all installed and supported devices. Users can expand a device to view specific devices installed. You can select any device and view its properties, resource and configuration settings. Device settings, including IRQs and I/O ranges, can be viewed and altered. The Device Manager will be discussed in greater detail later in this chapter.

Hardware Profiles

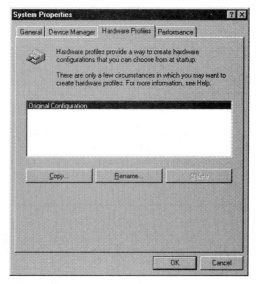

The **Hardware Profiles** tab is used for setting up multiple hardware configurations for a system. Providing different hardware configurations at startup allows the mobile user to have maximum control over the computer.

Hardware profiles will be discussed in greater detail later in this chapter.

Performance

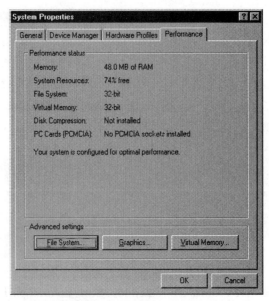

You can view and modify configuration settings relating to system performance through the **Performance** tab of the System utility. This includes settings for file systems (drives), graphics, and virtual memory. These settings will be discussed in greater detail later in the course.

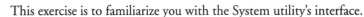

Exercise 5-3:
Using the System utility

This exercise is to familiarize you with the System utility's interface.

1. The Control Panel should be open since the last exercise was performed. Launch the System utility.

2. Click on the **Device Manager** tab.

3. Expand the **Floppy disk controllers** listing.

4. Select the floppy disk controller available on your system and click on **Properties**.

5. Click on the **Resources** tab. Notice that IRQ setting information is available here.

6. Click on **Cancel**.

7. Click on the option for **View devices by connection**. Notice that the listing changes the way it is displayed.

8. Click on the **Performance** tab.

9. Click on **Virtual Memory**.

10. Verify that the option to **Let Windows manage my virtual memory settings (recommended)** is enabled.

11. Click on **OK**.

12. Click on **Cancel**.

13. Close the System utility.

HARDWARE MANAGEMENT

This section discusses the Control Panel utilities that are used for hardware management. The following topics are discussed within this section:

*   Add New Hardware

*   Modems

*   Mouse

*   Multimedia

*   Power

*   Printers

Add New Hardware

Windows 95 includes the new Add New Hardware Wizard which enables users of any expertise level to add new hardware components to their computer system. Windows 95 includes many standard drivers for many available manufacturers. These may be used, as well as installing new device drivers. All this can be done using the new Add New Hardware Wizard.

The Add New Hardware utility leads the user through installing new hardware. We will discuss the use of this wizard in detail later in this chapter.

Modems

The Modems Properties page has two pages:

- General

The **General** tab allows the user to install new modems with the Install New Modem Wizard, configure modems, remove existing modems, view modem properties, and set up dialing preferences.

- Diagnostics

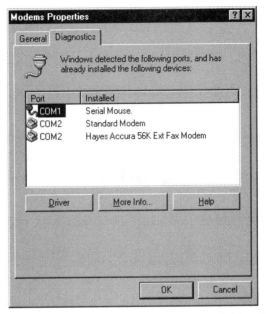

The **Diagnostics** tab displays the port status and driver information for the selected port. Modem diagnostics occurs when **More Info...** is selected.

The Modems utility will be discussed in more detail later in the course.

Mouse

The Mouse utility allows the user to configure or change the current mouse. This utility contains four property pages.

Buttons

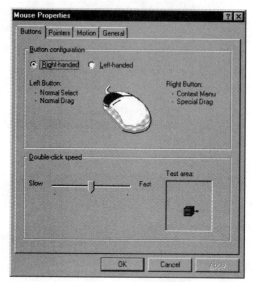

Button configuration

This option configures the mouse for right-handed or left-handed users. For example, if the user is right-handed, the left mouse button operates as mouse button 1. The right mouse button is used to display pop-up menus. For left-handed users, the mouse buttons operate in reverse.

Double-click speed

This options sets the speed of the double-clicking action of the mouse. To test any new configurations, users may double-click in the test area.

Pointers

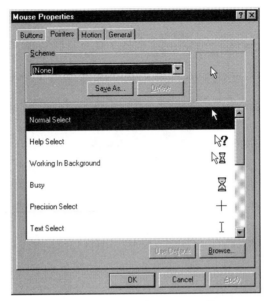

Scheme

This option allows you to change the scheme of the cursor using selections provided by Windows 95. As a new scheme is selected, all cursor icons will change accordingly in the display. You can select different cursors and cursor schemes. If you want to change a particular pointer within a scheme, you can click on the **Browse** button to select a different pointer. Then, to save the new scheme, click on **Save As**. You will need to enter the new name of the scheme.

Motion

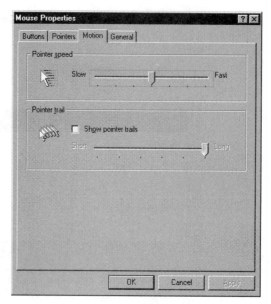

Pointer speed

This option configures the speed of the pointer's movement on the screen.

Pointer trail

This option sets the speed of the pointer's trail during movement on the screen. To view the trail on screen, click on the checkbox for **Show pointer trails.** Users may want to enable this option if they are using an LCD screen.

General

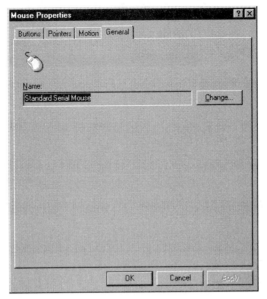

The **General** tab allows the user to select a new mouse. Click on **Change** to select a new mouse from the following dialog:

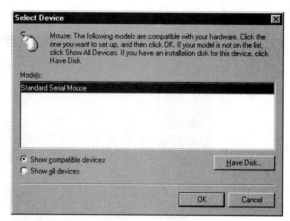

If **Show all devices** is selected, the list will change to display manufacturers and models of various mouse devices.

Exercise 5-4:
Configuring a Mouse

1. Launch the Control Panel.

2. Open the Mouse utility. Click on the **Motion** tab.

3. Click on the checkbox for **Show pointer trails**.

4. Move your mouse and observe the effect of the new setting on your screen.

5. Disable the **Show pointer trails** option. This setting will not affect later exercises.

6. Click on **OK** to exit the Mouse utility.

8. Close the Control Panel.

Multimedia

As the number of multimedia applications grows, so does the desire for multimedia on the desktop. Windows 95 has enhanced that desire by making multimedia capability readily available. The Windows 95 multimedia architecture offers certain benefits:

- Media Control Interface (MCI) allows multimedia devices to run independently from each other.

- Built-in tools allow recording, editing, and playing of digital audio and video.

- Simplified installation of additional multimedia hardware through the use of the Add New Hardware Wizard.

- Enhanced file-sharing allows the sharing of CD-ROM drives across a network.

- Support for playing multimedia files is built-in and includes:

    Digital Video (AVI) files

    Waveform Audio (WAV) files

    Musical Instrument Digital Interface (MIDI) files

- Built-in audio support allows the user to:

    Assign sound clips to system events.

    Play audio CDs with the CD player.

    Record sound with the Sound Recorder.

    Link audio clips to documents using OLE support.

The Multimedia utility allows configuration for multimedia devices. Let's take a closer look at each of the property pages within this utility.

Audio

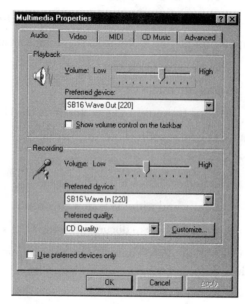

The **Audio** tab provides configuration settings for any available audio devices.

Playback

This option allows you to set the **Volume** of sounds played through the audio hardware on your system. The Preferred device settings display all available audio hardware. You can also display an icon for Volume control on the taskbar.

Recording

This option allows you to set the Volume for sounds that you wish to record using the audio hardware on your system. This setting will affect the volume of the recorded sound when played back.

Display the Preferred device list to select an audio device from your available audio hardware. You can also select the Preferred quality of your recording as CD quality, Radio quality, or Telephone quality.

To create a new sound quality format or customize the existing preferred quality types, click on **Customize**. The following dialog will appear:

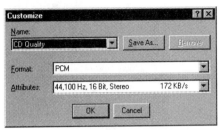

To create a new audio format, select **Untitled** from the list of names. Then select the Format type from the available list. Finally, you must select the Attributes of the new audio format. To save the new format, click on **Save As**. You should also save any modifications to the existing preferred quality types using **Save As**. The option to remove a format is also available.

Video

The **Video** tab contains configuration settings for viewing video clips.

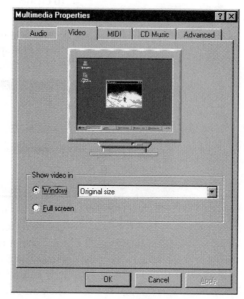

Show video in

To select the viewing window size for a video clip, you can select from Original size, Double original size, 1/16 of screen size, 1/4 of screen size, 1/2 of screen size, and Maximized. You can also view the clip at full screen.

MIDI

This **MIDI** tab displays and configures MIDI output and MIDI schemes.

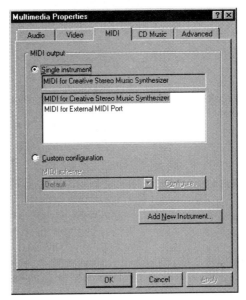

MIDI output

The **Single instrument** option displays the instrument on which MIDI is played in Windows. The open space beneath Single instrument displays all available instruments for your system. To select a new instrument, simply click on it.

The **Custom configuration** option allows you to select or modify an existing MIDI scheme or create a brand new scheme. Click on **Configure** to display the following dialog:

Schemes

To modify a scheme, you must first select one from the list of schemes. Next, select a Channel. To change the configuration of a MIDI instrument, click on **Change**. The instruments available will depend on whatever MIDI instruments are installed on your computer.

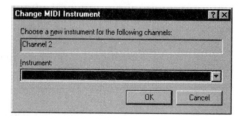

The **MIDI** tab also allows you to add a new instrument using the MIDI Instrument Installation Wizard. To launch the Wizard, click on the **Add New Instrument** button. The following introductory dialog will be displayed:

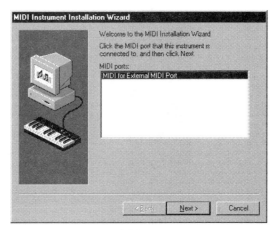

If there is more than one MIDI port available on your computer, you can select the desired port on this screen. Then click on **Next**.

If you are installing an instrument that is not a general MIDI instrument, you must select the appropriate instrument definition. Then click on **Next**. You can also **Browse** to locate the instrument definition.

You can either accept the default name of the MIDI instrument or create a new name. Click on **Finish** when you are done. The new instrument will be listed on the **MIDI** tab.

CD Music

The **CD Music** tab displays any or all CD-ROMs available on your system. To set the volume of your headphones, first select the CD-ROM drive that the headphones are connected to. Then, set the volume setting for the headphones. If you have more than one CD-ROM device on your system, set the volume settings for each CD-ROM headphone one at a time.

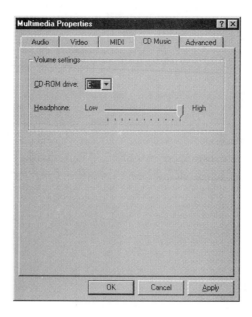

Advanced

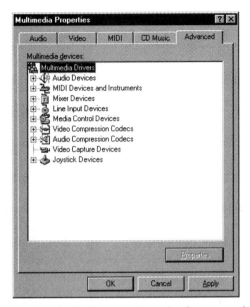

The **Advanced** tab displays a tree of all the multimedia devices available on your system. To view the device drivers for each entry, simply click on the *plus symbol* next to each device. To view properties for a desired device driver, select the device driver and click on **Properties**. A dialog similar to the following will be displayed:

The **General** tab on this property page allows you to enable or disable the driver for a selected device. To disable a device driver, click on the **Do not use this Media Control device** option. The status of the device will then change to "disabled." To view additional settings for the device driver, click on **Settings**. The dialog displayed below is specific to the selected device driver:

You can remove the device driver for a multimedia device by clicking on **Remove**.

Power

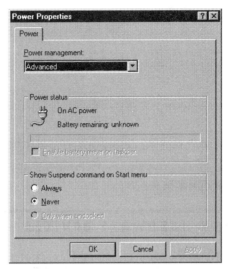

The Power utility allows configuration of power management for your computer. Users can select three different types of power management: Advanced, Standard, or Off. Advanced power management allows the system to use additional power-saving features provided by Windows. Standard power management allows the system to use the power-saving features available on your system. The Off feature turns power management off.

Power status
> This option allows you to view an icon for battery power on the taskbar. This feature is useful for portable computers.

Show Suspend command on Start menu
> The **Suspend** command can be displayed on the Start menu always, never, or only when a portable computer is undocked.

Printers

The Printers utility is a shortcut to the Printers folder. Printer setup and management will be discussed later in the course.

PLUG AND PLAY HARDWARE DEVICES

This section will introduce the Plug and Play features of Windows 95. Plug and Play is designed to automate and simplify system hardware configuration. The following topics are discussed within this section:

- Plug and Play
- The Plug and Play Standard
- Plug and Play: Bus Support
- Plug and Play: Windows 95 Support
- Plug and Play: Docking Systems

Plug and Play architecture has helped make Windows 95 a popular product. It enables users with any level of experience to set up a computer system with new hardware components without assistance.

Plug and Play

Windows 95 is the first operating system to provide full support for the new Plug and Play standard.

Prior to Plug and Play, installing new hardware was a trying exercise. Typically, you would purchase a compatible piece of hardware, set the hardware jumpers, physically install the card, install configuration software (if included), reboot the PC, and hope for the best.

Hardware communicates with the PC by means of I/O addresses, interrupt requests (IRQs), and frequently, a direct memory access channel (DMA). When you install a legacy hardware device and an existing piece of hardware is using these values, a conflict occurs, causing you to start the entire hardware configuration again.

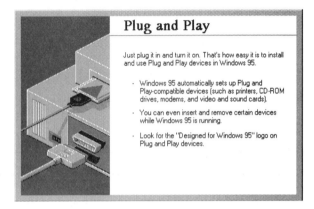

To combat this problem, Intel, Compaq, and Microsoft originated an undertaking to create the Plug and Play architecture. The Plug and Play Association of hardware manufacturers governs this standard.

The Plug and Play Standard

The Plug and Play architecture consists of three components:

*   Plug and Play BIOS

    The Plug and Play BIOS detects and configures Plug and Play cards as part of the Power On Self Test (POST) process. In addition, the Plug and Play BIOS provides run-time services that allow system software to coordinate configuration management with the BIOS.

- Plug and Play hardware devices

  The ESCD (Extended System Configuration Data) data structure holds the current configuration of all devices in the system in some form of non-volatile storage. Plug and Play hardware devices must have the capability to access the information stored in the ESCD.

- Plug and Play operating system

  The Windows 95 operating system is Plug and Play-compatible. It is centered around a new feature, known as the Configuration Manager, which integrates the automatic hardware configuration process.

Many of the devices available on the market today include Plug and Play hardware devices.

Plug and Play: Bus Support

Information travels from the device to the computer via a bus. Information pertaining to standard bus types and any special Plug and Play concerns must adhere to one of the following standards:

- Industry Standard Architecture (ISA)

  Plug and Play and legacy ISA devices can be installed and maintained on the same system.

  Plug and Play ISA devices are dynamically configured by the operating system.

  If both Plug and Play and legacy ISA devices exist on the computer, static configuration values are stored in the registry.

- Enhanced Industry Standard Architecture (EISA)

  EISA cards generally meet Plug and Play specifications.

  EISA cards contain non-volatile RAM to store configuration values.

  The Windows 95 Configuration Manager makes the configuration information stored on the card available to system components.

- Small Computer Standard Interface (SCSI)

    Plug and Play SCSI devices support automatic and dynamic configuration of device ID and termination.

    Windows 95 Setup frequently has problems detecting multiple SCSI devices sharing the same SCSI host adapter.

    SCSI devices not detected by Windows 95 Setup can be installed through the use of the Add New Hardware Wizard, bypassing automatic detection.

- PCMCIA (Personal Computer Memory Card International Association)

    PCMCIA supports all facets of Plug and Play technology.

    The PCMCIA device must contain information that Windows 95 can use to create a unique ID for the device.

    Most PCMCIA devices support *hot* swapping.

- Video Electronics Standards Association (VESA) Local (VL)

    VL devices do not totally comply with the Plug and Play standard.

    VL devices work similar to ISA devices.

    Most VL devices are high-performance video cards.

- Peripheral Component Interconnect (PCI)

    This bus is found in most Pentiums and PowerPCs. It is frequently used as a secondary bus.

    If the primary bus is not Plug and Play-compliant, the secondary PCI bus cannot utilize Plug and Play functionality.

    PCI meets most Plug and Play specifications, storing configuration information in non-volatile RAM.

Plug and Play: Windows 95 Support

Windows 95 implements Plug and Play functionality in all components. Windows 95 Plug and Play features include:

- Full compatibility and support for legacy hardware.

- Support for mobile computing, including *hot* docking and *hot* swapping of Plug and Play devices.

- Automated configuration and installation of Plug and Play peripherals.

- Centralized hardware configuration information in the Windows 95 Registry.

- Reduced user support requirements.

Immediately after installing a Plug and Play device and powering up the computer, Windows 95 notifies the user that a new device has been found. If the operating system does not have a driver available for the device, the user will be prompted to insert a diskette with the manufacturer's Windows 95 driver. The system configures the device and it is available immediately. PCMCIA devices are immediately identified upon insertion. Windows 95 loads the appropriate driver, and the computer beeps to notify the user that the device is ready for use.

Here is an overview of the components that make this process work:

- Configuration Manager

    The Configuration Manager can be thought of as a type of *traffic cop*. It monitors the system for changes in device configuration and can notify the appropriate applications and device drivers when such changes occur. As a result, device conflicts are essentially eliminated. The Configuration Manager works with sub-components, such as bus enumerators, to identify each bus structure and required device configuration.

- Bus Enumerators

    Bus enumerators collect information from the hardware devices, device drivers, and BIOS during the enumeration process. When a Plug and Play device is added to or removed from the system, the bus enumerators notify the Configuration Manager. The Configuration Manager uses resource arbitrators to allocate resources such as IRQs and interrupt levels. The resource information is then passed to the device driver.

Parallel ports, and the peripherals connected to them, can utilize Plug and Play through the use of Compatibility mode and Nibble mode protocols. Compatibility mode furnishes a byte-wide communication path between the computer and the peripheral. Data is sent in 4-bit nibbles if Nibble mode is used. Nibble mode is also used during device enumeration.

For non-Plug and Play devices, Windows 95 checks for known hardware devices by checking I/O ports and known memory addresses to attempt to identify whether the ports or addresses are being used by specific devices.

Installation of legacy hardware requires the use of the Add New Hardware Wizard. This process is discussed later in the chapter.

Plug and Play: Docking Systems

A significant advantage of Windows 95 Plug and Play is that it allows support for mobile computers with docking stations. Windows 95 supports two types of docking:

- *Cold* docking

    The computer must be powered down prior to docking or undocking.

    Multiple hardware configurations are useful in managing devices when docked or undocked.

    Legacy docking systems utilize *cold* docking.

- *Hot* docking

    The computer may be docked or undocked without first powering down.

    BIOS or bus enumerators inform the Configuration Manager of the configuration change, and the Configuration Manager passes the information to the device drivers.

    Plug and Play docking systems utilize *hot* docking.

In order to support *hot* docking, Windows 95 supports two different types of undocking systems:

- Manual ejection

    The user undocks the system without using a software interface.

    The user must close programs, save files, and complete all *closing* tasks prior to undocking.

    Data can be lost if the user does not intervene.

- Auto-ejection

    The user undocks the system using a software interface similar to a VCR mechanism.

    Windows 95 prompts for user intervention as necessary to close any open resources that will be affected.

    Data is not lost in the process.

Certain systems require steps to be performed prior to *hot* docking. If a system is undocked without allowing Windows 95 to close open files or save information to disk, data loss will occur. This is the case with manual ejection systems.

The principles described for the docking of mobile computers apply to other types of dynamic hardware, such as removable mass storage devices.

INSTALLING NEW HARDWARE

Windows 95 makes it easier to add new peripheral or internal hardware devices through the use of the Add New Hardware Wizard. You may add either legacy or Plug and Play hardware. The Add New Hardware Wizard will do the majority of the configurations for you. The following topics are discussed within this section:

- Add New Hardware Wizard
- Hardware Conflict Troubleshooter
- Reconfiguring Resource Settings Due to Hardware Conflicts

You will also be introduced to the troubleshooter that is provided by Windows 95. This utility helps users determine why and where hardware conflicts occur.

Add New Hardware Wizard

The Add New Hardware wizard walks you through all the steps necessary to add and configure new hardware devices that are non-Plug and Play. After physically installing the new piece of hardware, start your system to begin configuration.

NOTE: *Windows 95 will automatically recognize Plug and Play devices after their physical installation. The following procedure is used primarily for legacy hardware.*

To access the Add New Hardware Wizard, run **Start/Settings/Control Panel**. Double-click on the Add New Hardware utility.

To begin installing the new hardware, click on **Next**.

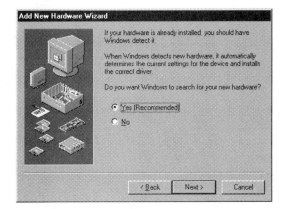

It is recommended that you let Windows 95 detect new hardware. As Windows finds new hardware, it will determine the settings for the device and the drivers required. You should close all open applications before starting the Add New Hardware Wizard.

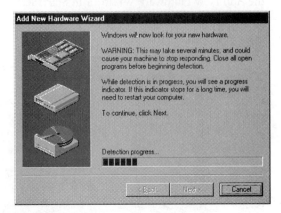

After Windows finds new hardware, you will have the option of viewing the settings or proceeding with the configuration process. Upon successful hardware installation, Windows may ask you to reboot the system to complete the device installation.

If Windows cannot detect the new hardware, the following dialog will be displayed:

You must then select the type of hardware you wish to install. Hardware types include: CD-ROM controllers, Display adapters, Floppy disk controllers, Hard disk controllers, Infrared, Keyboard, Memory Technology Drivers, Modem, Mouse, Multi-function adapters, Network adapters, Other devices, PCMCIA sockets, Ports, Printers, SCSI controllers, Sound, video, and game controllers, and System devices. Once you have made your selection, click on Next.

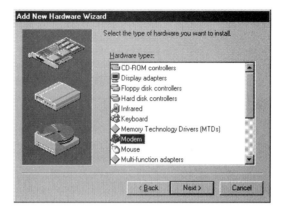

You can then manually specify the hardware device's manufacturer and model from the available list. If you want to install from a disk, you can click on the **Have Disk** button. This will then install the hardware device and close the Add New Hardware Wizard.

Hardware Conflict Troubleshooter

Although Windows 95 makes several checks to ensure that hardware devices do not conflict with each other, there is always the possibility that a conflict can occur. To assist the user in resolving hardware conflicts, Windows includes the Hardware Conflict Troubleshooter.

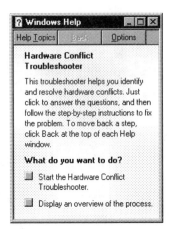

To display this help utility, run **Start/Help**. On the **Contents** tab, expand the Troubleshooting selection. Locate the **If you have a hardware conflict** option. Select the option and click on the **Display** button or double-click on the option to display the above dialog. You can also access this troubleshooting utility using the **Index** tab. You can either type "troubleshooting" or "hardware conflicts" to minimize the available listing of help utilities. This Hardware Conflict Troubleshooter will walk you through all the steps necessary to resolve the conflict.

Reconfiguring Resource Settings Due to Hardware Conflicts

Since legacy devices have fixed resource settings, conflicts occur when a new device attempts to use previously assigned settings. To solve this problem, the Device Manager can be used to configure a hardware device manually.

> *NOTE:*   *Changing the resource settings for a device using the Device Manager causes these changes to appear in the registry. Use the Device Manager to change these settings instead of directly editing the registry to avoid problems.*

Devices that are in a state of conflict display an exclamation point on their icon within the Device Manager.

Mitsumi CD-ROM Controller with Double Speed Drive

Click on the **Properties** button to view a device's **Resources** settings.

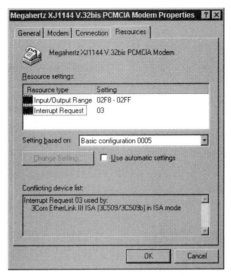

In the example above, we see the resource settings for a device in conflict. A listing of all conflicting devices appears at the bottom of this window. You can see that the IRQ set for the modem conflicts with the network interface card.

To change the resource settings, highlight the value that you wish to change and click on **Change Setting**. A dialog appears that allows the user to view alternate resource settings and select an available value.

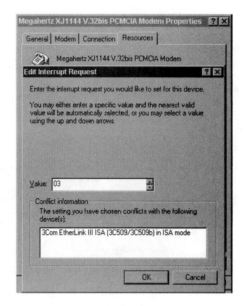

The new value takes effect after Windows 95 restarts.

Do not change resource settings for Plug and Play devices unless it is absolutely necessary. Manual configuration of these settings fixes their values. Fixed values render Windows unable to dynamically manage resources used by Plug and Play devices.

HARDWARE ADMINISTRATION

This section will present the properties within the Control Panel System utility. You can view and modify configuration information regarding hardware and user profiles, startup/shutdown, performance, and environment here. The following topics are discussed within this section:

- System Properties
- Reconfiguring Device Drivers
- Hardware Profiles

Many times, it is necessary to consider current system settings and alter configurations accordingly. As an administrator, it is especially important to understand the functions of each of these properties.

System Properties

To open the System utility, run **Start/Settings/Control Panel**. Then, launch the System utility by double-clicking on its icon. You can also open this utility by right-clicking on the My Computer desktop object and selecting **Properties**. System properties were introduced earlier in the chapter. Let's take a closer look at the settings available on the **Device Manager** tab.

The Device Manager

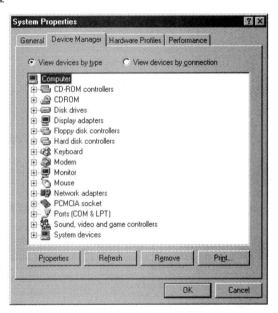

The **Device Manager** tab allows the user to view all devices graphically. You can view devices by type or by connection.

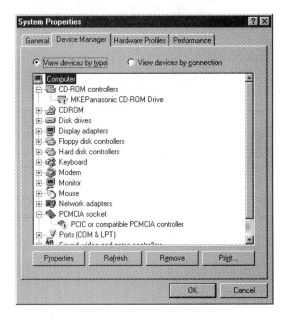

This tree of devices is expandable. Click on the plus symbol to expand the tree and see the specific devices by category.

Disabled devices in the current hardware configuration have an "X" through their icons. A device displaying a circled exclamation point through its icon denotes a problem. Detailed information about problems are displayed when you view properties for the device.

You can access the property page for a selected device by highlighting its icon and clicking on **Properties**, or by double-clicking on the object.

To view the resource settings for a device, select the **Resources** tab.

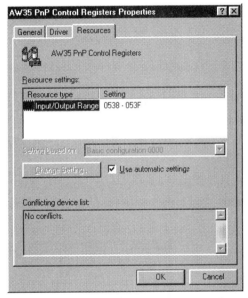

Note that you can clear the checkmark in the **Use Automatic Settings** checkbox and configure the device manually. Once you have done so, click on **Change Settings**.

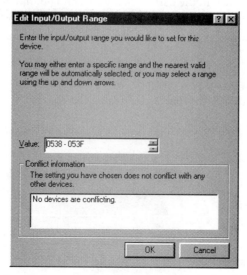

If a conflict with another device occurs while changing the value for the Input/Output range for the device, conflict information will be displayed in the box on the bottom of this property page.

Each object will display a specific set of properties for a selected device. The graphic below illustrates the **Driver** properties for a sound controller:

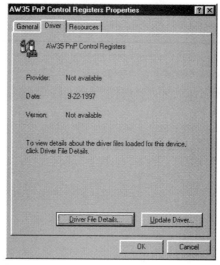

To display the list of current drivers available for this device, click on **Driver File Details**.

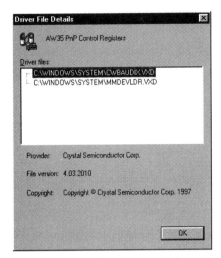

The Computer object at the top of the Device Manager has properties as well:

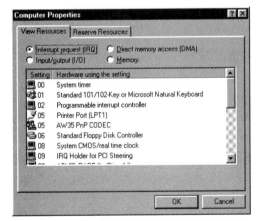

You can view IRQ, I/O, DMA, and Memory settings from this dialog. To view and add system-wide reserved resources, select the **Reserved Resources** tab.

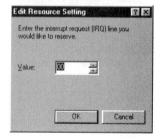

Then, select the reserve resource you wish to add, and click on **Add**. The dialogs below display the types of configurations that can be made for each type of reserve resource.

- IRQ

- I/O

- DMA

- Memory

Reconfiguring Device Drivers

The Device Manager also assists in correcting problems relating to incorrect device drivers. To view the device drivers for an installed device, highlight the desired component, click on **Properties**, and select the **Driver** tab.

To update the driver for a given device, click on the **Update driver** button. This launches the Update Device Driver Wizard. You are given two choices for updating drivers. You can either allow Windows to search for the driver or you can select it yourself from a list.

If you allow Windows to search for the driver, the system will attempt to locate the files on the floppy drive, CD-ROM drive, or the network. If it is unable to find the updated drivers, you can click on the **Other Location** button to display the dialog below. You can now browse the system yourself to locate the files.

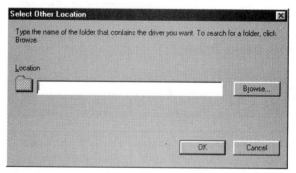

If you choose to select the new drivers from a list, you can click on the option to **No, select driver from list** on the initial screen of the Update Device Driver Wizard. You can display device drivers by **Show compatible hardware** or **Show all hardware**. Once you have made your selection, click on **Finish** to update the drivers for the device.

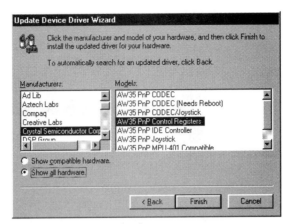

The device drivers currently in use are listed, along with file details.

Hardware Profiles

Windows 95 allows you to create hardware profiles to provide you with the capability of using your PC in different hardware configurations. For example, a laptop has different hardware available to it when it is in a docking station.

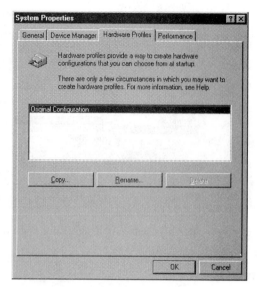

After defining different hardware configurations, Windows 95 can detect the PC's configuration at startup and load the appropriate device drivers. If Windows cannot determine the PC's startup configuration, the system will ask the user to choose from a list of possible configurations.

To configure a hardware profile for a portable computer, first select the hardware profile upon which you would like to base the portable profile. Click on **Copy**. Enter a new name for the new portable hardware profile and click on **OK**. Next, use the Device Manager to enable or disable those devices that will not be necessary for the portable computer. You can do so by viewing the Properties for the selected device and changing the Device usage to the new portable hardware profile.

Exercise 5-5: System Utility

The purpose of this exercise is to give you practice working with the Windows 95 System utility to create a hardware profile. You should be logged on as your primary user at the beginning of this exercise.

1. Run **Start/Settings/Control Panel** and launch the System utility. This displays the System properties.

2. Close the System property page and Control Panel.

3. Right-click on the My Computer Desktop object and select **Properties**. This is an alternate way of displaying system properties.

4. Click on the **Device Manager** tab.

5. Expand the entry for Floppy disk controllers.

6. Select your floppy disk controller and click on **Properties**.

7. Click on the **Resources** tab. This displays the I/O (Input/Output Range), IRQ (Interrupt Request), and DMA (Direct Memory Access) settings for the controller. It also contains the conflicting device list.

   Record the DMA setting below:

   ....

   ....

8. Click on **Cancel**.

9. Scroll to the top of the list and select **Computer**.

10. Click on **Properties**. The Computer Properties dialog has two tabs.

11. If not selected in the foreground, select the **View Resources** tab. This will display your selection of IRQ, I/O, DMA, or Memory usage.

12. Click on the **Direct memory access** option. You will see your floppy controller listed at the value you recorded earlier.

13. Click on the **Reserve Resources** tab. This is to set aside resources so they will not be assigned. This is blank at default for most systems.

14. Click on **Cancel**.

15. Click on the **Hardware Profiles** tab.

16. With **Original Configuration** selected, click on **Copy**.

17. Type the following as the new name and click on **OK**:

    ```
    Test Configuration
    ```

18. Click on the **Device Manager** tab and select your floppy disk controller.

19. Click on **Properties**.

20. Disable the **Test Configuration** option and click on **OK**.

    NOTE: Remove the check from Test Configuration ONLY.

21. Click on **Close**.

22. Shut down and restart your computer.

23. When prompted to select a configuration, select **2** and press *ENTER*.

24. Log on normally.

25. Using the procedures described earlier, launch the System utility.

26. Click on the **Device Manager** tab. You will see a red "X" on the floppy disk controller.

27. Shut down and restart your system, selecting to use the Original Configuration (1). Log on normally.

28. Using the procedures described earlier, launch the System utility.

29. Click on the **Hardware Profiles** tab.

30. Select **Test Configuration** and click on **Delete**. When prompted to verify the deletion, click on **Yes**.

31. Click on **OK**.

SCENARIOS

Scenario 1

Jane will be traveling to Spain next month for a temporary relocation period of 3 months. She is fluent in Spanish. She will be using her laptop computer primarily for her work in Spain. She will be communicating with all her peers in Spanish. How can you enable her system to use the native language?

....

....

Scenario 2

Joel, your sales representative, travels quite often between the home office and several national sales offices. He has a laptop which is connected to a docking station when he comes in to the home office. At the home office, he uses the network card to connect to network servers. While at the national sales offices, he has no need for the network adapter. How can you configure a hardware profile to disable the network card when he is traveling?

....

....

SUMMARY

During this chapter, you examined some advanced system configuration issues, including:

- Using Control Panel utilities to configure Windows 95 workstations
- The Plug and Play standard
- Adding new hardware to a computer
- Concerns for docking mobile computers
- Using the Device Manager to configure device drivers and resource settings for hardware devices
- Creating multiple hardware profiles

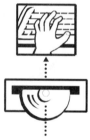

Stop now and complete the Chapter 5 NEXTSim simulation exercise on the Interactive Learning CD-ROM.

POST-TEST QUESTIONS

The answers to these questions are in Appendix A at the end of this manual.

1. List the tabs in the Passwords utility.

....

....

2. How can you enable mouse trails to be visible?

....

....

3. Settings changes on the **Regional Settings** tab of the Regional Settings utility will affect which other property pages?

....

....

4. How can you identify a disabled device in the System Device Manager?

....

....

5. What terms are used to describe the two docking types supported by Windows 95?

....

....

6. What are the three components in Plug and Play architecture?

....

....

7. Which property page of the System utility displays installed devices and drivers?

....

....

CHAPTER ⑥

Disk Management

OBJECTIVES

At the completion of this chapter, you will be able to:

- Discuss the characteristics of a hard disk.
- Use the FDISK utility to create a disk partition.
- Perform a file or disk back up using Microsoft Backup.
- Perform disk compression using DriveSpace.
- Use the Disk Defragmenter to repair fragmented files.
- Use ScanDisk to scan system and data areas on the disk for errors.
- List the file systems utilized by Windows 95.

PRE-TEST QUESTIONS

The answers to these questions are in Appendix A at the end of this manual.

1. What is the function of the master boot record?

   ....

   ....

2. What is the most familiar file system in the Windows 95 operating environment?

   ....

   ....

3. Why is it important to perform backups on a routine basis?

   ....

   ....

4. What two files are created on a compressed floppy disk?

   ....

   ....

INTRODUCTION

Proper hard disk configuration and maintenance plays a key role in system stability and performance. Windows 95 provides many tools that make disk configuration and optimization easy. This chapter investigates the purpose of these tools and why they should be used.

The chapter begins with a discussion on disk partitioning. Disk partitioning allows administrators to make the most efficient use of disk space. Next, the focus will change to the various disk utilities available to administrators. These are: DriveSpace, Backup, Disk Defragmenter, ScanDisk, and System Agent. You will learn how to defragment hard drives, use ScanDisk to troubleshoot disk problems, and utilize Windows 95 DriveSpace to achieve disk compression.

The chapter will end with a discussion on file system problems. We will use the System utility's **Performance** tab to evaluate configurations that can help you diagnose and resolve file system problems.

PARTITIONING

This section will discuss how to create a partition on the hard disk. Disk partitioning allows you to create logical divisions on the hard disk. This optimizes the hard disk space available on the system. The following topics are discussed within this section:

- Disk Characteristics
- File Management
- FDISK

Let's begin with a brief discussion of how a hard disk works.

Disk Characteristics

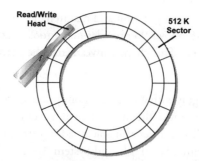

The physical characteristics of all disk drives are similar. Cylinders represent the data storage areas on the drive media. The cylinder area under a single read/write head is a data track. Tracks are divided into sectors, usually 512 bytes in length. Different drives are, however, also unique. They have different numbers of cylinders, heads, and sectors, which means that they have different storage capacities. They are also logically different, according to how disk partitions are set up on the drives.

System hardware, usually the ROM BIOS or hard disk controller, keeps track of a drive's physical characteristics. Windows 95 has a way of tracking the logical characteristics.

- Master Boot Record (MBR)

    The MBR contains information about the hard disk partitions.

- DOS boot record

    The boot record contains information about partition (or diskette) characteristics.

Let's take a closer look at each of these.

MBR

Each hard disk will have a Master Boot Record (MBR). It is a one-sector file stored at physical sector 0, head 0, and cylinder 0. It is created when you run FDISK to partition the hard disk and contains hard disk partition information.

The MBR:

- Identifies the active (bootable) partition.

- Identifies the operating system for each partition by its system indicator.

- Identifies the starting location and size of each partition.

• Contains a signature of 55AAh, which indicates a valid MBR.

The MBR is found on hard disks only.

Logical Characteristics of a Hard Drive or Diskette

As previously mentioned, a drive is physically divided into heads, cylinders, and sectors. However, Windows 95 does not simply write information to a drive a single sector at a time. Instead, it divides the drive into logical units, called clusters, that it uses to read, write, and keep track of the information stored on the drive.

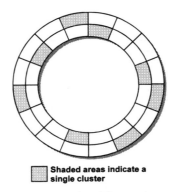

Shaded areas indicate a
single cluster

You can configure a drive either as one large partition or divide it into several smaller partitions. Depending on the size of the partition, the drive will have different-sized allocation units, or clusters. The larger the partition, the larger the cluster size.

A cluster is composed of at least one, but usually multiple, sectors. When Windows 95 writes information to hard disk, it finds enough free sectors to make up a cluster and sets the entire cluster aside for that piece of information, even if that information does not fill the entire cluster. This means that a very large partition may result in wasted sectors on a hard drive.

The clusters used to save data do not need to be contiguous. However, the less contiguous the clusters are, the more the read/write heads of the drive will have to move in order to access and save the data. For this reason, a fragmented drive can result in decreased performance.

Determining the Optimal Partition Size

In order to determine the optimal partition size for your hard drive, you need to consider the size of data files that will most often be stored on the drive. Remember, leftover sectors in a cluster are not reassigned. The hard drive space is simply wasted. The chart below should help you determine optimal partition sizes given your drive usage pattern:

Partition Size	Sectors per cluster	Cluster size
< 16 MB	8	4 KB
16-127 MB	4	2 KB
128-255 MB	8	4 KB
256-511 MB	16	8 KB
512-1023 MB	32	16 KB
1024-2048 MB	64	32 KB

When using this chart, it may help to think about cluster size as equivalent to minimum file size. For example, if a drive is going to be used to store data files that are typically 16 KB, the most optimal partitioning scheme for a 4-GB drive would be to create four partitions that are each 1 GB. Drives with more than 2 GB must be partitioned into 2-GB or smaller partitions.

File Management

The 32-bit, protected-mode file system in Windows 95 allows administrators and users to gain enhanced utilization of hard disks, CD-ROM devices, and network resources. The file system supports long filenames and directories. It is no longer necessary to be limited to the eight-character naming convention that was used in prior Windows products.

The Windows 95 operating system includes the following file systems:

- File Allocation Table (FAT)

    The FAT file system is the most commonly used in the world. It provides operating system compatibility, allowing users to access FAT partitions when booting up with DOS for example. This file system also has a number of disk utilities available for management and recovery operations.

- Virtual File Allocation Table (VFAT)

    The 32-bit Virtual File Allocation Table is the primary file system. It uses either real-mode or protected-mode drivers. The structure of FAT on the disk remains the same as in previous versions. VFAT uses 32-bit code to handle all file access.

- CD-ROM File System (CDFS)

    The Virtual CDFS (VCDFS) handles information on CD-ROMs just as VFAT handles information on a hard disk. This file system's drivers load dynamically upon detection of an attached CD-ROM. CDFS is a protected-mode version of MSCDEX.EXE.

- Network Redirectors

    Network redirectors include the Microsoft Client for NetWare Networks and the Client for Microsoft Networks. Network redirectors access the network file system.

Network support is discussed later in the book.

FDISK

FDISK lets you partition a hard disk. Use FDISK to:

- Create a primary DOS partition.
- Create an extended DOS partition.
- Create logical drives within an extended DOS partition.

- Identify the active (bootable) partition.
- Delete disk partitions.
- Delete logical drives.
- Display partition information.

With versions of DOS later than 5.0, FDISK allows you to remove a non-FAT partition and replace it with a FAT partition. Hard disk partition information is recorded in the MBR. FDISK supports two option switches:

/status	This switch reports the partition information without taking you into the interactive portion of FDISK.
/mbr	This switch rebuilds the MBR without recreating the partitions and losing all partition data.

In some cases, it may be necessary to rebuild the MBR to recover from viral infection. Do not run **fdisk** with the **/mbr** switch if a hard disk contains more than four partitions.

FDISK has a Windows 95 equivalent. This version of FDISK runs as an MS-DOS application. Start **fdisk** by selecting **Run** from the **Start** menu and entering the **fdisk** command, or by running **fdisk** at a command prompt. The functionality of this version equals that of previous versions.

SYSTEM TOOLS

This section lists a summary of the various system tools available in Windows 95. Administrators can use these tools to utilize hard disk space efficiently. The following topic will be discussed in this section:

- Disk Management

We will discuss the installation and implementation of each of the system tools later in this chapter.

Disk Management

Disk Management under Windows 95 involves using updated disk utilities. These new graphical tools perform the same basic functions as their MS-DOS and Windows 3.x-based predecessors. They include:

- Disk Defragmenter

    Fragmentation of a hard disk results in performance penalties due to files residing in non-contiguous blocks on the drive. The Windows 95 Disk Defragmenter allows for defragmentation of the drive while performing other tasks. This is also referred to as drive optimization. Disk Defragmenter should be run as a part of your periodic routine maintenance procedure or when there is a noticeable reduction in the file access rate. When you run Disk Defragmenter, Windows 95 will analyze the degree to which your disk is fragmented and recommend whether or not to continue with the defragmentation process.

- ScanDisk

    ScanDisk can uncover and fix disk problems, such as lost clusters, cross-linked files, DoubleSpace or DriveSpace errors, incorrect FAT entries, and bad drive sectors. This new version of ScanDisk also has the ability to run in the background while the user performs other tasks. Like Disk Defragmenter, ScanDisk should be run as routine maintenance. Additionally, run ScanDisk any time a system is shut down as a result of an abnormality–such as a General Protection Fault (GPF) or a system crash.

- DriveSpace

    The Windows 95 DriveSpace program allows maintenance of compressed drives created by DoubleSpace or DriveSpace.

Disk Defragmenter and ScanDisk utilities can all be accessed from the **Start** menu. You can also access these tools using the **Tools** tab for a desired drive's properties. For example, open the My Computer desktop object. Right-click on the desired drive and click on **Properties**. Click on the **Tools** tab. You will see three buttons available: **Check Now, Backup Now,** and **Defragment Now**. These buttons correspond to the ScanDisk, Backup, and Defragmenter utilities respectively.

You will also learn how to schedule these utilities using the System Agent. System Agent will be discussed at the end of this chapter.

DRIVESPACE

This section introduces the DriveSpace system tool. Installation steps for DriveSpace are listed. We will also discuss the implementation of the system tools' various options such as compressing a drive, mounting drives, compression ratios, and more. The following topics are discussed within this section:

- Introduction to DriveSpace
- Compressing a Drive
- Uncompressing a Drive
- Compression Ratios
- Other Menu Options
- DriveSpace and Dual-Boot
- Compressing the System Drive

Drive compression enables you to use disk space efficiently. Compressing disk drives enhances the performance of your operating system.

Introduction to DriveSpace

DriveSpace can be used to compress and uncompress data on floppy disks, removable media, or hard disk drives. The first time it is used, the drive will have 50 to 100 percent more free space than it did before. The DriveSpace included with Windows 95:

- Can only compress drives with at least 512 KB free space.
- Can only create a compressed drive of up to 512 MB.
- Supports long filenames.
- Is compatible with the VFAT file system.

A compressed drive is really a compressed volume file (CVF) on an uncompressed host drive. The CVF file has read-only, hidden, and system attributes. All CVFs are located on uncompressed drives and are stored in the root directory of that host drive. Make sure not to delete a CVF file, as you will not be able to recover the files it contains. You can use a compressed drive the same way you did before it was compressed.

The executable file for this utility is located in the \WINDOWS directory. To launch this utility, run **Start/Programs/Accessories/System Tools/DriveSpace** or run **drvspace** from the Run dialog.

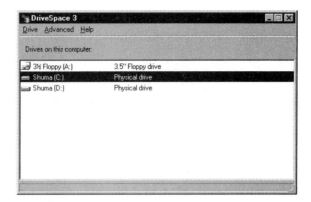

Compressing a Drive

To compress a drive, first select the drive from the Drives on this computer: list. Then, run **Drive/Compress** from the menu. This will display information regarding the drive you have selected for compression. The dialog will tell you how much space DriveSpace will compress on the selected drive. You will also be told the drive letter of the host drive that will be created and the amount of uncompressed free space it will contain.

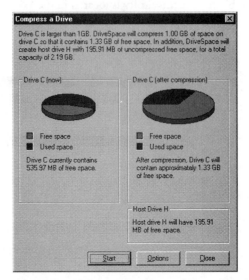

Note the graphical representation of the drive's current free and used space. Next to that, there is another graph displaying free and used space that will be available after disk compression.

To change the host's drive letter, click on **Options**. Select the new drive letter using the available list. You can also change the free space on the host drive to a value other than what DriveSpace has allocated. If you do not want to view the host drive, you can enable the **Hide host drive** option. Click on **OK** once you have made your selections to return to the Compress a drive dialog.

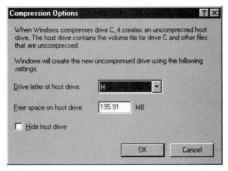

To begin compression, click on **Start**.

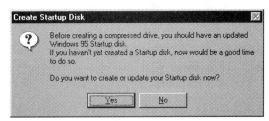

DriveSpace reminds you that you should have an updated Startup disk available in case of system problems that may occur after disk compression. If you have not created a Startup disk as of this point, you can do so by clicking on **Yes**. If you select **No**, the next dialog will appear.

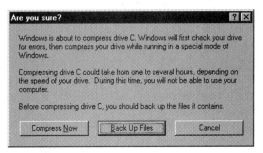

NOTE: *It is highly recommended that you create a Startup disk or update the existing disk prior to starting disk compression.*

DriveSpace displays this dialog to confirm that you do want to compress the selected disk drive. It is also highly recommended that you back up all files on the drive prior to performing the compression. If you click on **Back Up Files**, Microsoft Backup will be launched. This utility will be covered in detail later in this chapter. If you are ready to proceed with compression, click on **Compress Now**. Once compression begins, several additional operations occur. First, ScanDisk performs a thorough scan of the drive to be compressed. Next, the CVF file, which is named Dblspace.000 is created, prepared, and resized.

Once compression is complete, exact capacity, free space, and used space amounts will be displayed for before compression and after compression. Click on **Close** to close the dialog.

> NOTE: *DriveSpace creates compressed drives of up to 512 MB. To utilize DriveSpace on larger hard disks, partition the hard disks into volumes of 512 MB or less.*

After compression, the estimated compression ratio is used to predict the available space on the drive. The compression ratio can be changed to provide a more accurate estimation of available storage space. Changing the ratio does not affect the actual size of the available space but DriveSpace's estimation of the available space.

> NOTE: *Microsoft Plus! For Windows 95 includes a more advanced version of DriveSpace known as DriveSpace3. DriveSpace3 provides compression for drives up to 2 GB in size, as well as faster compression on Pentium-based computers. Note that when you install DriveSpace3, it installs over DriveSpace almost like an upgrade.*

You can also compress a floppy disk to maximize its storage space. The procedures used to compress a hard drive can be used to compress a floppy disk.

> NOTE: *A compressed floppy disk can be used only on computers using Windows 95 DriveSpace or MS-DOS v6.x DoubleSpace.*

Once compression is complete, the DriveSpace dialog displays the host drive that was created for the floppy drive. The contents of this compressed drive include two files: Dblspace.000 and Readthis. This means that the floppy is not empty. However, it is compressed. The Readthis file is a text document stating instructions for mounting the disk.

To mount a compressed floppy disk in the DriveSpace utility, you must first insert the floppy disk into the floppy disk drive. Run **Advanced/Mount** from the menu.

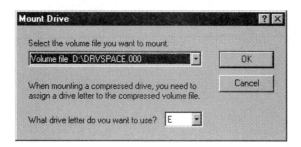

Next, click on the volume that you wish to mount. You can also select the drive letter that you wish to use. If you choose to change the host drive letter after compression, run **Advanced/Change Letter**. Once you have finished making your selections, click on **OK** to close the dialog. Exit from DriveSpace. The next time you launch DriveSpace, the utility will automatically mount compressed disks that are inserted in the floppy drive. Mounting a compressed floppy disk allows you to use the disk as if it were uncompressed.

Uncompressing a Drive

You can also uncompress a drive. Select the drive you wish to uncompress and run **Drive/Uncompress** from the menu. Click on **Start** to begin uncompressing a selected drive.

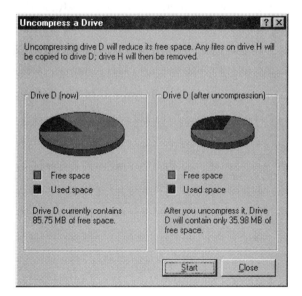

Compression Ratios

On an uncompressed drive, the amount of additional data you can store is determined by the amount of free space left. The free space on a compressed drive is only an estimate. DriveSpace compresses a file as efficiently as possible. However, some files can be compressed more than others. For example, a text file can be compressed more than an executable. DriveSpace calculates "available" free space based on an estimated compression ratio, which can be set by the user. Changing the compression ratio does not change the way DriveSpace compresses the files; it only changes the way it estimates the free space left available on the compressed drive. You can specify a ratio between 1.0 to 16.0.

To change the estimated compression ratio, run **Advanced/Change Ratio** from the menu.

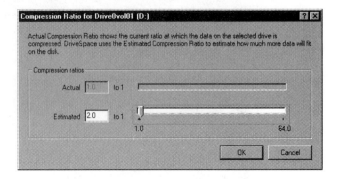

Other Menu Options

To adjust the free space on a compressed drive, run **Drive/Adjust Free Space** from the menu.

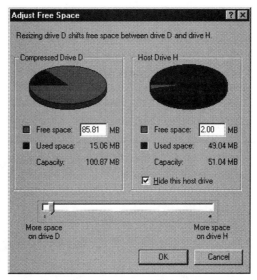

Use the scroll bar on the dialog to shift the free space between the compressed drive and the host drive. If a red area appears in the scroll area, and you move your scroll bar on top of the red area, DriveSpace will defragment the drive.

To view properties of your compressed drive, you can either double-click on the drive or run **Drive/Properties**.

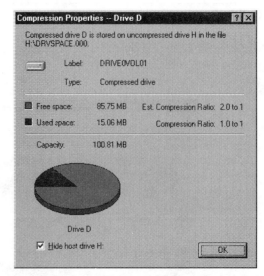

To create a new compressed drive, run **Advanced/Create Empty**. The following dialog appears:

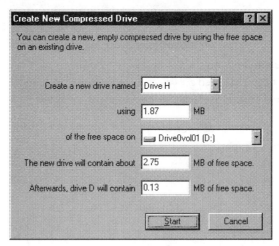

First, you must select the drive letter for the new compressed drive. Next, select the drive from which you want to use free space to create the new compressed drive. Specify disk space allocation for the new drive. As you change the specified amount of space to be used on the new compressed drive, two values on this dialog will change: The new drive will contain about... and Afterwards, drive *driveletter* will contain....

Various types of information are displayed for the user. These include:

- The location of compressed data on the host drive
- The label of the drive.
- The type of drive (compressed or uncompressed).
- Free space.
- Used space.
- The capacity of the selected drive.

You can select to hide the host drive from this dialog as well.

You can also format a drive using the DriveSpace utility. Run **Drive/Format** from the menu to begin formatting procedures. DriveSpace also allows you to delete a drive. However, the drive cannot be a compressed drive.

DriveSpace and Dual-Boot

It is important to keep in mind that DriveSpace compression occurs within the Windows 95 operating system. The CVF file will not be visible when the Windows NT operating system is in use. If you are configuring a computer for dual-boot, it is best to use uncompressed FAT partitions.

Compressing the System Drive

It is possible to compress the Windows 95 system drive. When you do, DriveSpace will restart the system under a very limited operating system. Since DriveSpace can only compress closed files, this process will allow the majority of system files to be compressed.

Exercise 6-1:
Using DriveSpace

The purpose of this exercise is to give you practice compressing a floppy disk.

1. Launch DriveSpace from **Start/Programs/Accessories/System Tools**.

2. Verify that the 3-1/2 Floppy is selected. If it is not, select it.

3. Run **Drive/Compress**.

4. Click on **Start** to begin compressing the floppy drive. Once compression begins, several additional operations occur. First, ScanDisk performs a thorough scan of the drive to be compressed. Next, the CVF file, which is named Dblspace.000 is created, prepared, and resized.

5. Once compression is complete, exact capacity, free space, and used space amounts will be displayed for before compression and after compression. Click on **Close** to close the Compress A Drive dialog.

BACKUP

This section discusses the Backup system tool. As you will see, this tool is used to restore files, directories, or entire servers when a system crash occurs. The following topics are discussed within this section:

- Introduction to Backup
- File Filtering in Microsoft Backup
- Drag and Drop in Microsoft Backup
- Settings Options for Microsoft Backup
- Performing a Backup of the Entire System
- Performing a Backup of a Selected Folder
- Restoring a File, Directory, Hard Drive, or an Entire System
- Comparing File Contents With a Backup File Set
- Scheduling a Backup
- Other Microsoft Backup Features
- Compatible Tape Drives

For a network administrator, this tool is among the favorites. It is what saves administrators the deadly fear of loss of information when a server crashes. Therefore, it should be a habit to use this utility to back up information on a regular basis.

Introduction to Backup

Microsoft Backup for Windows 95 provides the ability to back up files to disk or tape. The QIC 133 backup tape specification that provides support for long filenames is supported. To install Microsoft Backup, run **Start/Settings/Control Panel**. Double-click on the Add/Remove Programs utility. Click on the **Windows Setup** tab. Select the **Disk Tools** component and click on **Details**. Select **Backup** and click on **OK**. Click on **OK** to close Add/Remove Program Properties. A shortcut is then added to **Start/Programs/Accessories/System Tools**.

You can also launch Backup from the **Start** menu by using the Run command. To do so, select **Run** from the **Start** menu. Type **Backup** and click on **OK**. On initial launch, the following dialog will be displayed:

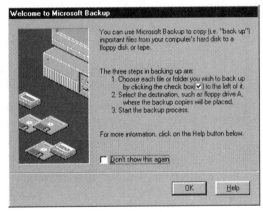

This dialog describes the three basic steps in performing a backup:

1. Select the folder or drive that you wish to back up by clicking on its checkbox.

2. Select your destination for the backup.

3. Begin the backup process by clicking on **Next Step**.

Microsoft Backup creates a full backup file set automatically. It is stored in the C:\PROGRAM FILES\ACCESSORIES directory. As the dialog states, you must use this file set if you would like to back up an entire hard drive. Registry files are stored on the file set as well. By performing a backup of your hard drive, you are protected from any hard drive crashes that may occur in the future. If your system has more than one hard drive on it, it is a good idea to save the backup to a location other than the hard drive being backed up. You can open this full backup file set by running **File/Open File Set**.

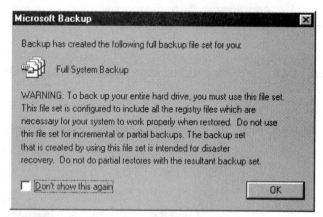

There are two types of backups available with Microsoft Backup for Windows 95. These are:

- Full

    A full backup will back up all selected files.

- Incremental

    An incremental backup will back up only the files that have changed since the last full backup.

A full backup offers the highest level of protection for the contents of your hard drive. However, with large capacity disks, it can be a very time-consuming and tedious process.

File Filtering in Microsoft Backup

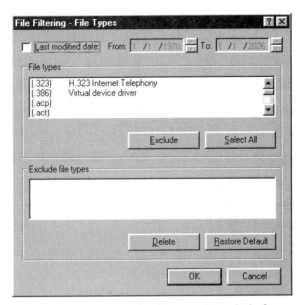

File Filtering allows you to specify particular file types to exclude from your backup. For example, you might decide to not back up .EXE files because you can reinstall all of your applications if the hard drive fails. To display File Filtering Settings, run **Settings/File Filtering**. You can configure the program to only back up files that were modified within a range of dates. Depending on the information you are backing up, it may not be necessary to back up all files. To exclude a specific file type, select the file type that you do not wish to back up. Then click on **Exclude**. If you do not wish to back up a majority of file types, you can click on **Select All**, and then deselect the file types you do not want to exclude.

Drag and Drop in Microsoft Backup

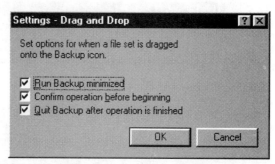

Drag and Drop allows you to administer Microsoft Backup with drag and drop capabilities. To display Drag and Drop Settings, run **Settings/Drag and Drop**. You can then drag and drop a file set onto the Backup icon as long as the Backup window is minimized. You can also require that a confirmation dialog be displayed when backup is about to begin. The third option that is available allows you to quit Backup once the sequence is complete.

Settings Options for Microsoft Backup

The Settings option in Microsoft Backup allows administrators to configure settings for backup operations such as enabling drag and drop backup, incremental or full backups, restore, and compare operations.

General Settings

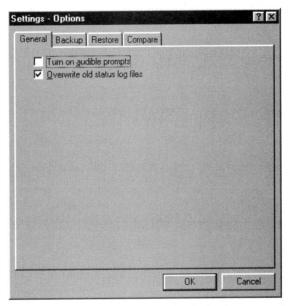

The **General** tab allows you to enable audio prompts for backup operations. You can also select to overwrite old status log files on this property page.

Backup Settings

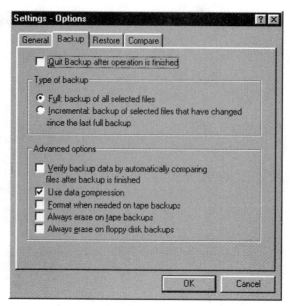

The **Backup** tab allows you to configure the following properties:

Quit Backup after operation is finished

This selection allows you to quit backup when backup is complete.

Types of Backup

This option allows you to choose either a Full backup or an Incremental backup. Incremental allows you to back up files that have changed since they were last backed up. It is recommended that you perform a full backup weekly, and an incremental backup daily. Full backup is selected by default.

Advanced Options

You can perform the Compare operation automatically once backup is complete. Data compression is used by default in backup operations. This option also allows you to set properties for tape backups, such as format and erase functions, depending on the type of backup tape used.

Restore Settings

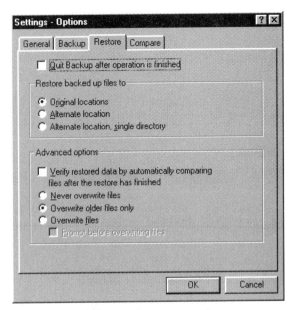

The following properties are available on the **Restore** tab:

Quit Backup after operation is finished

> This selection allows you to quit backup when backup is complete.

Restore backed up files to

> This selection allows you to set the location for restoration of files. You can restore to the original location, an alternate location, or a single specific directory in an alternate location.

Advanced options

You can set data to be compared automatically after restoration has taken place in this selection. You can also allow restore to never overwrite files, overwrite older files only, or overwrite files during the restore operation. When **Overwrite files** is selected, you can set a prompt to display before files are overwritten. **Overwrite older files only** is selected by default.

Compare Settings

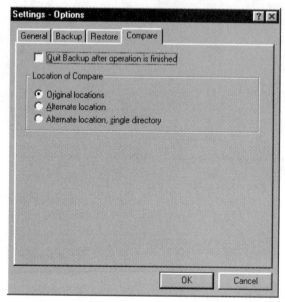

The **Compare** tab allows you to set the following options:

Quit Backup when operation is complete

This selection allows you to quit backup when backup is complete.

Location of Compare

This selection allows you to set the location for the comparison of files. You can compare files to either the original location, an alternate location, or a single specific directory in an alternate location.

Performing a Backup of the Entire System

To back up your entire system, first launch Microsoft Backup from **Start/Programs/ Accessories/System Tools**. Click on **OK** to verify that Backup has created a full backup file set for you. Next, run **File/Open File Set**.

Open the Full System Backup file set located in C:\PROGRAM FILES\ACCESSORIES. You will need to wait a few minutes while Microsoft Backup copies settings to the local registry. Note that all local hard drives now have a checkbox filled. Click on **Next Step**.

Now select the destination where you'd like the backup files to be stored. This can be a network drive, a compatible tape drive, or even a floppy disk. Click on **Start Backup**. Enter a backup set label name. You will recognize the file set by this label name. To enter a password, click on **Password Protect**. Enter a password and type it again for confirmation. Then click on **OK**.

To correctly perform a backup for an entire system, you must follow these procedures. If you were to select the hard disk itself, Backup would not perform operations on vital parts of the system, such as the Registry.

Any time you perform a backup to a network drive, you are utilizing network resources. Therefore, the network may experience performance degradation. If you choose to perform backups to a network drive, perform the backup during off-hours.

Performing a Backup of a Selected Folder

To perform a backup of a selected folder, verify that you are on the **Backup** tab. Select the folder that you wish to backup. You may back up a specific subdirectory instead of the entire folder. Expand the directories until you reach the subdirectory you wish to back up. Once you reach the level you want, select the checkbox for the subdirectory from the right. In the following example, the MB1dir is the directory that needs to be backed up. It is at the following path: C:\WINDOWS\CCMAIL\MB1dir. As you can see, you can select any of the files listed on the right for backup simply by clicking on its checkbox.

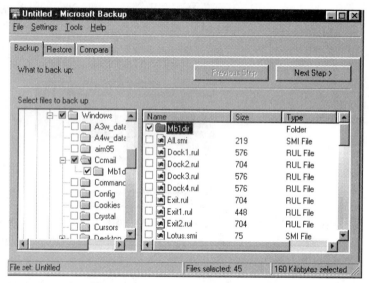

Once you have made your selection, click on **Next Step**. Select a destination for the backup file set to be stored. Then click on **Start Backup**.

Enter a backup set label name. You will recognize the file set by this label name. To enter a password, click on **Password Protect**. Once you have entered a password and confirmed it, click on **OK**. Using password protection on file sets is a good security measure. This will prevent users from accessing file sets and causing corruption. Click on **OK** to verify that the operation is complete.

Click on **OK** to close the summary report on Backup.

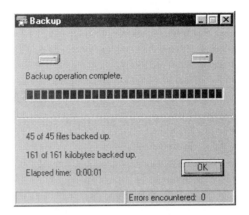

Restoring a File, Directory, Hard Drive, or an Entire System

Microsoft Backup also allows you to restore files, directories, hard drives, or your entire system after experiencing a system crash. To effectively do so, you must have performed a backup recently. For this reason, it is very important to back up data on a regular basis. Administrators should make it a practice to perform regular backups either to network servers, other hard drives, or tape drives.

To begin restoring a file, verify that you are on the **Restore** tab of Microsoft Backup. Select the drive that contains the backup file set. Select the backup set label from the list on the right. Click on **Next Step**.

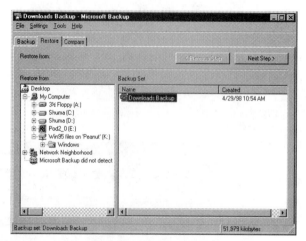

Click on the checkbox next to the full system backup file set. Click on **Start Restore** to begin restoring the file.

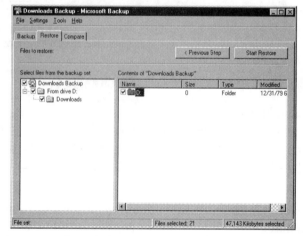

Once the operation is complete, click on **OK** to close the verification dialog. Then click on **OK** to close the summary report.

The same procedures apply for restoring folders, disks, and even an entire system.

Comparing File Contents With a Backup File Set

Microsoft Backup allows you to compare file contents with a backup file set. This function allows you to compare if any changes or updates to files have been made since you last performed a backup. To use the Compare operation, verify that the **Compare** tab is displayed. Select the drive that contains the backup file set from the left-hand side. Select the backup file set that you want to compare against from the right-hand side. Click on **Next Step**.

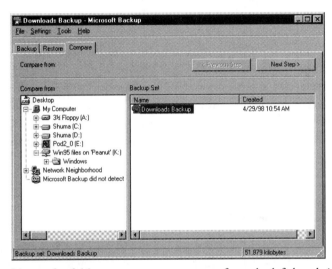

Select the checkboxes for folders you want to compare from the left-hand side. Click on **Start Compare**. Once the operation is complete, click on **OK** to close the verification dialog. Then, click on **OK** to close the summary report.

Scheduling a Backup

You can define a set of files that you want to back up periodically. Verify that the **Backup** tab is displayed and expand the drive to locate the path storing the files you wish to select. Click on the checkboxes for those files you wish to back up periodically from the list on the right-hand side. Click on **Next Step**. Select the destination drive and/or folder for storing the backup file set.

Run **Settings/Options** from the menu. Display the **Backup** tab. You can select an **Incremental: backup of selected…backup** method. This will allow you to back up only selected files that have changed since the last backup. Click on **OK**. Select the destination where you would like to store the backup file set. Click on **Start Backup**. Enter the backup set label that you will use to recognize the backup file set. You can enable password protection by adding a password. We have discussed password protection previously in this section. If you choose not to enable password protection, click on **OK** to close the Backup Set Label dialog. Click on **OK** to verify that the backup operation is complete. Close the summary report by clicking on **OK**. The next time you want to perform a backup of these selected files, you can open the file set and let it set all configurations for the backup.

Other Microsoft Backup Features

Microsoft Backup also allows you to format and erase your tape backup. To format a tape, run **Tools/Format Tape**. You will need to enter a name for the tape backup. Depending on the size of the tape, it may take several hours to format the tape. If the format moves very slowly or does not perform correctly, you may have a conflict between your video display driver and the floppy disk controller. To solve this problem, restart the format and open an MS-DOS window at full screen. If your MS-DOS window opens up minimized, press *ALT+ENTER* to maximize.

You can also erase a tape

by running **Tools/Erase Tape**. This will erase the entire tape. There is no tool or option to erase a partial area of the tape. If your tape is not connected properly or if you do not have a tape backup, you will see the following dialog.

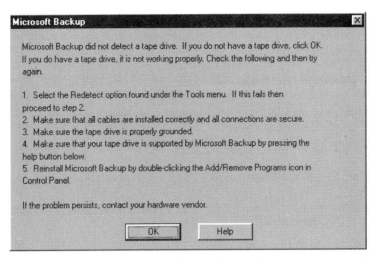

If you do receive this message, check to make sure the tape backup is connected properly. If the problem persists, check to make sure the tape backup is grounded. If problems still continue, you can verify whether or not your tape backup is compatible with Microsoft Backup. Click on **Help** to do this. Finally, you can try to reinstall the Microsoft Backup utility. Once you feel the problem has been resolved, redetect the tape backup by running **Tools/Redetect Tape Backup**.

Compatible Tape Drives

The Windows 95 Backup utility is compatible with the QIC 40, QIC 80, and QIC 3010 tape drives that are manufactured by the following companies:

- Colorado Memory Systems
- Conner
- Iomega

These tape drives connect to the primary floppy disk controller of the Windows 95 machine.

The Windows 95 Backup utility cannot be used with tape drives connected to a secondary floppy disk controller or an accelerator card. In addition, the following devices are incompatible:

- Archive drives
- Irwin drives
- Mountain drives
- QIC wide tapes
- QIC 3020 drives
- SCSI tape drives
- Summit drives
- Travan drives

DISK DEFRAGMENTER

This section discusses the installation and implementation of the Disk Defragmenter system tool. We will discuss the various additional options that may be set for disk defragmentation to be an optimal operation. The following topics are discussed within this section:

- Introduction to Disk Defragmenter
- Using Disk Defragmenter As a Command-Line Command

Many times, when you have installed, uninstalled, and reinstalled several different software applications, sectors may become misarranged, causing system performance to deteriorate over time. That is why it is important to use the Disk Defragmenter tool on a regular basis when disk usage is rather high.

Introduction to Disk Defragmenter

Windows 95 comes with a graphical disk defragmentation tool. The Disk Defragmenter utility (DEFRAG) is used to reallocate the disk space so that a file contains contiguous sectors. This improves access time because the processor can take advantage of more optimal algorithms for reading data. You can use this utility to defragment uncompressed drives and drives that have been compressed with DriveSpace or DoubleSpace. Third-party vendor compression software is not compatible with the Windows 95 version of Disk Defragmenter.

Because DriveSpace assigns space sector by sector, a DriveSpace volume can contain fairly small fragments. Therefore, it is advisable to periodically run DEFRAG on your compressed volume to improve file access time. Running DEFRAG on a compressed volume is no different from running it on any other drive. However, the drive must be mounted before DEFRAG can be run. Drives are usually mounted automatically.

To launch the Disk Defragmenter tool, run **Start/Programs/Accessories/System Tools**. Select the drive you wish to defragment and click on **OK**.

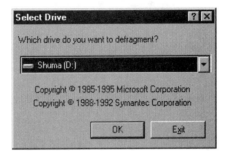

The following dialog may appear, stating that the selected drive is already defragmented by a certain percentage. If you have been experiencing system trouble, you should go ahead and defragment the drive. You can click on **Start** to begin defragmentation or click on **Advanced** to select additional configurations.

The **Advanced** option will allow you to configure the defragmentation method, as well as a few additional options. You can enable Disk Defragmenter to check the disk for any errors. This option is similar to what you would see in ScanDisk. ScanDisk is discussed later in this chapter. Any options selected in the **Advanced Options** dialog may be set for this session only or for all future sessions.

Defragmentation method

Full defragmentation (both files and free space)

> This option will arrange data so that it is stored in a location, one right after the other. Free space will be stored at the *end* of the disk all in one location.

Defragment files only

> This option will arrange all file data in one location. This option will not arrange the free space. This allows the defragmentation method to run faster than a full defragmentation.

Consolidate free space only

> This option will arrange all free space into one location. Doing so will enable all future files to be saved without fragmented sectors. The drawback to this option is that any existing files that may be fragmented may become more fragmented.

You can also allow Disk Defragmenter to check for any existing errors on the disk drive. These options may be saved for future use. Or, you may also select to use them during the current operation, and use defaults the next time.

Once you start the Disk Defragmenter, you will see a progress status dialog. Depending on the size of the disk and the number of fragmented sectors, this process could take some time. If you wish to view the details of the disk defragmentation, click on **Show Details**.

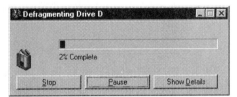

The dialog will display the defrag process as it works through the disk. This program can run in the background while the user continues on with other tasks.

The Disk Defragmenter runs more quickly when minimized or when showing only summary information. To better understand the color-coded squares displayed on the detailed dialog, click on **Legend**.

> *NOTE: The defragmentation program will start over if the drive contents change during the process.*

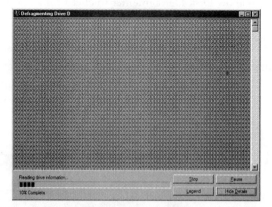

Definitions for optimized data, unoptimized data, free space, data that will not be moved, bad areas of the disk, data that's currently being read, and data that's currently being written are displayed in the **Legend**.

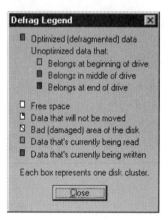

NOTE: *The Fast Indexer Tool that installs with Microsoft Office will cause the DEFRAG program to stop and restart continuously. This is caused by the fact that the indexer is continually writing to the hard disk to update its index. Whenever DEFRAG detects that the hard disk has been written to, it restarts. It is best to pause this indexing before starting DEFRAG.*

Using Disk Defragmenter As a Command-Line Command

DEFRAG can be placed in a batch file with switches for unattended operation. The command-line syntax is:

```
DEFRAG drive: /ALL /F /U /Q /NOPROMPT /CONCISE /DETAILED
```

where:

drive:	The drive to be optimized
/all	Defragment all local hard drives
/f	Defragment files and free space
/u	Defragment files only
/q	Defragment free space only
/noprompt	Requires no user intervention
/concise	Displays summary information while running
/detailed	Displays detailed information while running

SCANDISK

This section describes the usage of the ScanDisk system tool. We will also discuss the command-line commands available for ScanDisk. The following topics are discussed within this section:

- Introduction to ScanDisk
- Using ScanDisk As a Command-Line Command

Later in the chapter, we will discuss how you can schedule the ScanDisk system tool for operation at a regularly scheduled time.

Introduction to ScanDisk

The ScanDisk utility helps users identify and correct problems with hard drives. It is a graphical system tool that can run in the background while the user works on other files.

To launch ScanDisk, run **Start/Programs/Accessories/System Tools**. From this dialog, you must select the drive you wish to check for errors. Next, select the type of test you wish to run: Standard or Thorough. A Standard test will check only files and folders for errors. A Thorough test will perform the functions of a Standard test, as well as checking the disk for errors. The Standard test performs faster. However, the Thorough test is the best method to use, since it will check the hard disk itself for any possible errors. The checkbox for **Automatically fix errors** allows ScanDisk to automatically fix any errors it finds.

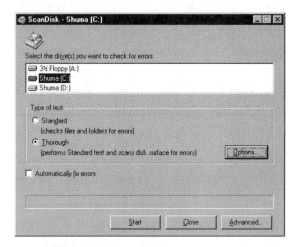

Additional Settings For a Thorough Test

To configure additional settings for the Thorough test selection, click on **Options**. This dialog allows you to select which area of the disk you want to scan. You can select **System and data areas**, **System area only**, or **Data area only**. These selections will alter the time spent performing the ScanDisk operation. This will depend on the size of the disk and the size of system and data areas. You can also enable ScanDisk to not perform write testing during its operation. If you choose to allow ScanDisk to automatically fix disk errors, you can also select to not repair bad sectors in hidden and system files.

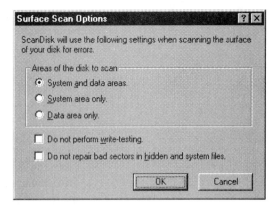

Clicking on **Advanced** from the ScanDisk dialog allows the user to configure additional options. This dialog allows you to specify that ScanDisk should check the host drive first. Host drives were discussed previously in this chapter.

Display Summary

This option allows you to view a summary report each time ScanDisk finishes its operation. You can select to view it always, never, or only if errors were found.

Log file

This option allows you to keep a log file for ScanDisk reports. You can replace the log each time ScanDisk is used or append new reports to the existing log. You can also choose to not keep a log at all. ScanDisk stores the log file in the root directory of the drive being scanned as SCANDISK.LOG at the root of your system drive.

Cross-linked files

This option can delete, make copies, or ignore any cross-linked files found during ScanDisk operation.

Lost file fragments

This option allows you to convert any lost file fragments into a file. These files are named as File0000.chk in the root directory of the disk you are scanning. The number of the file will increment as lost file fragments are found.

Check files for

This option will check files for any invalid file names and invalid dates or times. If you allow ScanDisk to check files for invalid names, you may not be able to open certain files after its operation is complete.

Using ScanDisk As a Command-Line Command

ScanDisk can be placed in a batch file with switches for unattended operation. The command-line syntax is:

```
SCANDISK [drive:] /A /N /P
```

where:

drive:

This identifies the drive(s) to be scanned.

/a

All local hard drives are scanned.

/n

User intervention is not required.

/p   Preview Mode, where ScanDisk seems to report and make
                                changes to the hard drive, but no changes actually occur.

NOTE: *When running the MS-DOS version of this program from the command line*
           (SCANDISK.EXE), the same switches apply.

If you need to run ScanDisk on an unmounted compressed drive, you should use the
following syntax:

```
scandisk drive:\drvspace.nnn
```

    or

```
scandisk drive:\dblspace.nnn
```

The *nnn* refers to the file extension of the compressed volume.

Exercise 6-2:
Using ScanDisk and Disk Defragmenter

The purpose of this exercise is to give you practice in basic disk and file management
procedures. You should be logged on as your primary user at the beginning of this
exercise.

1. Open the My Computer Desktop object.

2. Right-click on drive C: and select **Properties**.

3. Select the **Tools** tab.

4. Click on the **Check Now** button.

5. Verify that drive C: is selected and click on the **Standard** test option.

6. Click on **Start**. Let the test run to completion.

   NOTE: *If you encounter any errors, you will generally want to allow the system to fix*
              them.

7. When the Results dialog appears, click on **Close**.

8. Place a formatted diskette, such as the one you have used in earlier exercises, into drive A:. Select the **3 ½ Floppy (A:)** from the ScanDisk dialog.

9. Click on **Thorough** test option.

10. Click on the **Options** button.

11. Click on the **Data area only** option.

12. Click on **OK**.

13. Click on **Advanced**.

14. Click on the log file option to **Append to log**.

15. Click on **OK**.

16. Click on **Start**. Let it run to completion.

17. When the scan is finished, click on **Close**.

18. Remove the diskette from the drive. Then, click on **Close** to close ScanDisk.

19. Now, we are going to see if the system thinks that the C: drive needs to be defragmented. Click on **Defragment Now**.

20. The dialog should tell you that you do not need to defragment this drive now. Click on **Exit**.

21. Click on **OK** to exit the disk properties.

22. Run **Start/Programs/Accessories/System Tools/ScanDisk**. This will display the same ScanDisk dialog you saw from the disk properties.

23. Click on **Close**.

24. Close the window for My Computer.

ROUTINE MAINTENANCE

This section discusses how System Agent is used to schedule the operations of the various system tools discussed thus far. The following topics are discussed within this section:

- System Agent
- The Program Menu
- Scheduling a New Program
- Advanced Configurations for Changing a Schedule
- Advanced Menu Options
- The Notification Dialog
- Available System Resources

When you are an administrator, it is not always possible for you to administer system tools to improve system performance on a user's computer. System Agent allows you to schedule these operations for routine performance.

System Agent

System Agent is a scheduling utility that you can use to determine when certain programs should run. Once a program has been scheduled, System Agent will initiate it for you automatically. It can also be set up to check available disk space and run hard disk checks using system tools, such as ScanDisk, at certain times of the day, week, or month.

System Agent is loaded into memory when Windows 95 is booted up and remains in effect until the computer is turned off. An icon is displayed in the Taskbar. If you rest your mouse over the icon, information about System Agent is displayed. You can right-click on the icon to display a context menu that lets you either **Open** the System Agent utility or **Suspend the System Agent**.

You must have the Microsoft Plus! Package to install System Agent. Installation procedures for System Agent are discussed in Appendix C. To launch System Agent, open **Programs/Accessories/System Tools/System Agent** or you can double-click on the icon located on the Taskbar.

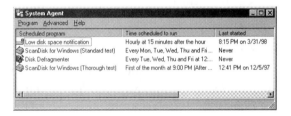

The Program Menu

The **Program** menu allows you to schedule a new program, change a scheduled program, set properties, run a program, disable a program, and remove a program.

To add a new program, run **Program/Schedule a New Program**. The following dialog is displayed:

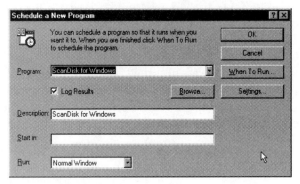

Select a program from the drop-down list. Available programs are:

- ScanDisk
- Disk Defragmenter
- DriveSpace
- Low disk space notification

You should verify that the **Log Results** checkbox is enabled if you would like a log file to be recorded. The log file is called SAGELOG.TXT and is stored in the C:\PROGRAM FILES\PLUS directory. It can automatically be viewed by selecting **View Log** from the **Advanced** menu. The Notepad application opens and displays the log file. The most recent entry is at the bottom of the file. Important information is recorded, including when a program started and finished and whether it was successful.

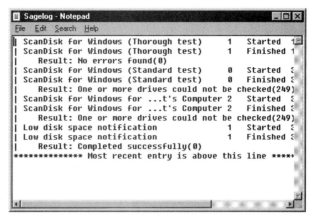

Once you have selected the program you would like to schedule, you must configure additional settings. First, enter a description that will be displayed on the main dialog of System Agent. If you want the application to start from a specific directory, you can specify a directory path in the Start in field. Then choose the mode in which you would like the new program to run. Your options are as follows: normal windows, minimized, or maximized.

Click on **Settings** to open the Settings dialog. The Settings dialog which appears is dependent upon the program selected. For example, the following dialog represents the Settings for Low Disk-Space Notification:

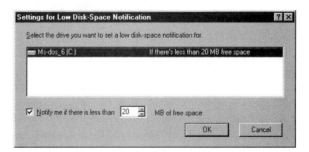

The Disk Defragmenter Settings dialog looks like this:

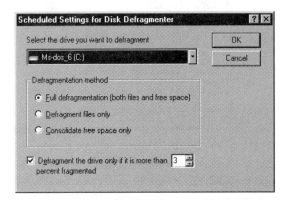

Scheduling a New Program

To schedule a new program, click on the **When to Run** button from the **Schedule a New Program** dialog. The following dialog appears:

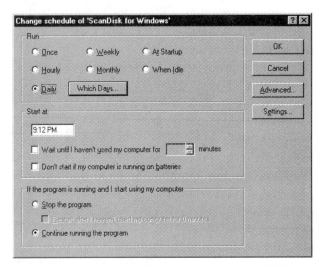

Click on the desired Run option. The following options are available:

Once	If you select the option to start **Once**, you must enter a start time including an hh:mm (AM/PM) entry as well as the month, day, and year.

Weekly	If you select the **Weekly** option, you must enter a start time including an hh:mm (AM/PM) entry, as well as the day of the week you wish to run the scheduled program.
At Startup	This selection will run the scheduled program each time the system starts. You can specify to not start the scheduled program if the computer is running off of a battery.
Hourly	If you select the **Hourly** option, you must enter a time within an hour to start the scheduled program. You can select between 0 and 59 minutes.
Monthly	The **Monthly** option requires you to enter a start time in hh:mm (AM/PM) on a certain day of every month. You can choose between 1 and 31.
When Idle	This option will start the scheduled program when the computer is idle for the specified amount of time. You must enter the amount of time in the Start at section of the dialog. Time can be specified between 1 and 999 minutes.
Daily	The **Daily** option requires you to click on the **Which Days** button to select the days on which you would like the program to run. You must select any or all of the days listed: Monday, Tuesday, Wednesday, Thursday, Friday, Saturday, and Sunday.

The Start at section of the Change Schedule dialog requires you to specify three types of information. The first field which is used to specify start times will change depending on the Run mode selected. The **Wait until I haven't used my computer for...** option is available for all run modes except At Startup and When Idle. If you choose to set an idle time, enter the number of idle minutes between 1 and 999. You can also disable the schedule from running if your computer is running on battery power.

The last setting that you can configure on the Change Schedule dialog is to stop or continue running the scheduled program if the user starts to use the computer. If you set the schedule to stop the program while the computer is in use, you can set an idle time. If you select **Stop the Program** and have also selected the **Wait until I haven't used my computer for ... minutes** option, the number of minutes will appear in the **Restart after the I haven't used my computer for ... minutes** option.

You have two additional configuration options available from the Change Schedule dialog: Advanced and Settings.

Advanced Configurations for Changing a Schedule

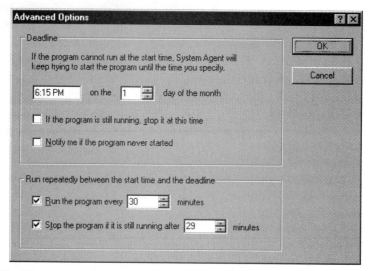

Deadline

This option will start System Agent over and over again until the time you specify is reached. You can also specify the day of the month on which to keep trying to run the program.

If the program is still running, stop it at this time will stop System Agent when the specified time is reached.

The **Notify me if the program never started** option notifies the user if the scheduled program didn't start. This could happen because the computer is running using battery power, the system is turned off, or if the user is using the computer.

You can also configure times for the scheduled program to run repeatedly between the specified start time and the deadline.

The **Settings** option available on the Change Schedule dialog displays the same dialog as the **Settings** option on the **Properties** dialog.

Advanced Menu Options

Suspend System Agent

Select **Suspend System Agent** from the **Advanced** menu or right-click the System Agent icon in the Taskbar and run **Suspend System Agent**.

A checkmark will appear to the left of **Suspend System Agent** in the **Advanced** menu.

If you try to shut down System Agent while it is suspended, you will be notified that none of the scheduled programs will be started and you will be asked if you want to Exit anyway.

To Reinitiate System Agent   Select **Suspend System Agent** from the **Advanced** menu or right-click the System Agent icon in the Taskbar and run **Suspend System Agent**.

To Stop Using System Agent   Select **Stop Using System Agent** from the **Advanced** menu. The following dialog will appear:

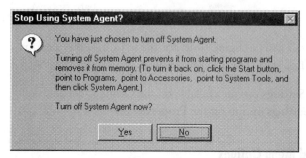

Click on **Yes** if you are sure you want to turn the System Agent off or click on **No** to return to the System Agent screen.

If System Agent has been turned off, but you want to restart the utility, launch System Agent from **Start/Programs/Accessories/System Tools**. The following dialog will be displayed:

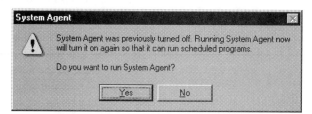

Click on **Yes** if you are sure you want to run System Agent or click on **No** to return to Windows.

The Notification Dialog

When a program runs through System Agent, it will either be successful or not. If it is successful, the information will be recorded in the SAGELOG.TXT file. If it is not successful, a dialog will be displayed providing information about the problem encountered. The following Low Disk Space Notification dialog shows what happens when System Agent realizes there is less available disk space than the setting specifies:

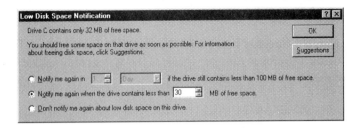

Available System Resources

Although system information can be obtained through the System utility in the Control Panel, System Resources are displayed by selecting **About System Agent** from the **Help** menu. The amount of memory on the system is also displayed.

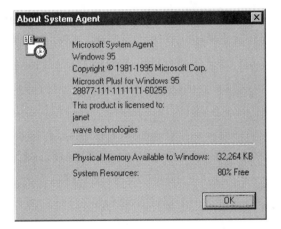

FILE SYSTEM PROBLEMS

This section discusses detailed information on troubleshooting File System problems using the Performance property page of the System utility. The following topics are discussed within this section:

- System Performance
- Optimizing Hard Disk Performance
- Optimizing CD-ROM Performance
- Troubleshooting Incompatible Applications Performance

System Performance

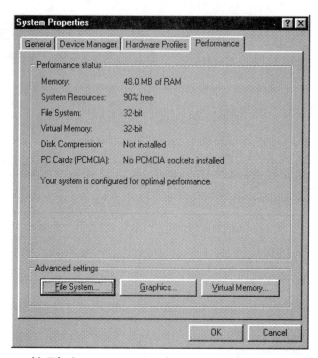

The **Performance** tab's **File System** option in the System utility allows you to display hard disk, CD-ROM optimization, and troubleshooting options for the file system.

Optimizing Hard Disk Performance

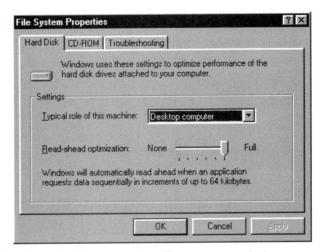

The **Hard Disk** tab for File System options allows you to optimize system performance depending on the typical role of the machine. A machine can participate in one of three roles: Desktop computer, Mobile or docking computer, or network server. These settings help to define how much RAM is allocated for cache memory. For example, a desktop computer uses a smaller cache size leaving more RAM available for applications. A mobile or docking system uses a larger cache size which reduces the amount of power needed to access local hard drives. The case is opposite for a network server. A network server uses a larger cache size which leaves less RAM for applications.

The **Read-ahead optimization** setting is set to full by default. This enables Windows 95 to cache 64 KB of data read from the disk. This data is cached because the program may need to read data again and on a drive that is not fragmented, chances are good that the data will be contiguous. To reduce the read-ahead optimization cache, change the setting from the default. This cache setting allows settings from none, up to 4 KB, 8 KB, 16 KB, 32 KB, or 64 KB. As you scroll to each line on the scroll bar, these values will be displayed in the corresponding description.

Optimizing CD-ROM Performance

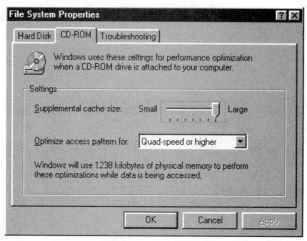

The **CD-ROM** tab allows you to optimize system performance when a CD-ROM is accessed. The supplemental cache size allows you to increase the CD-ROM cache. This setting should be changed to a higher size if the computer uses many multimedia programs. You can change the optimize access pattern settings from Quad-speed or higher, Triple-speed drives, Double-speed drives, Single-speed drives, and No read-ahead. Each of these settings allows Windows to use a certain amount of memory for CD-ROM cache flush.

No read-ahead	1088 KB
Single-speed drives	1088 KB
Double-speed drives	1138 KB
Triple-speed drives	1188 KB
Quad-speed drives	1238 KB

Note that the default supplemental cache size is dependent on the optimize access pattern setting.

Troubleshooting Incompatible Applications Performance

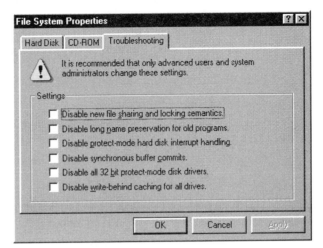

These settings can be used to resolve problems resulting from applications that may not be compatible with the Windows 95 operating environment and system. It is important to note that these settings should be used only during troubleshooting, and not for regular system settings. Changes made to these settings could damage system performance greatly.

- Disable new file sharing and locking semantics

    This option should be selected only when an MS-DOS application is experiencing problems with sharing (SHARE.EXE) in Windows 95.

- Disable long name preservation for old programs

    This option should be selected only when legacy applications do not provide support for long filenames. It causes long filenames to be lost when a file is opened and saved in an application that does not support them. Normally, Windows 95 uses a process called tunneling to ensure that long filenames are preserved under these conditions.

- Disable protect-mode hard disk interrupt handling

  Normally, Windows 95 captures interrupts to be processed by a 32-bit virtual driver (*.VXD). This option enables interrupts to be interpreted by the ROM routine. It is important to understand the impact of this setting as it will slow system performance. Sometimes, you may need to check this option depending on the hard disk controller. If the hard disk controller cannot handle interrupts automatically, you should enable this selection.

- Disable synchronous buffer commits

  This option should be used for the Commit File call only when an application's vendor requests the change. If changes are made randomly to this option, system performance will decrease dramatically.

- Disable all 32-bit protect-mode disk drivers

  This option should be enabled if you are having problems with a hard drive that is not fully compatible with Windows 95.

- Disable write-behind caching for all drives

  Disabling this option allows caching to be present for only read activities. This option is useful for situations where the power supply is questionable. For example, this selection should be made if you experience power surges or outages frequently. It will ensure that data is written directly to the file system.

SCENARIOS

Scenario 1

One of the graphic artists in your company's marketing department is perpetually running out of disk space. He must dual-boot between Windows 95 and Windows NT Workstation because one of his graphics programs will only run on Windows 95 and his 3D rendering program will only run under Windows NT. What Windows 95 tool can provide him with more disk space?

....

....

Scenario 2

You used DriveSpace to compress your D drive. When you run Properties on the D drive, it shows that you have 10 MB available. However, when you try to copy a 15-MB file, you are told that there is no space available. Your compression ratio is set to 3. What is the problem?

....

....

Scenario 3

You need to provide a computer for a new employee who will typically store data files that are 16 KB or less. The only computer available is one that you were using as a test machine for a SQL Server database. Windows NT is currently installed on the system. It has a 4-GB hard drive that is partitioned into two equal NTFS partitions. You need to install Windows 95 on the computer. What should you do to provide optimal disk usage?

....

....

Scenario 4

You are the network administrator. One of the employees keeps calling you because he continually runs out of disk space. How can you monitor disk space on an automated schedule?

....

....

Scenario 5

Your company has recently started performing tape backups to provide security against system breakdown. The administrator you have assigned to this task has been starting the backup right before he leaves for lunch since it does not need supervision. You have noticed that for the last two weeks, there has been an increase in the number of calls coming through to Tech Support. Users are complaining that their systems are running extremely slow. What could be causing these problems?

....

....

Scenario 6

You would like to use Microsoft Backup to back up a 4-GB drive that is 50% full. You have a SCSI tape drive that uses 500-MB tapes. You want the backup to run at night. How can you back up your data without someone staying all night to change tapes?

....

....

SUMMARY

In this chapter, you were introduced to issues relating to hardware management, as well as troubleshooting file system problems. These included:

- Understanding how the hard disk works
- Using the DriveSpace utility to perform disk compression
- Using the Backup utility to back up and restore files
- Using the Disk Defragmenter utility
- Using the ScanDisk utility to troubleshoot hard disk problems
- Understanding and troubleshooting file systems in Windows 95

In the next chapter, we will discuss file management in Windows 95.

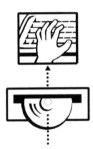

Stop now and complete the Chapter 6 NEXTSim simulation exercise on the Interactive Learning CD-ROM.

POST-TEST QUESTIONS

The answers to these questions are in Appendix A at the end of this manual.

1. What utility is used to create a partition on the hard disk?

   ....

   ....

2. What is the benefit of password protection for a backup file set?

   ....

   ....

3. You have recently purchased a tape backup for your department. You have been using Microsoft Backup for the past year, but you have always backed up information to a network server. How can you enable Microsoft Backup to recognize the new tape backup?

   ....

   ....

4. What is the benefit of using a tool such as System Agent?

   ....

   ....

5. When should an administrator make changes to the **Troubleshooting** tab of File System settings?

   ....

   ....

6. What types of settings can be configured through the **File System** option in the System utility.

   ....

   ....

7. How can you determine the best size for a partition on your hard disk?

   ....

   ....

8. What is the main difference between DriveSpace and DriveSpace3?

   ....

   ....

CHAPTER 7

File Management

OBJECTIVES

At the completion of this chapter, you will be able to:

- Create new directories in Windows Explorer and My Computer.
- Create shortcuts to file and folder resources within Windows Explorer and My Computer.
- Find a file or folder in Explorer.
- Display disk properties using Explorer and My Computer.
- Discuss the benefits of long filenames in Windows 95.

PRE-TEST QUESTIONS

The answers to these questions are in Appendix A at the end of this manual.

1. How can you use Windows Explorer to connect to a network server?

   ....

   ....

2. Which of the menu options in Explorer changes depending on the selection a user makes?

   ....

   ....

3. How can you view resources in the Explorer view when using My Computer?

   ....

   ....

4. Describe some of the advantages of long filenames.

   ....

   ....

INTRODUCTION

Previous versions of Windows products used the File Manager to manage files and directories on floppy drives, hard drives, or network drives. Windows 95 replaces the File Manager with Windows Explorer. Explorer, as it is often referred to, allows users complete functionality for managing resources on their system.

The chapter begins with a look at the various **File** menu options available to users depending on resources selected. Next, remaining menu options for Explorer will be discussed, including those available in context-sensitive pop-up menus.

Users can access local or network resources through Explorer. Files and folders can be located and accessed easily. Users are also able to drag and drop objects from Explorer to items within Explorer, to the desktop, or even to shortcuts on the desktop. This allows users to create a customized desktop environment as well as a customized file management system.

The chapter also discusses the use of the My Computer utility to access file and folder resources. Explorer and My Computer play a large role in resource management which will be discussed later in the course. Both utilities can be used to browse and locate available resources. As you will see, the functionality of Explorer is expanded over that available in the old File Manager utility. The chapter will conclude by discussing the new use of long filenames.

USING WINDOWS EXPLORER

The following section introduces the various features of Windows Explorer. We will discuss how to use the Explorer for managing files and folders, setting up shared resources, and connecting to network resources. The following topics are discussed within this section:

- Explorer
- Windows Explorer Menu Items

- Pop-up Menus In Explorer
- Drag-and-Drop Operations In Explorer

You will see the ease of drag-and-drop operations that can be used to customize the desktop environment as well as managing resources depending on user preferences.

Explorer

As mentioned earlier in the course, Windows Explorer is one of the tools available for viewing your system's files, folders, and network resources in a hierarchical arrangement. It has replaced the old File Manager in the Windows 95 environment.

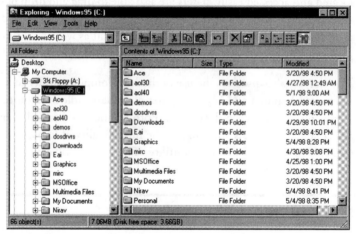

In the left pane, which is titled All Folders, Explorer lists the floppy drive (A:), all hard drives, external drives, and CD-ROM devices under the My Computer object. My Computer holds all of the local devices that can be accessed through Explorer. When you select an object in the All Folders pane, the Contents pane will display all contents within that object. For example, the graphic above displays the contents of the C: drive in the right pane.

To view the contents of a drive or folder, you can use one of two methods. You can double-click on the folder from either the All Folders pane or the Contents pane. The folder will then display an icon representing an open file folder. You can also view the contents of a drive or folder by expanding the folder. To expand a drive or folder, click on the "+" sign next to the folder. As you do so, the contents of that folder or drive will be listed directly below the selected item in the All Folders pane. The Contents pane will not display subdirectories or files within the drive or folder until you actually click or double-click to select an item. If there are no available items within a drive or folder, the "+" sign will not be visible. To contract the detailed view of a drive or folder, click on the "-" sign. You can also close a folder by double-clicking on it when the icon displays an open file folder. Once the folder is closed, its icon will appear as a closed file folder.

Explorer allows you to access additional Windows 95 utilities without using the Start menu or My Computer.

- Desktop

    The Desktop object in Explorer allows you to view all items stored on the Desktop. You can choose to save files, folders, applications, and shortcuts to the desktop as you would to a floppy or hard drive. You can also access the Network Neighborhood, Recycle Bin, and Briefcase utilities.

- Control Panel

    You can use Explorer to launch Control Panel utilities by clicking on Control Panel in the All Folders pane, and double-clicking on the desired utility in the Contents pane. The functionality of these utilities is not any different than when they are launched from **Start/Settings/Control Panel** or **My Computer**.

- Printers

    The Printers utility from Explorer allows you to access any installed printers or Microsoft Fax. You can also begin the installation of a new printer. Printers are discussed later in the course.

- Dial-Up Networking

    The Dial-Up Networking utility is the same as that available in the **Start/Programs/Accessories** menu item or through **My Computer**. Dial-Up Networking is discussed later in the course.

You can have more than one instance of Windows Explorer open. This is especially handy when you are copying many large files and directories from one location to another, yet you still want to launch a particular application using Explorer. Normally, you must wait for the copy operation to be completed before being able to maneuver around in Explorer. However, while the copy operation is running, you can open another instance of Explorer and perform other activities as desired.

For those users who still prefer to use the File Manager, you can do so by typing **winfile** in the **Start/Run** command utility.

Windows Explorer Menu Items

Similar to the File Manager utility in previous versions of Windows, Explorer allows you to create new folders and copy, move, or delete files and folders.

File Menu Options

The **File** menu changes depending on what the user has selected in Explorer. If the user has selected a floppy drive, hard drive, CD-ROM device, or folder in the All Folders pane, the following menu options are available:

The **New** menu option in the **File** menu allows you to create a new folder, shortcut, or file within the selected object. The type of file you can create depends on the software installed on your Windows 95 system. For example, the graphic below lists the types of files that may be created on a system where Microsoft Office is installed.

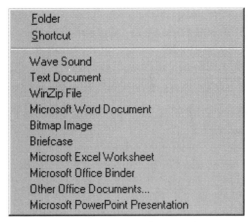

These menu options are available only when the cursor is focused on the previously mentioned devices in the All Folders pane. The **File** menu options change if a folder item is selected from the Contents pane. When a folder is selected, the following dialog appears listing the available options.

These options are also available through the pop-up menu that is displayed when the user uses the right mouse button. The **Open** menu option allows you to open the selected item, whether it is a folder or a file. If it is a folder, a new window will open displaying the file items contained within that folder. If it is a file, the appropriate application will launch first. Then, the file will open within the application.

Explore will open the folder and display the contents in the Contents pane. **Find** can be selected to search for a file within the selected folder. By launching the Find utility through a selected folder, the path leading to the selected directory is automatically entered for the search. The Find utility will be discussed later in the chapter.

Sharing is an available **File** menu option only if File and Print Sharing services are installed on the system. Resource and printer sharing will be discussed later in the course.

Send To is used to send the selected file or folder to a floppy disk or any other available resource that has been installed on Windows 95. If you have a fax client installed, you can send a selected file or folder to the fax application. If you have dial-up networking installed or any mail client such as Microsoft Exchange, you can send a file as a mail attachment.

The **File** menu also allows you to create shortcuts, delete, rename, and display properties for the selected file or folder. Finally, the **File** menu allows you to close Windows Explorer.

Edit Menu Options

The **Edit** menu has the standard options available such as **Undo**, **Cut**, **Copy**, **Paste**, and **Select All**. There is one additional menu option that allows you to paste a shortcut. To paste a shortcut, you must first copy the desired file or folder, go to the destination location, and select **Edit/Paste Shortcut**.

View Menu Options

The **View** menu is primarily used to change how the items inside the Contents pane are displayed. You can view items as Large Icons, Small Icons, List, or Details. The Details view of the contents of a folder or drive displays Name, Size, Type, and Modified information for each and every file and folder. The **View** menu also enables you to arrange or line up icons. The **Refresh** command can be used to refresh Windows Explorer contents when changes have been made. Finally, the **View** menu allows you to set **Options** relating to which files are displayed and how.

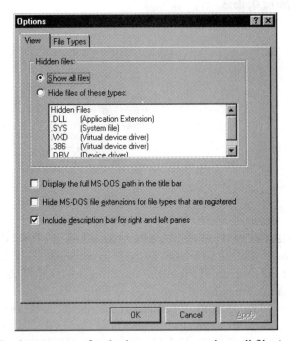

The Options dialog lets you specify whether you want to show all files in Explorer or hide selected files. You can also display the full MS-DOS file path, hide MS-DOS file extensions for registered file types, and include the description bar for both panes in Explorer. These options can be used for user preference. Some users like to view detailed information while others do not. Administrators can use the **Hide files of this type** option to hide certain system files. By restricting users from viewing the files in Explorer, they will not be able to delete or corrupt files of such importance. The **File Types** tab was discussed earlier in the course. This tab lists all of the registered file types available on the system. Windows 95 installs certain file types for the system to associate with applications. As you begin to install additional software, your list of registered file types will grow, allowing you to associate files with an application.

Tools Menu Options

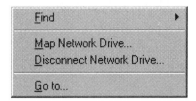

The **Tools** menu allows users to directly access the Find utility from within Explorer. Find is used to find files and folders on the system, as well as network drives. This utility has been discussed previously in the course. Users can also map direct connections to network resources from within Explorer. To map a network drive, open **Tools/Map Network Drive**. The following dialog appears:

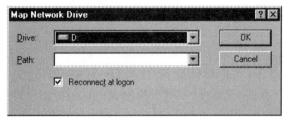

Select the drive that you want to use for identifying the network drive on your system. For connections to network resources, Explorer displays current connections, available servers, and shared resources. These are displayed either as connected resources or through Network Neighborhood.

The **Tools** menu also allows you to specify a folder name using the **Go to** option. Type in the name of the folder and click on **OK**. The folder will display its contents in the Contents pane. The folder will appear as an opened file folder in the All Folders pane.

Pop-up Menus In Explorer

Pop-up menus in Explorer depend on the item being selected. As previously mentioned, the pop-up menus for items selected in the Contents pane display the same menu options as those in the **File** menu. When you select a hard disk device from the All Folders pane, Windows 95 displays the following popup menu:

Users are allowed to perform the following functions: **Explore, Open, Find, Sharing, Format, Paste, Create Shortcut,** and **Properties.** All of these menu options have been discussed previously. The menu items on the pop-up menu for the floppy disk drive change a little bit. The **Copy Disk** command allows you to copy one floppy to another. Of course, this operation can be performed using the MS-DOS Command prompt along with the command line **copy** utility. However, end users may find the guided interface prompts easier to use. Explorer will begin to read the information from the floppy that is in the floppy drive at that time. Once it has completed reading the information, the user interface will prompt you to insert a second disk. This is sometimes called a target disk.

Drag and Drop Operations In Explorer

Windows 95 has added the ability to move and copy folders and files through drag and drop. To drag and drop a desired file, click on the file with the left mouse button and drag the object to the desired location. This copies the selected file. To move the file, you can hold down the *SHIFT* key, select the file, and then drag the object to the desired location. You can also move a file by selecting it first, then holding down the *SHIFT* key while dragging the file to the new destination. You can also copy and move files or folders using the right mouse button. To select the file you wish to copy or move, click on the file object with the right mouse button and drag to the desired location. Release the right mouse button to choose from the following options:

You can select **Move Here** to move the file or **Copy Here** to copy the file to the desired location. You can also create a shortcut for the selected file using **Create Shortcut(s) Here**. If you want to cancel the drag and drop operation, you can click on **Cancel**.

Disk Properties

To view the properties of a disk device on your system, right-click on the device you wish to examine. Select **Properties** from the pop-up menu.

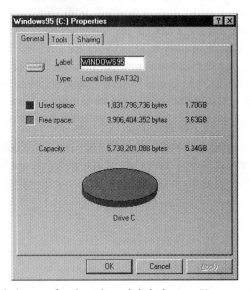

You can change the label name for the selected disk device. You can also view statistics for the disk device such as free space and used space. You can also determine the size of the selected device.

USING MY COMPUTER

This section discusses file management using My Computer. My Computer displays files, folders, existing network connections, as well as some Windows 95 utilities. The following topics are discussed within this section:

- My Computer
- My Computer Menu Options

My Computer can also be used to access the Control Panel and Printers utilities. We have already discussed the Control Panel. Printers will be discussed later in the course.

My Computer

My Computer is a tool available to users either from the desktop or within Windows Explorer. My Computer is simply another way to view, access, and use available file resources such as files, folders, network resources, disk devices such as floppy, hard disk, or CD-ROM. To open My Computer, double-click on its icon on the Desktop.

The various devices available on the system are visible in this window. Also available to the user are three additional utilities: Control Panel, Printers, and Dial-Up Networking. As you can see, users have the ability to access utilities in a few different ways, depending on their preferences.

My Computer Menu Options

The My Computer utility's menus are similar to Explorer's. However, the **File** menu does not change based on a user's selection. Users can either create a shortcut, delete or rename a selected item, or view the properties of a selected item. The following menu appears when the user displays the pop-up menu for any items within the My Computer window:

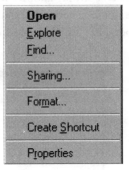

Open displays the contents of the selected item in a new window. This is applicable for a disk device or a folder item within a disk device. **Explore** launches Explorer to view the selected item. **Find** launches the Find utility. **Sharing** is only available when users have File and Print Sharing services installed on the system. **Format** is available when the user selects a disk drive. Before selecting format, you should make sure that any vital information has been backed up using a back up device, such as a tape drive or network server. Format erases all information on the selected drive, so use caution before beginning this procedure. **Create Shortcut** allows the user to create a shortcut on the desktop only. **Properties** displays the Properties dialog for the selected drive, folder, or file. The **Tools** tab available in the Properties dialog allows users to use the hard disk management tools discussed earlier in the course.

Once a drive is selected, you can view its contents by double-clicking on its icon within the My Computer window. Contents are displayed within a window environment rather than in a hierarchical listing such as that provided by Explorer.

Exercise 7-1:
Using My Computer

This exercise allows the student to become familiar with menu options and object drag and drop operations in My Computer.

1. Double-click on the My Computer desktop object.

2. Click on the C: drive once to select it.

3. Open **File/Properties** to display the properties available for this disk device. Notice that the label of this disk device can be changed simply by entering a new name in the Label field. We will discuss the other available tab options later in the course.

4. Click on **Cancel** to close the Properties dialog.

5. Double-click on the C: drive.

6. Click on the My Documents folder once with your right mouse button. Drag the folder to the desktop and release the mouse button.

7. Click on **Create Shortcut(s) Here**. Notice that you now have a shortcut to the My Documents folder on your desktop.

8. Close the C: window.

9. Close the window for My Computer.

LONG FILENAMES

This section discusses the usage of long filenames in Windows 95. In previous versions of Windows, users had been limited to using 8 characters for filenames. Characters other than alphanumeric characters were not valid. The following topics are discussed within this section:

- Filenames
- Viewing Aliases

However, as Windows 95 supports the use of long filenames, users can name their files up to 255 characters in length and may include certain non-alphanumeric characters.

Filenames

Windows 95 supports filenames of up to 255 characters, and paths of up to 260 characters on FAT file partitions. Long filenames can include spaces and punctuation except any of the following characters:

$$\backslash / : ? * \text{ “ } < > |$$

The term *long filename* may be a little confusing. A long filename is any filename that is not legal under DOS. For example, a name as short as "a...a" would be considered a long filename.

For each file with a long filename, an alias in the 8.3 format is automatically created. Since these are both stored in the directory table, the number of directory entries required is doubled when you use long filenames.

When converting long filenames:

- All spaces are dropped.

- Characters illegal under DOS are replaced by the underscore (_) character.

- The first six characters are used, then a tilde (~) and number, starting with 1, are added. If enough files exist to force the number to increment past 9, Windows 95 will use the first five characters, then a tilde (~) and number starting with 10 is added.

- The first three characters after the last period become the file extension.

Let's look at some examples:

Original Filename	8.3 Filename
This is my file.doc	THISIS~1.DOC
Financials.January.1995	FINANC~1.199
a.......a	a~1.a
No, I won't do that.ever	NO_IWO~1.EVE

Viewing Aliases

To view the alias for a file, right-click on the desired file and select **Properties**. Select the **General** tab to view the alias.

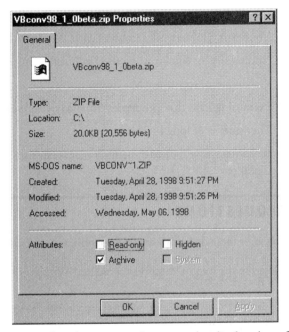

Running the **dir** command at the command prompt also displays long filenames and their associated aliases.

NOTE: *The root directory is limited to 512 directory entries. Using long filenames in the root directory creates two entries for each item: the long filename and the alias. Therefore, the root directory can fill up quickly with fewer files and folders present.*

SUMMARY

During this chapter, you were introduced to file management using Windows Explorer and My Computer. This included:

- Menu options within Windows Explorer

- Connecting to network resources with Windows Explorer

- Finding files or folders using the Find utility in Explorer

- Viewing resources using My Computer

- Examining hard disk properties using My Computer

- The benefits of long filenames

In the next chapter, we will discuss memory management issues involving virtual memory and multitasking.

POST-TEST QUESTIONS

The answers to these questions are in Appendix A at the end of this manual.

1. Describe the two methods for launching Windows Explorer.

....

....

2. How can you format a disk drive using My Computer?

....

....

3. What happens when a filename is converted from a long filename to an alias?

....

....

Memory Management

OBJECTIVES

At the completion of this chapter, you will be able to:

- Define the relationship between a process and a thread.
- Define the importance of virtual memory.
- Describe the differences between 16-bit and 32-bit multitasking.
- Customize virtual memory settings.

PRE-TEST QUESTIONS

The answers to these questions are in Appendix A at the end of this manual.

1. Describe the differences between processes and threads.

    ....

    ....

2. Compare cooperative and preemptive multitasking.

    ....

    ....

3. How does virtual memory fit in to the process of running applications on a Windows 95 system?

    ....

    ....

INTRODUCTION

Windows 95 has made memory management an easier task. In the previous version of Windows products, such as Windows 3.1, multitasking was available. Multitasking is what allows you to switch between various tasks and applications. Windows 3.1 used cooperative multitasking which gave up control to the new task. Windows 95 continues to use cooperative multitasking for 16-bit applications. However, 32-bit applications now use preemptive multitasking which uses a scheduler to allocate memory.

This chapter begins with a brief discussion of virtual memory architecture including process, threads, cooperative multitasking, and preemptive multitasking. We will then discuss virtual memory in the Windows 95 environment.

MEMORY MANAGEMENT

This section will discuss the fundamentals of memory management. This consists of the system's ability to monitor virtual memory and current running applications. You will also learn basic concepts relating to virtual memory. The following are topics discussed within this section:

- Virtual Memory
- Processes and Threads
- 16-Bit Multitasking
- 32-Bit Multitasking
- Ending a Task
- Virtual Memory Architecture

Memory management is often directly related to system performance in many ways. Determining the right amount of RAM, as well as appropriate virtual memory swapfile configuration, will ensure optimum performance.

Virtual Memory

Windows 95 takes the virtual memory and swap file concept that is familiar to Windows 3.x users and simplifies the required user intervention. Using a new virtual memory process, Windows 95 combines the flexibility of a temporary swapfile with the performance of a permanent swapfile.

Virtual memory is the scheme for permitting several programs to run at the same time, sharing the available physical memory of the computer. The virtual memory manager accomplishes this by *swapping* information from physical memory to a portion of the hard disk. Programs treat virtual memory exactly like physical memory. Every 32-bit Windows program, the 16-bit Windows session, and each MS-DOS program is allocated its own virtual memory space.

Windows 95 improves on the end-user interface for virtual memory. In Windows 3.x, a user had to decide whether to set up a temporary or permanent swapfile and the swapfile size. Windows 95 intelligently adjusts the swapfile size according to system demands.

The improved virtual memory scheme has the following major features:

- Dynamic swapfile sizing

- Ability to use fragmented portions of the hard drive for swapfiles

- Ability to create a swapfile on a compressed hard drive

- Improved virtual memory algorithms and access methods

Processes and Threads

Before discussing the Windows 95 virtual memory architecture, it is important that you understand processes and threads and the relationship between them.

What is a Process?

When a 32-bit application is launched, it is loaded into memory and receives a block of memory addresses. This is known as a process.

A process cannot execute any commands and does not use any processor time. It merely creates a holding place to keep its code, data, and resources accessible, but secure.

Think of a process as a walled city. Inside the walls, there are food, clothing, and tools that everyone who lives inside the city can access. However, no one outside the city can get to the resources within the city walls. Similarly, the code and data that belong to a process cannot be altered by any other process.

An application can have more than one process, providing increased security for mission-critical data.

Threads

A 32-bit application requires each process to have at least one thread. The thread of the process is responsible for executing its code.

A process must have at least one thread, but can have many more. However, under Windows 95 the threads only *seem* to be working simultaneously. Windows 95 does not support multiple processors and a computer with only one CPU can actually execute only one thread at a time. Nevertheless, because a time slice is so short, an application that uses multiple threads effectively can give the illusion that all threads are executing at the same time. This is known as multitasking.

16-Bit Multitasking

Another topic to discuss before moving on to the virtual memory architecture is multitasking. Windows 3.1 allowed applications to run concurrently through the process of cooperative multitasking. Each application would give up control to another active application by periodically checking the message queue. Windows 95 continues to use cooperative multitasking for 16-bit Windows applications. It creates one thread of execution that is shared between all 16-bit applications.

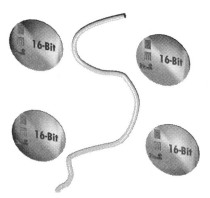

An application will keep control of the thread until the application either terminates or returns control to the operating system. It is up to the application to return control to the operating system. If an application performs a long task without giving up control to the operating system, all 16-bit applications can appear hung.

32-Bit Multitasking

Windows 95 utilizes a different scheme of multitasking for 32-bit Windows applications. Windows 95 uses a scheduler or dispatcher to allocate time to each thread that is running on the machine. This is known as preemptive multitasking because the operating system can preempt a thread's execution to give control to a thread with a higher priority or that has been waiting longer.

Since the operating system never loses control, an application is not nearly as likely to cause the operating system to hang. Even if a bug in an application causes the application to enter an endless loop, the user will generally still be able to gain access to the operating system and terminate the application gracefully.

The Windows 95 shell provides an illustration of preemptive multitasking. The shell itself is a process, and multiple windows performing file copies, file deletions, and other tasks have individual threads of execution.

Ending a Task

Sometimes, your computer system may stop responding to user activity. An application running on the system may have caused the system to become *hung*. This can mean that the application you are working in stops responding or maybe the entire system stops responding including the mouse. When this type of event occurs, you can press *CONTROL+ALT+DELETE* to bring up the task manager.

A dialog box that lists all active applications appears. Locked programs have a notation that they are not responding. You may select the program to close, or you may shut down the entire system.

A window opens listing each and every application or system activity running on the system. You can do one of three things at that point:

- End Task

    End Task allows you to end the task that is not responding. The application or activity that is *hung* will be listed in the task manager with "Not responding" next to the application name.

- Shut Down

    If there is more than one application causing the system to hang, or perhaps the entire system is hung, you can shut the computer down using this option.

- Cancel

    Cancel allows you to close the task manager.

Once you select to end the hung task, another window will appear stating that the application is busy. The user is then advised to wait 15 seconds and then try to end the task. The user is offered three options: Wait, End Task, or Cancel. Wait enables you to give the application a chance to gain control again. End Task allows you to end the task.

> *NOTE:* *You should realize that if you end a task that is not responding, you will lose any work you may have done. For example, if you are working in a word processing application, and you have created a document of several pages without having saved, you may lose your work. Fortunately, applications such as Microsoft Word does have an autorecovery feature which can help you recover some of your work. But most times, some piece of work is lost.*

Virtual Memory Architecture

The Windows 95 virtual memory scheme uses a demand-paged system based on a flat, linear address space which is accessed using 32-bit addresses. Windows NT uses a similar scheme. Demand paging is the method by which executable code and data move from physical memory to a paging file on a hard disk. If a process requires the paged data, the information returns to physical memory and other information in physical memory moves to disk as necessary. In this scheme, each process appears to have 4 GB of space available. The lower 2 GB is private to the process, but the upper 2 GB is shared by other processes.

The Intel 80386 family of processors incorporates protected-mode validation in the form of four protection rings. Protection rings used by the Windows 95 operating system include Ring 0 and Ring 3. Ring 0 components can do anything they want. Windows 95 uses Ring 0 for operating system components. Ring 3 components are prevented from executing certain instructions, such as interrupt handling, task switching or accessing defined memory regions. Windows 95 places application processes in Ring 3.

In the Windows 95 virtual memory scheme, system and application components reside in certain areas of virtual memory:

- Real-mode device drivers reside in the initial 640-KB block.

- 32-bit Windows applications reside in the area between 4 MB and 2 GB with each application assigned its own address space.

- 16-bit Windows applications, core system components, and shared DLLs reside in the area between 2 GB and 3 GB.

- Ring 0 components reside in the area between 3 GB and 4 GB.

Although it is recommended that you allow Windows to manage virtual memory settings, you can change them if you like. To do so, you must use the System control panel's Performance options.

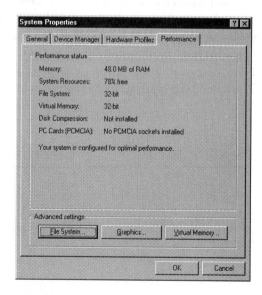

Click on the **Virtual Memory** button to display the following dialog:

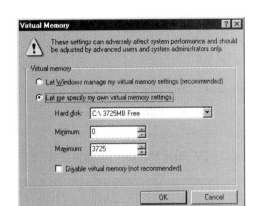

This dialog allows you to specify which hard disk you want to use for virtual memory as well as the amount of free space to use. You can also specify the minimum and maximum amount hard disk space to be used for virtual memory. By setting the maximum to zero, you can run Windows 95 without a virtual memory paging file. However, this is not recommended, since many applications require more memory than is available on most machines.

Normally, it is best to keep the **Let Windows manage my virtual memory settings** option enabled. However, if you are frequently use an application that requires a large amount of memory resources, you will want to increase the minimum size of paging file. When the size of the paging file must be increased dynamically, it causes a performance hit. A paging file that begins at its optimal size will result in better performance.

Exercise 8-1:
Configuring the Paging File

This exercise walks you through changing the size of your paging file so that Windows 95 can run without one.

1. Launch the Control Panel.

2. Launch the System utility.

3. Click on the **Performance** tab.

4. Click on the **Virtual Memory** button.

5. Click on the option **Let me specify my own virtual memory settings**.

6. Change the maximum value to 0.

7. Click on **OK**.

8. Click on **Virtual Memory** again.

9. Click on the option **Let Windows manage my virtual memory settings (recommended)**.

10. Click on **OK**.

11. Click on **OK**.

12. Close the Control Panel.

SUMMARY

In this chapter, you were introduced to issues related to multitasking and memory management. These included:

- Virtual Memory

- Processes and Threads

- 16-bit and 32-bit multitasking

- Virtual Memory settings

In the next chapter, we will discuss application management for 16-bit and 32-bit applications using virtual machines.

POST-TEST QUESTIONS

The answers to these questions are in Appendix A at the end of this manual.

1. Why would you want to manually increase the minimum amount of hard disk space used for virtual memory?

   ....

   ....

2. Where in virtual memory are real-mode device drivers stored?

   ....

   ....

3. What term refers to task scheduling where the operating system assigns time slices to threads?

   ....

   ....

4. Can a process have more than one thread?

   ....

   ....

5. A swapfile can be created on what type of drive?

   ....

   ....

6. Which combination of keys can be used to end a hung task?

    ....

    ....

CHAPTER 9

Application Management

OBJECTIVES

At the completion of this chapter, you will be able to:

- Describe the application types supported by Windows 95.
- Customize MS-DOS program settings.
- Describe MS-DOS mode.
- Compare memory usage of MS-DOS, Win16, and Win32 applications.
- Describe a Virtual Machine.
- Resolve application errors.
- Perform a local reboot to terminate a malfunctioning application.
- List changes in MS-DOS commands.
- Describe Windows 95 multimedia implementation.

PRE-TEST QUESTIONS

The answers to these questions are in Appendix A at the end of this manual.

1. What is the term for the technique where 16-bit code can call 32-bit code and vice versa?

   ....

   ....

2. What type or types of applications run in a shared address space?

   ....

   ....

3. How can you configure an MS-DOS program to shut down Windows 95 before the program can run?

   ....

   ....

4. What is displayed when you press *CONTROL+ALT+DELETE*?

....

....

INTRODUCTION

The true test of an operating system is the manner in which it manages applications. As you will see in this chapter, the Windows 95 operating system provides support for MS-DOS, 16-bit Windows, and 32-bit Windows applications. You will learn how the operating system accomplishes this by using Virtual Machines, and will see how to optimize application support.

The chapter continues with a discussion on customizing an MS-DOS program, manipulating basic and advanced settings, and when to use MS-DOS mode.

You will then be shown the steps you should take to intervene when an application fails, including selectively terminating an application by performing a local reboot. The chapter continues with a review of the changes in common MS-DOS commands.

MANAGING APPLICATIONS

This section will discuss application support under Windows 95. This includes both what applications types are supported, and some information on how support is implemented. The following topics are discussed within this section:

- Supported Applications
- Virtual Machines
- Support for MS-DOS Applications
- Support For 16-Bit Windows Applications
- Support For 32-Bit Windows Applications

As you will see, you will be able to continue using most of your existing applications. It is typically suggested that you upgrade to 32-bit versions of applications to help improve performance and take advantage of features such as long filenames.

Supported Applications

Great pains were taken during Windows 95 development to assure compatibility with the large installed base of MS-DOS-based and Windows 16-bit applications.

Windows 95 supports MS-DOS-based applications, 16-bit Windows (Win16) applications, and 32-bit Windows (Win32) applications. Support is provided through the Win32 API (Application Programming Interface).

To assure compatibility between 16-bit and 32-bit Windows applications, Windows 95 *thunks* between 16-bit and 32-bit code execution. Thunking is the technique where 16-bit code can call 32-bit code, and vice versa.

Virtual Machines

Essential to understanding how Windows 95 handles these three types of applications is the concept of Virtual Machines. A Virtual Machine consists of a virtual address space in physical or virtual memory, processor registers, and privileges. The Virtual Machine Manager coordinates resources provided to each application and system process. There are different virtual machines at work while you use Windows 95.

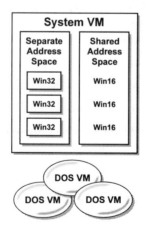

- The System Virtual Machine contains:

    Base system components (GDI, USER, Kernel)

    Shared memory address space shared by all 16-bit Windows applications

    Individual memory address spaces for each 32-bit Windows application

- A separate MS-DOS Virtual Machine (VM) for each MS-DOS application

As is apparent from the above graphic, all applications running under Windows 95 are run inside of virtual machines.

Support for MS-DOS Applications

Each MS-DOS program runs in its own Virtual Machine (VM). This allows multiple 8086-compatible sessions to run concurrently on the processor. This means that several MS-DOS applications can run concurrently. Any MS-DOS application that attempts to access memory outside of its VM is terminated by the operating system. This provides protection for Win16 and Win32 applications, as well as for system components.

Through the use of virtual device drivers (VxDs), each MS-DOS application receives access to hardware components. Since Windows 95 provides many 32-bit, protected-mode drivers to replace real-mode drivers previously loaded into conventional memory, MS-DOS applications have additional conventional memory for their use.

By default, Windows 95 runs all MS-DOS applications in a window. You may choose to run them full-screen. MS-DOS applications are set to run in background mode by default.

Windows 95 also supports an MS-DOS mode that allows an MS-DOS application to have 100% access to system resources. Most MS-DOS programs do not need to access this mode due to the enhanced support for MS-DOS applications within Windows 95.

Support for 16-Bit Windows Applications

Most applications designed for Windows 3.x (Win16-based applications) run under Windows 95 without modification. The design of Windows 95 ensures that Win16-based applications running on a computer with at least 4 MB RAM should perform as well as or better than they did under Windows 3.1. In general, Win16-based applications perform better under Windows 95, due to its 32-bit operating system services and 32-bit subsystems.

Some facts to remember about Win16-based applications:

- The operating system provides the same system resources to both Win32-based and Win16-based applications.

- Win16-based applications cannot utilize preemptive multitasking or long filename support.

- Win16-based applications share memory address space in the System VM, a common input queue, and a common message queue.

- Win16-based processes are scheduled cooperatively.

- Win16-based applications make use of 32-bit print and communications subsystems.

Because all Win16-based applications share a memory address space and common system queues, a malfunctioning Win16-based application can cause other Win16-based applications to fail. However, it will not adversely affect Win32-based applications. The operating system tracks resources utilized by Win16-based applications and uses this information to clean up the system after an application terminates abnormally. This frees up unused resources for additional processes. If an application does fail and hang, you can perform a local reboot, which is described later in this chapter.

Support for 32-Bit Windows Applications

Applications designed for Windows 95 utilizing the Win32 API take full advantage of all Windows 95 operating system enhancements. Advantages of Win32-based applications include:

- Preemptive multitasking

    The Windows 95 kernel schedules the time allotted to active processes and prevents one application from using all system resources.

- Long filename support

   Win16 applications access files through their 8.3 alias names.

- Memory protection

   Separate memory address space in the System VM protects Win32-based applications from errors generated by other applications.

- Separate message queue for each application

   Under Windows 3.x, applications multitask cooperatively, checking the message queue for information from the operating system. If an application stops checking the queue, other applications will be locked out of the message queue. Under Windows 95, failed Win32-based or Win16-based applications do not lock out a 32-bit application from its dedicated message queue.

The operating system tracks resources allocated to each Win32-based application on a per-thread basis. These resources are automatically freed when the application ends. If an application stops responding, you can perform a local reboot. The local reboot process is described later in this chapter.

> *NOTE: Win32-based applications for Windows NT will run under Windows 95 if the application does not use any Windows NT-specific APIs. Most Win32-based applications should be designed to run under both Windows 95 and Windows NT, unless they require a specific operating system feature that is not available under both operating systems.*

MS-DOS APPLICATIONS

This section will teach you how to configure and customize an MS-DOS application. Each of the properties settings have been outlined for you. The following topics are discussed within this section:

- Customizing MS-DOS Programs
- General Settings

- Program Settings
- Advanced Settings
- Font Settings
- Memory Settings
- Screen Settings
- Miscellaneous Settings
- Memory Available to MS-DOS Applications
- Windowed MS-DOS Toolbar

In many cases, you can improve the stability and performance of MS-DOS applications through customization. In other cases, it is necessary just to get the applications to run.

MS-DOS APPLICATION GUIDELINES

There is usually little, if any, difference when installing applications to run under MS-DOS or inside an MS-DOS session under Windows 95. In general, you should:

- Read all installation instructions.
- Read any included READ.ME (or similar) files.
- Watch for special requirements for the application to run.
- Make any necessary changes through the Properties dialog.

When you run MS-DOS applications, Windows 95 will always use a PIF file to define the application environment. This will either be a PIF that you have created, the PIF listed in APPS.INF, or the default PIF, _DEFAULT.PIF. While this file will work with most applications, it is written for a *worst-case* application and may not contain optimum settings for your applications. Also, some programs will have special requirements, forcing you to create a PIF.

When a DOS application is launched, Windows 95 looks for its PIF file in the same directory as the executable. If it is not there, it checks the APPS.INF for a listing. If there is no listing, it uses the default PIF. If you upgraded from Windows 3.1 or Windows for Workgroups 3.11, the default PIF will be named _DEFAULT.PIF. If you did not, you can create a default PIF by copying DOSPRMPT.PIF to _DEFAULT.PIF. Then you can customize it to provide a default that is best for your configuration and applications.

Customizing MS-DOS Programs

MS-DOS programs are written without Windows-type multitasking in mind. Due to this, these programs use as many resources as are available to the system. Therefore, Windows must have information on how to handle such programs. Properties sheets provide this information to Windows.

The properties sheet for an MS-DOS application contains six options.

- General

    Information such as type, location, size, MS-DOS filename, and attributes are displayed.

- Program

    This includes the command line, working directory, and window type information. Advanced program settings, including MS-DOS mode, are also available from this page.

- Font

    This allows you to set the font that the application uses to display information.

- Memory

    Information about conventional, expanded, and extended memory usage can be modified on this page.

- Screen

    This sets window usage, size, and performance values.

- Misc

    This includes Windows shortcut keys, mouse environment, and termination settings.

The MS-DOS properties sheet replaces the program information files and PIF Editor used in Windows 3.x.

General Settings

Opening a properties sheet for an MS-DOS application and selecting the **General** tab displays the following information:

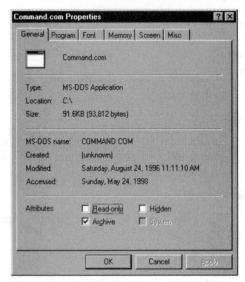

General information pertaining to the application, such as the MS-DOS name, size, location, and file attributes, can be found on this properties sheet. To change file attributes, check the appropriate box. File attributes have the same meaning in Windows 95 as they do in MS-DOS.

Program Settings

Selecting the **Program** tab displays the following information:

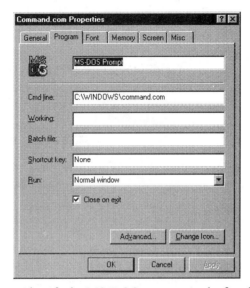

You can enter a name to identify the MS-DOS program in the first field available on this properties sheet. The Cmd line field must include the path leading to the MS-DOS program. You must also include the name of the application itself. The Batch file field allows you to designate a batch file for the program. Windows 95 will run the specified batch file prior to starting the program. You can also specify a shortcut key which must include the *CONTROL* key or *ALT* key as well as a character entry. For example, you can use *CONTROL+N*. Lastly, you can set whether you want the program to run in a normal window, minimized, or maximized. There are two additional settings available for the Program properties sheet: **Advanced** and **Change** Icon.

To access Advanced program settings, click on the **Advanced** button.

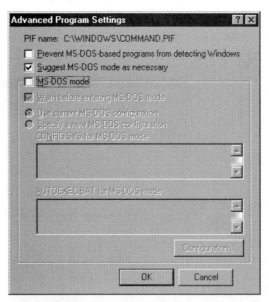

Entering MS-DOS mode forces Windows 95 to shut down upon launching the program. All system resources are then released to the MS-DOS application. Since this application takes complete control of the system, you may specify customized CONFIG.SYS and AUTOEXEC.BAT values for the application.

To enter MS-DOS application mode, Windows 95 unloads itself (actually, a small footprint remains in memory) and gives full control of the machine to the MS-DOS program. When the MS-DOS application terminates, the system restarts and returns the user to Windows 95.

Clicking on **Configuration** on this page presents the user with options to be used each time this program enters MS-DOS mode. You may view a description of what each item means by clicking on the desired object.

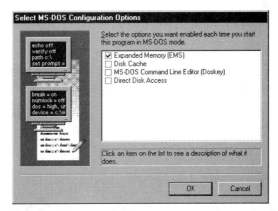

The manipulation of these properties creates a custom configuration for each MS-DOS application installed on the system. Certain programs written for MS-DOS must use the MS-DOS mode to run under Windows 95.

You can also change the icon of the selected program application by clicking on **Change Icon** on the **Program** tab.

You can select from the icons showing in the Current icon field or **Browse** to locate a different icon.

Font Settings

Selecting the **Font Settings** tab displays the following dialog:

Windows 95 provides a preview of the window and font settings selected. Note that both TrueType and Bitmap fonts are available.

Memory Settings

Selecting the **Memory** tab displays the following information:

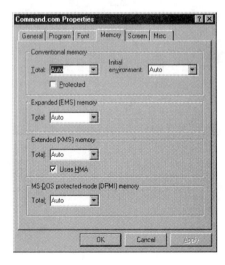

Conventional memory	Users can specify the total amount of conventional memory that is required to run the DOS application. If you are unsure of what this value should be, you should set it to Auto.
Expanded (EMS) memory	This option is enabled only if the CONFIG.SYS file does not include the NOEMS keyword. If this file does include this keyword, and you wish to enable expanded memory, you must manually remove the keyword from the file.
Extended (XMS) memory	This option allows you to specify the maximum amount of extended memory that you wish to allocate to the program. The HMA checkbox allows you to specify whether you would like the program to use High Memory Area (HMA).
MS-DOS protected-mode	Windows 95 provides DPMI (DOS Protected-Mode Interface) memory to applications that require specification. If a CONFIG.SYS loads EMM386 with the NOEMS parameter, DPMI memory will not be available. The default configuration is to have EMS enabled.

Conventional, expanded, extended, and DPMI values allow the user to specify the memory allocated to the application.

Screen Settings

Screen settings include the following:

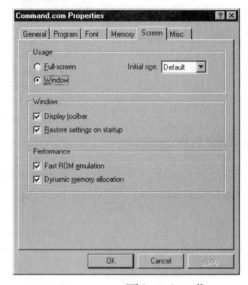

Usage	This option allows you to select whether the application will run at full screen or in a window. You can select the initial number of lines to view on screen.
Window	You can select to have the MS-DOS toolbar visible when an MS-DOS application runs in a window environment. You can also allow settings to be restored to their defaults when exiting the application.
Performance	**Fast ROM Emulation** should be enabled if you want the application to write to the screen faster using display drivers. These drivers will then emulate video functions in ROM emulation.
	You should enable **Dynamic memory allocation** if you plan to be running this application along with other non-DOS applications, especially if the DOS application uses text and graphic modes.

Dynamic memory allocation uses the Windows 95 video ROM-handling capacity. Fast ROM Emulation enables virtual device driver emulation of video ROM services to speed up video operations.

Misc Settings

Selecting the **Misc** tab displays the following:

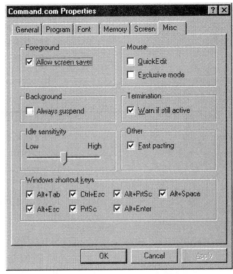

Foreground	This option is used to enable screen savers even when the MS-DOS program is the active running program.
Mouse	**QuickEdit** allows users to cut and paste text information. If you do not enable this option for an MS-DOS program, you must use the **Mark** menu option of the **Edit** menu to mark the text prior to selecting it for a copy operation.

	You can also specify that the mouse be used strictly for the selected MS-DOS program. If the user is running other Windows applications and this option is selected, the mouse pointer will not be available.
Background	This option allows system resources to remain unused when the program is idle.
Termination	This option should be used if you want to display a warning message when trying to close the program window while it is running.
Idle sensitivity	This option can be used to allocate resources to other applications when the program is idle for the specified amount of time.
Other	This option allows you to enable an operation known as Fast Pasting. Most programs include the ability to use this option. However, if you paste your text and it does not appear correctly, you should disable this option.
Windows shortcut keys	Selecting the available shortcut keys allows these to be associated with Windows applications only.

Idle Sensitivity provides the user with the ability to allocate additional CPU resources to an application running in the background by moving the slider toward the low end of the scale.

Program Information Files

PIFs (Program Information Files) are used to define requirements for your DOS applications. If you do not specifically define a PIF for your DOS applications, a default PIF is used. PIFs are defined:

- Automatically during Setup.

  Windows 95 uses the APPS.INF file to identify DOS applications. Many popular DOS applications are listed, along with suggested PIF settings. Since DOS applications are recognized by filename, some programs may be incorrectly identified.

- By Software Manufacturers.

  Some manufacturers are now providing PIFs with their DOS applications. These contain the manufacturer's suggested settings. It may be necessary to edit the PIF to meet your particular operational needs.

- Through the application's properties sheet.

  The properties sheet allows you to create custom PIFs. You can also modify existing PIFs.

Upgrading from Windows 3.1

Windows 95 stores PIF files in a different format than Windows 3.1. If you upgrade Windows 3.1 to Windows 95, your PIF files will be converted to the Windows 95 format.

Memory Available to MS-DOS Applications

Windows 95 makes much more conventional memory available to your MS-DOS applications by replacing 16-bit real mode drivers with 32-bit protected mode drivers. For example, these protected mode drivers replace 16-bit drivers for:

SHARE.EXE	File sharing and locking
MOUSE.COM	Microsoft mouse driver
SMARTDRV.EXE	Disk caching device
MSCDEX.EXE	CD-ROM extensions
DRVSPACE.SYS	Disk compression driver
Novell and Microsoft network client software	

The resulting conventional memory savings can be dramatic. On a PC with network client software, a CD-ROM device, and disk compression, the conventional memory available to MS-DOS applications is approximately 602 KB.

Memory in MS-DOS

The best place to start a discussion of MS-DOS memory is memory terms. This has traditionally been an area that has generated a great deal of confusion.

- Conventional memory

    This is the first 640 KB of system memory. Traditionally, this was the only memory available to DOS applications. It contains the interrupts table, BIOS table (and hardware settings), DOS kernel files, device drivers, environmental variables, the DOS command processor, TSRs, application programs, and data.

- Upper memory area (UMA)

    The UMA is located between 640 KB and 1 MB. It contains the ROM BIOS, device controller ROM, and video controller ROM and RAM. When supporting expanded memory, it will contain the expanded memory page frames. Free areas can be utilized as upper memory blocks.

- Upper memory blocks (UMB)

    UMBs are free areas within the UMA. UMBs can be used to contain device drivers and memory-resident programs (TSRs). Access to UMBs requires HIMEM.SYS loaded as an extended memory manager and EMM386.EXE loaded as the UMB manager.

- Extended memory (XMS)

    XMS memory is directly addressable memory starting at 1 MB. This is physically limited to 16 MB for 80286 microprocessors and 4 GB for 80386 and above microprocessors. An XMS driver, such as HIMEM.SYS, is required for applications to use extended memory.

- High memory area (HMA)

    The HMA is the first 64 KB of extended memory; that is, the first 64 KB above 1 MB. An XMS driver, such as HIMEM.SYS, is required for DOS to use the HMA. It is commonly used for loading DOS components, but may be used for a different memory resident program. However, only one program at a time may reside in the HMA.

- Expanded memory (EMS)

  EMS was developed as a way of working around the limitations of DOS and early microprocessors. It is based on the LIM (Lotus-Intel-Microsoft) specification, either LIM 3.2 or LIM 4.0. On an 80286-based system, an EMS memory board and driver are required; 80386 and above systems support emulation of EMS in XMS memory. EMS emulation requires HIMEM.SYS and EMM386.EXE loaded as part of CONFIG.SYS.

Memory Management for DOS Applications

Some of the most commonly used memory management commands, drivers, and utilities include:

- DOS=

  This command is used as a CONFIG.SYS memory management command statement. It is also used to determine the DOS location for UMB management.

- EMM386.EXE

  EMM386.EXE is the MS-DOS EMS emulator and UMB management program.

- HIMEM.SYS

  This is used as the MS-DOS XMS device driver.

Extended Memory

Extended (XMS) memory, as defined earlier, is directly addressable memory starting at 1 MB. The first 64 KB of XMS is the high memory area (HMA). While any one program (that will fit) can be loaded into the HMA, it normally is used to load part of MS-DOS, freeing up conventional memory for application use.

XMS memory is used by DOS for:

- Applications

    Many large applications, such as multimedia applications and games, are written to use XMS, if available.

- Disk caching

    Part of XMS is commonly used for setting up a disk cache. This helps to improve both read and write performance of local hard disks.

- EMS emulation

    Physical EMS memory boards are quickly becoming a rarity, with users instead using part of XMS as emulated EMS.

You must load HIMEM.SYS, or its equivalent, as part of CONFIG.SYS to make extended memory available. The default syntax for this statement is:

```
DEVICE=C:\DOS\HIMEM.SYS
```

HIMEM.SYS must be loaded before any other memory drivers or programs that use extended memory. For example, you must load HIMEM.SYS before EMM386.EXE and before executing the DOS= statement.

Windowed MS-DOS Toolbar

The new toolbar feature at the top of the MS-DOS window is apparent the first time you run an MS-DOS application under Windows 95.

The toolbar allows you to perform the following functions:

- Scaling window to any size with TrueType font support.

- Cutting, copying, and pasting into and out of the MS-DOS window.

- One-click access to the application's properties sheet.
- Quick switching between exclusive and background modes.

MS-DOS Mode

Some MS-DOS applications will require that you run them in MS-DOS mode. In this mode, Windows 95 is essentially shut down. Windows applications will also be shut down. The Warn Before Entering MS-DOS Mode property instructs Windows 95 to issue a warning before beginning to shut down. This will allow you to cancel the shutdown process.

Exercise 9-1:
MS-DOS Support

The purpose of this exercise is to work with MS-DOS application support. There are no special requirements for completing this exercise. You should be logged on as your primary username at the start of this exercise.

If you have selected a different primary logon during any exercises, you should launch the **Network Control Panel object** and change your logon type to Windows Logon. You will need to restart your system after making changes.

1. Launch the Windows Explorer.
2. Select the **WINDOWS/COMMAND** directory.
3. Right-click on **EDIT.COM** and select **Properties**.
4. Click on the **Screen** tab.
5. Select **Full-screen** as your screen usage.
6. Click on **OK**.
7. Double-click on EDIT.COM. The command will run full screen.
8. Close the window by running **File/Exit**.

9. Right-click on **EDIT.COM** and select **Properties**.

10. Click on the **Program** tab.

11. Click on **Advanced**.

12. Click on the checkbox to select **MS-DOS mode**.

13. Leave the remaining settings at default and click on **OK**.

14. Click on **OK**.

15. Double-click on **EDIT.COM**.

16. When prompted with a warning that all other programs will have to close, click on **Yes**.

17. Depending on your system, the system may restart after the command runs. If so, log on with your primary Windows logon username.

18. Run **File/Exit** from the menu to close the MS-DOS window. The computer will restart to Windows.

POTENTIAL APPLICATION PITFALLS

This section will discuss troubleshooting application-related failures. Common problems, their symptoms, and, in many cases, potential solutions are discussed. The following topics are discussed within this section:

- Working Directories for Win16-Based Applications

- Applications That Work Intimately With Hardware

- When Applications Fail

- Local Reboot Support

- Changes In MS-DOS Commands

Application troubleshooting is a critical part of end-user support. It is important that you understand the tools available and how to best use them to improve your troubleshooting, detection, and correction procedures.

Working Directories for Win16-Based Applications

Certain Win16-based applications require a defined working directory. However, Windows 95 does not allow you to specify a working directory in the properties sheet of a Win16-based application. To solve this problem, create a shortcut for the Win16-based application and view the shortcut's properties sheet.

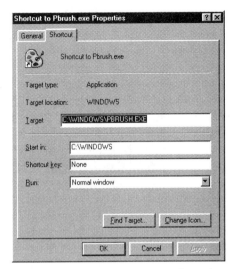

Selecting the **Shortcut** tab allows you to designate a working directory (Start In) for the Win16-based application.

> *NOTE:*   *Installing Windows 95 in a directory other than \WINDOWS causes some Win16-based applications to not find required DLL files. In this case, create a shortcut that starts in the\WINDOWS\SYSTEM directory to run the application.*

Applications That Work Intimately with Hardware

Windows 16-bit applications that work directly with hardware, such as virus protection utilities, may not function correctly under Windows 95. This is due to enhancements to the Windows 95 file system, such as long filenames.

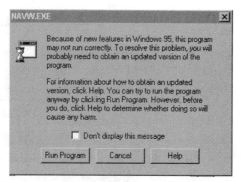

Virus protection utilities may be able to detect, but not remove viruses on a Windows 95 machine. These utilities may also detect virus activity where there is none.

When Applications Fail

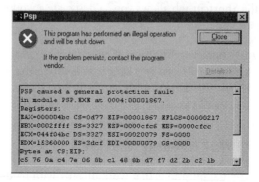

Applications can fail in two ways. Either an application can violate system integrity by performing a prohibited command, or an application can lock up by failing to respond to messages sent to it from the operating system.

Recalling our discussion of virtual machines earlier in this section, all 16-bit Windows applications share the same virtual machine. Therefore, if a 16-bit application fails, all other active 16-bit applications lock up until the problem is resolved.

Remember that 32-bit Windows applications run in separate virtual address spaces This means that a failed 32-bit application does not affect any other 32-bit applications that are active.

MS-DOS applications each have their own virtual machine. Therefore, if an MS-DOS application locks up, only the virtual machine that it is located on is terminated, not affecting any other active application.

Local Reboot Support

It is possible to reboot a computer by pressing *CONTROL+ALT+DELETE* twice. However, this should only be done as a last resort. Shutting down Windows 95 appropriately allows the system to save current registry information as well as assuring that any attached users do not lose data.

Changes in MS-DOS Commands

Due to new features in Windows 95, many familiar MS-DOS commands have been modified. The location of these new MS-DOS commands is the \WINDOWS\COMMAND directory. These include:

ANSI.SYS	ATTRIB.EXE	CHKDSK.EXE	CHOICE.COM
COUNTRY.SYS	DEBUG.EXE	DELTREE.EXE	DISKCOPY.COM
DISPLAY.SYS	DOSKEY.COM	EDIT.COM	FC.EXE
FDISK.EXE	FIND.EXE	FORMAT.COM	KEYB.COM
LABEL.EXE	MEM.EXE	MODE.COM	MORE.COM
MOVE.EXE	SCANDISK.EXE	SHARE.EXE	SORT.EXE
START.EXE	XCOPY.EXE	XCOPY32.EXE	

You can also start MS-DOS or Windows applications from an MS-DOS command prompt using START.EXE. The syntax is:

```
START application_name
```

You can also view a document with the **Start** command with the following syntax:

```
START document_name
```

Windows 95 will start the appropriate application for the document as long as there is an association between the document filename extension and an application.

Options for START.EXE include:

/m	(minimized)	Starts the program minimized (in the background)
/max	(maximized)	Starts the program maximized (in the foreground)
/r	(restored)	Starts the program restored (in the foreground)
/w	(wait)	Does not return until the other program exits

SCENARIOS

Scenario 1

You have just installed Windows 95 and you are trying to run a game that runs under MS-DOS. You launch the game in a window, but it fails. What can you try?

....

....

Scenario 2

You are trying to run an old MS-DOS based accounting program so that you can pull some old data off a backup. When you try to launch the program, you receive an error that it requires expanded memory. You can run other MS-DOS based programs. What is most likely the problem?

....

....

SUMMARY

In this chapter, you learned about many facets of application management under Windows 95 including:

- Types of applications supported by Windows 95
- Installation and removal of programs
- Windows 95 Virtual Machine implementation
- Win16 application support
- Win32 application support
- MS-DOS application support
- Customization of MS-DOS applications
- Changes in MS-DOS command-line utilities
- Resolution of application failures
- Windows 95 Multimedia features

The next chapter discusses the Registry and its components.

POST-TEST QUESTIONS

The answers to these questions are in Appendix A at the end of this manual.

1. Name the two types of Virtual Machines used by Windows 95.

   ....

   ....

2. What application types are supported by Windows 95?

    ....

    ....

3. Name two ways an application can fail.

    ....

    ....

4. How would you use the command line START.EXE to open a document named MYFINA~1.DOC?

    ....

    ....

5. How can you perform a local reboot?

    ....

    ....

CHAPTER 10

Registry

OBJECTIVES

At the completion of this chapter, you will be able to:

- Discuss the differences between the registry and INI files.
- Define the characteristics of the registry.
- List the components of the registry.
- Use the Registry Editor to import and export registry files.
- Edit the Registry using REGEDIT.
- Describe the relationship between Root Keys and Value Entries within the Registry.
- Troubleshoot problems with the registry.

PRE-TEST QUESTIONS

The answers to these questions are in Appendix A at the end of this manual.

1. The Windows 95 registry contains how many root keys? What are they?

   ....

   ....

2. What is the program provided with Windows 95 used to edit the registry?

   ....

   ....

INTRODUCTION

The chapter begins with a discussion of the Windows 95 Registry. Windows 95 tracks hardware, device drivers, system-wide configurations, as well as user-specific configurations using the registry. The registry resembles a database using root keys for each of the areas the operating system must track. As you modify configurations through Setup or the Control Panel utilities, you are actually modifying the contents of the registry. There are also some limited circumstances where you may need to modify the registry directly using the REGEDIT utility which will be discussed. As you will see, it is recommended that you use the administrative tools available to you for system and user configurations. The Registry Editor tool should be used only when necessary.

Stop now and view the following video presentation on the Interactive Learning CD-ROM:

Windows 95 Administration

Registry

INTRODUCTION TO THE REGISTRY

This section will introduce the basics of the Registry. The structure of the Registry will be discussed to help you better understand registry management procedures. The following topics are discussed within this section:

- The Registry
- Characteristics of the Registry
- Registry Components
- Registry Editor

- Editing the Registry
- Registry Structure
- Registry Configuration: Root Keys
- Registry Configuration: Value Entries
- Troubleshooting Registry Problems
- Registry During Startup

When changing system and device configurations, it is important to note that during that same time, corresponding registry entries are also created. The Registry is an important and informative tool available to you as an administrator.

The Registry

The Windows 95 Registry is the central repository for all information needed by the operating system to set up and configure the computer. In essence, the registry contains information previously stored in the AUTOEXEC.BAT, CONFIG.SYS, and initialization (INI) files.

The registry can be compared to the INI files used in Windows 3.x. In fact, certain information contained within the WIN.INI and SYSTEM.INI files has been migrated to the registry. Each key in the registry is similar to a bracketed heading in an INI file, and values within the keys are correspond to the information under the bracketed heading. Significant differences between the registry and INI files include:

- The registry provides a centralized location for all information.
- The registry can contain subkeys.
- The registry can contain binary data.
- The registry can store user preferences for multiple users of the same computer.

Windows 95 supports existing INI files solely for compatibility with 16-bit Windows and MS-DOS applications. New applications written for Windows 95 store initialization information in the registry.

Characteristics of the Registry

The Windows 95 Registry:

- Provides a single source for configuration information.

- Enumerates, tracks, and configures the hardware, applications, device drivers, and operating system control parameters.

- Allows users and administrators to configure computer options by using a standardized set of Control Panel tools and other administrative tools, reducing the likelihood of syntax errors in configuration information.

- Separates information related to users, applications, and computers, so that specific data for multiple users can be maintained on a single computer.

- Provides a set of network-independent functions for setting and querying configuration information, enabling direct examination of configuration data over a network.

- Provides storage of system configuration information that is recoverable after system failures.

Registry Components

The registry performs as if it were a single database, but actually it is composed of two separate files: USER.DAT and SYSTEM.DAT. By default, the files are located in the \WINDOWS directory.

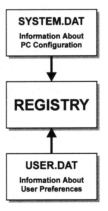

USER.DAT contains user-specific information relating to user profiles. This includes **Start** menu items, desktop configurations, and preference information. SYSTEM.DAT contains hardware-specific and computer-specific information. This information includes hardware profiles and settings displayed in the Device Manager.

To launch the Registry Editor utility, type **regedit** in the Run dialog. REGEDIT.EXE is installed automatically when Windows 95 is installed from a CD-ROM. It is located in the \Windows directory. However, if Windows 95 is installed from diskettes, REGEDIT.EXE is not included.

Registry Editor

There are several menu options which are available to help you maneuver through the Registry directly using the Registry Editor. The **Registry** menu includes the following options:

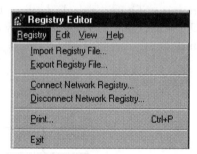

Let's look at two of the menu options: Import Registry File and Export Registry File. Connecting to and disconnecting from network registries will be discussed later in the course.

Registry Structure

To view the registry, launch the REGEDIT utility using the **Start/Run** command.

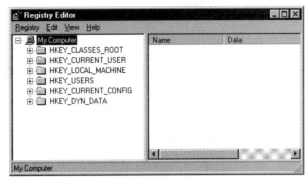

Each registry root key has a unique name beginning with HKEY_. Root keys contain data items called value entries. Additional subkeys off the root key may be present. The Registry Editor displays the root keys and subkeys in the left pane, and associated value entries in the right pane.

The Registry Editor displays registry information in much the same fashion as Windows Explorer displays directory information. For example, root keys are similar to folders while value entries are similar to files. The two main root keys are HKEY_LOCAL_MACHINE, which relates to the SYSTEM.DAT file, and HKEY_USERS, which relates to the USER.DAT file.

Registry Configuration: Root Keys

The registry root keys consist of the following:

- HKEY_LOCAL_MACHINE

    This key contains computer-specific information pertaining to hardware devices present, software settings, and similar data. This information is made available to all users of this computer. The contents of this root key relate directly to the SYSTEM.DAT file.

- HKEY_USERS

    This key contains information about all users of the computer, including generic entries for all users and user-specific information. Each user of the computer contains subkeys that define specific configuration and preference information. The contents of this root key relate directly to the USER.DAT file.

- HKEY_CLASSES_ROOT

    This key points to a branch of HKEY_LOCAL_MACHINE that describes certain software settings, such as information about OLE links, OLE associations, and aspects of the Windows 95 UI.

- HKEY_CURRENT_USER

    This key points to a branch of HKEY_USERS for the currently logged-on user.

- HKEY_CURRENT_CONFIG

    This key points to a branch of HKEY_LOCAL_MACHINE for the current hardware configuration.

- HKEY_DYN_DATA

    This key points to a branch of HKEY_LOCAL_MACHINE that tracks Plug and Play hardware information, including hot swappable devices.

Registry Configuration: Value Entries

The actual data tracked by the registry consists of Value Entries. A value entry has three parts:

- Data Type

    The data type of the value appears as an icon. The graphic below displays the icon used for binary data on the left and the icon used for text-based data on the right.

- Name of Value

    The descriptive name of the value entry is displayed.

- Value

    As stated earlier, values can be text-based or binary. Sample entries are shown below.

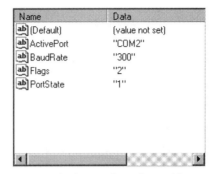

A value entry cannot be larger than about 64K.

Exporting a Registry File

A Registry file can be backed up or stored for later use by using the **Export Registry File** command. A Registry file can also be used on another computer to allow consistent settings to be used on multiple computers. You can export the entire registry or one specific level or branch of the registry to a saved file. This option may prove to be especially useful when making changes to only one branch of the registry.

To Export a Registry File, run **Registry/Export Registry File**.

Type a name for the file that will contain the exported registry information. Next, select the appropriate Export range.

All   This option will include all of the files in the registry.

Selected branch   This option will include a specific branch of the registry. The name of the branch should be specified.

NOTE: *If the branch is selected prior to opening **Registry/Export Registry File** from the menu, the branch name automatically appears in the Selected branch text box.*

Finally, click on **Save** to save the exported file.

Importing a Registry File

The **Import Registry File** command is used to bring back a previously stored Registry file or to retrieve a Registry file which exists on another computer on a network.

NOTE: *An imported file does not retrieve changed values or delete values which were added under a name that did not previously exist in the registry file. Therefore, importing is not the safest way to restore a registry file.*

To import a registry file, open **Registry/Import Registry File** from the menu to display the dialog below. You can browse to locate the registry file that you wish to import.

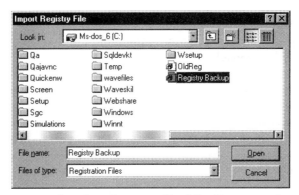

Click on **Open** to import the selected registry file. The filename and a progress bar appear.

When the operation is complete, a dialog similar to the one below is displayed. It states that the information in the selected registry file has been entered successfully into the Registry.

Editing the Registry

The registry stores all system and user information, therefore, practically everything about the operating system can be manipulated.

In most cases, it is not necessary to modify the registry directly using the Registry Editor. Administrators should use tools such as the System Policy Editor or the Device Manager to make configuration changes. Using the appropriate administrative tools is safer because these applications know how to store values properly in the registry. However, due to such things as a change in tuning parameters or the need to customize an application, you may be required to directly edit the registry.

If the need to directly edit the registry arises, keep in mind that if you make errors while changing values with Registry Editor, no warning occurs because the Registry Editor does not check for or recognize syntax or semantic errors. It is wise to test the system after each change to the registry so changes can be easily reversed should a problem occur.

There are several editing options available in the **Edit** menu of the Registry Editor. New keys can be created as either string values, binary values, or DWORD values. You can also Delete, Rename, Modify, and Find existing values and/or keys.

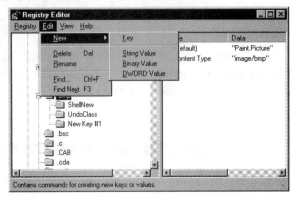

New/Key   This selection can be used to create a new key within a root key or a subkey.

New/String Value   String values allow you to store alpha and numeric characters representing a string name.

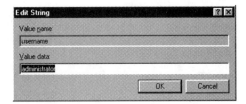

New/Binary Value

Binary values store information about hardware components.

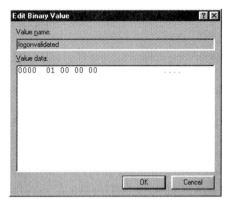

New/DWORD Value

DWORD value is a type of binary value. To modify the DWORD value entry, right-click on the selected value and run **Modify**. The following dialog will appear:

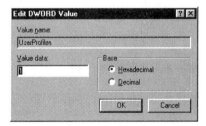

This allows the value of the represented data to be changed. These values will depend on the registry entry that is being set. If a key or value is selected, the **Edit** menu offers a new option. **Modify** allows you to modify the selected key. A dialog appropriate to the type of key will be displayed, and modifications can be made. Click on **OK** to save any changes.

The **Find** command in the **Edit** menu allows you to search the Registry for any combination of words. You can search for a key, a subkey, or a local key.

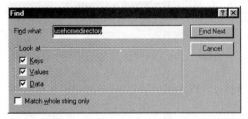

You can limit your search to look for keys, values, and/or data. To search the entire registry, select **My Computer** prior to starting the search. You may also use **Find** to identify a match only when it matches the entire string. That means partial matches will not be displayed. To find the next match, you can either:

- Run **Edit/Find** and click on **Find Next**.
- Run **Edit/Find Next**.
- Press *F3*.

The **Edit** menu also enables you to delete or rename keys. These are also available in the pop-up menu for a selected item.

Troubleshooting Registry Problems

The Registry Editor supports exporting and importing of registry files in either the editor's Windows-based interface or the real-mode version on the Windows 95 startup disk. Use the export capabilities of the Registry Editor to save the registry, in whole or in part, as a .REG file. REG files are in plain text and can be edited with any text editor.

If the registry becomes corrupted beyond repair, the real-mode REGEDIT.EXE utility can be utilized to import a REG file. The command-line syntax for using the REGEDIT utility is:

```
REGEDIT [/L:system] [/R:user] file1.reg, file1a.reg,
    file1b.reg...

REGEDIT [/L:system] [/R:user] /e file2.reg [regkey]

REGEDIT [/L:system] [/R:user] /c file3.reg
```

where:

/L:*system*   This specifies the path to SYSTEM.DAT.

/R:*user*	This specifies the path to USER.DAT.
file1.reg	This specifies one or more REG files to import into the Registry.
/e *file2.reg*	This specifies the filename to which the Registry should be exported
[*regkey*]	Through this parameter, you can select the starting Registry key from which to export a portion of the Registry. This value is optional and if no value is specified, regedit /e exports the entire Registry.
/c *file3.reg*	This specifies the REG file to use to replace the entire contents of the Registry.

It is a sensible idea to export the registry to a *.REG file and archive that file to assist in restoring the Registry if it becomes corrupt.

Registry During Startup

After a successful startup, the registry is automatically backed up by copying SYSTEM.DAT and USER.DAT to SYSTEM.DA0 and USER.DA0 respectively. If startup fails on a subsequent attempt, the DA0 files can be restored, returning you to a known good configuration.

This gives you the ability to sometimes recover from a system that will not boot due to registry errors. To recover from a boot failure, you must boot from the startup diskette that was created at installation. Change to the \WINDOWS directory. Copy the SYSTEM.DA0 file to SYSTEM.DAT. Copy the USER.DA0 file to USER.DAT.

Exercise 10-1:
Windows 95 Registry

The purpose of this exercise is to give you practice working with the Windows 95 registry and Registry Editor. You should be logged on as Student (or your primary user) at the beginning of this exercise.

You will need a formatted, blank diskette to complete this exercise.

Navigating the registry tree is similar to using Windows Explorer. Click on the "+" next to any folder to expand the folder one level. Click on a "-" at a folder to collapse the tree up to that level.

1. Open the **Start/Run** utility.

2. Type the following and press *ENTER*:

    ```
    regedit
    ```

3. Run **Registry/Export Registry File** from the menu.

4. Double-click on **My Computer** in the destination window.

5. Double-click to select the C: drive.

6. Type the following as the filename:

    ```
    TestBack
    ```

7. Under the Export Range, click to select the radio button next to **All**.

8. Click on **Save**.

9. Launch Windows Explorer and select to view the contents of drive C:. You should see a file named TestBack.reg.

10. Exit Windows Explorer.

11. In the Registry Editor, click to expand HKEY_LOCAL_MACHINE.

12. Work down through the registry tree by clicking to expand each of the following:

    ```
    System

    CurrentControlSet

    Control
    ```

13. Locate and select **TimeZoneInformation**.

14. In the details window, click on **DaylightName**.

15. Run **Edit/Modify** from the menu.

16. Overwrite the value data as the following and press *ENTER*:

    My Daylight Time

17. In the details window, click on **StandardName**.

18. Run **Edit/Modify** from the menu.

19. Overwrite the value data as the following and press *ENTER*:

    My Standard Time

20. Run **Registry/Exit** from the menu to exit Registry Editor.

21. Run **Start/Shut Down** to shut down your system.

22. Select **Restart your computer.**

23. After your system starts, log on as your primary user.

24. Launch the Control Panel and open the Date/Time utility. You should see your new time zone information listed.

25. Close the Day/Time Properties dialog and the Control Panel.

26. Using the procedures listed earlier in this exercise, launch the Registry Editor.

27. Run **Registry/Import Registry File** from the menu.

28. Browse to locate the C: drive.

29. Select TESTBACK.REG and click on **Open**.

30. After the import has finished, click on **OK** in the information dialog and then exit the Registry Editor.

31. Shut down and restart your system.

32. After your system starts, log on as your primary user.

33. Launch the **Control Panel** and open the Day/Time utility. You should see the original time zone information listed.

34. Close the Day/Time Properties dialog and the Control Panel.

SUMMARY

In this chapter, you were introduced to the features of the Registry, as well as the Registry Editor in Windows 95. This included:

- The differences between the registry and INI files
- Characteristics of the registry
- Components of the registry
- Importing and exporting registry files
- Editing and modifying registry entries
- Evaluating the differences between Root Keys and Value Entries in the Registry
- Recovering from a failed bootup due to incorrect registry entries

The next chapter discusses network components and TCP/IP implementation in Windows 95.

POST-TEST QUESTIONS

The answers to these questions are in Appendix A at the end of this manual.

1. Where is the registry stored? Which files make up the registry?

....

....

2. How can you import a registry file when the registry is damaged beyond repair?

....

....

3. Which of the registry keys contains computer-specific information pertaining to hardware devices present and software settings?

....

....

4. After a successful startup, what two files are created in order to back up the registry?

    ....

    ....

Networking Support

OBJECTIVES

At the completion of this chapter, you will be able to:

- Describe the basic features of Windows 95 networking support.

- Discuss the various different protocols available on a Windows 95 system.

- Install clients, adapters, protocols, and services.

- Identify currently installed network components.

- Configure the primary network logon.

- Install and configure TCP/IP on a Windows 95 workstation.

- Configure a subnet mask for an IP address.

- Describe the functions of DHCP, WINS, and DNS servers.

- Describe the function of the SNMP Agent.

- Use the PING and TRACERT utilities to test TCP/IP communication.

PRE-TEST QUESTIONS

The answers to these questions are in Appendix A at the end of this manual.

1. From what four network component types can you select components to install?

   ....

   ....

2. A unique computer name using the NetBIOS naming scheme has a limit of how many characters?

   ....

   ....

3. Which of the following are routable protocols: NetBEUI, NWLink, or TCP/IP?

   ....

   ....

INTRODUCTION

Network design, implementation, and support are seldom easy. There is no such thing as a *one-size-fits-all* network environment. The day of the single-vendor network, if there ever was such a time, is long past. Decisions are frequently made to accommodate the exceptions rather than being based on predetermined rules.

This chapter starts by looking at network environments in general. It discusses networking concepts and compares local and wide area network environments. From there, it proceeds to introduce the various protocols available for networking on a Windows 95 system. The chapter concludes with a focused discussion about Windows 95 networking.

NETWORK FUNDAMENTALS

This section will introduce the fundamentals of a network environment. Basic concepts and definitions are introduced. The following are topics discussed within this section:

- Network Environment
- What is a LAN?
- What is a WAN?
- Network Devices
- Networking Terms
- Picking the Right Protocol

To set up a network for your work environment, there are many aspects to consider. The key to properly setting up a network is to understand the fundamental network components and available protocol options.

Network Environment

One of the potential problems is defining what, exactly, constitutes an enterprise. In general usage, an enterprise is thought of as all of your corporate computers and support devices taken as a whole. This means that each organization's specific definition of an enterprise is going to be slightly different.

There are some general expectations which, though they may not be present in all environments, are common to many modern networks.

- Mixed network clients

    You are likely to encounter a mix of MS-DOS, Windows, Windows 95, and Windows NT clients on a network. Often, you will also find it necessary to add Macintosh clients to the mix.

- Mixed network servers

    You will seldom find a *pure* environment. It is common to have to support Windows NT Server domains on the same network as Novell NetWare, or Windows NT Servers implemented as part of a NetWare network. You may also need to support other platforms as well, including minicomputer or mainframe connectivity.

- Multiple LANs

    Usually, it is more accurate to refer to these as multiple subnetworks. As a network grows, divisions often must be imposed for performance, geographic, or security reasons.

- Multiple domains

    When supporting a Windows NT Server network environment, you may find it advantageous, or physically necessary, to break the network into multiple domains. The exact configuration will depend on a number of factors, including security requirements and, to some extent, physical system locations.

- Remote access requirements

    Physically separated networks require a means to communicate. Often, mobile employees need a way of attaching to a home network. In addition, the Internet is quickly becoming a vital part of how companies do business.

What is a LAN?

A Local Area Network (LAN) is the fundamental unit for network organization. A LAN is a group of systems in the same geographic location. In the most common usage, a network is described as a LAN if all of the systems are attached to the same network, even though the network may be divided into segments.

It is important to keep in mind that even though a LAN is considered a fundamental unit, it does not necessarily imply a simple, easy-to-manage environment. A LAN will commonly have a mix of client stations with variations in hardware, operating systems, and applications. It is not uncommon for a LAN to include multiple network operating systems, typically Novell NetWare and Microsoft NT Server. It may also include non-PC systems, such as UNIX servers.

LANs may even include what has traditionally been considered more a feature of wide area networks, remote connectivity. The most prevalent example of this is an Internet connection to allow users to access the Internet through the LAN rather than trying to support a dial-up connection for each user.

What is a WAN?

A Wide Area Network (WAN) is similar to a LAN in that it is made up of a collection of systems. It might be more accurate to describe a WAN as being composed of a collection of LANs. Typically, a WAN covers a wider geographic area than a LAN and requires some type of connectivity between its component LANs.

Management problems encountered in a LAN environment are multiplied due to scale. In addition, WANs have their own particular concerns. Many of the planning and design concerns will relate to connectivity, not only in how the systems connect, but the amount of traffic that can be carried across the connection.

Network Devices

You are likely to encounter a wide variety of devices in a network environment, especially in a WAN environment. Some of the most common you are likely to see include:

- Servers

    Servers provide resources to the network and typically act as a central point for security and access management. File and print servers are the most common type, but you are also likely to see specialized application servers.

- Client workstations

    By far, PC-based clients are the most common network clients, though it is not unusual to encounter at least some Macintosh systems. Even when you have a PC-based network, you are going to see variations in system hardware and client operating systems.

- Cable plants

    The cable plant refers to the media over which the systems communicate. Along with the cabling, you will have to concern yourself with network adapters, connection hardware, and in many implementations, central hubs tying the systems together.

- Connectivity devices

    In a WAN, as well as in many LANs, you are going to be supporting connectivity devices. Routers and bridges are common. In many cases, so are modems and other remote connectivity devices.

This is far from a complete list of what you will encounter in a network, but should give you an idea of the complex environment in which you will be working.

Networking Terms

To grasp the concept of networking, there are a few terms that you will need to understand. These terms further define the communication process between machines on a network.

Packet

Information being sent across the network is referred to as a packet. A message will often contain several packets, which must be delivered in order with the data intact. Upper-level protocols, such as TCP and UDP, are used to help ensure proper delivery and sequencing.

Protocol

A protocol is a set of rules defining how two processes communicate. The TCP/IP suite contains multiple protocols, each with its own packet type. The TCP/IP suite of protocols will be discussed later in this chapter.

Host

Also referred to as an end node, the term host refers to the devices configured as part of the network. It acts as the destination for an IP packet. Hosts can include mainframes, minicomputers, workstations, file servers, and even intelligent peripheral devices such as printers.

Address

Each node must have a unique address to communicate via TCP/IP. The address must follow the IP address format. The four-octet IP address identifies the host and the network on which that host resides. Each host will also have a six-byte MAC (Media Access Control) address, which is encoded on the network adapter. You will learn how to configure an IP address later in this chapter.

Names

Each host will also have a unique name. A common method for managing names is Domain Name System (DNS). DNS servers map IP addresses to DNS names. Microsoft networks also use a NetBIOS-based naming convention, with support provided through a name file or dynamically through the Windows Internet Naming Service (WINS). DNS servers and WINS servers are used for resolving host names and NetBIOS names respectively when the TCP/IP protocol is used. Using these servers for name resolution will be discussed later in the chapter.

Routers

Routers connect networks together, using the network portion of the IP address to identify the appropriate subnet. Once the subnet is located by passing the packet to a router directly connected to the network, the packet is delivered using the host address.

As you continue through this chapter, you will begin to see how these terms relate to networking in the Windows 95 environment. These concepts will become even more important later in the manual when implementing Windows 95 clients in a Windows NT and Novell NetWare environment are discussed.

Picking the Right Protocol

The best protocol selection for your networking environment will depend on your routing requirements, existing protocols, and connectivity requirements. It is important to remember that you aren't limited to picking one best protocol. Windows 95 is able to bind multiple protocols to the same network adapter. Therefore, it is possible to have multiple protocols installed on a Windows 95 computer.

NetBEUI

NetBEUI was originally introduced by IBM in 1985. It is written to the NetBIOS interface. It was designed to be an efficient protocol, requiring minimal overhead. If you do not need NetBEUI, it can be removed to save on system resources. You will see how to remove a network component a little later in this chapter.

NetBEUI is optimized for use on small LANs because it is small and fast. There is minimal configuration or management overhead. The biggest disadvantage to NetBEUI is that it is not a routable protocol, so it does not do well in a Wide Area Network (WAN) environment. It also cannot be used to communicate with NetWare or UNIX computers.

Use NetBEUI:

- On small LANs with no routing requirements.

- In environments where NetBEUI is already in use, such as Microsoft LAN Manager.

NWLink

NWLink provides Windows NT connectivity with Novell NetWare networks using the IPX/SPX-compatible transport protocol . NWLink lets your system talk with NetWare servers, other systems running NWLink, and other workstations running IPX/SPX. NWLink also supports the transfer of Novell NetBIOS communications packets across IPX/SPX.

If you do not need NWLink, it can be removed to save on system resources. NWLink is a fully routable protocol.

Use NWLink:

- When you have routing requirements.

- In environments where IPX/SPX is already in use, such as an existing Novell NetWare network.

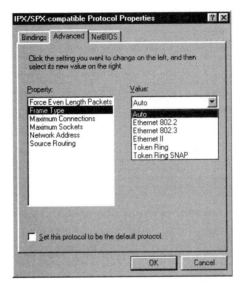

If you are trying to connect to a NetWare network and you receive a message stating that the servers cannot be found, you may need to change the Frame Type for the IPX/SPX protocol. By default, Windows attempts to detect the frame type automatically. However, if it does not accurately detect the server's frame type, you can manually set it on the **Advanced** tab of the IPX/SPX-compatible transport protocol properties sheet of the Network utility.

By default, the Windows 95 client should automatically detect the frame type for the IPX/SPX-compatible transport protocol to be used depending on the network. However, if a user complains of receiving either the "File server not found" or "A network server could not be found" error, you may need to change the frame type for the protocol manually.

If you are wanting to use the IPX/SPX protocol for a NetWare server 3.x or older, you must use the Ethernet 802.3 frame type. With NetWare 4.x, they have changed the standard frame type to Ethernet 802.2.

TCP/IP

TCP/IP is a term used in the industry to refer to the Internet family of protocols. It is the default protocol for UNIX and has become a de facto standard for wide area networking. It is fully routable and is available on most system platforms. It provides utilities to facilitate communications and information sharing between dissimilar hardware platforms. Interest in the Internet and in setting up corporate intranets has helped to fuel TCP/IP's growth.

Windows NT provides tools that help to make TCP/IP an excellent platform for client/server applications. In addition, a wide variety of management utilities and tools are available for supporting, testing, and troubleshooting TCP/IP networks.

Use TCP/IP:

- When you have significant routing requirements.
- When UNIX connectivity is required.
- If you wish to employ TCP/IP utilities in network management.
- In environments where TCP/IP is already in use.
- In Internet/intranet environments.

Microsoft DLC

The Microsoft Data Link Control (DLC) protocol has two primary functions in a Windows 95 environment. These are:

- Mainframe connectivity

    Some mainframe computers run DLC. If you need to communicate with one of these computers, you will need to install DLC.

- Directly connected printers

    Printers that are connected directly to the network rather than to a port on a computer communicate over DLC. An example is the HP Jetdirect printer.

When printing to a printer that is connected directly to the network, only the print server must be running Microsoft DLC. It is not necessary to install DLC on print server clients. Clients send the document to the Windows 95 computer that is acting as a print server. That computer uses DLC to communicate with the printer.

NETWORKING WINDOWS 95

This section will discuss network configuration. Configuration fundamentals are discussed first. The discussion will then move to the components necessary for systems within a network to communicate. The following topics are discussed within this section:

- Network Overview
- Clients
- Adapters
- Protocols
- Services
- Network Configuration
- Workstation Identification

As discussed earlier in the course, it is important to understand the process by which systems communicate across a network. The types of security available for a Windows 95 system in various networking environments are discussed later in the course.

Network Overview

Windows 95 incorporates network support. It includes everything you need to connect to a wide range of network configurations and even supports attaching as a remote client across standard telephone lines through the use of Dial-Up Networking. Dial-Up Networking connections will be covered later in the course.

Windows 95 supports a wide variety of network options. These include:

- Clients

    Windows 95 supports the most common network operating systems.

- Adapters

    The drivers for many popular network adapters are shipped with Windows 95, including a driver for dial-up access.

- Protocols

    Windows 95 supports common network protocols, including many vendor-specific protocol implementations.

- Services

    A number of specialized services are supported, including file and printer sharing for both NetWare and Microsoft networks.

Windows 95 Setup automatically detects most network adapters and installs network client support. For example, if Setup detects NetWare components, the 32-bit protected-mode Microsoft Client for NetWare Networks is installed. The components installed depend on your system configuration when you launch Setup. You can also modify the network components that are installed through the Network utility in the Control Panel.

Clients

Selecting a network client installs software to enable the workstation to utilize the network. Both the new 32-bit protected-mode clients and older real-mode clients are supported.

Network clients included with Windows 95 include:

- Banyan VINES DOS/Windows 3.1
- FTP Software NFS Client (InterDrive 95)

- Microsoft's Client for Microsoft Networks

- Microsoft's Client for NetWare Networks

- Novell NetWare Workstation Shell 3.x (NETX)

- Novell NetWare Workstation Shell 4.0 and above (VLM)

- SunSoft PC-NFS (5.0)

Windows 95 provides two protected-mode clients: Microsoft's Client for NetWare Networks and Client for Microsoft Networks. These clients use only 32-bit, protected-mode support files, such as protocols and adapter drivers. An advantage of using these clients is that they use no conventional memory.

> *NOTE: Only one real-mode client can be installed at any time. An unlimited number of protected-mode clients may be used concurrently.*

Adapters

The network adapter connects the computer to the cable plant. Windows 95 features new 32-bit drivers for network adapters that allow automatic binding of adapters to protocols. Windows 95 also furnishes support for Network Device Interface Specification (NDIS) 2.x and 3.1 adapter and protocol drivers.

The NDIS 3.1 specification provides support for many types of network media, such as Ethernet, Token Ring, and ArcNet. NDIS 3.1 drivers operate in 32-bit protected mode. Adapters that utilize the NDIS 3.1-compliant adapter drivers can be removed or added dynamically through Plug and Play. An example of this would be PCMCIA network adapters. Adapters using NDIS 2.x drivers use conventional memory due to the fact that NDIS 2.x drivers load in real mode. ODI drivers continue to be supported by Windows 95. These drivers are 16-bit and load in real mode.

Recalling our discussion of the Device Manager earlier in the course, each network adapter has resource settings that can be manipulated. These settings include:

- I/O Address Range

- IRQ setting
- Memory Address

To access advanced properties for network adapters, select the **Advanced** tab while viewing the adapter's properties sheet in the Network control panel. Advanced values vary from adapter to adapter. They could include:

- Transceiver Type
- Network Address
- Ring Speed
- I/O Port Base Address

Protocols

A protocol is a set of strict rules that governs the exchange of information between networked computers. Computers that wish to communicate across a network must use identical protocols.

Protocols included with Windows 95 include:

- Banyan VINES Ethernet Protocol
- Banyan VINES Token Ring Protocol
- DEC PATHWORKS 4.1 Ethernet
- DEC PATHWORKS 4.1 Token Ring
- DEC PATHWORKS 5.0 and above Ethernet
- DEC PATHWORKS 5.0 and above Ethernet (ODI)
- DEC PATHWORKS 5.0 and above Token Ring
- IBM DLC Protocol
- Microsoft IPX/SPX-compatible Transport Protocol
- Microsoft DLC
- Microsoft NetBEUI
- Microsoft TCP/IP
- Novell IPX ODI Protocol
- SunSoft PC-NFS Protocol

The Microsoft NetBEUI, TCP/IP, and IPX/SPX-compatible protocols are 32-bit, protected-mode virtual device drivers. Advantages of these protocols include the fact that their protocol stacks can be shared by multiple installed network clients and that they do not load in conventional memory.

Services

Windows 95 can provide the following services:

- File and Printer Sharing

    Windows 95 includes File and Printer Sharing for Microsoft networks and File and Printer Sharing for NetWare networks. A computer using the protected-mode Microsoft Client for NetWare or Client for Microsoft Networks can be configured as a file or print server on the network through the use of these services.

- Automated backup services

    You can install support for automated system backup with the Arcadia Software Backup Exec Agent or the Cheyenne Software ARCserve Agent.

- Direct-connect printer administration

    You can install Hewlett-Packard JetAdmin print server administration support.

- Microsoft Remote Registry services

    You can install support for remote administration. This service is required if you want to edit the registry from a remote computer either through the Registry editor or through the System Policy editor.

To protect shared resources on a NetWare network, Windows 95 supports the use of user-level security. Workstations on a peer-to-peer Microsoft network protect their resources with share-level security. Windows NT network clients can utilize either user-level or share-level security. Discussion of user-level versus share-level security follows later in this course.

Network Configuration

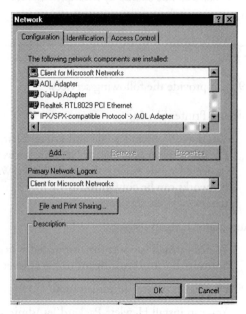

The Network control panel allows you to install, manage, and remove network components. The **Configuration** tab allows you to:

- Add client support, adapters, protocols, or services.
- Select the primary network logon.
- Enable or disable file and printer sharing.

The **Configuration** tab is displayed above. The additional tabs displayed at the top of the dialog let you enter the identification parameters for your workstation and select an access control method for resources you share to the network. The **Access Control** properties sheet will be discussed later in the course.

After making changes, you will be prompted for any necessary source files, either Windows 95 installation files or vendor-provided files. You must shut down and restart your system before most changes take effect.

Installing Network Components

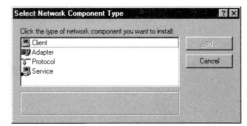

Click on **Add** from the Network dialog to display the Select Network Component Type dialog. Select the type of component you wish to install and click on **Add** to display your available selections.

Available selections are somewhat determined by the network driver and shell files already installed on your machine when you install Windows 95. Microsoft components are always available.

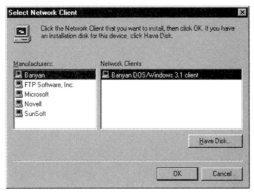

Select the manufacturer from the list on the left to view the available network clients, adapters, protocols, and services. You may see other manufacturers listed than those shown in the above graphic depending on the client software that was installed on your system when you ran Windows 95 Setup.

Removing a Network Component

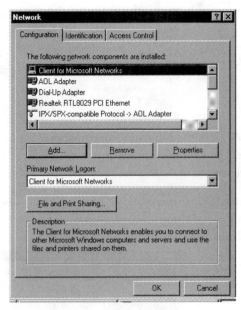

To remove a network component, select the component from the Network dialog. Then click on **Remove**. You will need to restart your computer to allow changes to take effect.

Workstation Identification

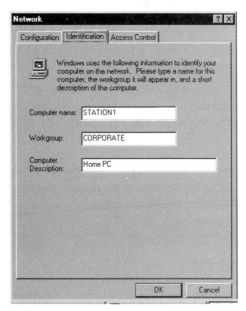

The **Identification** tab lets you define your system on the network using a unique computer name. This computer name must be unique to the network.

The computer name you assign to your workstation on the **Identification** tab of the Network property page is referred to as the NetBIOS name. NetBIOS (Network Basic Input/Output System) is actually an application interface, rather than a protocol. NetBIOS:

- Allows applications to communicate with NetBIOS-compliant protocols

    Originally, this was limited to communication over NetBEUI, but NetBIOS applications can be supported over TCP/IP and IPX.

- Manages communication sessions between computers

    This is the session-level management required for a 2-way interchange between computers.

- Tracks computers by computer name

    Under NetBIOS, each system has a unique computer name (up to 15 characters) that identifies it to NetBIOS sessions.

If you give a computer a name that is already assigned to another computer on the network and restart the computer, you will receive an error 38. You will need to change the computer's name on the **Identification** tab of the Network utility and restart the computer.

The Workgroup name identifies the workgroup, if any, to which your system belongs. The Computer Description is simply a text string used to describe your system, defaulting to your name as it was entered during Setup.

Exercise 11-1:
Using the Network Utility

This exercise demonstrates installing network components and configuring identification information for a computer workstation.

You should record the following pieces of information: current installed network protocols and workstation information.

Once you have done so, remove all protocols and restart your computer.

1. Run **Start/Settings/Control Panel**.
2. Double-click on the Network utility.
3. Click on **Add**.
4. Select **Protocol** and click on **Add**.
5. Select **Microsoft** from the list of manufacturers and **NetBEUI** from the list of network protocols.
6. Click on **OK**.
7. Click on the **Identification** tab.
8. Change the computer name to STUDENT.
9. Change the workgroup to CLASS.
10. Enter the description as SAMPLE.

11.   Click on **OK**.

12.   Click on **Yes** to restart your computer.

TCP/IP AND WINDOWS 95

This section discusses the fundamentals of TCP/IP as well as implementation of the protocol on a Windows 95 system. TCP/IP Properties are also defined along with a description of each properties sheet's function. The following topics are discussed within this section:

- TCP/IP Suite

- TCP/IP at the Desktop

- TCP/IP Installation

- TCP/IP Configuration

As the Internet and corporate intranets continue to grow in importance, it will be necessary for you to understand TCP/IP. TCP/IP configuration is necessary for a system to access the Internet, or for any system to operate on a TCP/IP-based network.

TCP/IP Suite

All TCP/IP protocols are defined through Requests For Comment (RFCs). The specification documents are part of the public domain. They may be acquired and reproduced free of charge.

It may be helpful to introduce a few terms and concepts relating to the protocol. Core protocols, utilities, and services associated with the TCP/IP suite include:

- IP (Internet Protocol)

    IP provides connectionless delivery between computer systems. Since this is a connectionless protocol, there is no guarantee of proper sequencing or even arrival at the destination. Higher-level protocols are required to ensure data integrity and proper sequencing.

- TCP (Transmission Control Protocol)

    TCP provides acknowledged, connection-oriented communications. It includes fields for packet sequencing and acknowledgment as well as source and destination socket identifiers to allow communications with higher-level protocols. Through these, TCP provides guaranteed delivery, proper sequencing, and data integrity checks. Should errors occur during transmission, TCP is responsible for retransmitting the data.

- ICMP (Internet Control Message Protocol)

    ICMP is used to control and manage information transmitted using TCP/IP. It allows nodes to share status and error information. This information can be passed to higher-level protocols, informing transmitting stations of unreachable hosts and providing insight into the detection and resolution of transmission problems. ICMP also helps to reroute messages when a route is busy or has failed.

- ARP/RARP (Address Resolution Protocol/Reverse Address Resolution Protocol)

    ARP and RARP are maintenance protocols. They are used on Local Area Networks to enable hosts to translate IP addresses to the low-level MAC addresses which are needed to communicate at the Data Link level.

    ARP is used to request a station's MAC address when only its IP address is known. Once obtained, this information is stored in the requesting system's ARP cache for later use. Since the information can be broadcast, it can also be used to update other systems. RARP is used when the MAC address is known, but not the IP address. Updated information, when received, is also cached.

- UDP (User Datagram Protocol)

    UDP is designed for connectionless, unacknowledged communications. Using IP as its underlying protocol carrier, UDP adds information about the source and destination socket identifiers. UDP also supports optional checksums for verifying header and data integrity.

- TELNET

    TELNET may be more accurately described as a connectivity utility. It is a simple remote terminal emulation application, allowing one host to connect to and run a session on another. Variants have been implemented to handle different terminal data streams. For example, there are 3270 and 5250 variants for communications with IBM mainframe and minicomputers. TELNET uses TCP for acknowledged communications.

- FTP (File Transfer Protocol)

  FTP supports file transport between dissimilar systems. TELNET is used for initial user authentication and interactive use is supported. Assuming sufficient rights, directory searches and file operations are supported, as well as file format and character conversion.

- SMTP (Simple Mail Transfer Protocol)

  SMTP provides a mechanism for the exchange of mail information between systems. It is not concerned with the mail format, just the means by which it is transferred. SMTP is the most widely used service on the Internet.

- SNMP (Simple Network Management Protocol)

  SNMP uses UDP to send control and management information between TCP/IP hosts. SNMP can collect management statistics and trap error events from a wide selection of devices on a TCP/IP network. An SNMP management station gives you the capabilities of remote device control and parameter management.

- DNS (Domain Name System)

  Through DNS, a common naming convention is provided throughout the Internet. It is implemented as a distributed database supporting a hierarchical naming system. DNS requires a static name to IP address mapping.

- NFS (Network File Services)

  NFS is the industry standard for UNIX environment distributed file systems. It provides a common, transparent environment in which users can share files, regardless of their hardware platform.

TCP/IP at the Desktop

TCP/IP is accepted as the standard for internetwork communications. Its popularity at the desktop continues to grow. However, TCP/IP was never designed for use with PCs. In fact, PCs didn't exist when TCP/IP was developed. This has led to some potential problems.

- Population size

    TCP/IP was designed for use with a limited population of mainframes and minicomputers. The large number of PCs in modern networks leads to problems in allocation of unique IP addresses and may eventually create an address shortage.

- Portability

    PCs, by design, are portable. They can move easily between different physical locations. This means that they can be moved between logical subnets. Doing so requires reconfiguration of IP addresses or the need for dynamic address management.

- End users

    The average PC user lacks the sophistication required to fully understand IP address and subnetting concerns. This can sometimes lead to errors in address and configuration parameters.

Although they are beyond the scope of this course, some manufacturers, including Microsoft, have developed products and procedures to help work around these problems and simplify TCP/IP management.

TCP/IP Installation

Follow these steps to install TCP/IP on your Windows 95 computer:

- Launch the Network control panel.
- Click on **Add**.
- When the Select Network Component Type dialog appears, select **Protocol** and click on **Add**.
- When the Select Network Protocol dialog appears, select **Microsoft** from the Manufacturers list and **TCP/IP** from the Network Protocols list.
- Click on **OK**.
- Click on **OK** to close the Network utility.

- If prompted, supply the path to the Windows 95 installation files.

- When prompted to restart the computer, click on **Yes**.

TCP/IP Configuration

To configure TCP/IP, launch the Network utility and select TCP/IP. Click on **Properties** to display the properties dialog for this protocol. You can also double-click on **TCP/IP** from the Network dialog to display the same properties dialog. The TCP/IP Properties dialog has several properties sheets. Let's look at each of them.

IP Address

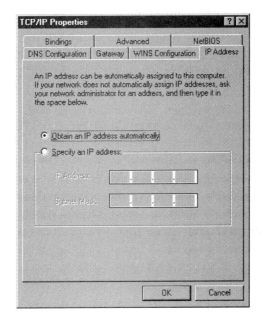

The **IP Address** tab allows you to either specify an IP address and subnet mask for the computer, or have the computer obtain the information automatically using a DHCP (Dynamic Host Configuration Protocol) server. Both of these options will be discussed in detail a little later in the chapter.

What Is an IP Address?

In order to use the TCP/IP protocol, each computer or node must provide an IP address to the network. An IP address consists of a four-octet address, such as 195.143.67.2. You must also provide a subnet mask that is used to identify the network and host portions of the address.

Later in the course, we will be discussing connections to the Internet. When connecting to an Internet Service Provider, your system obtains an IP address that allows it to connect to the Internet.

Another important fact for IP addressing is that two computers cannot have the same IP address. If they do, then it can cause the systems to hang. We will be discussing how DHCP servers help to eliminate duplicate IP addresses by automatically configuring TCP/IP on client machines. We will discuss the configuration of an IP address later in this chapter.

DHCP Configuration

DHCP servers can be used to assign an IP address to a DHCP client. The IP address assigned is available for use for a certain period of time. The next time a user logs on to the system, a new IP address is obtained for the system. If you plan to use a DHCP server to assign IP addresses for your client machines, you must also have a WINS server running for name resolution.

WINS Configuration

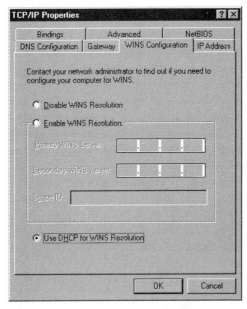

Windows Internet Naming Service, or WINS is an automated way of supporting NetBIOS name resolution. Through the **WINS Configuration** tab, you can choose to:

- Disable WINS Resolution

    Choose this option if WINS resolution is not available.

- Enable WINS Resolution

    Choose this option if a WINS server is available. If you enable WINS resolution, you must also provide the IP address of the primary WINS server. You can also specify a secondary WINS server if available.

- Use DHCP for WINS Resolution

    Choose this option if a DHCP server is available and configured to provide information about WINS servers.

Gateway

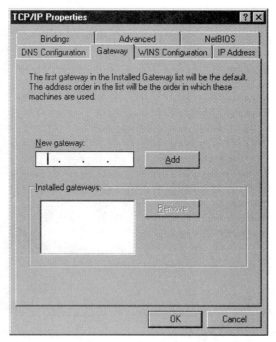

The **Gateway** tab is used to specify the default gateway. The default gateway is the IP Address that is used as a doorway to a different subnet. For example, if you are connected to the Internet and to a LAN that uses TCP/IP, the default gateway would be the IP Address through which you access the Internet. If you are connected to a LAN with multiple subnets, the default gateway would be the router's IP Address that is in the same subnet as your computer.

Type the IP address of the default gateway in the New gateway field and click on **Add**. If more than one default gateway is listed, they will be used in the order in which they appear in the Installed gateways field. To remove an installed gateway, select the gateway IP address and click on **Remove**.

> *NOTE:*   *If your computer is part of a network with only one subnet and you do not need to connect to any computer outside that subnet, including the Internet, you will not need to specify a default gateway.*

NetBIOS

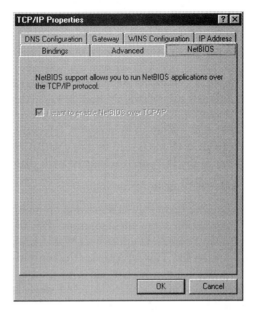

All NetBIOS activity is based on NetBIOS names. Each network device supporting NetBIOS communications must have a unique NetBIOS name, up to 15 characters long.

NetBIOS over TCP/IP is the network component that performs computer name to IP address mapping name resolution.

Name Resolution Methods

There are four methods for name resolution:

- B-Node

    A computer using B-node name resolution creates broadcasts to register the computer name as well as name resolution. If you do not configure the IP address to forward the name registration broadcasts, computers using a different subnet will not be able to see this computer. B-node name resolution is not recommended for use on large networks. When your network includes a Windows NT Server, the workstation will check the LMHOSTS file first to find the NetBIOS name. If it finds one, then it will return the IP address associated with that NetBIOS name.

- P-Node (or Point to Point Node)

    This method of name resolution does not use broadcasts for name registration and name resolution. P-node uses a NetBIOS Name Server (NBNS) which is similar to a WINS server to register all computer systems on startup. This server maps the computer name to the IP address so that no duplicate names are registered on the network. There is only one drawback to using P-node. If the server is not accessible, name resolution will be unavailable for systems.

- M-Node (or Mixed Node)

    M-node uses both B-node and P-node for name resolution. It uses B-node first to create broadcasts for name registration and name resolution. It also has the ability to use the NBNS server for name resolution. However, if P-node is unavailable, name resolution can still occur.

- H-node (or Hybrid node)

    H-node combines the use of B-node and P-node just like M-node names resolution. However, H-node uses B-node name resolution only if P-node fails.

DNS Configuration

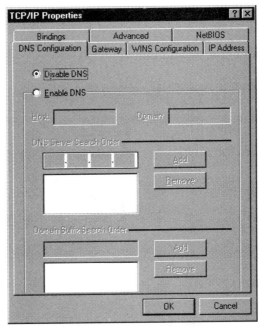

On the **DNS Configuration** tab, you can either disable or enable DNS. If you choose to enable DNS you must also provide the following information:

- Host

    This is the name that is used to identify your computer on the network.

- Domain

    This is the name of your DNS domain.

- DNS Server Search Order

    This field is used to specify the IP address of the DNS server that will be used. If more than one IP address is provided, they will be used in the order in which they appear until the name is resolved.

• Domain Suffix Search Order

   When DNS performs name resolution, it first appends the local domain name to the host name. If the host is not located, it will then append the domains listed in the Domain Suffix Search Order field.

Advanced

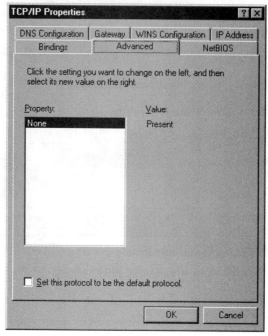

The **Advanced** tab allows you to change the value of a particular property. It also enables you to set the current protocol, in this case TCP/IP, as the default protocol when more than one protocol is installed.

Bindings

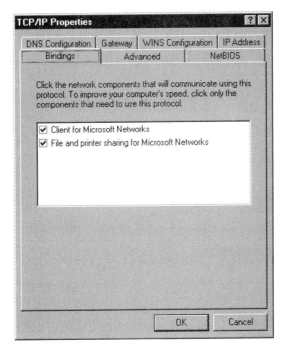

The **Bindings** tab allows you to place a checkmark next to the components that will utilize the TCP/IP protocol. Clear the checkmark next to a component if you do not want it to use TCP/IP.

CONFIGURING A TCP/IP ADDRESS

This section discusses the various issues for configuring an IP address. You will learn about the classes available for TCP/IP addressing as well as the limitations for each class. The following topics are discussed within this section:

- IP Address Fundamentals
- IP Address Planning

- IP Address Coordination
- Organizing Addresses
- IP Address Classes
- Class A Network
- Class B Network
- Class C Network
- Special Addressing

There are many factors and rules you must consider prior to selecting an IP address. It is very important to understand the rules for configuring an IP address. This knowledge will enable you to better understand how to configure a subnet mask. Subnetting is covered next in this chapter.

IP Address Fundamentals

Let's look at some basic concepts and terminology related to the TCP/IP protocol.

Each host, or computer, is assigned a unique IP address for each network connection or installed network adapter. The IP address is used to identify a packet's source and destination hosts.

An IP address is a 32-bit address, written as four octets (bytes) separated by periods. For example:

```
195.143.67.2
```

This way of representing an IP address is also known as dotted decimal notation. Each address will also have an associated subnet mask, dividing the address into its network prefix and host suffix. For example, you might have the following defined as a subnet mask:

```
255.255.255.0
```

The subnet mask is used to identify the network and host portions of the address.

Network	Host

The network portion identifies where the host is located, and the host portion identifies the device connected to that network. Using the previous example of 195.143.67.2 with a subnet mask of 255.255.255.0, the first three octets (195.143.67) would represent the network portion of the address and the last octet (2) would represent the host portion.

IP Address Planning

One of the most challenging jobs with any new TCP/IP-based network is address definition and management. Planning is a vital part of the process. This includes:

- Determining network address requirements.

    You must determine the maximum number of networks and the maximum number of hosts per network you must support. Leave room for growth, both planned and unplanned expansion. Be sure to include router interfaces, printers, and all other managed network equipment in your count.

- Determining your class address(es).

    If connecting directly to the Internet, you must apply for an appropriate range of addresses. If not, you can invent an address range to use, keeping in mind the future possibility of Internet connection.

- Define your subnet mask.

    Define a subnet mask that meets your addressing requirements. It is possible to have different-sized subnet masks on your network, but this is not suggested. It can lead to confusion and make the management process more difficult.

- Determine the valid IP address ranges on each subnet.

    These are the addresses that can be assigned to the hosts. Review your addresses carefully to ensure you have not included any invalid addresses.

The details of IP address planning and management are beyond the scope of this course. They are covered in *Microsoft Implementations of TCP/IP on Windows NT 4.0.*

IP Address For Internet Connections

Address assignments on the Internet must be carefully coordinated. With millions of hosts operating on thousands of networks, the potential for duplicate addresses is significant. If you are connected to the Internet, your network address will be assigned to you through the Internet Network Information Center, or InterNIC. An assigned address is only required if your network is connecting to the Internet.

To get your own address, contact InterNIC at:

Internet Network Information Center

c/o Network Solutions, Inc.

505 Huntmar Park Drive

Herndon, Virginia 22070

(703) 742-4777

hostmaster@internic.net

An organization is assigned a network address. The organization can further divide this into its own subnets and assign the host addresses.

Rather than going to InterNIC, it is more likely that an organization will work through a local provider for address assignment. The organization will then subdivide the address, if necessary, and assign host addresses. There are five classes, or levels, of IP addresses defined. We will discuss these briefly.

Organizing Addresses

Let's take a look at some theoretical limits. Keep in mind, these are theoretical maximums only. In practical applications, the values are significantly reduced.

If all the available bits in an address were all used for host addresses, 32 address bits would support approximately 4 billion hosts.

```
hhhhhhhh.hhhhhhhh.hhhhhhhh.hhhhhhhh
```

The problem is, all of the systems would be on a single network. This would result in a situation not unlike 4 billion people all trying to talk at the same time.

As already mentioned, TCP/IP gets around this through subnetting. If the first octet were given to network addresses, you could, in theory, support 256 networks and about 16 million hosts on each.

nnnnnnnn.hhhhhhh.hhhhhhhh.hhhhhhh

This would result in some obvious problems. One, you still have a very limited number of networks, and you still have a very large number of hosts on each network.

This can be taken down further by dedicating two octets to the network address and two octets to the host address. You could then support 65,536 networks with 65,536 hosts on each.

nnnnnnnn.nnnnnnnn.hhhhhhhh.hhhhhhhh

Large organizations would likely find this a more appropriate solution, but for most businesses, this is far more host addresses than required.

Taking the process one more step, the first three octets could be dedicated to the network address.

nnnnnnnn.nnnnnnnn.nnnnnnnn.hhhhhhhh

Potentially, this would support up to 16 million networks with 256 hosts on each. Remember that these are theoretical maximums. Real-world values are smaller.

Obviously, no one solution meets every organization's needs. IP addresses have been set up to support different levels of addressing called address classes.

IP Address Classes

Five address classes are supported, classified as A through E. Only the first three are ever assigned to the general user community: Classes A, B, and C. Class D addresses are reserved for multicasting, and Class E addresses are reserved for experimental purposes. A value of 127 in the first octet is reserved for loopback testing.

Class	Opening Bits	Default Subnets Mask	Network Range	# of Networks	# of Hosts per Network
A	0	255.0.0.0	1-126	126	16,777,214
B	10	255.255.0.0	128.0-191.255	16,384	65,534
C	110	255.255.255.0	192.0.0-223.255.255	2,097,152	254
D	1110	N/A	224-239	N/A	N/A

Your subnet mask is restricted by your choice of network ID. With a Class A network, your subnet mask must be at least 8 bits long. A Class B subnet mask must be at least 16 bits long, and for a Class C address, at least 24 bits.

All Class A addresses are already allocated, and Class B addresses are difficult to obtain. New connections to the Internet are assigned Class C addresses. If this does not meet an organization's needs, multiple Class C addresses are assigned.

Even if you are not planning to connect to the Internet, you must select an IP address from the appropriate class to provide the host address range needed. You should plan wisely should the need to connect to the Internet arise at a later date. A Class B address is flexible, but conversion to multiple Class C addresses at a later date will most likely be difficult.

Class A Networks

In a Class A network, the first octet defines the network portion of the address. The last three octets are used for subnet masking and host addresses.

In the first octet, the first, and most significant, bit must be set to 0. Only the seven least significant bits are used for addressing, and may be set to either 0 or 1. This defines 128 Class A networks with network addresses ranging from 0 to 127. Out of these, only 126 are useable. Addresses 0 and 127 are reserved.

A default subnet mask of 255.0.0.0 is assigned for a Class A network. This means that you may not change the value of any number positioned in the first octet. The octet is masked since this number cannot be changed once assigned.

Class A networks support up to 16,777,214 (2^{24}-2) hosts. The values 0 and 255 cannot be used as address values. 0 means "this network" and 255 means "broadcast to all nodes."

Class B Networks

In a Class B network, the first two octets are used for the network address. The last two octets are used for subnetting and host addresses.

The most significant bit of the first octet must be set to 1. The second most significant bit must be set to 0. The next 14 bits are used for addressing purposes. This gives us 16,384 Class B networks, ranging from 128.0 to 191.255.

A default subnet mask of 255.255.0.0 is assigned for a Class B network. This means that you may not change the value of any number positioned in the first two octets.

Class B networks support 65,534 (2^{16}-2) hosts. The values of all 0s or all 1s cannot be used as address values. All 0s means "this network" and all 1s means "broadcast to all nodes."

A Class B address is often used when setting up a moderate to large-sized network. Since Class B addresses have all been assigned, you can do this as long as you aren't connecting to the Internet, or are connecting through a firewall or some other means of isolating your network.

Class C Networks

In a Class C network, the first three octets are used for the network address. The last octet is used for subnetting and host addresses.

The first two bits of the first octet must be set to 1, and the following bit set to 0. The following five bits are used for addressing purposes in the first octet, plus the following 16 bits from the next two octets, providing 21 bits for the network address. This provides 2,097,152 Class C networks, ranging from 192.0.0 to 223.255.255.0.

A default subnet mask of 255.255.255.0 is assigned for a Class C network. This means that you may not change the value of any number positioned in the first three octets.

Class C networks support 254 (2^8-2) hosts. The values 0 and 255 cannot be used as address values in the last octet. 0 means "this network" and 255 means "broadcast to all nodes."

Special Addressing

There are several special addresses that are useful when troubleshooting a TCP/IP connection. These conventions are documented and used on the Internet as they are part of the Internet Protocol.

This Host	All Zeros	
Host on this Net	All Zeros	Host ID
Local Broadcast	All Ones	
Directed Broadcast	Network ID	All Ones
Loopback	127 Anything	

Since these addresses are defined as having a special use, they are not available as host addresses. Other invalid addresses include:

- Inappropriate subnet mask
- Class D address
- Class E address
- Duplicate address
- Two systems, separated by a router, with the same network address
- Two systems on the same physical network with different network addresses

A valid address will be unique, have a network address falling in the defined class range, and have an appropriate subnet mask.

CONFIGURING A SUBNET MASK

The following section is going to demonstrate how to configure a subnet mask for a given IP address. The following are topics discussed within this section:

- Subnetting Fundamentals

- Why Subnet?

- Defining Subnets

- Default Gateways

- Private Internets

Read through all the examples to better understand the process of selecting a subnet mask. If you understand the concept of the different classes of IP addresses, subnet masks should be easy to configure.

Subnetting Fundamentals

Let's review a little about addressing and network configurations.

- Each network must have its own network address.

- Networks are linked by routers.

- The subnet mask identifies the network and host addresses.

- An assigned address class, using the default subnet mask, provides a single network address.

If you were limited to the subnet mask definitions provided with the address classes, you would have to place all of your hosts on a single network. While you may do this with some Class C configurations, it is very unlikely with Class A or B. Realistically, many organizations find it necessary to subdivide a Class C license into two or more subnets.

You can use the subnet mask to identify your own network addresses within the class address you have been assigned. This is done by adding additional bits to the default subnet, which are then used to identify the physical subnet.

Why Subnet?

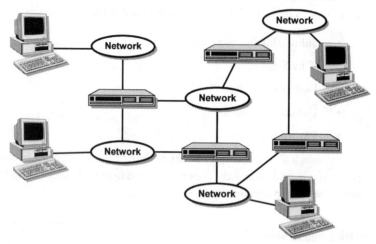

Why is it necessary to define additional subnets on an internetwork? Through proper use of subnets, you can improve network efficiency and better design your internetwork to meet your particular requirements. A primary reason for subnetting is to improve performance by not overloading available bandwidth. Without separate networks, each transmission is broadcast across the internetwork, waiting for the destination system to respond. As the network grows, traffic increases until it exceeds the available bandwidth. Dividing a network into subnets provides the following advantages:

- Keep local traffic local.

    By setting up subnets and keeping systems that need to share information together, you can cut the overall traffic levels on the network.

- Accurately locate remote hosts.

    In a well-organized network it is much easier to set up and manage routers.

- Make the best use of assigned addresses.

    You can organize the network to best meet your organizational requirements.

Any time you want to communicate with a remote host in an internetwork environment, you need three pieces of information:

- IP Address

    This uniquely identifies the host.

- Subnet mask

    This locates the network on which the host is located.

- Default gateway

    This is the path to be used if one is not defined for the host.

Only the IP address and subnet mask are needed when locating a local host.

Default Gateways

A default gateway is an intermediate system that forwards packets from an originating system to a destination system. For example, in the following graphic, the router would act as the default gateway for the two subnets.

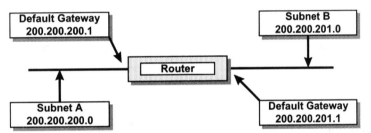

When configuring TCP/IP on a Windows 95 machine, think of the default gateway as the *exit door* for the subnet. Using the previous graphic as an example, the default gateway address (or *exit door*) for subnet A would be 200.200.200.1. Likewise, the default gateway address for subnet B would be 200.200.201.1.

Private Internets

A private internet is one that will not be connecting directly to the Internet. The term *intranet* is commonly being used to refer to internetwork environments of this type. The two most common examples of these are:

- Networks with no need to connect to the Internet.

- Networks connecting to the Internet through an application gateway (such as Microsoft's Proxy Server) that remaps IP addresses.

The Internet Assigned Numbers Authority (IANA) has set aside three sets of addresses for use on intranets:

```
10.0.0.0 - 10.255.255.255

172.16.0.0 - 172.31.255.255

192.168.0.0 - 192.168.255.255
```

There are some obvious disadvantages to using these addresses, the foremost being that it will be impossible to connect directly to the Internet or reference these addresses from the Internet. They have no meaning in the global Internet community. Routers connecting to the Internet should filter out any reference to these addresses.

Exercise 11-2:
Installation and Configuration of the TCP/IP Protocol

This exercise will have you install and configure the TCP/IP protocol for two Windows 95 clients. You will also need to configure workstation information for both computers.

1. Run **Start/Settings/Control Panel**.

2. Double-click on the Network utility.

3. Click on **Add**.

4. Select **Protocol** and click on **Add**.

5. Select **Microsoft** from the list of manufacturers and **TCP/IP** from the list of network protocols.

6. Click on **OK**.

7. Select TCP/IP from the **Configuration** tab and click on **Properties**.

8. Click on the option to **Specify an IP address:**.

9. Enter 172.10.10.10 as the IP address.

10. Enter 255.255.0.0 as the subnet mask.

11. Click on **OK**.

12. Click on the **Identification** tab.

13. Enter the computer name as STUDENT1.

14. Enter the workgroup as CLASSROOM.

15. Click on **OK** to close the Network dialog.

16. Click on **Yes** to restart the computer.

17. Now, on the second computer, open the Network utility.

18. Click on **Add**.

19. Select **Protocol** and click on **Add**.

20. Select **Microsoft** from the list of manufacturers and **TCP/IP** from the list of network protocols.

21. Click on **OK**.

22. Select TCP/IP from the **Configuration** tab and click on **Properties**.

23. Click on the option to **Specify an IP address:**.

24. Enter 172.10.10.9 as the IP address.

25. Enter 255.255.0.0 as the subnet mask.

26. Click on **OK**.

27. Click on the **Identification** tab.

28. Enter the computer name as STUDENT2.

29. Enter the workgroup as CLASSROOM.

30. Click on **OK** to close the Network dialog.

31. Click on **Yes** to restart the computer.

32. On the Student1 computer, run **Start/Programs/MS-DOS Prompt**.

33. Type the following and press *ENTER*:

    ```
    PING 172.10.10.9
    ```

34. You should receive information showing the reply of communication from Student2's computer.

35. Run **Start/Programs/MS-DOS Prompt** on Student2.

36. Type the following and press *ENTER*:

    ```
    edit lmhosts
    ```

37. Type the following and press *ENTER*:

    ```
    172.10.10.10 STUDENT2
    ```

38. Press *ALT+F* to display the **File** menu.

39. Press *S* to save the LMHOSTS file.

40. Press *ALT+F* to display the **File** menu again.

41. Press *X* to close the LMHOSTS file.

42. On Student1 at the MS-DOS Prompt, type the following and press *ENTER*:

    ```
    PING Student2
    ```

43. You should receive the same type of information that you did when you used the PING command.

USING DHCP, WINS, AND DNS SERVERS WITH TCP/IP

This section discusses the benefits of using DHCP, WINS, and DNS servers with the TCP/IP protocol. DHCP enables systems using the TCP/IP protocol to obtain a TCP/IP address. This replaces the need to manually configure a TCP/IP address for each and every machine. WINS servers allow machines to be identified with a NetBIOS naming scheme at startup. The following topics are discussed within this section:

- DHCP
- WINIPCFG
- Network Naming
- WINS
- DNS
- DNS Domains
- Name Resolution Basics
- DNS and Windows 95

You will also learn the naming schemes of DNS domains. If you have ever surfed the Internet, you may have noticed that site addresses are identified by names such as microsoft.com, yahoo.com, lycos.com, and so forth. These are examples of the DNS naming scheme.

DHCP

Dynamic Host Configuration Protocol (DHCP) allows TCP/IP systems configured as DHCP clients to automatically receive configuration parameters. Microsoft was the first manufacturer to implement DHCP, but other companies have since introduced both clients that use DHCP and servers that implement it.

DHCP is well suited to the PC environment. PC-based networks are volatile. It's a simple matter to move a PC from one location to another. Notebook computers are especially likely to move around on a regular basis. The problem is that when you move a computer to a different physical location, you are likely moving it to a different subnet as well. DHCP supports rapid release of IP addresses and reassignment as necessary.

Even if a PC remains stationary, DHCP leases addresses for a limited time only. During that time period, the PC can apply for renewal of the address. If that is not possible, the PC can bid for a new address.

WINIPCFG

The WINIPCFG utility displays current network configuration values. It is especially helpful when working with DHCP clients. IP addresses are assigned automatically for DHCP clients and WINIPCFG gives you an easy way of viewing the IP address assigned.

To launch WINIPCFG, access the **Run** command on the **Start** menu and type:

```
winipcfg
```

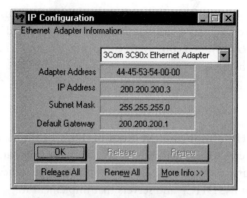

If the computer is connected to a LAN but not connected directly to the Internet, it may have more that one adapter and IP address. For example, if the computer is on a LAN and also uses TCP/IP with dial-up networking, it may have PPP listed as an adapter type. WINIPCFG enables you to view the settings for each adapter. If DHCP is used to supply configuration information, the following buttons will be available:

- Release

    This button is used to release the current DHCP configuration parameters and disable TCP/IP support.

- Renew

    The **Renew** button is used to renew the DHCP configuration parameters.

If the computer is configured with more than one adapter, the followings buttons will be available:

- Release All

    This button is used to release the current DHCP configuration parameters and disable TCP/IP support on each adapter.

- Renew All

    The **Renew All** button is used to renew the DHCP configuration parameters for each adapter.

The **More Info>>** button is available at all times. When it is selected, detailed TCP/IP configuration information is provided.

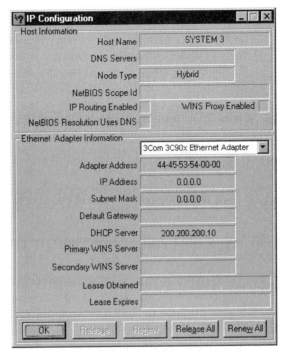

If a DHCP client displays an address of 0.0.0.0 (as displayed in the graphic), it has been unable to get an address from the DHCP server. Correct any problems with the server or the configured path, then select the **Renew** or **Renew All** button to bid for an address.

Network Naming

Addresses work well when computers need to communicate. If a user needs to locate a system, however, it is much easier if recognizable names are used. Let's discuss two naming systems:

- Domain Name System (DNS)

    In a DNS environment, each system will have a Fully Qualified Domain Name (FQDN), uniquely identifying it on the network. DNS uses a distributed, hierarchical naming system. For example: www.wavetech.com

- NetBIOS

    NetBIOS compatibility is essential in all Microsoft Networking engine-based network operating systems. NetBIOS is a common interface for creation of network applications. Under NetBIOS, each device must have a unique name.

It is likely that you will encounter networks where it is necessary to manage both DNS and NetBIOS names for network devices.

WINS

Windows Internet Naming Service (WINS) is commonly used for name resolution for Windows family clients. WINS is an automated way of supporting NetBIOS address resolution. It is a modification to NetBIOS Name Server (NBNS), using dynamic name registration. As each WINS client system starts up, it registers itself with a WINS server. When a client issues a command to a NetBIOS name, the client will try the following:

- Check to see if the name is on the local machine.
- Check the local cache of remote NetBIOS names.
- Query the WINS Server for address resolution.
- Issue a local name query broadcast.
- Parse the LMHOSTS file if LMHOSTS support is configured at the client.
- Parse the HOSTS file if one exists.
- Query DNS, if supported.

Each of the above will be attempted until address resolution occurs.

DNS

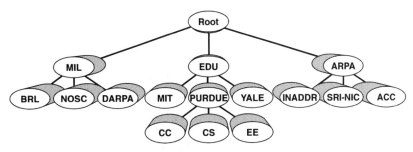

Domain Name Space Extract

DNS is a hierarchical naming system for identifying hosts on the Internet in the format *somewhere.domain;* for example, wavetech.com. The format is sometimes described as *host.subdomain.domain.* DNS requires a static DNS name to IP address mapping.

The hierarchical structure identifying domain names is called the domain name space. Each domain can be divided into subdomains, and these into host names, with a period acting as delimiter between each portion of the name.

Domains are the root level of the DNS identifiers and include organization types and countries. Each domain name is unique. This root is managed by the Internet Network Information Center. Each domain is managed by a different organization which administers its own subdomain. Each subdomain must be unique to the domain, and administration of that subdomain is normally assigned to the organization it represents.

DNS Domains

The following are some DNS domains you may encounter.

Organizational domains:

com	Usually a company, commercial institution, or an organization. For example, the DNS name for Wave Technologies International is wavetech.com.
edu	This identifies educational institutions. For example, mit.edu is the name of Massachusetts Institute of Technology.
gov	These are government organizations, such as nasa.gov for the National Aeronautics and Space Administration.
mil	This represents a military site, such as af.mil for the United States Air Force.
net	This is used for Internet gateways and administrative hosts.
org	This identifies non-commercial organizations or organizations that don't fit easily into other domain classes. For example, the address for National Public Radio is npr.org.

Examples of country domains include:

us	United States
au	Australia
ca	Canada
fr	France
uk	United Kingdom

Country domains also support subdomains. For example, the United States has a subdomain for each of the 50 states. The United Kingdom supports subdomains, such as co.uk for commercial organizations and ac.uk for educational institutions.

Name Resolution Basics

DNS names are maintained and managed through DNS servers. Each top-level domain, such as com, will have one or more DNS servers. It contains information about all of the domains that it supports. DNS servers are also supported at the subdomain level, which will contain the host name information. Subdomains can be further divided into logical zones, with a server managing all of the hosts for that zone.

When name resolution is required, the request is handled through name servers. A name server interprets the FQDN it receives to determine its specific address. If the local name server doesn't contain the requested information, the request is passed on to other name servers that are likely to contain the information. The query continues until the name and IP address are located.

DNS and Windows 95

DNS is the global name system used by TCP/IP hosts on the Internet. It is also sometimes used for name management on large private internetworks. A hierarchy of DNS servers responds to name resolution requests from TCP/IP hosts (clients).

Under DNS, millions of host names can be configured and managed. The database(s) containing the host names can be centrally managed.

Windows NT 4.0 includes a DNS Server service and a graphical interface for managing DNS entries. You can configure Windows 95 clients to query DNS running on NT or DNS servers on other platforms. One or more DNS servers can be specified for name resolution.

Follow these steps to enable DNS name resolution on a Windows 95 computer:

- Launch the Control Panel Networks utility.
- Select **TCP/IP** from the list of installed network components.
- Click on **Properties**.

- When the TCP/IP properties sheet appears, select the **DNS Configurations** tab.

SIMPLE NETWORK MANAGEMENT PROTOCOL

This section will discuss the use for SNMP, or Simple Network Management Protocol. You will learn how to use the SNMP management station as well. The following topics are discussed within this section:

- Introduction to SNMP
- SNMP Commands
- MIBs
- SNMP Installation
- Configuring the SNMP Agent

The System Policy Editor was discussed earlier in the course. Now, you will see how the System Policy Editor is used to set certain restrictions and parameters for the SNMP agent on a Windows 95 system.

Introduction to SNMP

Simple Network Management Protocol, otherwise known as SNMP, is a network management protocol that is part of the TCP/IP suite of protocols. A network management protocol can solve communication problems with various devices and networks. SNMP is comprised of the Management Information Base (MIB), the manager, and the agent.

Agents are any component running the SNMP agent service and capable of being managed remotely. Management stations are workstations running a product such as HP OpenView, Cabletron Spectrum or Novell's Managewise. Management stations provide a graphical representation of the network, letting you move through the network hierarchy to the individual device level.

The agent is installed on a node (host) on the network. The agent's job is to collect information as specified in the MIB. The manager is located on a host computer on the network. The manager's job is to poll the agents for certain requested information. The information SNMP can attain from a network is defined as an MIB (management information base). The MIB is structured hierarchically, similar to a tree. At the top of the tree is the most general network information available. Each branch of the tree then provides more detailed information on a specific area. Finally, the leaves of the tree provide the most specific information.

SNMP exchanges network information through the use of messages. SNMP has conversations between SNMP agents and SNMP management systems. Through these conversations, the SNMP management systems can collect statistics from and modify configuration parameters on agents.

SNMP Commands

There are three basic commands used in SNMP conversations:

get	The management station uses the **get** command to retrieve a specific parameter value from an SNMP agent. If a combination of parameters is grouped together on an agent, **get-next** retrieves the next item in a group. For example, a management system's graphic representation of a hub includes the state of all status lights. This information is gathered through **get** and **get-next**.
set	The management system uses a **set** command to change a selected parameter on an SNMP agent. For example, **set** would be used by the management system to disable a failing port on a hub.
trap	SNMP agents send TRAP packets to the management system in response to extraordinary events, such as a line failure on a hub. When the hub status light goes red on the management system's representation, it is in response to a TRAP.

An SNMP management station generates **get** and **set** commands. Agents are able to respond to **set** and **get** and to generate **trap** commands. If a user wants to see whether a device is attached to the network, he would use SNMP to issue a **get** command to that device. If the device were attached to the network, the user would receive back a response of "Yes, the device is attached to the network," from the device's SNMP agent. If a device is shut off, the user receives a packet sent out by the device's SNMP agent. This is known as a TRAP message.

MIBs

The term Management Information Base (MIB) contains information about objects that are available for management via SNMP. Each object has a unique identifier. MIBs are required for every object used as a statistics source or managed by a management system. MIBs can be defined as read-only (only responding to **get** commands) or read-write (able to respond to both **get** and **set** commands). Third-party manufacturers may define other MIBs and associated DLLs for management and control of other objects under Windows 95 or Windows NT.

SNMP Installation

1. Open the Network utility in Control Panel.

2. Click on **Add**.

3. Select **Service** and click on **Add**.

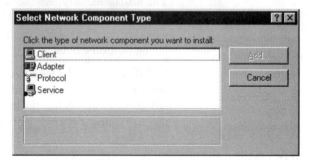

4. From the Select Network Service window, choose **Have Disk**.

5. Enter the path to the \ADMIN\NETTOOLS\SNMP directory on the Windows 95 CD and click on **OK**.

6. From the Select Network Service window, click on Microsoft SNMP **Agent** and then click on **OK**.

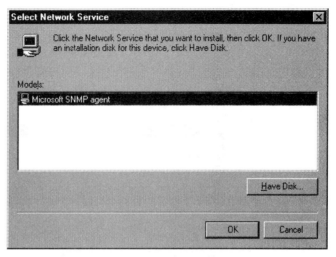

7. Close the Network dialog.

8. Restart your computer for the SNMP Agent service to take effect.

Before installing SNMP on a Windows 95 station, you need to gather your configuration information. Use the System Policy Editor to set the following:

Community
: A community is a group of systems that exchange SNMP information. You can specify to have your system send traps to one or more communities. You can use the community name to limit your SNMP messages from going out on an internetwork and clogging bandwidth.

Permitted Managers
: Specifies IP or IPX addresses that are allowed to retrieve information from an SNMP agent. If this policy is not checked, any SNMP console can query the agent.

Internet MIB (RFC 1156)
: Allows you to specify the contact name and location if you are using Internet MIB.

Trap Destinations   These are either IP or IPX addresses to which the SNMP service will send traps with the community name.

An SNMP agent must specify at least one trap destination. By default the SNMP agent will send traps to the public community. If you want the SNMP agent to send traps to any other community, you must edit the Registry or change the system policy.

Configuring the SNMP Agent

To configure the SNMP Agent using the Registry:

1. Use REGEDIT to locate the following key:

   ```
   HKEY_LOCAL_MACHINE\System\CurrentControlSet\Services\SNMP
       \Parameters\TrapConfiguration
   ```

2. Run **New** from the **Edit** menu and select **Key**.

3. Rename New Key #1 to the name of your new community and press *ENTER*.

4. Create a new string for each console to which SNMP should send traps.

5. Highlight your community. Run **New** from the **Edit** menu and select **String Value**. The first value name should be 1, the second value name should be 2, the third value name should be 3, etc. The value's data must be the IP or IPX address of the host to which the SNMP console's traps will be sent.

The following illustration shows an example of what the Registry should look like after adding a new community named MelrosePlace.

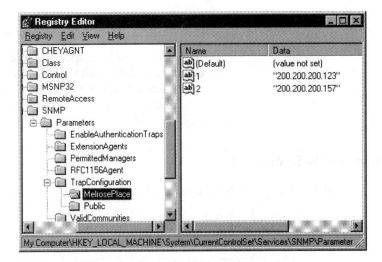

Removing the SNMP Agent

You can remove the SNMP Agent by removing the Microsoft SNMP Agent from the Network utility in Control Panel. You can also use System Policy Editor to turn off SNMP services by setting policies.

TCP/IP UTILITIES IN WINDOWS 95

This section will describe two of the utilities available to administrators for monitoring TCP/IP communication. They are PING and TRACERT. The following topics are discussed within this section:

- PING
- PING Options
- TRACERT
- TRACERT Options

These utilities can be used to test whether the TCP/IP protocol is communicating within a network environment or even across the Internet.

PING

The Ping utility is commonly used to test for the presence of other systems. To test for a particular system, enter the command and the host's IP address at the command line.

```
ping 150.4.5.21
```

A successful response would look something like this:

```
Reply from 150.4.5.21:bytes=32time=101ms TTL=243

Reply from 150.4.5.21:bytes=32time=100ms TTL=243

Reply from 150.4.5.21:bytes=32time=120ms TTL=243

Reply from 150.4.5.21:bytes=32time=120ms TTL=243
```

This shows that you received four replies, each 32 bytes long, and each taking just over 100 ms to reach you. Ping can be used when troubleshooting a networking problem. For example, you can:

- Ping yourself with the loopback address (127.0.0.1) to determine if you have a working TCP/IP stack.

- Ping yourself with your IP address to see if it is configured properly and to see if the address is duplicated on the network.

- Ping another system on the local network to test network integrity.

- Ping another system on a different subnetwork to verify that default gateways are operational and that network components are working properly.

- Ping each intermediate router between you and a remote host to test the route.

If you can ping a computer by specifying its IP address, but cannot ping it by specifying its host name, that means host name resolution is not working properly. Check to make sure that you can ping the DNS server. If you can, check to make sure that Windows 95 is configured to use the correct DNS server.

PING Options

Ping supports the following command-line options:

-t	The command will ping the specified host until interrupted.
-a	This option is used to resolve addresses to host names.

-n *count*	This will send the number of ECHO packets you specify in the count, defaulting to four.
-l *length*	This is used to set the size of ECHO packets, defaulting to 64 bytes. You can specify a packet size of up to 8192 bytes.
-f	Use this option to send a Do Not Fragment flag in the packet, so that it will not be fragmented by gateways on the route.
-i *ttl*	This is used to set the Time to Live field to a specified value.
-v *tos*	Use this to set the Type of Service field to a specified value.
-r *count*	The option records the outgoing and returning packet routes in the Record Route field. You must specify a host count value between 1 and 9.
-s *count*	This is used to specify the timestamp for the number of hops set in the count value.
-j *computer-list*	This is used to route packets via the hosts in the computer-list, up to a maximum of 9. Intermediate gateways may separate consecutive hosts.
-k *computer-list*	This is used to route packets via the hosts in the computer-list, up to a maximum of 9. Intermediate gateways may not separate consecutive hosts.
-w *timeout*	This sets the timeout value. The timeout value is in milliseconds.
destination_list	As the final command-line parameter, you can specify the list of hosts to ping.

TRACERT

The **tracert** command is helpful to determine what route your communication takes when you access a particular host. This can help in troubleshooting slow connections. The **tracert** command will report information about the route that is used between you and a remote host. For example:

```
C:\WINDOWS>tracert www.microsoft.com

Tracing route to www.microsoft.com [207.68.156.16]
```

```
1 236ms 216ms 228ms border3-serial2- 2.KansasCity.mci.net
  [204.70.42.17]

2 260ms 273ms 258ms core1-fddi-0.KansasCity.mci.net
  [204.70.2.65]

3 254ms 308ms 236ms KansasCity.mci.net [204.70.4.249]

4 288ms 235ms 280ms core2-hssi-2.Denver.mci.net [204.70.1.157]

5 286ms 284ms 261ms borderx1-fddi-1.Seattle.mci.net
  [204.70.203.52]

6 268ms 278ms 285ms borderx1-fddi- 1.Seattle.mci.net
  [204.70.203.52]

7 338ms 319ms 308ms microsoft.Seattle.mci.net [204.70.203.106]

8 260ms 294ms 282ms 207.68.145.54

9 286ms 478ms 278ms www.microsoft.com [207.68.156.16]

Trace complete.
```

TRACERT uses a series of packets to discover the route. The first is sent with a TTL of one. The TTL is increased by one on each packet until the destination is found.

Each router will decrement the TTL by (at least) one before forwarding to the next router in the path. When the TTL on a packet goes to zero, the router should send back an "ICMP time exceeded" message to the source. These are intercepted by TRACERT and used to build the route.

It should be noted that some routers drop expired packets without generating an error message. These routers will be invisible to TRACERT.

TRACERT Options

The **tracert** command uses the following syntax:

```
tracert [-d] [-h max_hops] [-j host_list] [-w timeout]
    target_name
```

The following options are supported:

-d	This specifies that IP addresses should not be resolved to hostnames.
-h *max_hops*	This sets a limit on the number of hops that will be attempted when trying to reach the target, defaulting to 30.
-j *host_list*	This is used to specify an informal source routing along the hosts listed.
-w *timeout*	The timeout value sets the maximum time that the command will wait for a reply to an Echo packet it has sent out.
target_name	This identifies the name of the target host.

Unless otherwise specified, an attempt will be made to resolve the host name for any returned IP addresses.

SCENARIOS

Scenario 1

You have decided to add the customer service representative's Windows 95 computer to the network so that she can access a network printer that is shared from her manager's Windows 95 computer. The computer where the printer is connected is running NetBEUI. Which networking components do you need to add to the customer service representative's computer?

....

....

Scenario 2

You are setting up a network for a small pharmaceutical distributor. There are four people in the office and all of them will be running Windows 95. The accounting database will be shared from an additional Windows 95 computer. The accounting software is written to the NetBIOS interface. Which protocol will provide the best performance?

....

....

Scenario 3

You have installed Windows 95 on a computer that is attached to a NetWare network. The NetWare network runs IPX/SPX, so you have installed IPX/SPX as the only protocol. You have also installed the Microsoft Client for NetWare Networks and set up your preferred server. However, you still cannot see the NetWare servers. What is most likely wrong?

....

....

Scenario 4

You are setting up a small network with four departmental subnetworks. The maximum number of devices on any subnet is 14, but may go as high as 26 in the future. You have been assigned the following address:

    213.191.22.0

Determine the following:

```
Subnet mask

Subnetwork addresses

All valid IP addresses

Subnetwork Broadcast Addresses
```

....

....

Scenario 5

You are the administrator of a Windows NT network with Windows 95 clients. You are running TCP/IP as your only protocol. The company's accounting program uses NetBIOS names to communicate with the accounting database. One of the accountants complains that his accounting program cannot access the database. You can ping the database computer's IP address from his machine. None of the other accountants are having a problem. What should you check next?

....

....

SUMMARY

In this chapter, you were introduced to the networking capabilities of Windows 95. These included:

- Features of Windows 95 network support

- The role of network clients, adapters, protocols, and services

- Identification of currently installed network components

- The basic features of Windows 95 networking support

- Installation and configuration of TCP/IP on Windows 95

- The functions of DHCP, WINS, and DNS servers

- Testing TCP/IP communication using the PING and TRACERT utilities

In the next chapter, we will be discussing how to set up peer-to-peer networks. The chapter also includes a discussion on user profiles and system policies. You will learn how and when to implement each type of user management method.

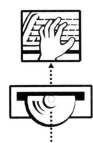

Stop now and complete the Chapter 11 NEXTSim simulation exercise on the Learning CD-ROM.

POST-TEST QUESTIONS

The answers to these questions are in Appendix A at the end of this manual.

1. Name the 32-bit, protected-mode network clients included with Windows 95.

   ....

   ....

2. List three network protocols utilized by Windows 95 that use 32-bit, protected-mode device drivers.

   ....

   ....

3. Which Windows 95 tool displays information about the TCP/IP protocol in regards to IP addresses?

    ....

    ....

Peer-to-Peer Networking

OBJECTIVES

At the completion of this chapter, you will be able to:

- Describe the benefits and drawbacks of a peer-to-peer network.
- Describe advantages and limitations of peer servers.
- Share workstation resources to the network using share-level security.
- Share workstation resources on a Microsoft network using user-level security.
- Access shared resources with the Windows Explorer.
- Access shared resources with the Network Neighborhood.
- Map Network Drives.
- Work with persistent shares.
- Browse available network resources.
- Configure the Browse Master for Microsoft Networks.

PRE-TEST QUESTIONS

The answers to these questions are in Appendix A at the end of this manual.

1. What is a persistent share?

   ....

   ....

2. When referring to resource access, what two types of resources are normally considered?

   ....

   ....

3. When you open the Network Neighborhood, what is listed in addition to the Entire Network icon?

   ....

   ....

4. When manually typing a non-mapped network path, what format must be used to enter it?

....

....

INTRODUCTION

The chapter begins with a discussion of the Windows 95 Microsoft networking client, otherwise known as peer-to-peer networking. We will discuss how to install the Microsoft Client for Microsoft Networks as well as additional configurations for allowing Windows 95 clients to communicate with one another. The chapter then discusses the advantages of Windows 95 computers serving as peer servers in the networking environment.

The discussion will then turn to issues involving Resource Management. You will see how the Network Neighborhood and Windows Explorer can allow you to browse for resources.

The differences between the peer sharing schemes utilized by Microsoft and NetWare networks will be identified. The process for setting up shares using user-level and share-level security will be highlighted during this segment. The discussion of Resource Access covers the following topics:

- Accessing shared file resources
- Accessing shared printer resources
- Browsing with the Network Neighborhood
- Browsing with the Windows Explorer
- Mapping network drives to file resources

The chapter concludes with a discussion about network browsing and persistent shares.

MICROSOFT NETWORKS

This section describes how to set up a peer-to-peer network. A peer-to-peer network is simply a network consisting of Windows 95 clients. You will learn the necessary steps that must be followed to allow communication between all clients on the network. The following topics are discussed within this section:

- Setting Up a Peer-to-Peer Network
- Installing the Client for Microsoft Networks
- Configuring the Primary Network Logon
- Selecting the Appropriate Logon Option
- Verifying Protocols
- Assigning a Workgroup
- Viewing the Network

Logon validation will not be discussed at this time. Since we are dealing with peer-to-peer networks only in this chapter, this option is not applicable. It will be discussed in the next chapter in conjunction with how to implement Windows 95 in a Windows NT domain.

Setting Up a Peer-to-Peer Network

Peer-to-peer networking allows Windows 95 machines to communicate across a network without the existence of a Windows NT Server or NetWare server. The following must be performed on each computer before it can be part of a peer-to-peer network:

- Install Client for Microsoft Networks.
- Configure the Client for Microsoft Networks as the primary network logon.
- Select the appropriate logon options.
- Verify that the appropriate protocols have been loaded.

Let's take a close look at each of these steps in creating a peer-to-peer network.

Installing the Client for Microsoft Networks

To install the Client for Microsoft Networks, you must first launch the Network control panel. You can do so using **Start/Settings/Control Panel** or right-clicking on the Network Neighborhood desktop object and running **Properties**.

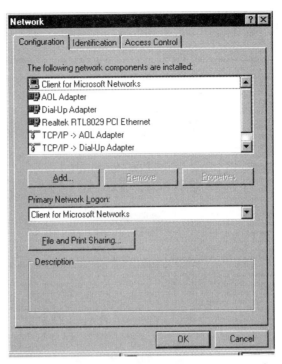

Once the Network dialog opens, click on the **Add** button. Select **Client** from the Select Network Component Type dialog. Click on the **Add** button. Select **Microsoft** from the list of Manufacturers. Then select **Client for Microsoft Networks** from the list of network clients.

Configuring the Primary Network Logon

Once the client has been installed, the system should automatically change the Primary Network Logon to Client for Microsoft Networks. If it does not, manually change it so that the Client for Microsoft Networks will be used.

Selecting the Appropriate Logon Option

Once you have installed the Client for Microsoft Networks, you can choose whether you would like to use **Quick logon** or **Logon and restore network connections** by displaying the properties sheet for the Client for Microsoft Networks.

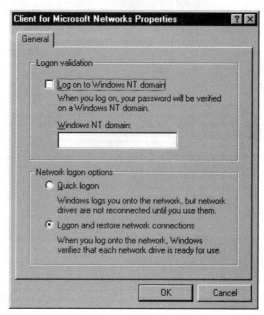

Selecting **Quick logon** causes you to connect to network drives the first time you access them. Selecting **Logon and restore network connections** causes all of your connections to be made as soon as you restart the computer. While the **Quick logon** option allows you to begin working more quickly, there may be a slight delay when a connection is accessed for the first time. Quick logon is the default setting.

To change the current network logon option, select Client for Microsoft Networks from the **Configuration** tab of the Network dialog and click on the **Properties** button. You can also display the properties sheet by double-clicking on Client for Microsoft Networks from the Network dialog. Set the appropriate option. Then, click on **OK** to close the Client for Microsoft Networks Properties dialog.

Verifying Protocols

In order for your clients to communicate across the network, they must have the same protocol installed. Only one matching protocol is required. However, multiple protocols can be installed. The details of installing a protocol were discussed earlier in the course. Simply use the Network control panel to add the desired protocol that will be used for communication across the peer-to-peer network.

Finally, click on **OK** to close the Network dialog. The system will install the necessary drivers for the newly installed client and protocols. You will need to restart your computer for these changes to take effect.

Assigning a Workgroup

You can also create workgroups for your Windows 95 clients. Workgroups can be used as a means of grouping clients together, for example, by department. To assign a workgroup to a Windows 95 client, click on the **Identification** tab of the Network properties dialog. Enter the name of the computer. An entry may already exist if the name was supplied at installation. Then enter the name of the workgroup, such as Accounting or Sales. You can also enter a computer description if you like. This information can be left blank. It will not affect network communication. Finally, click on **OK**. You will need to restart your computer. Once the computer has rebooted, the client will appear in the assigned workgroup.

NOTE: *Workgroup assignments do not provide access security. Resources in one workgroup are available to users in another workgroup. Their only purpose is to organize shared resources according to a logical scheme.*

Viewing the Network

Once your Windows 95 client has been configured to be part of a peer-to-peer network, you can use the Network Neighborhood to view all clients and workgroups within the network. Double-click on the **Network Neighborhood** desktop object. You should see two listings, Entire Network and your computer's identification name. To view the other computers in the network, double-click on **Entire Network**.

You can double-click on a workgroup to view the clients contained in that group. Any computers that do not belong to a workgroup are listed once you double-click on **Entire Network**. If you receive a message stating that you are unable to browse the network, you can use the Network Troubleshooter available in the Help utility for Windows 95. It is a guided help utility that poses questions to which you must respond.

Exercise 12-1:
Microsoft Client for Microsoft Networks

This exercise discusses installing the client component for Client for Microsoft Networks. We will also go through the additional steps for setting up a Windows 95 client for a peer-to-peer networking environment.

1. Launch the Network control panel.
2. Click on **Add**.
3. Select **Client** and click on **Add**.
4. Select Microsoft from the list of manufacturers and Client for Microsoft Networks from the list of network clients.
5. Click on **OK**.
6. Verify that the primary network logon is Client for Microsoft Networks.
7. Click on **Add**.
8. Select **Protocol** and click on **Add**.
9. Select Microsoft from the list of manufacturers and NetBEUI from the list of network protocols.
10. Click on **OK**.

11. Click on the **Identification** tab.

12. Enter the workgroup name as Corporate.

13. Click on **OK**.

14. When prompted to restart your computer, do so.

ACCESS SECURITY

This section describes the use of share-level security available on a peer-to-peer network. The following topics are discussed within this section:

- Access Control
- Share-level Security
- User-level Security

Windows 95 clients can be configured to use user-level security. However, this cannot be done without a validation server such as Windows NT or NetWare. The next two chapters will cover these environments.

Access Control

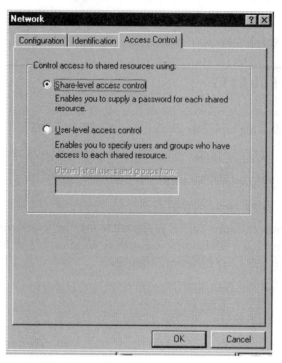

The **Access Control** tab of the Network utility is used for selecting a method of controlling access to resources shared to the network by your workstation.

* Share-level access control

    Share-level security consists of providing passwords to protect each shared folder, printer, and additional resource, such as a CD-ROM drive. Share-level security can still be used even if a Windows NT Server is available. However, it is most commonly used in a small peer-to-peer environment.

* User-level access control

    Access permissions are set on a user-by-user basis. You must specify the location of the master list containing authorized users. Only users on the master list may access the shared resources. The master list can be provided by a validating logon server such as a Windows NT domain controller or Novell NetWare server, or by an additional Windows NT Server or Windows NT Workstation. You cannot implement user-level security in a purely peer-to-peer environment.

In a workgroup or peer-to-peer environment, users manage their own shared resources. It is best suited to a small number of workstations with relatively experienced users. A network composed entirely of Windows 95 computers, such as a peer-to-peer network, can only use share-level security.

Let's take a closer look at each type of access control available on a Windows 95 client.

Share-level Security

Share-level security controls access for shared components with individually assigned passwords for each resource. You may assign a password to a directory or a locally attached printer. If other users wish to access the resource, they must supply the appropriate password. Passwords are not required, and if a password for a resource is not assigned, every user with access to the network can access that resource.

A directory may be shared, but hidden from the Network Neighborhood browsing list by adding a dollar-sign character ($) to the end of its share name, as in SECRET$.

Advantages of share-level security include:

- Ease of setup and use

- No requirement for a network security provider

- Good security method for small workgroups

User-level Security

User-level security controls access to shared network resources by requiring that a security provider, such as a Windows NT domain controller or a NetWare server, authenticates a user's request to access resources. This provider grants access to the shared resources by checking the username and password against those in the user account list security provider. The network security provider maintains the listing of user passwords and accounts. Therefore, each computer running Windows 95 does not have to store its own list of accounts.

> *NOTE: For Windows NT Server domains, enter the domain name instead of a server name.*

To use File and printer sharing for Microsoft Networks, the security provider must be either a Windows NT domain controller, a Windows NT backup domain controller, or a Windows NT workstation. To use File and printer sharing for NetWare Networks, the security provider must be either a NetWare 2.x server, a NetWare 3.x server, or a NetWare 4.x server running bindery emulation. File and print sharing for Microsoft Networks will be discussed later in this chapter.

Advantages of user-level security over share-level security include:

- Centralized administration of users and passwords by a network administrator.

- Greater security due to user validation by a network security provider.

- Group assignments of resource access.

- Elimination of individual password tracking for shared resources.

Sharing resources with user-level security will be discussed in the next chapter.

ACCESSING RESOURCES

This section will describe the methods by which a user can connect to a network resource. This includes a discussion of tools supporting network access. The following topics are discussed within this section:

- Accessing Shared Resources

- Universal Naming Conventions (UNC)

- Network Neighborhood

- Explorer

- Viewing Network Resources

- Persistent Connections

In many work environments, a network will consist of several servers. Windows 95 provides tools using a simple, graphical interface to locate and access network-based resources.

Accessing Shared Resources

Windows 95 provides a flexible network client environment. You can browse for available network resources with the same utilities used to access local workstation resources. As you have already seen, Windows 95 often provides a number of ways to perform the same action, allowing you to select the most appropriate or easiest one for you to use. Network resource access is handled in the same way.

- File resources

    The primary tools for working with file resources are Network Neighborhood, My Computer, and Windows Explorer. Once a network resource has been mapped and established, it can be accessed just as if it were a local drive.

- Printer resources

    You can set up access to printer resources through the Network Neighborhood desktop object or the Printers folder. The Printers folder can be accessed from the taskbar or the Control Panel.

You can also set up shared resources such as hard drives and CD-ROM devices.

Universal Naming Conventions (UNC)

First, let's discuss the naming convention used to access resources on a different computer. UNC is a naming convention that describes network servers and any share points on those servers. UNC names begin with two backslashes, followed by the server's computer name. Other fields in the name are separated by a single backslash. A typical UNC name would appear as:

    \\computer_name\share_name\subdirectory\filename

For example, a Windows 95 workstation with a computer name of 95Workstation and a shared directory called SHARED would have the UNC name:

    \\95Workstation\SHARED

At the command prompt, you can obtain directory listings of a shared directory using the following syntax:

```
DIR \\computer_name\share_name
```

Network Neighborhood

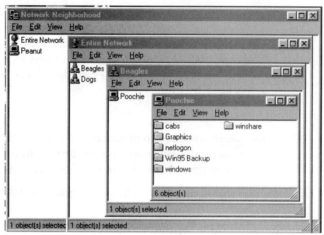

When you open the Network Neighborhood desktop object, currently connected servers are displayed along with an icon for Entire Network. Opening the Entire Network icon displays all available peer clients and servers including workgroups. Double-clicking on a client displays any shared resources.

Once you have selected a network resource in Network Neighborhood, the **File** menu offers three new options that have not been discussed yet in this course:

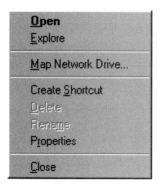

Open	This option allows you to open a window displaying the resources within the selected item which may be a server or folder.
Explore	**Explore** displays the contents of the selected item using Windows Explorer.
Map Network Drive	This option allows you to create a direct connection to the network resource. This connection is displayed in Windows Explorer or My Computer.

You can view and use shared directory contents from this utility without creating a persistent network connection. However, creating this connection is an available option.

Explorer

As mentioned earlier in the course, Windows Explorer is used to view your system's files, folders, and network resources in a hierarchical (tree) arrangement. This tree is displayed in the left pane of the Explorer window; the right pane shows the contents of the object selected in the graph. You can also access Network Neighborhood resources by clicking the plus sign (+) next to Network Neighborhood.

Viewing Network Resources

On a peer-to-peer Windows 95 network, all resources assigned to a certain workgroup are grouped together according to the workgroup assigned on the **Identification** tab in the Network utility. They can be viewed through Network Neighborhood.

To view shared resources assigned to a workgroup computer, first open Network Neighborhood using the desktop object or Windows Explorer. Double-click on the Entire Network icon. Any workgroups on the network appear along with any clients not belonging to a workgroup. Double-click on the desired workgroup. All computers in that workgroup that have File and Print Sharing enabled will be displayed, provided they are connected to the network and accessible. Double-click on a computer to view its shared resources.

Persistent Connections

Drive letters can also be assigned to another computer's shared resource. This allows you to directly access the shared resource from My Computer, Windows Explorer, or a shortcut that has been created. This can be done by mapping a network drive to the path of the resource on another computer.

To view currently mapped drives, open My Computer. My Computer displays all network drives like the icon labeled Cabs on 'Poochie' (D:) in the following graphic.

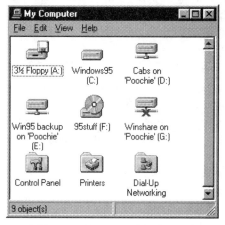

If a network drive is not available, it is designated with a red "X".

If a shared resource is going to be accessed on a routine basis, it is a good idea to place a shortcut to the resource on the desktop. To place a shortcut on the desktop, right-click on the folder in Network Neighborhood and drag it to the desktop. When you release the mouse button, you will be prompted to **Create a Shortcut** or **Cancel**. Select **Create a Shortcut** and an icon containing a name of Shortcut to *sharename* will appear on the desktop. When the shortcut icon is opened, all of the directories and files contained in the folder appear.

Many applications, such as Microsoft Word, allow you to open a file via the **File/Open** command and browse to Network Neighborhood. This method allows you to locate the particular file that you are seeking.

Another way to access a resource is to type the UNC path to the resource into the Run utility in the **Start** menu. When you click on **OK**, a window containing the contents of the folder is opened.

RESOURCE SHARING

This section will discuss how to set file and directory security permissions. These permissions may be set for users and groups. The following topics are discussed within this section:

- Sharing Resources
- File and Printer Sharing
- Peer Resource Sharing
- Performance Enhancement

As an administrator, it is important to be familiar with the types of access available through file, directory, and share permissions. Often times, users or groups will need to share critical files with others in their organization.

Sharing Resources

To utilize File and printer sharing for Microsoft Networks, the 32-bit Client for Microsoft Networks must be installed .

Using File and Printer Sharing services allows other users running a compatible network client to connect to resources on the peer server. Shared resources could include volumes, printers, folders, CD-ROM drives, and directories.

File and Printer Sharing

To install File and printer sharing for Microsoft Networks, launch the Network control panel first. Click on the **Add** button on the tab of the Network dialog. Select **Service** from the Select Network Component Type dialog. Click on **Add**. Select **Microsoft** from the list of manufacturers. Click on **File and printer sharing for Microsoft Networks**. Then click on **OK**.

Next, you must enable File and printer sharing on the client machine. To do so, click on the **File and Print Sharing** button on the **Configuration** tab of the Network dialog.

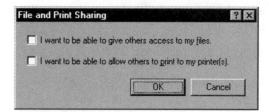

You can select **I want to be able to give others access to my files, I want to be able to allow others to print to my printer(s)**, or both.

In many cases it is appropriate to group computers by workgroup. Logical workgroups can make it easier to find resources on a network. For example, if all of the accountants are assigned to the Accounting workgroup and all of the sales people are assigned to a Sales workgroup, it will be easier to find the shared list of sales leads.

Peer Resource Sharing

To share a resource to the network using the Windows Explorer and share-level security, highlight the desired item and right-click to view the context-sensitive menu.

Select **Sharing** from the options presented. The following dialog appears:

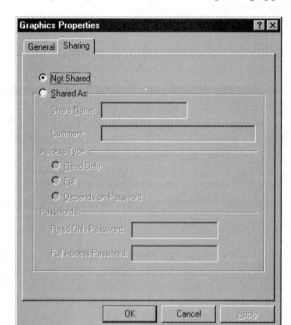

Click on **Shared As** and provide the resource with a Share Name. The share name you provide must be fifteen characters or less if the computers on your network use NetBIOS names.

You may also include an optional Comment. Select the appropriate access type.

Read-only   If the appropriate password is entered, the user will be able to open and read files within the directory. If the file is an executable, the user will be able to run the application.

Full   If the appropriate password is entered, the user will be allowed to view, modify, add, and delete files in the folder.

Depends on Password
                     A different password can be assigned for Read-only and Full Access. A user will be allowed the appropriate type of access once the password is entered.

Click on **OK**. If you selected the **Depends on Password** option, and entered a password for either Read-Only Password or Full Access Password, you are asked to confirm the password again.

After clicking on **OK**, the resource is displayed within Windows Explorer with an icon that denotes that it is now shared. The icon looks like a small hand.

Share-level security for folders, printers, and additional resources, such as a CD-ROM is handled by assigning a password to the resource and requiring the password to be typed from any other computer on the Windows 95 network the first time the resource is accessed. You can avoid typing the password on subsequent access attempts by using Password Caching. Password Caching is covered a little later in this chapter. As long as the user knows the appropriate password when prompted, he will be allowed access to the folder. If no password is assigned to the shared folder, then it is automatically available to the entire network.

Performance Enhancement

Windows 95 does an adequate job in adjusting system parameters for user demands and different network configurations. Manual tuning of system parameters is not usually needed to improve network performance; however, you can take other steps to increase file-sharing performance. Performance can be enhanced by:

- Using a 32-bit, protected mode network client.

- Using the NDIS 3.1 network adapter drivers that come with Windows 95.

- Installing the latest network adapters.

To improve network performance for file or print servers, do the following:

- Let Windows 95 adjust the swap file size.

- Ensure that the server has sufficient memory based on the number of users and network size.

- Using the Control Panel System utility, set the computer's role to Network Server.

- Install a high-performance (at least a 16- or 32-bit) adapter on the peer server.

- Remove unnecessary network protocols.

- Install faster disk drives or disk controllers.

Exercise 12-2:
Network Resources

The purpose of this exercise is to give you practice sharing resources in a network environment. You must be configured as a network client with the appropriate file and printer sharing service loaded. At the start of this exercise, you should be logged on using the username and password provided for your network environment.

1. Open the **My Computer** desktop object.

2. Open the **Printers** folder.

3. Right-click on a printer and select **Sharing**.

4. Click on the radio button next to **Shared As**.

5. Leave the share name at default and enter a password.

6. Click on **OK**.

7. Reconfirm the password by typing it in again.

8. Click on **OK**.

9. Close the printer folder.

10. Right-click on **drive C:** and select **Open**.

11. Right-click on the **DOS** directory and select **Sharing**.

12. Click on the radio button for **Shared As**.

13. Change the access type to **Depends on password**.

14. Enter the following password for full access:

    abcd

15. Click on **OK**.

16. Confirm the password for full access by typing:

abcd

17. Click on **OK**.

18. Close the drive C: window and My Computer.

PASSWORD SECURITY

This section discusses password synchronization and the importance of using passwords in the Windows 95 environment. The following topics are discussed within this section:

- Security in Windows 95

- Screen Saver Passwords

- Synchronizing Passwords

- Password Caching

- Editing the Password List

Understanding passwords and password synchronization is key to making your peer-to-peer network as secure as possible.

Security in Windows 95

In a peer-to-peer network, Windows 95 implements security through the use of locally defined passwords. There are passwords that unlock user-specific settings, passwords that provide access to the system, and passwords that provide access to the network and to network resources. It is important to understand the distinction between these types of passwords in order to implement security on your peer-to-peer network and identify potential security holes. Let's look at how these passwords interact.

Windows Password

The Windows logon and password give you access to all of the resources on the local system. Some restrictions may be enforced through the use of policies, which will be discussed a little later. In addition, typing a Windows logon and password will give you access to the Network Neighborhood and all shared resources that do not require a password. The first time you log on, a password file is created and you automatically become a valid user on that computer. If you cancel from the logon dialog, you will be able to access local resources, but you will not have access to network resources. You will even be able to access Regedit and System Policy Editor. Under these circumstances, the Passwords properties dialog will not allow you to set a Windows password or synchronize passwords. You are essentially logged on as a *nobody*.

Screen Saver Password

A screen saver can protect your system from unauthorized access while you are away from your computer. The screen saver password is not cached in the password cache. However, you can synchronize it with your Windows password so that you do not have to remember multiple passwords. This will be discussed a little later.

Resource Passwords

Passwords to share-level resources unlock the resources themselves. They can be cached in a password cache so that you only have to remember one password.

Screen Saver Passwords

If you use a screen saver on your Windows 95 system, you can configure the screen saver to require a password before it returns control to the desktop. This will prevent your computer from being accessed by unauthorized users if you need to walk away.

> NOTE: *It does not prevent a user from restarting your system.*

To provide password protection for your screen saver, open the Display properties dialog box. You can do so by using the Control Panel or right-clicking on the Desktop and selecting **Properties** from the pop-up menu. Select the **Screen Saver** tab. Click on the checkbox for **Password Protected**. Click on the **Change** button. Type the old password (if there is one). Then assign and confirm a new password. Click on **OK**.

```
┌─────────────────────────────────────────────────┐
│ Change Password                          [?][X]  │
├─────────────────────────────────────────────────┤
│  Change password for Windows Screen Saver        │
│                                      ┌─────────┐  │
│                                      │   OK    │  │
│                                      └─────────┘  │
│  New password:       [           ]   ┌─────────┐  │
│                                      │ Cancel  │  │
│  Confirm new password: [           ] └─────────┘  │
│                                                   │
└─────────────────────────────────────────────────┘
```

The screen saver password can be changed by following the steps listed above or by using the Passwords Properties dialog box found in the Control Panel. To change the screen saver password using the Passwords utility, open the Passwords control panel first. Verify that the **Change Passwords** tab is displayed. This tab is only visible if the user logged on to the Windows network with the correct password. Click on **Change Other Passwords**. Select **Windows Screen Saver** and click on **Change**. Type the new password and confirm it. Click on **OK**. Click on **OK** to close the Passwords dialog.

Synchronizing Passwords

The screen saver and Windows passwords can be synchronized so that you only have to remember one password. The synchronized password is updated either by changing the Windows password or by changing the screen saver password. Once synchronization is established and a user has logged onto the computer with the appropriate Windows password, the synchronized password will also be required to clear the screen saver.

To synchronize the Windows Logon and the Screen Saver passwords, open the Passwords control panel. Verify that the **Change Passwords** tab is displayed. Click on **Change Windows Password**. Click on the checkbox for **Windows Screen Saver**. Click on **OK**. Click on **Cancel** to keep the existing Windows password or type a new password and click on **OK**.

NOTE: *Once the Windows password and the Screen Saver password have been synchronized, you should only change the password through the Change Windows Password option in the Passwords control panel or through the **Screen Saver** tab of the Display control panel. Changing it through the Change Other Passwords option will cause password synchronization to be disabled. The system will also become temporarily confused and you will not be allowed to change the Windows password or resynchronize the passwords. To correct the problem, log off and log back on using your Windows password.*

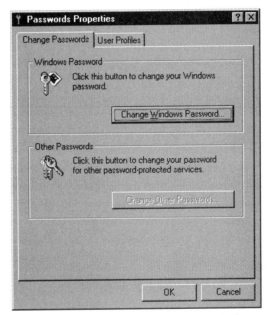

If a user presses **Cancel** on the logon dialog, the screen saver will appear after the appropriate elapsed time, but no password will be required to clear it. If this *nobody* user tries to update the screen saver password, he or she will be unable to do so. The following error box will be displayed:

If a user logs on with a new name, he is prompted to type and confirm the Windows password. The new Windows password automatically becomes the Screen Saver password.

The Screen Saver password dialog box is system modal. This means that no other activity, including *CONTROL+ALT+DELETE*, can occur until a password is successfully entered.

Password Caching

Password caching is automatically available when Windows 95 is installed. It is available to password-protected resources using share-level security, applications that have passwords stored using the Master Password API, Windows NT computers that are not in a domain or have a logon password that is not the primary network logon, and for NetWare servers.

The password file (.PWL) is stored in the WINDOWS directory of the local computer. It contains the passwords that have been successfully typed in for resources on the network. The first time you access a resource that has password protection, you must type the appropriate password to gain access to the resource.

To record a password in the .PWL file, access the resource and type in the correct password. Verify that the **Save this password in your password list** checkbox is checked. Password caching is on by default. Then click on **OK**.

As long as the user logs on properly and password caching has not been disabled through a system policy, the user will not be asked to type the password again. The password file will be accessed instead.

Editing the Password List

The Password List Editor (PWLEDIT) displays a list of resources with passwords stored in the user's .PWL file. The passwords themselves are not displayed but existing resource passwords can be deleted when necessary.

To install the Password List Editor, open the Add/Remove Programs control panel. Click on the **Windows Setup** tab. Click on the **Have Disk** button. Click on the **Browse** button. Locate ADMIN\APPTOOLS\PWLEDIT\PWLEDIT.INF and click on **OK**. Select **Password List Editor**. Click on **Install**. Click on **OK** to close the Add/Remove Programs dialog.

> NOTE: *The PWLEDIT program is not automatically installed, so if this is the first time it is being used, it must first be installed.*

Now you are able to use the Password List Editor by opening **Start/Run**. Type in PWLEDIT and press *ENTER*.

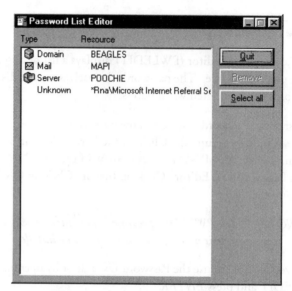

The Password List Editor lists all of the resources with cached passwords for the current logged on user. The user must have specified that password caching is to be used. The Editor allows you to delete resources from the list, but does not allow you to edit the list in any other way. If the password to a resource has changed, you can edit the password cache by accessing the resource with the new password. To delete a resource from the list, simply highlight the resource and click on the **Remove** button.

If you delete or rename the .PWL file, you will need to reenter the password the first time you access each resource.

Exercise 12-3:
Using Password Synchronization

This exercise is to familiarize you with setting passwords for both your screen saver as well as your Windows logon password. We will also synchronize the passwords for user ease of logon.

1. Open the Add/Remove Programs utility.
2. Click on the **Windows Setup** tab.
3. Click on **Accessories** from the list of components.
4. Click on **Details**.
5. Scroll down and select Screen Savers.

6. Click on **Details**.

7. Click on **Flying Windows**.

8. Click on **OK**.

9. Click on **OK** to close the Accessories dialog.

10. Click on **OK** to close the Add/Remove Programs Properties dialog. This installs the new screen saver on to your system.

11. Open the Display control panel.

12. Click on the **Screen Saver** tab.

13. Select **Flying Windows** as your screen saver.

14. Click on the checkbox for **Password protected**.

15. Click on the **Change** button.

16. Type the following and press *TAB*.

    ```
    Wave
    ```

17. Type "Wave" again to confirm the new screen saver password and click on **OK**.

18. Click on **OK** to verify that the password has been changed successfully.

19. Click on **OK** to close the Display Properties dialog.

20. Open the Passwords control panel.

21. Verify that you are on the **Change Passwords** tab and click on the **Change Windows Password** button.

22. Type the following and press *TAB*.

    ```
    wave
    ```

23. Type the following and press *TAB*.

    ```
    summer
    ```

24. Type "summer" again to confirm the new password and click on **OK**.

25. Click on **OK** to confirm that the password was changed successfully.

26. Click on **Close** to close the Passwords Properties dialog.

27. Close the Control Panel.

28. Run **Start/Shut Down**.

29. Select **Close all programs** and log on as a different user.

30. Try to type "wave" as the logon password. The system will display a dialog stating that the password is incorrect. Type "summer" and log on to your system.

BROWSING

This section will provide information about browsing. You will learn about master browsers. The following topics are discussed within this section:

- Network Browsing
- Browse Master For Microsoft Networks
- Browsing Network Resources
- Browse Master Updates
- Configuration

In this usage, the term *Browsing* refers to locating network servers and resources. This can include a mix of peer servers, such as Windows 95, and client/server file servers, such as Windows NT Server.

Network Browsing

The Network Neighborhood is the focal point for browsing network resources from a Windows 95 workstation. The Network Neighborhood provides the following benefits:

- Users browse available resources with a graphical interface.
- Shortcuts can be created within the Network Neighborhood for frequently accessed objects.
- Simple mapping of network drives is accomplished through the use of the toolbar, or by right-clicking the desired resource.
- Desktop shortcuts can be created for frequently accessed network resources.

A quick way to browse a server is to open **Start/Run** and type the UNC name of the server (such as \\MYSERVER). A window appears with the specified computer providing the user with the opportunity to double-click on its icon to browse the contents. After the window appears, press the *BACKSPACE* key to move the user up through the hierarchy of Workgroups, Entire Network, and Network Neighborhood.

Browse Master for Microsoft Networks

The Windows 95 browse service maintains the browse list through the use of a master browse server and a backup browse server. Each Windows 95 workgroup has one master browse server for each protocol used within the workgroup. In addition to the master browse server, there may be one or more backup browse servers for each protocol within a workgroup.

As Windows 95 starts up on a workstation, the computer checks to see if a master browse server is present for its workgroup. If one does not exist, an election appoints a master browse server for the workgroup.

If Windows 95 locates a master browse server existing in the workgroup, the system checks the number of computers in the workgroup and the number of browse servers present. If the ratio of computers to browse servers within a workgroup exceeds 15 to 1, an additional computer may be appointed to the role of a backup browse server.

Acting as a Master Browser can put a load on a system. Therefore, it is important to consider a computer's load when determining whether it can act as a Master Browser. A computer that does a lot of processor-intensive work should have the Browse Master set to **Disabled**. A fast computer that does not perform a lot of processor-intensive work can be selected as the preferred Master Browser by setting the Browse Master property to **Enabled**. A setting of **Automatic** causes the computer to become the Master Browser if it is the one elected. A Master Browser must be configured for each protocol in a particular workgroup. The configuration of the browse master will be discussed shortly.

Browsing Network Resources

To browse network resources at the command prompt, you can use the **net view** command. The **net view** command performs most of the same browsing actions as Windows Explorer or Network Neighborhood, except that it does not provide a list of workgroups.

The **net view** command uses the following syntax:

```
NET VIEW \\COMPUTERNAME

            or

NET VIEW /WORKGROUP:WORKGROUPNAME
```

The *COMPUTERNAME* is the name of the computer with shared resources you want to view. */WORKGROUP* specifies that you want to view the names of the computers that share resources in another workgroup. *WORKGROUPNAME* is the name of the workgroup for which you would like to view the list of computer names.

The browsing scheme used by Windows 95 on Microsoft networks has its roots in browsing method used by Windows for Workgroups and Windows NT. The Windows 95 browse service attempts to balance network traffic related to browsing activity while providing a scheme that works well when supporting both small and large networks.

On a peer-to-peer Windows 95 network, only computers with File and printer sharing for Microsoft Networks will be included on the browse list. They will be grouped by workgroup. If Windows NT or Windows for Workgroups systems are included in the network, they will be displayed in the list as well.

Browse Master Updates

When a Windows 95 computer starts up on the network, it sends an announcement to the master browse server for its workgroup. The master browse server then adds the new computer to the master list of available computers in the workgroup. The master browse server then notifies backup browse servers that a change to the browse list is available and should be obtained. The backup browse servers request the new information to update their local browse lists. Receipt of an updated browse list may take as long as 15 minutes, and new computers on the network will not show up in a user's request for a browse list until the update is received.

Since an update may take up to 15 minutes, it can sometimes lead you to believe that there is another problem with the network. A quick way to determine whether a specific computer is on the network, but not yet in the browse list, is to use the Find utility in the Start menu. Open **Start/Find/Find Computer** and type the computer's name. If the computer is connected to the network, Find Computer will locate it immediately. Another method is to type the UNC path of the computer in the **Start/Run** dialog.

If you suspect that the Master Browser is not maintaining an accurate list, you can request a list using the following command:

```
net view /workgroup:workgroupname
```

The workgroup's Master Browser is the only computer that can handle this request. The backup browse servers will not respond.

When a user shuts down Windows 95 properly, the system notifies the master browse server that it is shutting down. The master browse server then notifies backup browse servers that a change to the browse list is again available. The backup browse servers request the changes to the browse list.

If a user turns off the computer without shutting down Windows 95 in the proper manner, the system does not get a chance to send a message to its master browse server. In this case, the absent computer might appear in the master browse list until the name entry times out, which can take up to 45 minutes.

PROFILES ON A PEER-TO-PEER NETWORK

This section discusses the implementation of user profiles for Windows 95 clients within a peer-to-peer network. The following are the topics discussed within this section:

- User Profiles On a Peer-to-Peer Network
- Roving Profiles on Peer-to-Peer Networks

As you have seen earlier in the course, user profiles are an essential part of the user environment, especially when users may access more than one station using a given logon. Roving profiles are available on a peer-to-peer network. However, you must manually set the path to the roving user profiles.

Roving User Profiles On a Peer-to-Peer Network

A roving profile is one that can be accessed regardless of where a user logs on. This means that the profile must be stored somewhere on the network. On a peer-to-peer network, that profile is normally stored in a home directory for each user.

To let every computer in the network know where the home directories are located, you must create a text file listing each user's home directory on one of the network peers. Users should be given read-only rights to the directory containing this file. For security reasons, you should protect the directory from unauthorized modification by assigning a password for full access.

For example, you might create a file named PROFILES.INI in a SHARES\PROFILES directory, then share this directory to the network.

The file would have entries similar to those shown below:

```
[Profiles]

Frank=\\SHAREDIR\HOMEDIR\FRANK

Vic=\\SHAREDIR\HOMEDIR\VIC

Scott=\\SHAREDIR\HOMEDIR\SCOTT
```

In order to let Windows 95 know that this file exists, you need to add the following registry values to the HKEY_LOCAL_MACHINE\Network\Logon key:

DWORD Value	UseHomeDirectory
String Value	SharedProfileList

Edit the value of SharedProfileList so that it contains the UNC path and the filename of the text file containing the list of home directories.

SCENARIOS

Scenario 1

You want to add another computer to an existing peer-to-peer network composed of Windows 95 computers running NetBEUI. The computer's user needs to be able to share files with other users and to access shared files over the network. Windows 95 was installed on the computer, but no networking components were installed. What do you need to add to the computer?

....

....

Scenario 2

You are the administrator of a peer-to-peer Windows 95 network. There are many shared resources on the network and all of them have different passwords. Some of the users have started keeping password lists under their keyboards. When you ask them why, they say that they cannot remember so many passwords. Which feature of Windows 95 can help them keep track of their passwords without posing a security risk?

....

....

Scenario 3

The plant manager in your company often has to leave his desk to oversee operations. He is worried that someone will access the files on his computer. He wants additional security, but is concerned that he cannot remember more than one password. How can he configure his system to meet both of these objectives?

....

....

Scenario 4

You have installed a new printer driver on a Windows 95 computer and shared the printer to the network. You had to shut the computer down to add some additional memory. You restart the computer and try to see the printer in Network Neighborhood on another Windows 95 computer, but it is not there. How can you verify that the computer with the printer attached is still connected to the network?

....

....

Scenario 5

Your manager suspects that slow network performance on your peer-to-peer network is due to the fact that too many computers are acting as the Master Browser in the workgroup. You have disabled the Browse Master property on all of the computers in the network. Now users complain that no network computers are available in Network Neighborhood. What should you do?

....

....

SUMMARY

In this chapter, you saw how Windows 95 clients can share resources in a peer-to-peer environment. This included:

- Share-level vs. user-level security
- Sharing workstation resources utilizing share-level security
- Browsing network resources
- Mapping network drives
- Configuring the Browse Master for Microsoft Networks
- Creating persistent shares
- Using the Windows Explorer and the Network Neighborhood to view shared resources
- Utilizing Peer Servers with Windows 95 and MS-DOS based clients
- Optimizing the file-sharing performance of Windows 95

In the next chapter, you will see how to implement Windows 95 as a client in a Windows NT domain environment.

POST-TEST QUESTIONS

The answers to these questions are in Appendix A at the end of this manual.

1. Using user-level security, what types of rights can be granted to users for a resource?

....

....

2. List the three possible settings for the Microsoft Browse Master.

    ....

    ....

3. You are supporting a peer-to-peer network of Windows 95 computers. One of the managers would like to share the project progress sheets with the other users on the network. Other managers need to be able to modify the progress sheets. Other employees should only be able to read them. How will you tell her to configure access?

    ....

    ....

4. One of your users is complaining that he cannot browse the network. He seems to have access to all of his local resources. When he tries to set a password for his screen saver, he receives a dialog box with a red circle and no error message. What is most likely the problem?

    ....

    ....

Windows 95 as a Windows NT Client

OBJECTIVES

At the completion of this chapter, you will be able to:

- Describe the Windows NT environment including domains and trust relationships.

- Describe the advantages of user-level security in a Windows NT environment with regards to resource sharing.

- Define the process of password synchronization for a Windows 95 client in a Windows NT environment.

- Describe the master browse service.

- Implement user profiles on a Windows NT network.

- Implement system and user policies on a Windows NT network.

PRE-TEST QUESTIONS

The answers to these questions are in Appendix A at the end of this manual.

1. Can you use Windows NT Workstation as an authenticator?

   ....

   ....

2. Where are profiles stored when you have a mixed network environment including Windows 95 clients and a Windows NT Server?

   ....

   ....

3. How can you keep a user from changing his Windows password when his logon is authenticated by a Windows NT Server?

   ....

   ....

INTRODUCTION

This chapter discusses the changes that occur when you have a mixed networking environment with Windows NT. The chapter begins with a discussion of the Microsoft networking environment when a Windows NT Server is part of the network. The chapter will first discuss the concept of domains and trust relationships. Next, the steps involved in configuring Windows 95 clients to be validated by a Windows NT Server will be identified.

Next, the chapter moves on to discuss resource sharing when Windows NT is used as the authenticator for user-level security. There are a few changes in the types of resource permissions available to the administrators and users.

The chapter then discusses the importance of passwords. Password synchronization is again discussed, but this time, for the Windows NT environment.

The chapter finishes with a discussion of the implementation of user profiles, policies, and group policies for Windows 95 clients who are being validated by a Windows NT Server.

MICROSOFT NETWORKS

This section will present some basics about NT Server domains, primary domain controllers (PDCs), and backup domain controllers (BDCs). Since a domain consists of a PDC and typically one or more BDCs, it is important to understand the role of each of these types of servers. The following are topics discussed within this section:

- Domain Organization
- Primary/Backup Domain Controllers
- Additional Server
- Trust Relationships
- One-Way Trusts

- Two-Way Trusts

As an administrator of a Windows NT 4.0 network, you need to understand the concept of a domain. By understanding the fundamentals, you will better be able to manage the domain clients.

Domain Organization

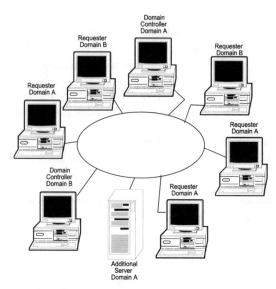

Microsoft networking is based around a domain model. A small network may contain only one domain to which all of the stations in the network belong. A larger network may contain many domains, which may or may not be set up to share resources with each other.

A domain is a logical, rather than physical, organization. Domain members do not need to be physically grouped together. In fact, they can reside in different cities, or even countries, as long as they have a way to communicate.

So what makes a group of systems a domain? Systems become part of a domain by being identified as domain members. Valid domain members include:

- Primary Domain Controller
- Backup Domain Controller
- Additional Servers

- Client Workstations

As members of the same domain, the systems work together. When a user logs on from any workstation, all of the domain servers become available as a group.

Primary/Backup Domain Controllers

Most servers are installed as either primary or backup domain controllers. Either, once defined, will remain a member of that domain for the life of the server. The only way to change domain membership for a primary or backup domain controller is to reinstall Windows NT Server.

- Primary domain controller

    Each domain will have one, and only one, primary domain controller. The primary domain controller holds the domain accounts database, the user and group database. Any time changes are made through User Manager for Domains, they are automatically made to the primary domain controller.

- Backup domain controller

    Each backup domain controller contains a backup copy of the domain accounts database. As changes are made to the database at the primary domain controller, these are replicated to any backup domain controllers in the domain.

    It is normally suggested that at least one other server in a domain be installed as a backup domain controller. A backup domain controller can help handle user account validations and can, should the need arise, be promoted to take the place of the primary domain controller.

If you have a domain that includes wide area links, you should install at least one backup domain controller at each remote location. That will allow for local processing of logon requests and help to reduce traffic across the link.

Additional Server

Specialty servers are sometimes set up as additional servers. An additional server is a machine that is running Windows NT Server, but not acting as a primary or backup domain controller. An additional server is also called a member server.

If integrated into a domain as a domain member, a server can grant access to resources through the use of group memberships. The server does not contain a copy of the domain's account database, so it cannot be used to validate domain logon attempts. Instead, it will contain its own local list of users and groups.

Possible uses of servers include:

- Time-critical or resource-intensive tasks

  If installed as additional servers, the machines do not assist in user logon validation. This means that there is not an additional strain placed on system resources for this.

- Separate management requirements

  Specialized servers, such as SQL servers, are often managed separately from the rest of the domain. Set up as a server, you can assign management duties to the appropriate administrator without giving him or her unnecessary access to domain controllers.

- *Mobile* server

  If there is a chance that the server will be moved in the future, it should be installed as an additional server rather than as a domain controller. Additional servers can be moved between domains simply by setting up a machine account in the domain and specifying a different domain name at the server.

Trust Relationships

Trusting Domain   Trusted Domain

Trust relationships are an important part of Windows NT Server domain management and security. Trust relationships give you a way of combining domains into a single management unit. It is a logical link implemented between two domains by the domain administrators. Trust relationships:

- Provide greater flexibility in network planning and design.

  Domains can be combined in different ways to meet operational needs.

- Simplify administrative overhead for multiple domains.

  Multiple domains can be managed from a central point. A single user database can be maintained and applied across multiple domains.

- Simplify network access for end users.

  End users only need to remember one global user account name and password to be able to access all necessary network resources.

- Allow domains to easily share resources.

  Domain boundaries do not have to act as barriers to resource access.

Let's take a closer look at what a trust relationship is and how it is implemented.

About Trust Relationships

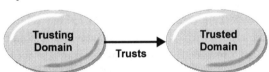

Each trust relationship is established between two domains, a trusting domain and a trusted domain. Once established, users and groups in the trusted domain can be assigned rights and permissions in the trusting domain. That is, the trusting domain trusts the users in the trusted domain. Of course, it is up to the administrator to determine how much each user and group should be trusted. Users and groups in the trusted domain **do not** automatically receive any rights and permissions. Just as users in the local domain, they must be explicitly granted permissions to resources.

Another important note is that the trust only works in one direction. Users in the trusting domain cannot access resources in the trusted domain.

The basic trust relationship can be expanded by establishing multiple trust relationships. Trust relationships can be established independent of physical locations, provided there is a connection between the domains.

SETTING UP DOMAIN CLIENTS

This section describes the process for setting up a Windows 95 client to log on to a Windows NT Server. The following topics are discussed within this section:

- Microsoft Network Clients
- Network Access Logon
- Validation

Follow these procedures to enable your Windows 95 clients to have their logon validated by a Windows NT domain.

Microsoft Network Clients

A Windows 95 client can be set up to connect to a Windows NT network. A Windows NT domain controller, a Windows NT Server, or a Windows NT Workstation can validate a user, provided that user has an account. To configure the Windows 95 client to be validated by a Windows NT computer, you must make sure that Client for Microsoft Networks is installed. Installation procedures for this client were earlier in the course. Once the client is installed, display its properties by selecting the client, and clicking on the **Properties** button. You can also double-click on the Client for Microsoft Networks to display the properties sheet. Next, click on the checkbox for **Log on to Windows NT domain**. This tells the Windows 95 client that you want logon to be validated by a Windows NT domain. You must enter the name of the Windows NT Server domain or Windows NT Workstation domain. Finally, click on **OK** to accept the validation configuration and close the Network dialog. You must restart your computer to let the changes take effect. Once the logon dialog appears, there will be an extra field of information that displays the name of the domain the user is logging in to.

> NOTE: *If you want the user to be validated by a Windows NT server that is not part of a domain or by a Windows NT Workstation, you will need to enter that computer's NetBIOS name instead of the domain name.*

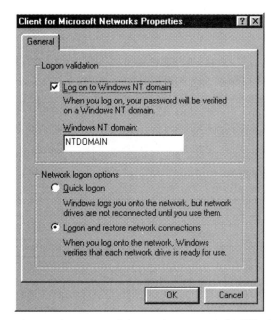

It is not necessary to change the name of the workgroup on the Windows 95 client to match the name of the Windows NT domain. You can have your Windows 95 clients remain in their workgroups and still be validated through the Windows NT server. A Windows 95 user will be able to see all workgroups in the Network Neighborhood. However, a workgroup and a domain share the same icon, so it is difficult to distinguish between them. If you want resources organized by domain rather than by workgroup, you will need to set the workgroup on the **Identification** tab of the Network utility to the domain name.

Validation

Both Windows NT Server and Windows NT Workstation can be used to provide a list of users and groups for user-level security. With Windows NT Server, users are often managed and provided by a domain controller. However, they can also be provided by a server that was installed as an additional server, also called a member server.

Exercise 13-1:
Microsoft Client

This exercise has special requirements. You will need a network adapter installed in your system and access to an NT Server domain. You will need to get a valid username, domain name, and server with shares to which you have access from the network administrator.

Start the exercise logged on as your primary user.

Username   _____

Domain name   _____

Server name   _____

Shares   _____

1.   Open the Network utility.

2.   If any client types are listed in the components list, select and delete each by clicking on **Remove**.

3.   Click on **Add**.

4.   Select Client and click on **Add**.

5.   Select Microsoft as the manufacturer and Client for Microsoft Networks as the client type. Click on **OK**.

6.   If prompted, provide the path to your installation files. The **Browse** button opens a dialog allowing you to locate the files.

   NOTE: *On this and later exercises, if Windows 95 cannot find files it needs, type in a path of either C:\WINDOWS or C:\WINDOWS\SYSTEM and try to install the particular file again.*

7.   Select **Client for Microsoft Networks** from the Network dialog and click on **Properties**.

8.   Check the box next to **Log on to Windows NT domain**.

9.   Type the domain name in the **Windows NT domain** field.

10.   Click on **OK**.

11.   Click on **OK** to close the Network dialog.

12.   When prompted, click on **Yes** to restart your system.

13.   After the system restarts, log on using the username provided for you.

14.   If prompted to retain your settings, click on **Yes**.

15. When prompted to confirm your password, type in your password and press *ENTER*.

16. Run **Start/Programs/MS-DOS Prompt**.

17. Type the following and press *ENTER*:

    ```
    net view \\server
    ```

    Replace server with the server name of your Windows NT Server. What happens?

    A list of shares is displayed (only if there are existing shares).

18. Type the following and press *ENTER*:

    ```
    EXIT
    ```

19. Double-click on the Network Neighborhood desktop object.

20. After a short delay, the Entire Network and any servers to which you are attached are listed.

21. Right-click on the server to which you have access and select **Open**. Any shared resources will be listed. You can also double-click on the server to display the shared resources.

22. Launch **Start/Programs/Windows Explorer**.

23. Scroll down to Network Neighborhood and expand the listing.

24. Select the server to which you have access and expand it.

25. Select a share. Its contents will be listed in the Contents window.

26. Run **Map Network Drive** from the **Tools** menu. You are prompted to enter the path to the share.

27. Click on **Cancel**.

28. Bring the server window into the foreground and select a share to which you have access.

29. Right-click on the share object and select **Map Network Drive**.

30. The share path is already entered. Leave the drive letter at default and click on **OK**.

31. Bring Windows Explorer into the foreground and run **Refresh** from the **View** menu.

32. You should now see a logical drive listed in Explorer for your shared network resource.

33. Right-click on the network drive and select **Properties**.

34. The drive type is shown as **Network Connection**. Click on **OK**.

35. Close all open windows on your system.

Network Access and Logon

When you start up your system, you are prompted automatically for your username and password. Windows 95 provides unified logon support in a mixed environment.

- Unified Logon

  Windows 95 provides a means of supporting unified logon to all of your network servers from a single prompt. When you first log on, you will be prompted for a username and password for each network operating system supported. If the username and password are the same for each, you are prompted for primary logon only on subsequent attempts, with automatic attachment to other networks through username and password caching.

- Logon script processing

  Logon script processing is supported for both Novell NetWare and Microsoft networks. A NetWare logon script processor is provided as part of the Microsoft Client for NetWare.

- Browsing

  No matter which system tool you prefer for browsing available resources, all resources to which your client has access are displayed. You also have the option of creating desktop shortcuts to commonly used network resources. If you lose your server connection, Windows 95 will automatically rebuild your network environment and resource connections when the server connection is restored.

In many cases, you will have client-specific logon options.

RESOURCE SHARING

This section describes resource sharing when a Windows NT domain is available. User-level security provides additional security since users must be validated by a security provider. Share-level security does not have this requirement. The following topics are discussed within this section:

- Microsoft Network Concerns
- Security Options
- Share-level Security On a Windows NT Network
- User-level Security On a Windows NT Network
- Sharing Folders and Subfolders
- Applying Permissions to Users and Groups
- Peer Servers

As you may know, Windows NT provides high security for all aspects of the operating system environment from logon validation to resource sharing. By implementing a Windows NT authenticator in your networking environment, security to resources is heightened.

Microsoft Network Concerns

You must install the Client for Microsoft Networks in order to use the File and printer sharing for Microsoft Networks service. File and printer sharing for Microsoft Networks is not supported if File and printer sharing for NetWare Networks is also installed. You can only support file and print sharing for one or the other.

In order to implement user-level security, you must identify a network security provider. The name you enter for the provider depends on your network configuration:

- Windows NT Workstation

    Enter the name of a Windows NT Workstation as security provider.

- Stand-alone Windows NT Server

    Enter the machine name of a Windows NT server as security provider.

- Windows NT Server domain

    Enter the domain name as security provider. An available domain controller will be queried for security information.

Configuration of the Windows NT domain has been discussed earlier in this chapter. Let's take a look at how to configure share-level and user-level securities.

Security Options

Share-level or user-level security is set on the **Access Control** tab of the Network utility. These security options are mutually exclusive. You cannot use share-level security for some resources and user-level security for others.

When you configure user-level security, you must specify the domain name or computer name that will provide your list of users and groups.

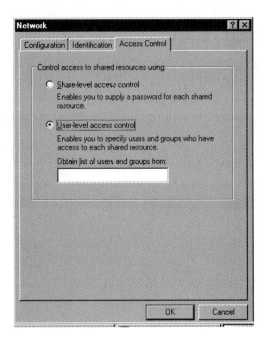

If the domain or computer you specify is not available, the following dialog will be displayed:

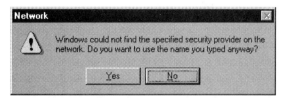

If you click on **Yes**, you will be prompted to select whether the security provider is a Windows NT Server or a Windows NT Domain.

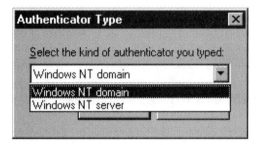

When switching between share-level and user-level security and vice-versa, all established shares are lost. The following warning dialog box is displayed:

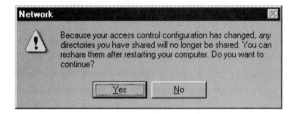

Share-level Security On a Windows NT Network

Shared resources are folders and printers that are made available to users. Although it can be used on a Windows NT network, share-level access is generally used in a peer-to-peer environment where there is not a security provider. The default Windows 95 computer setting is share-level.

You might use share-level security in a situation where some users are validated by a security provider, but others are not. Using share-level security allows users to gain access to resources based on a password, not their identity.

Another situation in which share-level security would be used is in a situation where no network administrator is available to manage user accounts.

In most situations, share-level security is less secure than user-level security.

User-level Security On a Windows NT Network

When a folder is configured for sharing, the following dialog box is displayed:

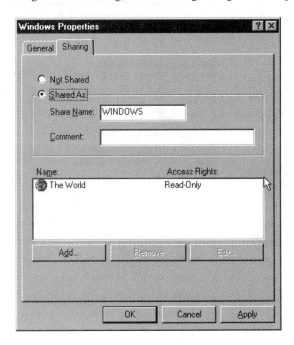

You will need to specify a share name. Adding a dollar sign ($) to the end of the share name will make it not appear in a list. A comment can be added. This comment is displayed in the browsing list. This gives the user more information about the folder's contents.

User-level access lets you grant users specific access rights to a folder and its contents. These users are stored on a Windows NT computer, NetWare 3.x server, or NetWare 4.x server. On a Windows NT domain, these user accounts are created and managed by User Manager for Domains. On a Windows NT Server that is not a domain controller or on a Windows NT Workstation, these user accounts are created in User Manager.

The list of users and groups is determined by the network security provider specified on the **Access Control** tab of the Network utility.

Granting Access Permission to Selected Users

Once you enabled the **Shared As** option from the above dialog, you can click on **Add** to select the users that you want to allow to access the shared resource. Then you can grant access permissions accordingly for each user or group. If that domain trusts other domains, you will be able to select a trusted domain from a drop-down list.

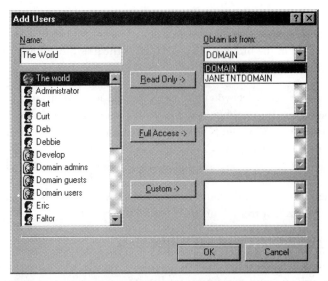

Users and global groups are displayed in the list. The Administrator is a built-in account for administering the computer or domain. The world represents all users in the domain, so if the world is given certain access, each user in the domain is allowed the same type of access. Read Only, Full Access, and Custom access settings can be established for The World, any number of groups of users, or specific user names.

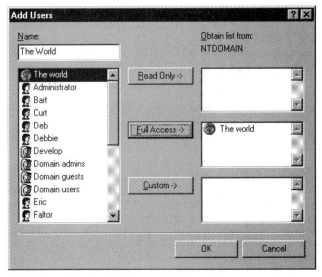

The **Custom** settings access is only available with user-level security. The Change Access Rights dialog is displayed when you click on **OK** to close the Add Users dialog.

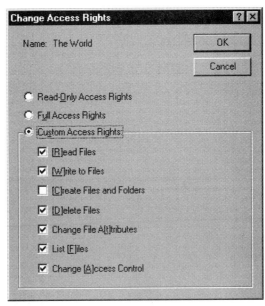

Any combination of these settings can be established for the selected group(s) or user(s). The settings are:

Read Files	The user can open and view files, but cannot modify them.
Write to Files	The user can edit existing files, but not create new files or folders.
Create Files and Folders	The user can create files and folders.
Delete Files	The user can delete files.
Change File Attributes	The user can change file attributes.
List Files	The user can list the contents of the shared folder.

| Change Access Control | The user can change access permissions on the shared folder. |

Sharing Folders and Subfolders

If a user has access to a parent folder, by default he is given the same level of access to any of the parent's subfolders. However, you can create subfolders with specific access permissions.

If you share a folder that contains other shared folders, the following dialog will be displayed:

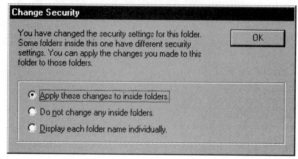

The available options are as follows:

- Apply these changes to inside folders

    This option will change the security settings of all child folders to match the parent folder.

- Do not change any inside folders

    This option will keep existing settings on all internal folders.

- Display each folder name individually

    This option will display a prompt for each shared subfolder. You can make independent decisions about whether or not to apply the security settings of the parent folder.

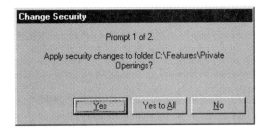

Applying Permissions to Users and Groups

Rights for Windows 95 shares are cumulative. First the user's rights are checked, then the rights for each group to which the user belongs. The user's rights take precedence over group rights. That means that if the user's rights are more restrictive than those of the group, the more restrictive rights will be granted. If a group's rights are more restrictive, the less restrictive rights will be granted.

If the user does not have explicit rights, rights will be the sum total of those granted to all of the user's groups. For example, suppose Bill belongs to the Accounting group and the Managers group. The Accounting group has read-only access to the Salaries share. The Managers group has write access to the Salaries share. Bill will be able to read and modify documents within the Salaries share. However, if Bill is explicitly given read-only access, he will not be able to modify the documents in the Salaries share.

Exercise 13-2:
Access Security Options and Share Network Resources

The purpose of this exercise is to give you practice sharing resources in a mixed network environment. You must be configured as a Microsoft Network client with the File and printer sharing for Microsoft Networks service loaded. You also need a Windows NT domain server available. At the start of this exercise, you should be logged on using the username and password provided for your network environment. You will not be able to complete this exercise without network access.

1. Launch the Network utility.

2. A list of currently installed components are listed. Verify that Client for Microsoft Networks is available in the list.

3. Select the Client for Microsoft Networks and click on the **Properties** button.

4. Click on the checkbox for **Log on to Windows NT domain**.

5. Enter the name of your Windows NT domain.

6. Click on **OK**.

7. Click on the **Access Control** tab. At this time, **Share-level access control** should be selected. Change the current setting to **User-level access control.**

8. Enter the name of your Windows NT domain to obtain the list of users and groups.

9. Click on **OK**.

10. When prompted to restart your computer, click on **Yes**.

11. When prompted, log on using the appropriate username and password.

12. Launch **Start/Programs/Windows Explorer**.

13. Right-click on the **WINDOWS** directory and select **Sharing**.

14. Click on the **Shared As** option.

15. Change the share name to SYSTEM.

16. Click on **Add** to add permitted users.

17. Select **The World** user.

18. Click on **Read Only** to add The World to the group of permitted users for this access right.

19. Select the **Domain admins** group.

20. Click on **Full Access**.

21. Select the **Domain users** group.

22. Click on **Custom**.

23. Click on **OK**.

24. Click on the checkbox for **List Files**. This gives the Domain users group the permission to list the files within the WINDOWS directory, but no other actions are permitted.

25. Click on **Apply**.

26. Click on **OK** to close the Windows Properties dialog.

27. Close Windows Explorer.

PASSWORDS

This section discusses the concept of password synchronization for an environment that includes a Windows NT Server. The following topics are discussed in this section:

- Microsoft Networking Password Settings
- User Must Change Password at Next Logon
- Password Synchronization For a Windows NT Client
- User Cannot Change Password
- Password Never Expires
- Troubleshooting Password Problems At Logon

As you read through the section about password synchronization, keep one fact in mind. If the Windows password and the Microsoft Networking password are the same, the user will only be prompted for the Microsoft Networking password when logging on.

Microsoft Networking Password Settings

A Windows 95 client can only log into the Microsoft Windows Network if the name and password established in the User Properties dialog of the User Manager for Domains are successfully entered and confirmed by the Windows NT security provider. The Windows NT User Manager for Domains allows you to specify three options that affect when and if a user can modify his password. They are shown in the graphic.

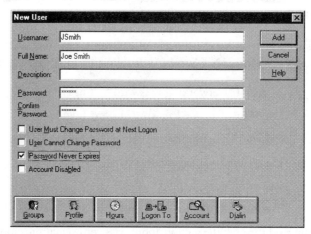

Let's take a close look at each of these password settings.

User Must Change Password at Next Logon

If the option **User Must Change Password at Next Logon** is selected, the user is prompted to change his password the first time he logs on to the Microsoft Windows Network using that username. An informational dialog box appears stating "Your password for *NTDOMAIN* has expired. You must specify a new one to log on." NTDOMAIN will be replaced by the name of the security authority you are using for validation.

When the user clicks the **OK** button at logon, the Change Password dialog box is displayed, prompting the user to change the password for Microsoft Networking. The user needs to enter the old password once and the new password twice. Once the new password is entered and confirmed, a message appears stating "The password has successfully changed," and the **User Must Change Password at Next Logon** checkbox becomes unchecked in the User Properties dialog of User Manager for Domains.

If this new username or password is different from those used for Windows logon, the Welcome to Windows dialog box appears the user is prompted to log on to Windows. The User Name field contains the username. The correct Windows password should be entered in the Password field to log on to Windows properly.

Password Synchronization For a Windows NT Client

The need to enter two passwords can be avoided by synchronizing the passwords. Synchronizing the screen saver password with the Windows password was covered in the previous chapter.

To synchronize the Microsoft Windows Network password with the Windows password, you must first open the Passwords control panel. Verify that the **Change Passwords** tab is displayed. Click on **Change Windows Password**. Click on the **Microsoft Networking** checkbox to enable synchronization. Then, click on **OK**.

> *NOTE: Now that there are two system passwords involved, the passwords must be validated on each. The first dialog will be the Change Windows Password dialog.*

Type the Old Windows password in the Old password field. Type a new password and confirm the new password. Click on **OK**. The following dialog box appears if the Windows and the Microsoft Networking passwords were not previously synchronized:

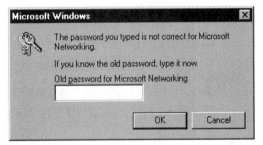

Type in the old password for the Windows NT user account and click on **OK**.

The newly synchronized password takes effect for Windows and the Microsoft Network as well as the screen saver, provided it has been set for synchronization. To view a list of all of the passwords that will be changed, click on the **Details** button on the Change Windows Password dialog box.

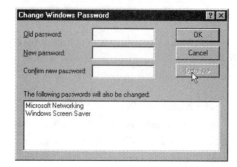

User Cannot Change Password

If the option **User Cannot Change Password** is selected, the user is not allowed to change his password at any time. The following error dialog appears when this User Properties setting is enabled and the user tries to change the password in the Passwords utility's **Change Other Passwords** option.

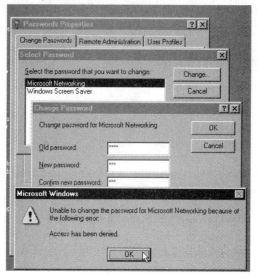

If you try to synchronize passwords for Microsoft Networking and Windows when the user password setting **User Cannot Change Password** is enabled, the following error will be displayed.

This dialog is followed by confirmation that the Windows password did change. The passwords will not be synchronized at this point.

Password Never Expires

If the option **Password Never Expires** is selected, the user's password never changes unless it is modified explicitly, either through synchronization or by changing it in either User Manager or in the Passwords control panel.

Troubleshooting Password Problems At Logon

If a user does not type the correct password for Microsoft Networking, he will not be prompted for a Windows logon even if the passwords are not synchronized. Users can access all resources on the local machine, except the **Change Passwords** tab of the Passwords control panel. Users can also see other computers through **Find Computer**, but are not allowed access to any other computers even if those computers are on the Microsoft Windows Network. The following error is encountered if the user tries to open a Windows client machine which was located in **Find Computer**:

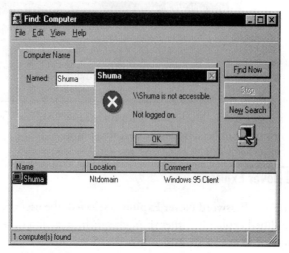

The error "Not logged on" reflects the fact that the local client is not logged on, not that Shuma's computer is not logged on. As long as the local client and any other client share a common protocol, they can be seen through **Find Computer**.

If the user successfully logs on to the Microsoft Network, but cancels the Windows password prompt, he will still be able to access the network.

BROWSER SERVICE FOR WINDOWS NT

This section discusses the browser service for a Windows NT network environment. The following topics are discussed within this section:

- Browse Master Updates
- Configuration of the Master Browser

Each master browse server maintains the master list of workgroups, domains, and computers for a specified workgroup. Backup browse servers assist with browse list requests as needed. Using backup browse servers helps minimize the network traffic handled by the master browse server. Typically, one master or backup browse server is assigned for every fifteen computers in a particular workgroup.

Configuration Of the Master Browser

To configure Browse Master settings, open the Network control panel. Select **File and printer sharing for Microsoft Networks** from the **Configuration** tab. Click on the **Properties** button to display the properties for this component. You can also double-click on **File and printer sharing for Microsoft Networks** to display the properties sheet.

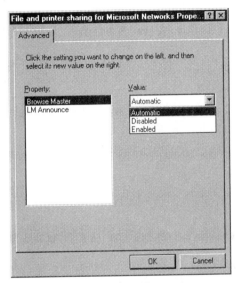

Browse Master settings include:

- Automatic

    The computer may maintain the browse list if elected.

- Enabled

    The computer may be used as the master browse server.

- Disabled

  The computer will not perform master browse server functions.

The Automatic setting is selected by default.

NOTE: *The LM Announce setting present on the property sheet for File and printer sharing for Microsoft Networks configures the computer to utilize a LAN Manager 2.x domain on the network.*

USER PROFILES ON A WINDOWS NT NETWORK

This section discusses the use of user profiles for a Windows 95 client on a Windows NT network. The following topics are discussed within this section:

- User Profiles On a Windows NT Network
- Establishing Mandatory User Profiles On a Windows NT Network
- Roving User Profiles On a Windows NT Network

Be sure to note the difference in where profiles are stored when the network is using a Windows NT Server for logon validation.

Establishing Mandatory User Profiles On a Windows NT Network

With Windows 95, you can create mandatory user profiles for use on Windows NT or NetWare networks. Through use of mandatory user profiles, the administrator can enforce a consistent desktop configuration for selected users. This feature can be used to create a standard user profile for each computer and make sure that implementation takes place at every logon.

To implement a mandatory user profile, you must first enable user profiles from the Passwords control panel, **User Profiles** tab. Customize the desktop and settings. Copy the files for the user profile to the home directory of each user who will use the mandatory profile. This profile may exist on a Windows NT network, a different domain controller, or a network server. You will need to share the home directory to access it on the Windows 95 client.

Next, locate the USER.DAT file in the home directory. Rename it to USER.MAN. You will receive a confirmation dialog asking whether you are sure you want to rename USER.DAT. Click on **Yes**.

When the user logs on, Windows 95 will apply the mandatory profile to the computer's registry. These settings will be loaded into the Registry, overriding any local profiles that may exist for the user. The user can change desktop settings while logged on. However, as the user logs off, changes will not be saved to the mandatory profile file. If changes were saved, this would defeat the purpose of a mandatory profile.

If a USER.MAN file is not found, the USER.DAT is used. If neither file is available, the user's desktop will be set up using the default profile.

Roving User Profiles On a Windows NT Network

To enable a roving user profile, you must first enable user profiles. Then you must specify the profile path in User Manager for Domains in Windows NT. To do so, display the User Properties dialog. Click on the **Profiles** button. To define a user's home directory, type it in the **Local Path** field of the Home Directory section of the User Environment Profile dialog. When the roving user next logs on to a machine, the user profile file will be downloaded and applied.

The network parent directory that contains user home directories should be shared out with Read-Only access. Users will then not be able to directly modify profile files on the network.

   NOTE: *Windows NT stores profiles for Windows NT computers at the specified profiles path. It does not use this path to store Windows 95 profiles.*

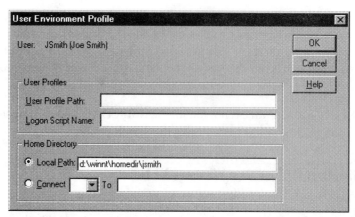

In this case, JSmith is the user's name.

Policies On a Windows NT Network

This section discusses the implementation of policies in a Microsoft network environment that includes a Windows NT Server. The following topics are discussed within this section:

- Using Policies On a Windows NT Network

- Creating User Policies in CONFIG.POL

- Group Policies

- Setting Group Priorities

- Logon Scripts

Using Policies On a Windows NT Network

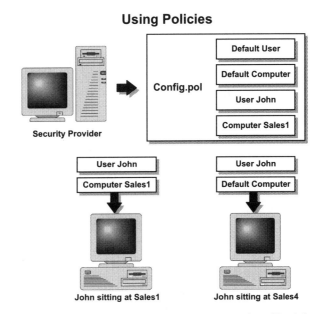

Using Policies

To create a policy, you must first create a CONFIG.POL policy file. This is the policy file to which you will add user and computer policies. To create this file, run **File/New File** in System Policy Editor. The System Policy Editor was discussed earlier in the course.

This will display two icons: default user and default computer. Policy settings created in these two items will apply to users who do not have a user-specific policy created or for users who do not log on to the domain.

It is this CONFIG.POL file that is downloaded automatically from the Windows NT network. This policy file should be stored on the network in the *servername*\netlogon share. The netlogon share is actually the share name for the \WINNT\SYSTEM32\REPL\IMPORT\SCRIPTS directory. If you choose to manually download policies, you must choose a network share other than netlogon.

These default locations can be overridden in the policy file setting by selecting the **Network** option for the default computer policy settings and expanding **Update**. Click on the checkbox for **Remote Update**. You must then enter the new path to where you want policy files to be stored.

Policy settings for the default user or a specific user will modify the registry settings in the HKEY_CURRENT_USER key. Policy settings for the default computer or a specific computer will modify the registry settings in the HKEY_LOCAL_MACHINE key.

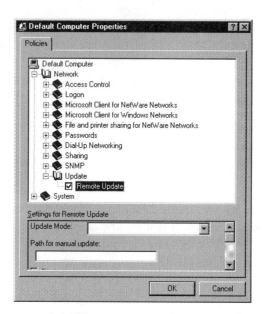

Creating User Policies With CONFIG.POL

To create default user and computer policies that will be stored on a Windows NT Server, first run **File/New File** to display the default user and default computer icons. Set policy settings for either the default user or default computer by double-clicking on the respective icon. This will display the properties where policy restrictions can be set. Be sure to check for specific settings that may need to be set for certain restrictions.

To add a user policy, run **Edit/Add User**. You may either type the name of the user or browse the list of users. This user policy will be contained in the CONFIG.POL file on the network. Once the user logs in, the policy will be downloaded from the network. Policy settings will then be enabled.

Double-click on the user icon to set policy restrictions. Once you have set the policy, click on **OK**. To set a policy for a machine, run **Edit/Add Computer**. You may either type the computer's name or browse the list of computers on the network. Double-click on the computer icon to set policy restrictions. Once you have set the policy, click on **OK**. Finally, run **File/Save As**. Save the policy as CONFIG.POL in the *servername*\netlogon share.

To confirm that policies will be stored in the default location on the Windows NT Server, open the local registry by running **File/Open Registry**. Double-click on the Local Computer icon to display its properties. Expand **Network**. Expand **Update**. Verify that the checkbox for **Remote Update** is selected. Also, verify that the update mode is set to **Automatic (use default path)**. Then click on **OK**.

You can create as many user and computer policies as needed within CONFIG.POL. Automatic download should usually be used for users who will be logging on to a Windows 95 machine in the local network.

Manual Remote Updates

Sometimes you may want to specify a path for remote update manually. For example, you might want to store policies on a server other than the primary domain controller. To do this, run **File/New File**. Add a user by running **Edit/Add User**. Enter the name of the user or browse the list of users to select. Click on **OK**. Then set policy settings for this specific user.

The policy name should reflect the name of the user. For example, if the user's name is Todd, then name the policy TODD.POL. You should note that the policy name cannot exceed 8 characters.

To change the download method to manual, run **File/Open Registry**. Double-click on the Local Computer icon. Expand **Network**. Expand **Update**. Verify that **Remote Update** is checked. Change the update mode to **Manual (use specific path)**. Then type the following in the path field:

`\\servername\sharename\USERNAME.POL`.

Finally, click on **OK**.

The policy will not be downloaded until the user logs on to the system again. The policy will then be downloaded from the specified path.

Group Policies

You can define group policies for users using Windows NT as an authenticator. On a Windows NT network, you can only use global groups created in Windows NT to define group policies. Local groups cannot be seen by Windows 95. They are used for assigning access to local resources on Windows NT computers.

To create group policies, you must confirm that GROUPPOL.DLL has been installed on all client machines. To create a global group in Windows NT, launch User Manager for Domains on your Windows NT system. Run **New Global Group** from the **User** menu.

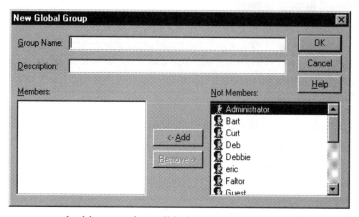

Type a group name and add users who will belong to this group. Click on **OK**.

Once you have created global groups on Windows NT, you will need to create the group policy on the Windows NT client. To create a group policy, you must use the CONFIG.POL policy file. This policy file overrides all other policy files. For example, if you have a specific user policy that is saved as *username*.POL, but you belong to a group with a group policy defined, the group policy settings will take precedence if there are conflicts. If CONFIG.POL contains policies for a specific user, the group policies of the groups to which that user belongs will be ignored.

To create a group policy, launch System Policy Editor. Run **Open File** from the **File** menu. Open the CONFIG.POL file which is stored in the Windows NT server's netlogon share. Run **Add Group** from the **Edit** menu. Type the name of the group you want to add. You can also browse the list of users and groups from the Windows NT domain to select a group. Then click on **OK**. Double-click on the group's icon to display Properties. Define policy settings for the group and click on **OK**.

Setting Group Priorities

Follow the steps to create a group policy for each group whose policy settings you wish to define. Once you have defined all policies, you must set the priorities of each group. This is necessary for cases where users belong to multiple groups. Groups placed highest on the list have highest priority. So, if a user belongs to two groups, the group that has highest priority will apply its policy settings.

To set group priority, verify that CONFIG.POL is still open. Run **Group Priority** from the **Options** menu in System Policy Editor.

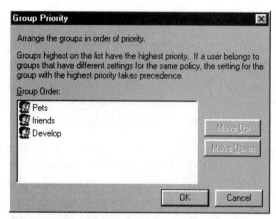

Use the **Move Up** and **Move Down** buttons to change the priority of the groups listed in the Group Order box. Confirm the priority level of each group and click on **OK**.

Logon Scripts

Logon Scripts are batch files that administrators use to automatically run certain applications on the user's machine. You must enable logon scripts from User Manager for Domains in the Windows NT environment. Logon scripts must be stored in the netlogon share of the Windows NT domain.

To specify the logon script path and batch file name, double-click on the user for whom you want to enable a logon script in User Manager for Domains or User Manager. This displays the User Environment Profile dialog. Type the path for the logon script. The path should begin with the netlogon share path (usually *SYSTEM*\SYSTEM32\REPL\IMPORT\SCRIPTS). The reference to *system* will be the WINNT directory if Windows NT was installed to its default location.

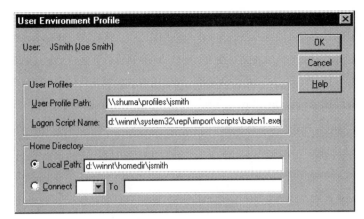

When the user logs on to the Windows 95 client, the logon script will be downloaded from the server. The batch file will then be executed. You can create specific logon scripts for each user, or one logon scripts for multiple users. If your network environment consists of a PDC and multiple BDCs, you can set up replication to ensure that the logon script is available even if the PDC is down.

SCENARIOS

Scenario 1

You are deploying Windows 95 on a network with multiple domains. The Sales domain trusts the Accounting domain and the Marketing domain. The DocumentControl domain trusts only the Accounting domain. The Accounting domain and the Marketing domain trust no one. You are setting up users who will need access to resources in both the Sales domain and the DocumentControl domain. In which domain will you create them?

....

....

Scenario 2

You have installed Windows 95. Now you want the computer to be validated by a Windows NT domain controller named EMPLOYEES in the SALES domain. The Windows NT network is running TCP/IP. What steps must you take?

....

....

Scenario 3

You have shared the HR folder and granted read-only permission to the Employees group in the SALES domain. You have configured the SALES domain as the security provider. You would like to give access to the Employees group in the MARKETING domain as well. However, the domain is not available from the Add User dialog. What most likely is the problem?

....

....

Scenario 4

Sam is a temporary employee. He will be working in technical support for several months. You want him to be able to access all of the shares that a permanent employee of technical support can access, except that you do not want him to be able to modify the items in the STATUS share. Permanent employees of technical support all belong to the TECHSUPPORT group. How can you configure Sam's access?

....

....

Scenario 5

John has the following settings in Windows NT User Manager:

User Properties		
Username: John		OK
Full Name: John Smith		Cancel
Description: Accountant		Help
Password: ************		
Confirm Password: ************		

☐ User Must Change Password at Next Logon
☑ User Cannot Change Password
☑ Password Never Expires
☐ Account Disabled
☐ Account Locked Out

Groups   Profile   Hours   Logon To   Account   Dialin

He wants to synchronize his Windows 95 password, his Screen Saver password, and his Microsoft Networking password. Which setting will you need to change so that he can do that?

....

....

Scenario 6

John, Sarah, Sam, and April are telemarketing representatives. Sam is in charge. All of them are members of the TELEMKT group in the CORPORATE domain. You want all of the telemarketing representatives to have a certain set of desktop items and start menu items. You want them to only be able to run approved programs. However, Sam needs to be able to run more programs than the other representatives. What is the easiest way to configure this?

....

....

SUMMARY

In this chapter, we examined the following factors of Windows 95 as a client in a Windows NT network:

- Features of the Windows NT environment
- Advantages of user-level security
- Implementing user-level security for resource sharing
- Password security
- Password synchronization with the Windows NT environment
- Browsing service in Windows NT
- Implementation of user profiles in a Windows NT environment
- Implementation of user and system policies in a Windows NT environment
- Implementation of group policies in a Windows NT environment
- Usage of logon scripts

POST-TEST QUESTIONS

The answers to these questions are in Appendix A at the end of this manual.

1. You want to provide user-level security using a single Windows NT Server. How will you need to install that server?

    ....

    ....

2. A user calls you at home because he forgot his Microsoft Networking password and critically needs access to a network resource. He is running Windows 95 and his passwords are not synchronized. You do not have a computer at home. What utility can you use to give him access to the network?

    ....

    ....

3. You suspect that a virus might have infected several computers in the company and caused severe fragmentation on the drives. You would like to run a virus scan and SCANDISK on each computer in the company the next time the user logs on. Which tool on Windows NT can enable you to do this?

    ....

    ....

Windows 95 as a Novell Netware Client

OBJECTIVES

At the completion of this chapter, you will be able to:

- Describe the Novell NetWare 3.x environment.
- Describe the Novell NetWare 4.x and Intranetware environments.
- Describe the process of setting up a NetWare client.
- Describe the browse service for a NetWare network.
- Configure SAP and Workgroup Advertising for NetWare Networks.
- Describe the advantages and limitations of peer servers.
- Describe the differences for implementing user profiles and system policies on a NetWare network.

PRE-TEST QUESTIONS

The answers to these questions are in Appendix A at the end of this manual.

1. What account must be present on the NetWare server to support Windows 95 file and printer sharing?

   ....

   ....

2. Where are profiles stored on a NetWare network?

   ....

   ....

3. Which NetWare utility is used to manage user and group account information?

   ....

   ....

4. What types of information does the Bindery store?

   ....

   ....

INTRODUCTION

This chapter discusses the changes that occur when you have a mixed networking environment that includes Novell NetWare 3.x servers , Novell NetWare 4.x servers, and/or Intranetware servers. The chapter begins with a discussion of the NetWare 3.x networking environment. Then the chapter discusses the NetWare 4.x and Intranetware networking environment. The chapter will also discuss resource sharing, the master browse service, and user profiles and policies.

NETWARE 3.X OVERVIEW

The following topics are discussed within this section:

- NetWare Disk Organization
- NetWare Logical Volumes
- NetWare 3.12 Disk Organization
- NetWare's Default System Directories
- Bindery

NetWare 3.x has a server-centric design, based on the bindery database files stored on each NetWare 3.x server. In order for users to be able to access resources on a NetWare 3.x server (in a strict 3.x environment), they must have an account on each server.

NetWare Disk Organization

Disks are organized in a way very similar, but not identical to, DOS. The basic organizational hierarchy is:

- File server

    Each file server is named to identify it on the network. The names may be up to 47 characters long. Short names are recommended.

- Volumes

    Volumes in NetWare are similar to logical drives in DOS. Each of the volumes within a single file server must have a unique name of 3 to 15 characters.

    NetWare 3.x can support up to 64 volumes. The maximum storage space is a total of 32 TB. A single volume can span multiple physical drives, up to a maximum of 32 TB. Up to 1,024 physical drives are supported.

- Directories

    The directory structure is effectively the same as in DOS. NetWare 3.x will convert 8-character directory names to the 8.3 naming convention.

- Files

    File structure is also effectively the same as in DOS.

The **slist** command will give you a list of file servers available on the network.

NetWare Logical Volumes

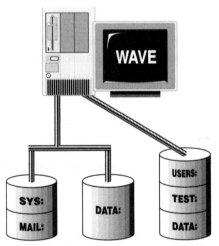

Internally, NetWare recognizes installed hard disks as a disk channel and disk drive address. However, this type of organization is inflexible and would be very difficult for most users.

As far as you and your end users are concerned, the top level of disk organization is the volume. NetWare volumes are similar to logical drives in DOS.

*NOTE   The volume "SYS:" is required as the first volume. This is set up as a system
default.*

The **CHKVOL** command will give you volume status information.

TIP: Create volumes with short names, as you will often need to type in the names.

The **CHKDIR** command gives you directory information, including directory size and
directory space remaining.

NetWare 3.12 Disk Organization

Each volume has its own directory structure. It has the same type of tree structure as is
used in DOS.

The top level of the directory is identified by the file server name and volume name. This
is like the root directory in DOS.

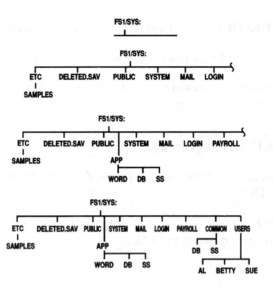

The volume SYS: has six default directories:

>PUBLIC
>
>SYSTEM
>
>MAIL
>
>LOGIN
>
>ETC
>
>DELETED.SAV (By default, this is hidden.)

These are required for NetWare to work. They must reside on the first volume, but need to appear only on the first volume. There are no mandatory directories on any other volumes.

The DELETED.SAV directory holds deleted files until purged or until their allotted space is required for other purposes. DELETED.SAV is hidden in a DOS directory scan, but can be seen with NetWare's NDIR command. This directory is not considered one of the five system default directories.

NetWare's Default System Directories

LOGIN

Loading the NetWare shell gives you access to the LOGIN directory, and only that directory. It contains:

> LOGIN.EXE – Allows you to Login to system.

> SLIST.EXE – Lists available file servers.

If you are using diskless workstations, you will also have:

> NET$DOS.SYS

Some non-Novell software will also occasionally install a file in the LOGIN directory to control access to the software.

MAIL

This is a holdover from when NetWare included a built-in electronic mail system. It will contain a numeric subdirectory for each user. The unique user ID number is used as the subdirectory name. These subdirectories are used by the system to store individual login scripts and printer configurations. Some non-Novell electronic mail packages use this area to store messages.

PUBLIC

Contains NetWare commands and utilities available to the users. Any executable files which will be accessible to all users can be stored in PUBLIC. DOS and common applications are usually stored in subdirectories under PUBLIC.

SYSTEM

Used for system files and supervisor-only utilities. The print queue subdirectories are also kept under the SYSTEM directory. It is strongly suggested that you not map a search drive to SYSTEM under any circumstances.

DELETED.SAV

Contains files deleted, but not purged. All files from deleted directories are put into DELETED.SAV until a global purge, unless files are flagged with the purge attribute.

ETC/SAMPLES

This directory holds the Internet database files for the TCP/IP NLMs. These NLMs are used for communications with Transmission Control Protocol/Internet Protocol (TCP/IP) networks.

> *NOTE:*   *An NLM is a NetWare Loadable Module. This is a utility that extends the normal functionality of the network.*

Bindery

The bindery stores information about users, groups, file servers, print servers, and other logical and physical entities on the network. Network information, such as passwords, account balances, and trustee assignments, are also kept in the bindery.

The bindery files are stored in SYS:SYSTEM. They are system files and do not appear in a normal directory search. The bindery files are NET$OBJ.SYS, NET$PROP.SYS, and NET$VAL.SYS.

SETTING UP NETWARE CLIENTS

The following topics are discussed within this section:

- Users and Groups: A Primer
- System Configuration Menu Utility
- SYSCON – User Information
- SYSCON Group Information
- The Microsoft Client for Novell Networks

Users and Groups: A Primer

- A user name allows access to network functions.

    In order to get onto the network, you must have a valid username. Each user should have his or her own username.

- A user account must be created on each NetWare 3.x server.

   NetWare 3.x does not have a centralized security model like Windows NT domains. You will need to specifically create a user account on each NetWare server the user will need to access.

- The system starts out with only two users defined:

   Supervisor, with all privileges on the system.

   Guest, with limited access. For security reasons, you should remove guest access from the system.

- Groups are sets of users that need access to the same resources.

   Groups are used to define access and privileges for users performing the same or similar functions.

- One default group is created during installation.

   The group Everyone is created by the system. As each user account is created, it is automatically made a member of the group Everyone.

- Only a Supervisor can create users and groups or change group memberships.

   Supervisor rights can be assigned to particular user accounts.

- A Workgroup Manager creates users and manages their access and privileges.

   They can delete or change users that they create or are assigned.

- An Account Manager manages access privileges.

   They cannot create users. They can delete users who are assigned to them.

The basic menu utility for creating users and groups is SYSCON.

System Configuration Menu Utility

SYSCON is the basic user and group utility. It is used to:

- Establish users and groups.
- Assign rights and privileges.

- Enforce security.
- Enable accounting to charge for services.
- Create login scripts.
- Perform system management functions.
- Define Workgroup Managers and User Account Managers.

NOTE: *SYSCON is commonly considered the primary supervisor utility.*

SYSCON is an MS-DOS application that can be launched from Windows 95.

You must have supervisor privileges to view and change user information. As a user, you can view all information about yourself. However, you are only able to change your password and modify your login script.

SYSCON - User Information

This is a brief listing of user information. Each entry is user specific. Modifications to one user do not affect other users.

Account Balance	Used with the NetWare accounting system to set balances for system access and use. This option is only available when the Accounting feature is installed.
Account Restrictions	Sets security information regarding the user.
Change Password	Allows the user or supervisor to change the user password. The password is never displayed.
Full Name	This entry contains the user's full name. The username is usually a shortened version of the user's full name.
Groups Belonged To	This entry is a list of group memberships. This selection can also be used to change group membership information.
Intruder Lockout Status	This is used with advanced security features to lock (or unlock) an account after an unauthorized login attempt. The entry appears when intruder detection is activated.
Login Script	Set custom login script for the user. This affects network startup for the user.

Managed Users and Groups	List or modify names of all users and groups that are being managed by the current user. You will see names listed in this section when the user is a Workgroup Manager or a User Account Manager.
Managers	Lists Workgroup Manager(s) with responsibility for managing this user record. The user may be deleted only by the Supervisor or by a Workgroup Manager for this particular user.
Other Information	Includes the unique user ID number, a system-generated number which identifies the user to the system. Even if the username is modified, the user ID number will remain the same.
Security Equivalences	Set security equal to another user. This is used to define supervisor equivalents (users whose permissions are the same as Supervisor's).
Station Restrictions	Limits login to specified workstations.
Time Restrictions	Sets allowed login times. Logs out users who have exceeded their approved times.
Trustee Directory Assignments	Sets allowed access to a directory. Affects that directory, its files, and all subdirectories.
Trustee File Assignments	Sets allowed access at a file level, allowing files to have different access privileges than those assigned to the directory.
Volume/Disk Restrictions	Allows you to limit the user's available storage space on any or all volumes on the network. It displays the user's limit and disk space currently in use.

SYSCON Group Information

Full Name	This contains the full name associated with the group.
Managed Users and Groups	This option displays and allows you to modify the list of users and groups managed (as Workgroup Managers or User Account Managers) by the members of this group.
Managers	This option displays and allows you to modify the list of users or groups who manage this group.
Member List	This option displays and allows you to modify the members of the group.
Other Information	This entry includes the unique group ID number.
Trustee Directory Assignments	This option displays and allows you to modify directory access privileges .
Trustee File Assignments	This option displays and allows you to modify file access privileges.

The Microsoft Client for Novell Networks

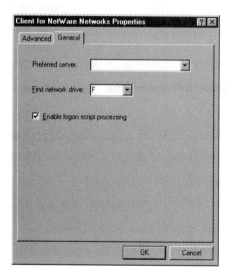

As mentioned earlier in the course, Windows 95 Setup automatically detects most network adapters and existing network client software and installs network client support. For example, if Setup detects NetWare components, the 32-bit protected-mode Microsoft Client for NetWare Networks is installed. The components installed depend somewhat on your system configuration when you launch Setup. You can also modify your setup through the Network utility.

As a NetWare client, you are prompted to identify your preferred server. This is the server with which your workstation will first attempt to communicate and query for logon validation. If you do not specify a preferred server, your workstation will attempt to log on to the first server responding.

The first network drive identifies the first drive ID available for connection to network resources. You must also specify whether or not to enable logon script processing. If you do not select to process logon scripts, your system will still attempt to make any persistent connections defined through Windows 95.

The Microsoft Client for NetWare does not support all features and services. Your requirements may force you to install Novell's Client 32 for Windows 95.

Exercise 14-1:
Novell NetWare Client

This exercise has special requirements. You will need a network adapter installed in your system and access to a Novell NetWare network. You will need to get a valid username and the server to which you have access from the network administrator.

Start the exercise logged on as your primary user.

Username   _____

Server name   _____

1. Launch the Control Panel and open the Network utility.

2. Click on **Add**.

3. Select Client and click on **Add**.

4. Select Microsoft as the manufacturer and Client for NetWare Networks and click on **OK**.

5. If prompted, type the path to the installation files.

   NOTE: *On this and later exercises, if Windows 95 cannot find files it needs, type in a path of either C:\WINDOWS or C:\WINDOWS\SYSTEM and try to install the particular file again.*

6. Select Client for NetWare Networks and click on **Properties**.

7. Type your server name in the Preferred server field and click on **OK**.

8. Verify that the default logon is Microsoft Client for NetWare Networks.

9. When prompted restart your system, click on **Yes**.

10. Log on using the username and password provided for you for the NetWare server.

11. When prompted that you have not logged on before, click on **Yes**.

12. When prompted, type your password again and press *ENTER*.

13. Right-click on Network Neighborhood and select **Open**.

14. You should see your preferred server listed. Right-click on the server and select **Explore**.

    This opens Explorer for the drive so you can walk through the directory structure.

15. Expand SYS and select Public. The directory's contents are displayed.

16. Run **Map Network Drive** from the **Tools** menu.

17. Type the following in the path and press *ENTER*:

    `\\servername\SYS\PUBLIC`

    Replace *servername* with your preferred server's name.

18. Double-click on My Computer. You will see all of the drives you have mapped to your NetWare server listed.

19. Close all open windows.

NETWARE 4.X AND INTRANETWARE OVERVIEW

The following topics are discussed in this section:

- NDS Database Logical Structure
- NDS Objects
- NDS Object Classes
- NDS Object Naming
- NDS Database Physical Structure
- NDS Partitions
- Bindery Emulation and the NDS Directory Database

NDS Database Logical Structure

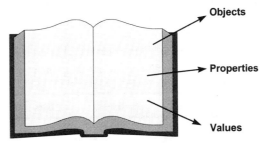

The NDS database is an enterprise-wide database containing information about network objects, such as NetWare servers, users, groups, print queues, printers, applications, and so on, as well as associated properties.

Each object has properties. Properties may have a single value or multiple values.

The properties of an object vary depending on the object type. For example, one property of a user object is titled Home Directory. The value of this property is the path to the user's home directory in the NetWare file system. A print queue object does not have a Home Directory property because a print queue does not log in to the network and use the file system.

NDS Objects

Because NDS is an enterprise-wide database, it is important to divorce the pre-NetWare 4.x concept of printers, servers, and users being associated with a particular server. NDS maintains these objects globally for the whole network, not on a per-server basis.

Each server on the network *looks* to the global NDS for information on objects. Therefore, all servers and clients have access to the same information.

When a network administrator makes any changes to the NDS, it is made one time only, and all servers *see* the new information.

Objects represent an item defined in the Directory Services database which is also referred to as the Directory or Directory tree. For example, a user is an object with a property titled Name. The value is the actual name itself.

Object	User	User	Printer
Property	Name	Telephone#	Name
Value	Chris	555-0011	Laser

Some properties, such as Name, are mandatory. Others, such as phone number, are optional.

NDS Object Classes

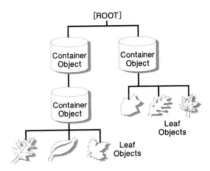

There are three classes of objects:

- [ROOT]
- Container
- Leaf

All objects make up the NDS Directory database. The logical organization of the NDS database is depicted as an inverted tree. At the top of each Directory tree is the [ROOT] object, created at the time of installation.

Only one [ROOT] object exists per NDS Directory tree. When referring to the [ROOT] object, brackets are required. Because the [ROOT] contains all objects, it is considered to be a Container object. The [ROOT] object cannot be deleted or renamed.

> *NOTE:*   *The [PUBLIC] object represents all nodes with a connection to the network whether they are logged in and authenticated or not. For this reason, be very careful when using the [PUBLIC] object as the target of file system or NDS security assignments.*

Container objects are used to hierarchically organize the NDS database and can contain other objects.

Leaf objects are resources found in a Container object, such as users, servers, or printers.

NDS Object Naming

All objects may use any of the following characters:

- A - Z (upper and lowercase)
- , - ( ) and spaces
- Numbers

TIP: *Although objects can be created with embedded spaces or special characters, a user may not be able to log in. Test any user IDs in which you have used these characters.*

The following characters cannot be used:

    { } [ ] . % @

Including spaces in object names can cause problems under some client operating systems. Some, including DOS, use spaces as delimiters.

NDS Database Physical Structure

Now that you understand the logical structure of the NDS database, let's explore its physical structure.

The NDS database is stored in a hidden directory on the SYS volume of a NetWare 4.11 server. The design of NDS allows the database to reside in whole, or in part, on NetWare 4.11 servers throughout the network. This distributed design makes NDS an extremely flexible and scaleable directory service.

NDS Partitions

The NDS database can be logically divided into partitions. By default, the entire database resides in a single partition known as the Root partition. Depending on the NDS design and physical layout of your network, it may be necessary to partition the database. Performance and fault tolerance are the primary reasons for partitioning an NDS database.

Bindery Emulation and the NDS Directory Database

The NDS Directory database replaces the bindery files used in previous versions of NetWare. Many applications and devices have been designed to operate on bindery versions (3.12 and prior) of NetWare. In order to provide backward compatibility with NetWare bindery applications and third-party bindery products, NetWare 4.11 provides Bindery Emulation.

The NetWare 3.x bindery consists of three files:

- NET$OBJ.SYS
- NET$PROP.SYS
- NET$VAL.SYS

These files contain the objects, properties, and values known to the server. Unlike NetWare 4.x and NDS, NetWare 3.x servers do not share bindery information. Separate bindery files are maintained and stored on each individual file server. NetWare 4.11 emulates these files through software, but NetWare 4.11 servers do not have bindery files.

Bindery Emulation is configured on a container-by-container basis. Each NetWare 4.11 server can provide bindery emulation for up to 16 containers in an NDS Directory. To enable bindery emulation, set the BINDERY CONTEXT= server configuration parameter in the server's AUTOEXEC.NCF file.

During installation, bindery emulation is enabled by default for the file server's parent container. When a client logs in to NetWare 4.11 using a bindery connection, only NDS Leaf objects whose parent container is listed in the server's bindery context are available. In addition, only those NDS objects that have an equivalent bindery object will appear. For example, the Directory Map object is unique to NDS. Any Directory Map object whose parent container is listed in a server's bindery context will not appear to bindery applications.

> *TIP:*   *You can disable the bindery emulation feature and also make changes to the bindery context through the file server's SET parameters. SET parameters are covered in detail in the Advanced Administration for NetWare 4.11 course.*

If multiple bindery objects have the same name, only the objects whose container is listed first in the bindery context will be visible.

SETTING UP INTRANETWARE CLIENTS

The following topic is discussed within this section:

*   NDS Administration Utilities
*   NDS and Client for NetWare Networks

NDS and Client for NetWare Networks

The Microsoft Client for NetWare Networks provides only bindery connections to NetWare servers. With this client, users cannot connect to NDS resources. NDS containers, profiles, and user login scripts are not executed by clients with bindery connections.

An additional software component named Service for NetWare Directory Services may be added to the Microsoft Client for Novell Networks in order to support NDS connections. This component provides access to NDS resources and login scripts. NDS services are only available with NetWare 4.x. If you plan to use the NDS service, you must install the VLM client.

Novell's Client 32 for Windows 95 is the clear choice for workstations that need access to NetWare-controlled NDS resources. Client 32 permits simultaneous connections to multiple NDS Directory trees. In addition, Client 32 can coexist with the Microsoft Client for Microsoft Networks; allowing transparent access to NetWare, Windows NT, and IBM LAN Server resources.

NDS Administration Utilities

You cannot administer an Intranetware server using SYSCON. However, NetWare 4.11 provides several administration utilities. These include graphical, character-based menu, and command-line utilities. The utility most likely to meet the needs of network administration tasks is the NetWare Administrator.

NetWare 4.11 includes both 16-bit and 32-bit versions NetWare Administrator designed to operate with Windows 3.x and Windows 95, respectively.

By default, this utility is located in the SYS:PUBLIC directory on a NetWare 4.11 server. NetWare Administrator consolidates most of the features previously found in several character-based menu and command-line utilities.

It is important to note that NetWare Administrator is used to manage both NDS security and file system security. There are, however, differences and care should be taken not to confuse the two.

There are very few visible differences between the 16-bit and 32-bit versions of NetWare Administrator. There are, however, some functional differences. The 16-bit version cannot show multiple trees and does not support multiple-object selection. It also does not support using *BACKSPACE* to move to the parent container of the current object. Due to these differences and the increased speed and stability of the Windows 95 operating system, you should use the 32-bit version whenever possible.

RESOURCE SHARING FOR A NETWARE CLIENT

The following topic is discussed within this section:

* NetWare Network Concerns

NetWare Network Concerns

To utilize File and printer sharing for NetWare Networks, the 32-bit Microsoft Client for NetWare Networks must be installed. NetWare workstations using the Novell-supplied NETX or VLM client may access shared resources, but cannot share their local resources to the network. File and printer sharing for Microsoft Networks must be installed to share file and print resources on a Microsoft network. However, you cannot have both File and printer sharing for NetWare Networks and File and printer sharing for Microsoft Networks installed on the same computer.

A NetWare 2.x, NetWare 3.x, or NetWare 4.x server running bindery emulation must be available to act as a network security provider in order to utilize File and printer sharing for NetWare Networks. In addition to this, the network security provider must include a WINDOWS_PASSTHRU account that does not have password protection in the account database. This account is used to provide validation for user-level security. It needs only access to the bindery to validate users.

A computer installed with File and printer sharing for NetWare Networks uses NCP (NetWare Core Protocol) file-sharing to share resources. NCP is the principal protocol for transmitting information between a NetWare server and its clients. IPX is the underlying protocol that carries NCP messages. MS-DOS based Novell NetWare clients, computers running Windows NT, and computers that have the Microsoft Client for NetWare Networks installed use NCP to share resources.

You can only use File and printer sharing for NetWare Networks if you are running Microsoft Client for NetWare Networks as your primary logon.

Installing the NetWare Client

To utilize File and printer sharing for NetWare Networks, the 32-bit Microsoft Client for NetWare Networks must be installed. To install the client, launch the Network utility panel. Click on **Add** from the **Configuration** tab. Select **Client** and click on **Add**. Select **Microsoft** from the list of manufacturers and **Client for NetWare Networks** from the list of components. Then click on **OK**. Click on **OK** to close the Network dialog. You will need to restart your computer to let changes take effect.

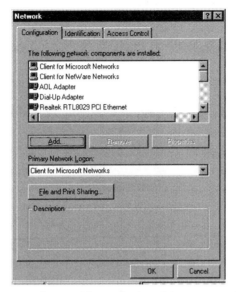

NetWare workstations using the Novell-supplied NETX or VLM client may access shared resources, but cannot share their local resources to the network. The 32-bit Client for Microsoft Networks must be installed to share file and print resources on a Microsoft network.

Novell also has a 32-bit client known as Client32. Client32 cannot be used with remote administration and user-level security on a Windows 95 client. The reason is that remote administration requires the File and printer sharing for NetWare Networks (FPNW) to be installed. Client32 cannot communicate with FPNW. Client32 does work with File and printer sharing for Microsoft Networks.

Using file and printer sharing services allows other users running a compatible network client to connect to resources on the peer server. Available resources could include printers, folders, CD-ROM drives, and directories.

These services are mutually exclusive. You can share resources to a NetWare or Microsoft network, but not both.

The properties sheet for the Client for NetWare Networks displays two tabs: **Advanced** and **General**.

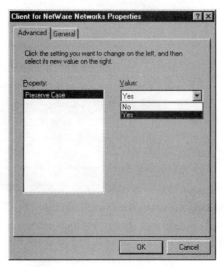

The **Advanced** tab allows you to configure the appropriate settings for any listed properties.

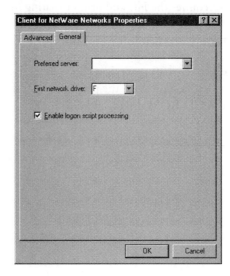

The **General** tab allows you to select the Preferred Server that you wish to use for the Client for NetWare Networks. You need to make this selection if you have more than one NetWare server operating in the network environment. Next, you must select the drive letter that you want to assign to your first network connection. You can also enable or disable logon script processing from this properties sheet.

Working with Persistent Shares

You can create a persistent connection to any drive by clicking on the **Reconnect At Logon** checkbox in the Map Network Drive dialog box.

Persistent connections are restored to the same drive letters at Windows 95 startup and can be viewed within the My Computer object.

With the Microsoft Client for NetWare Networks, persistent connections can be defined for NetWare volumes and directories. The need to use NetWare **map** commands in login scripts is eliminated when using persistent connections. However, you can still use **map**, **attach**, and other commands at the command prompt or in login scripts if desired.

Exercise 14-2:
Resource Configuration

You must be attached to a NetWare network to complete this exercise. You should start this exercise with Microsoft Client for NetWare as your primary logon.

1. Launch the Network utility.

2. Click on **Add**.

3. Select **Service** and click on **Add**.

4. Select Microsoft as the manufacturer and select File and printer sharing for NetWare Networks. If File and printer sharing for Microsoft Networks is installed on your computer, you must remove it before installing File and printer sharing for NetWare Networks.

5. Click on **OK**.

6. Select File and printer sharing for NetWare Networks from the installed list of components and click on **Properties**.

7. Select **SAP Advertising** and change its value to **Enabled**.

8. Verify that the **Workgroup Advertising** property is set to **Enabled: May Be Master**.

9. Click on **OK**.

10. Click on **OK** to close the Network dialog.

11. If prompted, provide the path to your installation files.

12. When prompted, click on **Yes** to restart your system.

BROWSING SERVICE FOR NETWARE NETWORKS

This section discusses the master browser service for NetWare networks. The following topic is discussed within this section:

- Browsing NetWare Networks

Provided the NetWare servers are running bindery emulation, browsing on an Intranetware network is identical to browsing on a NetWare 3.x network.

Browsing NetWare Networks

The Windows 95 operating system provides ample support for browsing and connecting to network resources on NetWare. Excluding the workgroup support provided by the Client for NetWare Networks, this support is the same whether you use Client for NetWare Networks or the Novell-supplied NETX or VLM client software.

NetWare networks do not use workgroups, so computers running Windows 95 with VLM or NETX clients cannot be members of workgroups. However, Windows 95 computers running File and printer sharing for NetWare Networks with Workgroup Advertising enabled may appear in workgroups.

The Network Neighborhood is the best way to browse network resources. Upon opening the Network Neighborhood on a computer running a NetWare networking client, all the NetWare bindery-based servers connected to your workstation are displayed. Computers running File and printer sharing for NetWare Networks with Workgroup Advertising enabled also appear in the Network Neighborhood.

Opening the Entire Network object provides a display of all NetWare servers on the network. A list of workgroups that include computers running File and printer sharing for NetWare Networks and Workgroup Advertising is also displayed. Available resources can be viewed by right-clicking on an object and running Explore.

If a computer has both the Client for Microsoft Networks and the Microsoft Client for NetWare Networks installed, a list of computers running Windows for Workgroups, Windows 95, and Windows NT will also be displayed. The list of NetWare servers is at the beginning of the list of workgroups, while domains are listed within the Entire Network listing.

Within the Network Neighborhood and Entire Network windows, a server can be opened to access its contents without having to map a network drive to the resource. You will be asked for security information, if necessary, and you can choose to save your password in the password cache so that the system will provide it as necessary.

For a computer running the Client for NetWare Networks, drive mappings are limited to the available drive letters. Despite this, Windows 95 supports unlimited UNC connections. If the computer is running NETX, it is limited to eight server connections. If running VLMs, it is limited to fifty server connections.

SAP and Workgroup Advertising for NetWare Networks

To configure SAP and Workgroup Advertising, open the Network property sheet. From the **Configuration** tab, highlight File and printer sharing for NetWare Networks and click on **Properties**.

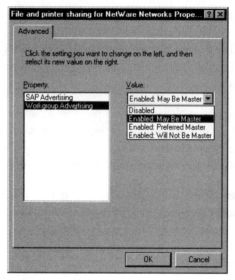

Settings for Workgroup Advertising include:

- Disabled

    The computer is not contained in the browse list and cannot be seen by other workstations.

- Enabled: May Be Master

    The computer is added to the browse list and can be elected the master browse server for the workgroup. This is the default setting.

- Enabled: Preferred Master

    The computer is added to the browse list and is the master browse server for the workgroup.

- Enabled: Will Not Be Master

    The computer is added to the browse list, but will not perform master browse server functions.

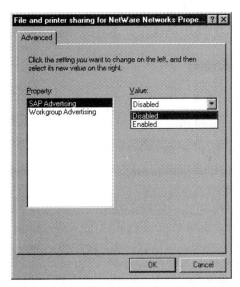

SAP Advertising can be either Disabled or Enabled. If SAP Advertising is **Enabled**, NetWare NETX or VLM clients can see the peer server and access its resources. If SAP Advertising is **Disabled**, only workstations running the Client for NetWare Networks can see the peer server and access its resources.

PEER SERVERS

This section will introduce peer servers. Windows 95 clients that are configured as peer servers expand the capabilities of your network. The following topics are discussed in this section:

- Why Use Peer Servers?

- Peer Server Client Support
- Peer Limitations On NetWare Networks

Using peer servers to provide resources to your network can be a necessary solution or an absolute nightmare. It is necessary to understand the capabilities of peer servers as well as their limitations to avoid these pitfalls.

Why Use Peer Servers?

Advantages of using computers running Windows 95 as peer servers include:

- Additional storage space for the network
- Additional printer support for users
- Central administration of peer servers through System Policies and NetWatcher utilities

If you are configuring a user's workstation to act as a peer server, it is recommended that you specify that the computer cannot run programs in MS-DOS mode. MS-DOS mode takes exclusive control of the operating system, causing File and printer sharing services to shut down. Prohibiting this application mode can be accomplished through the use of the system policy Disable Single-Mode MS-DOS Applications.

Peer Server Client Support

A peer server running File and printer sharing for NetWare Networks appears differently to users, depending upon the server advertising method.

Another computer running the Client for NetWare Networks views the peer server as a normal shared resource on the network. If the peer server utilizes Workgroup Advertising, it appears in a workgroup. A peer server configured to use SAP advertising will not appear in a workgroup, but it will appear in the Entire Network list.

A computer running NETX or VLMs views the shared directories on a peer server that uses SAP advertising exactly as volumes on a NetWare server. If the peer server is not using SAP advertising, then a NETX or VLM client cannot see or access resources on the peer server while browsing the network.

Shared printers appear as NetWare print queues. Most NetWare command-line utilities, including RIGHTS, FILER, SYSCON, MAP, VOLINFO, PCONSOLE, and CAPTURE, work exactly as if the peer server was a NetWare volume.

Peer Limitations On NetWare Networks

As you have seen, Windows 95 computers using the Client for NetWare Networks with File and printer sharing for NetWare Networks service installed and SAP advertising enabled appear as NetWare volumes to NETX and VLM clients. However, there are certain differences between NetWare servers and Windows 95 NetWare peer servers. These are:

- NETX or VLM clients cannot use LOGIN to access a Windows 95 peer server at the command line.

- NETX clients can use ATTACH to connect to a Windows 95 peer server at the command line.

- VLM users can run a **login /ns** command and use the **LOGIN** button on the Windows NWUSER utility.

- Using SYSCON displays Windows 95 peer servers. However, the user list displayed for the Windows 95 machine reflects the users and groups listing for the user-level security provider.

- VOLINFO displays volume information for Windows 95 peer servers.

PROFILES AND POLICIES ON A NETWARE NETWORK

This section discusses the implementation of user profiles and system policies in a mixed environment of Windows 95 clients and NetWare servers. The following are the topics discussed within this section:

- Using User Profiles On a NetWare Network

- System Policies On a NetWare Network

Provided the NetWare servers are running bindery emulation, the implementation of profiles and policies is identical for NetWare 3.x, NetWare 4.x, and Intranetware.

Using User Profiles On a NetWare Network

Roving user profiles are supported on Novell NetWare networks, as well as on Microsoft networks. The process for enabling roving profiles is similar. For a Novell NetWare network, you must define the Microsoft Client for NetWare networks as your primary network logon. User specific settings are stored on the preferred server, in the \SYS\MAIL*user_id* directory.

On a NetWare 3.x server, the network saves the user profile information in SYS:MAIL*UserID* the first time a user logs out after choosing to save user profiles. *UserID* is a NetWare-assigned 8-character hexadecimal ID. It is also saved on the local hard disk in the \WINDOWS\PROFILES directory in a subdirectory named after the user.

System Policies On a NetWare Network

If policies should be updated automatically, the CONFIG.POL file must be stored in SYS:PUBLIC on the NetWare server that validates the user (preferred server). If you want to store policies in another location, you will need to set the Remote Update option to manual and configure the appropriate path.

SCENARIOS

Scenario 1

You are the administrator for a NetWare 3.12 network running IPX/SPX that includes Windows 95 clients. You are setting up a computer for a new employee named Ralph. He will be running Windows 95. What do you need to do?

....

....

Scenario 2

You have followed the procedures in the previous scenario. Ralph can log in to the NetWare server, but he cannot access the shared HR directory. What do you need to do?

....

....

Scenario 3

You are the administrator of a NetWare 3.12 network that uses Windows 95 clients with Microsoft's Client for NetWare Networks. One of the project teams would like to share a few folders using share-level security. How can you configure the network so they can do that?

....

....

Scenario 4

You are migrating your network from NetWare 3.12 to Windows NT 4.0. Users have been sharing folders using user-level security. You have migrated about half of the employees in the company to the Windows NT server and installed Microsoft Client for Microsoft Networks on their computers. When you tried to install File and Printer Sharing for Microsoft Networks, you received an error. What is the problem?

....

....

Scenario 5

You have just upgraded your NetWare 3.12 network to Intranetware. Now none of the Windows 95 clients running Microsoft Client for NetWare Networks can see any NetWare servers. You have checked to make sure that they are running the same protocol. You have installed a client with Novell's Client 32 and it can see the servers fine. What most likely is the problem?

....

....

SUMMARY

In this chapter, you were given the information necessary to implement Windows 95 as a client in a Novell NetWare environment. This included:

- Novell NetWare 3.x, Novell NetWare 4.x, and Intranetware environments

- NetWare client configuration

- Browse services for a NetWare network

- SAP and Workgroup Advertising for NetWare Networks

- The advantages and limitations of peer servers

- User profiles and system policies on a NetWare network.

POST-TEST QUESTIONS

The answers to these questions are in Appendix A at the end of this manual.

1. Is it possible to have the Client for Microsoft Networks and Client for NetWare Networks running at the same time on a client? How about File and print sharing for Microsoft Networks and File and print sharing for NetWare Networks?

....

....

2. Where are system policies stored on a NetWare network?

   ....

   ....

3. When should you implement a peer server in your network environment?

   ....

   ....

4. What file is used to configure settings for NetWare protocols, bindings, and network adapters?

   ....

   ....

5. How is the preferred server configured for the Client for NetWare Networks?

   ....

   ....

6. Which NetWare server stores roving profiles stored?

   ....

   ....

7. When should SAP Advertising be used as compared to Workgroup Advertising?

   ....

   ....

8. How can you configure the master browser for Workgroup Advertising?

    ....

    ....

CHAPTER 15

Printer Management

OBJECTIVES

At the completion of this chapter, you will be able to:

- Configure printers for use with Windows 95.

- Install a local and network printer.

- Configure properties of a selected printer.

- Discuss the advantages and disadvantages of using peer servers in a networking environment.

- Configure Windows 95 to function as a NetWare print server.

- Troubleshoot various types of printing problems.

PRE-TEST QUESTIONS

The answers to these questions are in Appendix A at the end of this manual.

1. What account must be present on the NetWare server to support Windows 95 file and printer sharing?

   ....

   ....

2. What are the two methods you can use to install a network printer?

   ....

   ....

3. What is the purpose of HP JetAdmin?

   ....

   ....

4. How is deferred printing enabled?

   ....

   ....

INTRODUCTION

This chapter begins with a discussion about the architecture of printer drivers in the Windows 95 environment. We will discuss the Universal Printer Driver, which is used to communicate between printing and the environment. Next, the chapter discusses the different types of fonts that can be used for printing, such as raster fonts and truetype fonts.

The chapter then focuses on installation of local and network printers. Printers as well as most objects in the Windows 95 environment have property pages that allow you, the administrator, to specify additional configurations such as spooling, sharing, and capturing printer ports, as well as other specifications.

The following topics will also be discussed:

- Use of the Printers folder
- Installation and removal of printer drivers
- Setup of Point and Print printing
- Creation, reordering, and deletion of Windows 95 print queues
- Purpose and use of minidrivers and universal drivers
- Access of a printer via a NetWare network

The chapter concludes with a discussion of troubleshooting procedures for problems related to local printing problems as well as problems encountered with Windows.

PRINTING

This section presents the printer support features introduced with Windows 95. In many ways, printer installation and support have been simplified under Windows 95. The following topics are discussed within this section:

- Printing with Windows 95

- General Information

These new printing features allow users easy access to printer configuration and give them more control over the printing process.

Printing with Windows 95

Windows 95 features improvements in printing over its predecessor, Windows 3.x. These improvements include:

- Ease of printer setup and support because of improvements in the user interface and plug and play support.

- Better performance through the use of a new 32-bit printing architecture.

- Better integration of network printing through extension of the Windows 95 printing architecture to the network environment.

- Quicker *return-to-application* time because of the use of Enhanced MetaFile (EMF) spooling.

General Information

Any discussion of Windows 95 printing must start with the Printers folder. This folder is accessed through the My Computer object on the desktop, or via **Start/Settings/Printers**.

The Printers folder contains all installed printers on the Windows 95 computer. New printers also can be added from this folder.

NOTE: *The Registry contains all information about installed printers.*

Installation of printers takes place in one of five ways:

- During Setup, when prompted to add a printer
- During Setup, using a custom setup script
- After Setup, using the Add New Printer Wizard
- Automatically, using a Plug and Play printer
- Using Point and Print

PRINT DRIVER ARCHITECTURE

The following topics are discussed within this section:

- Windows 95 Device Driver Model
- Printer Drivers

Windows 95 Device Driver Model

The universal printer driver and minidriver make up the Windows 95 device driver model. The Universal Printer Driver (UNIDRV.DLL) is provided by Windows 95. It is responsible for communicating with the operating system. The minidriver is provided by the printer manufacturer and provides additional information to the universal printer driver and to the printer.

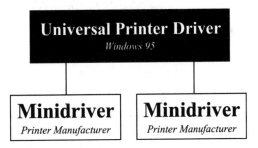

Universal printer drivers support a set of printers through the use of a single driver. For example, all HPPCL printers use the same driver (HPPCL.DRV), as do all PostScript printers (PSCRIPT.DRV). These drivers communicate with the minidriver provided by the printer's vendor.

Printer Drivers

The 32-bit printing architecture of Windows 95 uses a printer device driver scheme that consists of two parts: a universal print driver and a PostScript printer minidriver. The universal driver serves as the interface between the operating system and the mini-drivers. The minidrivers communicate with the universal driver and to the specific printer.

NOTE: *The universal driver supports most non-PostScript printers. PostScript printers require the appropriate minidriver.*

To change printer drivers for an installed printer, view the properties sheet for the desired printer and select the **Details** tab. Installing printer drivers will be discussed later in the chapter.

FONTS

The following topics are discussed within this section:

- Terminology
- Raster Fonts
- TrueType Fonts
- Installing Fonts

Terminology

An important part of understanding and managing printers under Windows 95 is having a good understanding of how Windows 95 works with fonts. Since Windows applications normally work in a WYSIWYG (What You See Is What You Get) environment, information is displayed on the screen the same way that it will appear when it prints. Before beginning a discussion of how Windows 95 manages fonts, let's define some terms.

Typeface	This refers to a character set in which all characters share common characteristics. Examples of common typefaces include Courier, Helvetica, and Times New Roman. Often, both the name and the typeface are copyrighted by the manufacturer (or designer).
Character Set	This defines the relationship between keystrokes or keyboard codes and assigned characters. The ANSI character set is used by Windows, where many non-Windows applications use the ASCII character set.
Font	In Windows usage, a font refers to a typeface name, not including attributes such as **bold** or *italic*.
Font Style	These are font characteristics that can be defined for a font. Windows supports **bold**, *italic*, ***bold italic***, and roman, which is usually referred to as regular or normal.
Font Size	This is the point size of the font, from highest ascender to lowest descender in the character set. It is measured in points (1/72 in.), a standard typesetting measure.
Font Effects	Windows supports special effects for fonts, such as underline, double underline, or color attributes.
Font Family	A group of typefaces with similar characteristics.
Pitch	Type size for fixed-width fonts (see "Spacing"), measured in Characters Per Inch (CPI).
Serif	A specific font characteristic indicating that the font has projections from the upper and lower strokes of letters.
Sans Serif	A specific font characteristic indicating that the font does not have projections from the upper and lower strokes of letters.
Slant	Angle of the font characters, which will normally be either *italic* or roman (no slant).

Spacing	Refers to character width, determining how characters are spaced on a line. A fixed font, also called a monospaced font, uses the same spacing for all characters, no matter what the character width, giving a constant CPI value. Proportional fonts vary the space given to each character depending upon the character's actual width. For example, an "M" receives significantly more space than an "I."
Weight	Stroke heaviness, referring to the width and *darkness* of a character. Common terms for describing weight include light, regular, book, demi, bold, heavy, black, and extra bold.
Width	A normal typeface may be expanded or compressed horizontally to create different widths, giving you compressed, normal, and expanded fonts.
X-Height	Defines the vertical size of lowercase characters within the character set.
System Fonts	This term does not refer to a specific font, but the fonts that are defined for system purposes, such as dialog boxes or those used to display OEM text.
Raster Fonts	Character definitions are stored as bitmaps and displayed as dots on the screen or printer. These fonts cannot be successfully scaled or rotated without loss of resolution.
Vector Font	Characters are defined from a mathematical model, making it easy for them to be scaled or rotated without loss of resolution.
TrueType Font	These are outline fonts using the TrueType technology. TrueType support and an assortment of TrueType fonts are installed with Windows 95.
PostScript Font	These are outline fonts based on the PostScript language.
Screen Fonts	There are font descriptions used to display characters on screen. These may be Raster, Vector, or TrueType fonts.
Printer Fonts	These are font descriptions used to print information. Windows supports Device fonts, Printable Screen fonts, and Downloadable Soft fonts.
Device Fonts	These are fonts that reside at the printer. These may be built into the printer or supplied through cartridges or font cards.

Printable Screen Fonts

> These are Windows screen fonts that Windows can translate into a printable version.

Downloadable Soft Fonts

> These are fonts that reside on the system hard disk. These fonts are transferred to printer memory as necessary.

Raster Fonts

Raster fonts are stored as bitmaps of the characters. Windows stores different sets for different font sizes and video resolutions. The Windows MS Serif, MS Sans Serif, Courier, System, and Terminal are all Raster fonts. Raster fonts:

- Are less processor intensive.

    Since the fonts are displayed as bitmaps, all Windows must do is locate the correct character and display it on screen.

- Are more disk intensive.

    Windows must store a font file for each size and resolution of the font.

- Provide limited scaling.

    Windows can scale Raster fonts in even increments (14, 16, 18, ...) only. The character quality becomes degraded, appearing ragged, at larger font sizes.

The Windows Setup program will normally install the screen and printer Raster fonts appropriate to your system.

> *NOTE: Some printer drivers do not support Raster fonts.*

A number of manufacturers sell additional Raster fonts. You can install additional fonts through the Fonts control panel.

TrueType Fonts

TrueType support and TrueType fonts are included with Windows 95. Fonts are scalable, stored on disk as a series of points and *hints* for displaying the characters. Hints are algorithms, used by a software device called the Rasterizer, to shift the scaled font outlines to improve the font appearance on screen.

TrueType fonts provide a number of benefits to Windows 95 users:

- What You See *Is* What You Get

    The same font is used as both the screen and printer font. As each font is used, a bitmap representation is built in the font cache and is available from that time on to all Windows applications.

- Scalable fonts

    TrueType fonts are fully scalable without loss of resolution. The fonts can be rotated as well, but only in 90-degree increments.

- Limited disk requirements

    Each font requires only two files: a .TTF and an .FOT file. Windows will scale these font definitions to meet user requirements. The .TTF file contains the character set's mathematical definition. The .FOT file contains hint information for the font.

- Included with Windows

    Since TrueType ships with Windows 95, there is nothing extra that you have to buy. Of course, there are typefaces available in addition to those you receive with Windows.

- Font embedding

    When sending a document to an outside source for printing, you can embed an encrypted copy of necessary fonts with the document. Fonts may be embedded as read-only (the document can be printed, but not edited) or read-write (the document may be edited and printed). All of the fonts included with Windows 95 may be embedded for read-write.

NOTE: *Font manufacturers have the option of setting the security on a font so that it cannot be embedded in a document.*

- Printer support

    TrueType allows you to support a wide range of printers and printer types. Font information is translated into a form that can be printed by the output device.

TrueType places the responsibility for generating printer fonts on Windows, rather than relying on the printer. While this reliance on the PC's CPU may reduce Windows' performance, the overall application performance is often better when print operations are involved.

Installing Fonts

To install a new font, you must first launch the Fonts control panel.

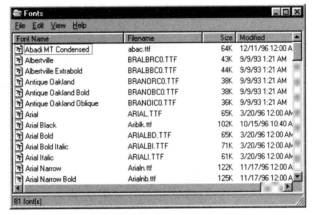

Once this dialog appears, run **File/Install New Font**.

You can install fonts from either a floppy, local, or network drive. If there is more than one font available in the source folder, you can click **Select All** to install all available fonts. Fonts other than TrueType may be installed as well. By default, new fonts will be copied to the c:\windows folder.

Click on **Done** when you have finished looking at the detailed font information.

If a TrueType font becomes corrupted, Windows will automatically mark the font as unavailable for the current Windows session. You should then remove and reinstall the font.

INSTALLATION AND CONFIGURATION OF A PRINTER

This section discusses the Add Printer Wizard. You will learn how to install a local printer and share it out on the network. You will also learn about the properties sheets available for a selected printer. The following topics are discussed in this section:

- Installing a Local Printer
- Printer Properties
- Printer Sharing
- Printing From MS-DOS Applications

In many ways, printer installation and support have been simplified under Windows 95.

Installing a Local Printer

Launch the Printers utility from My Computer, the Control Panel, or **Start/Settings/Printers**. Double-click on the Add Printer icon to run the Add Printer Wizard. Click on **Next** to begin installation.

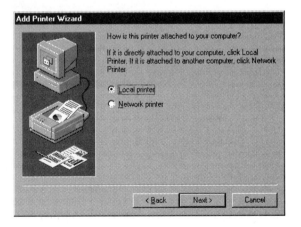

Verify that **Local Printer** is selected and click on **Next**. The installation of a network printer will be discussed later in this chapter.

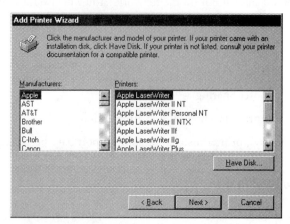

Select the manufacturer and the printer model from the available lists. Click on **Next**.

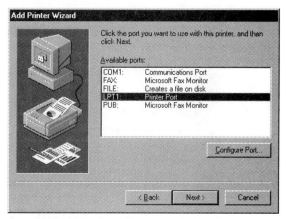

Select which port you would like to use for this printer. Click on **Next**.

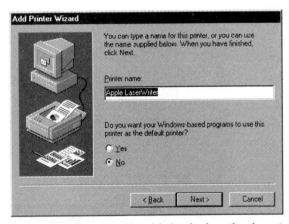

Type a name for the printer. This name should clearly describe the printer. You can also select whether or not you want this printer to be the default printer for all Windows-based applications. Click on **Next**.

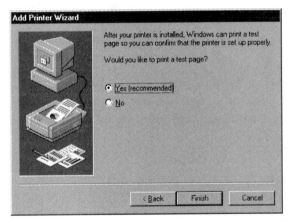

Select whether or not you would like the wizard to print a test page. Click on **Next**. If you choose to print a test page, you will receive the following dialog:

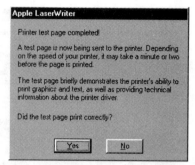

If the printer is offline or not plugged in properly, you will receive the following message:

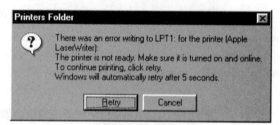

After printer installation, an icon for the printer appears in the Printers folder. As with other objects, you can create a shortcut for the printer and place it anywhere you wish. Having a shortcut to a printer in a readily available area such as the desktop, allows you to drag and print effectively.

To print a file with drag and print, drag the file onto the printer icon or shortcut to the printer and release. The file automatically adds itself to the print queue.

Exercise 15-1:
Local Printer Management

During this exercise, you will install the drivers for a local printer. You do not need a printer to complete this exercise. Your CD-ROM drive should contain your Windows 95 CD. If you installed from floppies, have them available at this time.

You should be logged on at your workstation before starting this exercise.

Instead of using double-click in this exercise, you can right-click and select **Open**.

1. Double-click to open the My Computer desktop object.

2. Double-click on the Printers folder.

3. Double-click on the Add Printer icon to launch the Add Printer Wizard.

4. When the opening dialog appears, click on **Next**.

5. Verify that **Local printer** is selected and click on **Next**.

6. Scroll through the Manufacturers list and select HP.

7. Scroll through the Printers list and select HP LaserJet 4.

8. Click on **Next**.

9. Verify that LPT1 is selected as the port and click on **Next**.

10. Overwrite the printer name as shown below and click on **Next**.

    MainPTR

11. When prompted to print a test page, click on the radio button next to No and click on **Finish**. Depending on your method of installation, you may be prompted to insert a Windows 95 installation diskette.

12. Right-click on your newly created printer object and select **Set As Default**.

13. Right-click on your newly created printer object and select **Properties**.

14. The properties screens are somewhat printer-specific and control all printer options. Click on **Cancel**.

15. Right-click and drag the printer to a clear area of the desktop.

16. Select **Create Shortcut(s) Here**.

17. Launch Windows Explorer.

18. Select the DOS directory.

19. Drag Drvspace.txt to the desktop printer object and drop it.

20. You will notice Notepad opens the file then closes. After a minute or so a printer folder dialog opens and you will receive an error that the job cannot be printed. Click on **Cancel**.

21. Close all open programs and windows.

Printer Properties

The Printers folder is located in the My Computer desktop icon, **Start/Settings/Printers**, or the Control Panel. To display the Properties sheet of an installed printer, first select the printer from the Printers folder. You can then either right-click and select **Properties** or run **File/Properties**. You should note that the icon in the Control Panel is a shortcut to the Printers folder. Since it is a shortcut, its context menu is different than the menu displayed from the original folder.

The context menu for the Printers folder in My Computer or **Start/Settings/Printers** displays the following items:

Open	This command opens the Printers folder.
Explore	This command views the Printers folder within Windows Explorer.
Capture Printer Port	This command displays the capture printer port dialog. You can select the device (port) you want to capture.
End Capture	This command displays a dialog listing all the present captures. To end a capture, select a printer from the list and click on **OK**.
Create Shortcut	This creates a shortcut to the Printers folder on the desktop. A shortcut to this item cannot be created anywhere other than on the desktop.
Properties	This option is not available but is listed.

The options menu for the Printers shortcut in the Control Panel displays **Open**, **Create Shortcut**, and **Properties** options. These provide the same functions as those listed above. As you can see, the list of options is more restrictive.

The Properties sheet for a selected printer can display up to eight tabs: **General**, **Details**, **Sharing**, **Paper**, **Graphics**, **Fonts**, **Device Options**, and **PostScript**. Depending on the type of printer you have installed, there may be only three or four tabs instead of the eight that will be discussed. The tabs that may be displayed in this situation are **General**, **Details**, **Sharing**, and **Paper**.

General Properties

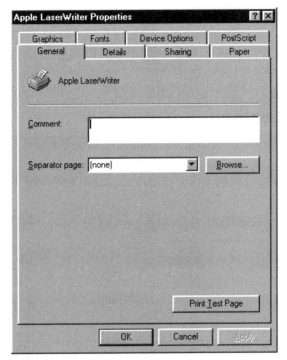

The properties available on the **General** tab include:

Comment

Comment allows you to add any pertinent information to identify the printer.

Separator page

A separator page is useful for situations where multiple users are printing to the same printer. The separator page displays the user name, which helps in identifying printouts. Available settings are:

Full

A full separator page includes graphics.

Simple

A simple separator page includes text only.

Browse	Browse allows you to set the path to a custom separator page.
Print Test Page	This selection allows you to print a test page to verify that the printer is installed and working properly.

If you have many users printing to the same printer, it is a good practice to have separator pages set up. This will help users easily identify their documents.

Details Properties

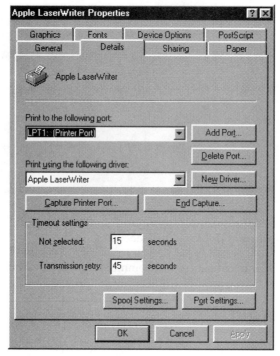

The **Details** tab displays the name of the selected printer. It also displays:

Print to the following port	This displays the network path for a network printer and/or the port number the printer is using.
Print using the following driver	This option should display the type of printer you are using or one that can be recognized by your printer's brand.

Add Port	This option allows you to set a network path to the port you would like to use or you may select from the local ports listed. If the printer was installed as a network printer, the Network option will be chosen by default.
Delete Port	This option allows you to select from the list of available ports for deletion. Network ports are also displayed.
New Driver	This option should be used when a new or updated driver is available for the printer. By clicking on **New Driver**, you will receive a warning that the settings for the new driver will be saved, but the new driver may look different. Then you will see a dialog listing the manufacturers and models of various different printers. If the driver is located on a local or network server, you can click on **Have Disk** to browse to the path of updated drivers.
Capture Printer Port	If you need to print from non-Windows applications, such as an MS-DOS application, you need to capture a printer port. Once the path to the port is chosen, you may select to reconnect this connection at logon. This option is also available in the Add Printer Wizard. You can also open this dialog by right-clicking on the Printers folder in My Computer or by running **File/Capture Printer Port** from the My Computer menu options. You must also capture a printer port for any network printers that may be used.

End Capture

This option is used to remove the network path to the MS-DOS application printing port. You can also open this dialog by right-clicking on the Printers folder in My Computer or by running **File/End Capture** from the My Computer menu options.

Timeout Settings

    Not selected

This option allows you to select the amount of time Windows will wait for the printer to be online before displaying an error dialog.

    Transmission retry

This option allows you to set the amount of time Windows will wait for the printer to be ready for printing.

Spool Settings

This selection is used to specify how print jobs should be spooled to the printer. You can select printing to begin either after the last page is spooled or after the first page is spooled. By selecting **Start printing after last page is spooled**, printing will not begin for a length of time, especially if the print job is large. The **Start printing after first page is spooled** option is often preferred by users who like to view the actual printout as soon as possible.

You can also select the spool data format as RAW or EMF. Raw data format is printer-specific and may require conversion before it can be printed on a different type of printer. This can extend the length of time it takes to print. EMF data format uses a set of Windows 95 internal commands to create images that represent textual data.

You can also enable or disable bi-directional support for a printer. Bi-directional support allows direct queries to the printer. This provides for less user intervention, which ultimately speeds up the spooling process.

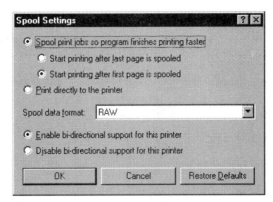

Port Settings

This button provides two selections for configuring the printer's LPT port: **Spool MS-DOS print jobs** and **Check port state before printing**. Each of these selections can be disabled by clearing the corresponding checkbox.

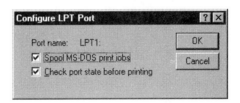

Sharing Properties

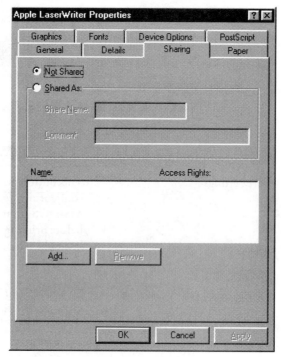

The **Sharing** tab allows you to share a local printer out as a network printer. To enable printer sharing, click on the **Shared As** option. You can either enter a new name for the share or keep the default name. Comments may be added for further clarification of the share. If user-level security is enabled, sharing may be configured for users and groups authenticated by a Windows NT domain, a Windows NT Server, a Windows NT Workstation, or a NetWare server. If share-level security is enabled, you can enter a new share name, a comment, and a password to allow users to log in to the network printer.

You can also display the **Sharing** tab for a selected printer by right-clicking on the selected Printer and selecting **Sharing**.

Paper Properties

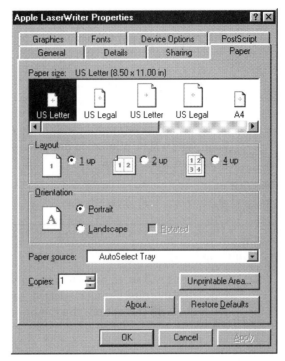

The **Paper** tab allows you to select the default type of paper to use for printing. It has the following options:

- Layout

    1 up

    One page will be printed per piece of paper.

    2 up

    Two pages will be printed on one piece of paper, thus dividing the paper into two sections.

    4 up

    Four pages will be printed on one piece of paper, thus dividing the paper into four sections.

- Orientation

    Portrait

    This setting will set all pages to print in this orientation by default.

    Landscape

    This setting will set all pages to print in this orientation by default. Once the landscape setting is selected, you have the option of selecting Rotated. With this option, you can print the text or image upside down.

- Paper source

    There are three types of paper source options available: AutoSelect Tray, Cassette, or Manual Feed.

- Copies

    The number of copies to print by default can be set here. Unless you are absolutely sure you want the designated number of copies to print each time, you can set the number of copies within the application from which you are printing. Make sure that the selection within the application does not set the number of copies as a default value.

- About

    This option displays copyright information for the selected printer.

- Restore Defaults

    This option restores defaults to any selection within the **Paper** tab of Printer Properties.

- Unprintable Area

    This selection allows you to manipulate the area of paper to which you do not want to print. If incorrect changes are made to this dialog, you can click on **Restore Defaults** to revert to the default values.

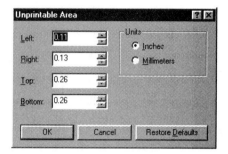

Graphics Properties

The **Graphics** tab allows you to set the following properties:

Resolution   This list allows you to select the resolution at which you
                      want to print. Resolution is measured in dots per inch, or
                      dpi.

Halftoning

    Use printer's settings

    Use settings below

      Screen frequency   You can specify the pattern frequency for
                              halftone printing. These settings should be
                              changed by users who have experience with
                              halftone printing.

      Screen angle   You can specify the angle of pattern for
                              halftone printing. These settings should be
                              changed by users who have experience with
                              halftone printing.

Special

Print as a negative image

If this option is enabled, your document or image will be printed as a negative image. For example, where the background color of the document may have been white and the text color black, it would now print with the background color of black and the text color white.

Print as a mirror image

If this option is enabled, your document or image will be printed as a mirror of the original.

Scaling

This option allows you to magnify or decrease the size of your image or document between 25% to 400%. It is important to be sure that you want all documents and images to print using this scale. If not, this option is generally available in Print Options or Print Setup of a Windows application.

Fonts Properties

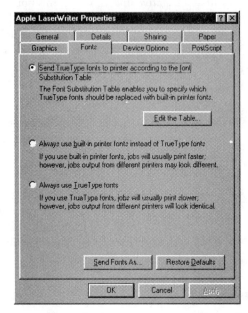

The **Fonts** tab allows you to select whether or not to use a font substitution table to map TrueType fonts to a close substitute if the font cannot be found. If you elect to do this, you can edit the substitution table.

For all available fonts, you may select to send them to the printer as Outlines, Courier, Helvetica, Symbol, and Times.

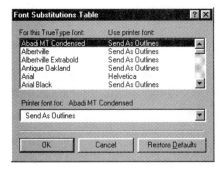

Other options on the **Fonts** tab include:

* Always use built-in printer fonts instead of TrueType fonts

    This option will translate TrueType fonts to PostScript fonts. This speeds
    up the printing process. However, since PostScript fonts are system-
    dependent, print jobs may look different from printer to printer.

* Always use TrueType fonts

    If you prefer to print using TrueType fonts, printing time will increase.
    However, since TrueType fonts are used, print jobs will look the same no
    matter which brand or model printer is used.

Device Options Properties

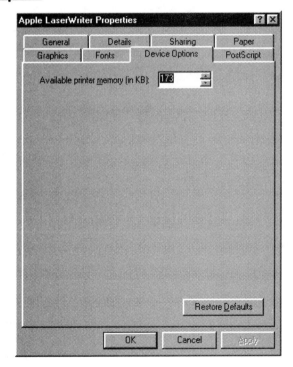

The **Device Options** tab allows you to set the amount of memory to be used for printing. If this value does not match the available memory on the printer, you may need to alter the memory allocation.

PostScript Properties

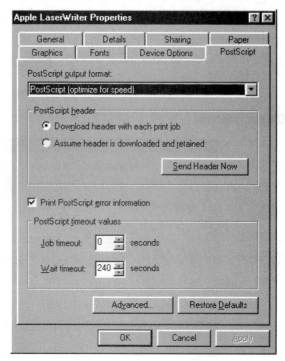

The **PostScript** tab allows you to set the following options:

PostScript output format

> This option allows you to select the output format for PostScript printing from the following selections: PostScript (optimize for speed), PostScript (optimize for Portability-ADSC), Encapsulated PostScript (EMS), and Archive Format.

Download header with each print job

> This selection enables the header to be printed each time a document is sent to the printer. This is good to use for users who print to a network server.

Assume header is downloaded and retained

> This selection enables the header to be printed only one time. This saves time when printing documents and images.

Send Header Now

> Once this selection is made, **Assume header is downloaded and retained** is automatically selected.

Job timeout

> This option enables you to set the waiting time for a document to travel from the computer to the printer. Once the set time has been reached, the printer does not try to retrieve information from the computer.

Wait timeout

> This option sets the timeout for the printer to wait for PostScript information.

Advanced options include:

PostScript language level

> This option allows you to select the language level used on your system. There are two levels: PostScript Level 1 and PostScript Level 2. Unless you are sure, you should not make any alterations to this selection.

Bitmap compression

> This selection allows you to choose whether graphics should be compressed before being sent to the printer. If you are using either PostScript Level 1 or PostScript Level 2 language levels and your printer is connected to a parallel port, you should select "Compress bitmap images." Otherwise, you should leave the default "No bitmap compression."

Data format	If your printer is connected by either serial, parallel, or a network port, you should select ASCII data format. ASCII data format takes some time to print. Binary communications protocol sends data in binary format over a serial or parallel port. This is a bit faster than ASCII data format. If you select Binary communications protocol, you must enable Send Mode to switch your printer to use the BCP protocol. Tagged binary communications protocol is the same as Binary communications protocol, except that there is no need to enable the Send Mode feature. Pure binary data can only be sent over network ports. However, it is the fastest printing data format.
Send CTRL+D before job	This option allows the printer to be notified that printing is complete. The printer is then reset. You must clear this setting if you are connected to a UNIX-based network.
Send CTRL+D after job	This option allows the printer to be notified that printing is complete. The printer is then reset. You must clear this setting if you are connected to a UNIX-based network.
Restore Defaults	This option restores all values on this tab page to defaults.

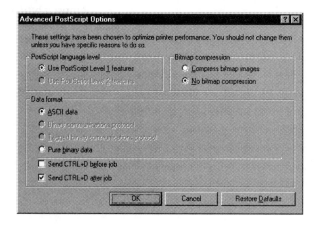

Exercise 15-2:
Setting Properties For a Local Printer

This exercise assumes that you have an Apple LaserWriter printer installed. If it is not installed on your system, use the Add Printer Wizard to install the printer. You do not need to have the driver disk available for installation.

1. Right-click on the Apple LaserWriter printer icon from within the Printers folder in My Computer or **Start/Settings/Printer**. Select **Properties**.

2. Click on the **Details** tab.

3. Click on **Spool Settings**.

4. Change the spool data format to **EMF**.

5. Click on **OK**.

6. Click on the **Fonts** tab.

7. Change the current option to **Always use built-in printer fonts instead of TrueType fonts**.

8. Click on **OK** to close the Apple LaserWriter Properties dialog.

Printer Sharing

Windows 95 provides a way to share a local printer to the network. This feature can work well in a workgroup environment. However, a Windows 95 production machine may not run efficiently if it is required to perform a large amount of printing. In other words, if your network users do a lot of printing, it would be better to set up a network print server rather than share a local printer. In addition, before a local printer can be shared to the network, a file and printer sharing service must be installed. Windows 95 includes File and printer sharing for Microsoft Networks and File and printer sharing for NetWare Networks. These services were discussed previously in the course.

To share a local printer across a network, open the Printers folder and right-click on the desired printer. Click on the **Sharing** tab. The following screen appears:

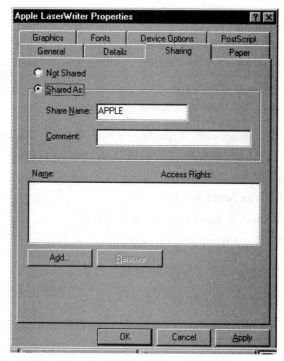

Click on **Shared As** to allow the printer to be a shared resource. You can keep the default share name or create one of your own. Adding a comment is optional. If you have user-level security enabled, you can click on **Add** to select users from your domain or server. The following dialog displays the list of users obtained from a Windows NT Server.

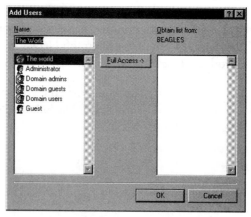

Note that users can be granted only full access to the printer.

If share-level security is enabled on the Windows 95 client, then you are not requiring users to be authenticated by a server or domain. Instead, you must specify a password that users will use to gain access to the shared printer.

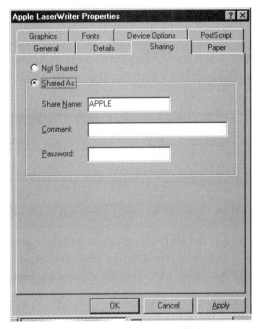

The printer now appears in the Printers folder as shared.

PRINTING FROM MS-DOS APPLICATIONS

The two main DOS application printing problems with Windows 3.1 were that the DOS print jobs did not spool and that there were conflicts when trying to print from a DOS application and a Windows application simultaneoulsy. Windows 95 fixed these problems by enabling DOS-based print jobs to be spooled into the 32-bit Windows 95 print spooler. The following graphic displays a Microsoft Word file in the Network Printer queue followed by a file printed from the MS-DOS Edit application.

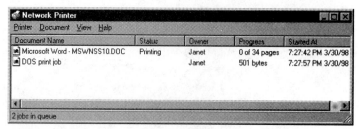

Windows 95 takes the DOS file, which would have printed directly to the printer in Windows 3.1, and sends it to a *virtual* print spooler. The virtual print spooler adds it into the actual 32-bit print spooler. This allows the application to become available more quickly.

NETWORK PRINTERS

This section defines the process for installing a network printer. It also discusses how to configure Windows 95 as a NetWare print server. The following topics are discussed within this section:

- Installing a Network Printer
- Windows 95 as a NetWare Print Server

Installing a Network Printer

Whether setting up a printer connection through the Network Neighborhood or Printers folder, you are prompted to supply much of the same information. Once again, you may find Network Neighborhood easier to use because you are prompted only for the parameters needed to configure the printer.

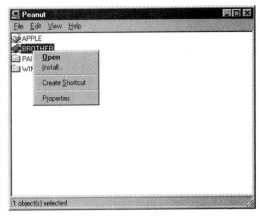

To install a network printer using Network Neighborhood, browse to the printer on the network. Right-click on the printer and run **Install**. The Add Printer Wizard will begin and walk you through installing the network printer.

You can also install a network printer by launching the Add Printer Wizard from **Start/ Settings/Printers**, My Computer, or the Control Panel.

At the introductory screen, click on **Next** to continue the wizard. The following dialog appears. Select **Network printer** and click on **Next**.

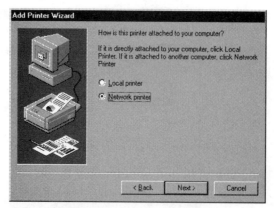

Click on **Browse** to find the network path.

You must also identify whether you print from MS-DOS programs so that the printer can be configured properly. The following dialog appears when you click on **Browse**:

Locate the printer on the network and click on **OK**.

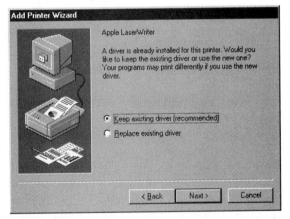

You must also select a printer device driver. Select the manufacturer first, then select the printer driver from the supplied list. If the driver is already installed on your machine, for local printer or network printer support, you are prompted to either keep or replace the existing driver. The default is to keep the existing driver.

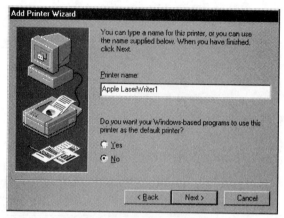

Give the printer a name that users can recognize easily. If you wish, you may set this up as the default printer for your Windows applications.

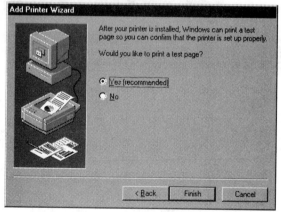

It is suggested that you print a test page. This lets you verify that your workstation is communicating properly with the printer and that you installed the correct device driver.

Finally, a printer object is created using the name you specified. Its icon identifies it as a network printer.

Windows 95 as a NetWare Print Server

Windows 95 includes the Microsoft Print Service for NetWare utility. This utility allows a Window 95 machine to function as a type of NetWare print server. Essentially, it enables a NetWare server to send print jobs to the Windows 95 computer. The Microsoft Print Service for NetWare utility runs in the background, therefore, unlike a NetWare print server, the Windows 95 computer can be used for other things as well. Microsoft Client for NetWare Networks must be installed and your system must be attached to a Novell Network before you can install the Microsoft Print Service for NetWare utility. You do not need to install file and printer sharing for NetWare Networks to take advantage of this feature.

To install the Microsoft Print Service for NetWare, open the Network utillity. Verify that you are on the **Configuration** tab and click on **Add**. Select **Service** in the Select Network Component Type dialog box and click on **Add**. In the Select Network Service dialog box, click on **Have Disk** and type the path to the ADMIN\NETTOOLS\PRTAGENT directory on the Windows 95 CD. Click on **OK**. When the Select Network Service window appears with Microsoft Print Agent for NetWare Networks highlighted, click on **OK**.

To enable the Microsoft Print Server for NetWare, right-click on the local printer in the Printers folder. Select **Properties**. Select the **Print Server** tab and click **Enable Microsoft Print Server for NetWare**. Access the **NetWare Server** pull-down menu and choose the NetWare server where the print queue resides. Only servers to which you have access will be listed.

The name of the print server should now appear in the Print Server field. Your Windows 95 computer should now be able to receive print jobs from the NetWare print server.

PRINTER MANAGEMENT

The following topics are discussed within this section:

- Using Point and Print
- Using Deferred Printing
- HP JetAdmin Service
- Windows 95 Print Queues

Using Point and Print

Point and Print allows the Windows 95 user to install drivers for a remote printer from a shared workstation, a Windows NT server, or a Novell NetWare file server.

> *NOTE:*   *Using a Novell NetWare server as a provider of Point and Print information requires configuration at the print server. Only a user with Supervisor privileges will be able to perform the required configuration. Using the Add New Printer Wizard to set up a printer and capture a print queue is an alternative to reconfiguring the NetWare file server.*

To set up a printer on a Windows NT network using Point and Print, follow these steps:

- Open the Network Neighborhood.
- Open the server icon for the associated print queue.
- Open the desired print queue.
- Windows 95 walks the user through the steps needed to install the appropriate printer drivers.

Depending on server configuration, the information supplied by the server could include:

- Printer driver files.
- Name of the server where the driver files are stored.
- Printer model information.

A Windows 95 print server, Windows NT print server, or NetWare print server can be used to automatically download the necessary files to install a printer locally. This Point and Print process can be started by dropping a file onto the printer, by browsing to the printer using the Add Printer utility, or by selecting the printer in Network Neighborhood. The following graphic demonstrates a file being dropped into a printer named "canon" on Shuma's computer, which is a Windows 95 print server.

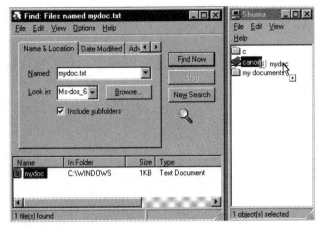

If you drop a file onto the Network printer icon and the printer has never been installed on your computer, the following screen appears prompting you to install the printer:

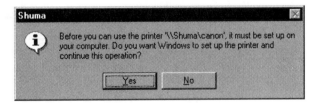

Installing a Remote Printer

To automatically install a remote printer, click on **Yes** when prompted to set up the printer. Click on **Yes** if you will print from MS-DOS applications or click on **No** if you will not. Click on **Next**. The following MS-DOS dialog appears:

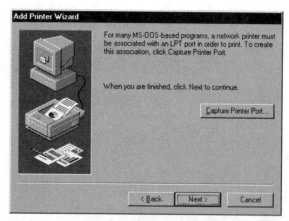

Click on **Capture Printer Port** to assign an LPT port to the path of the computer. The first available LPT port is automatically assigned as the Device and the Path to the printer is displayed.

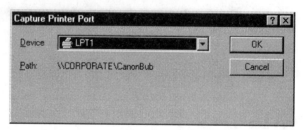

Click on **OK**. Click on **Next** to continue.

> *NOTE:*   *If you are installing a driver for a Windows NT print server, the printer name in Windows NT must have the same name as the printer in the Windows 95 MSPRINT.INF file. If they do not have the same name, the following Windows 95 dialog appears asking for the printer manufacturer and specific printer name.*

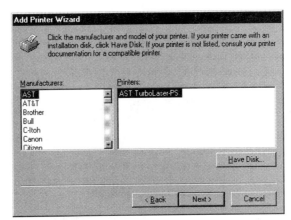

Regardless of whether the printer is attached to a Windows NT or Windows 95 computer, the remaining steps are the same.

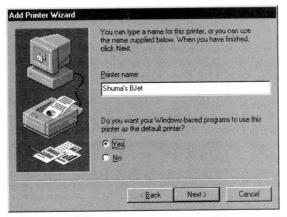

Type a different Printer name, if desired. Select **Yes** if you want your Windows-based programs to use this printer as default or **No**, if not. Click on **Next**. Select **Yes** to print a test page or **No** to not print a test page. Finally, click on **Finish**.

In Windows 95, when you click on **Finish**, the Wizard determines whether the drivers can be downloaded from CAB files on the local machine or whether the necessary driver files need to be downloaded from the print server. If they must be downloaded from the print server, the transfer happens automatically. A screen similar to the following appears listing the source of the files and the destination on the local machine:

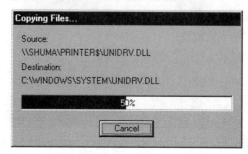

Notice that the source of files on the Windows 95 print server is a hidden shared directory named Printer$. When the transfer of the necessary files is complete, the printer is set up. If a file was dropped onto the printer to initiate the install, then the file will be printed.

In Windows NT, when you click on **Finish**, the Wizard requires that the necessary driver files be downloaded from the same media as was used for the original Windows 95 installation. If a CD-ROM was used to install Windows 95, for example, then you are prompted for the Windows 95 CD-ROM as in the following graphic:

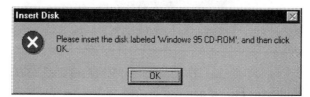

If Windows 95 was installed from the Windows NT server, the necessary driver files are automatically downloaded from the server.

Using Deferred Printing

Deferred Printing

Deferred Printing is enabled by setting a network printer to Work Offline or a local printer to Pause Printing. This is especially important for remote users who can only connect to a printer periodically or if the printer is being serviced.

To set up Deferred Printing:

1. Launch the Printers utility from the Control Panel.

2. Select the printer.

3. Right-click to display the available options and select **Pause Printing** (for a local printer) or **Work Offline** (for a network printer).

The status of the printer displays **Pause** (when Pause Printing is used) or the printer icon appears as dimmed (when Work Offline is used). The document is added to the print queue when the print job is sent to the printer. Once Work Offline or Pause Printing is turned off, the jobs begin to print in the order in which they were placed in the queue.

HP JetAdmin Service

The Hewlett Packard JetAdmin application allows you to control the setup and configuration of Hewlett Packard printers that are connected to an HP JetDirect print server. The HP JetDirect print server can be installed on a Novell NetWare server, Novell print server, or on every computer in a peer-to-peer setting.

To install the HP JetAdmin Service, open the Network utility. Click on **Add**. Select **Service** and click on **Add**. Select **Hewlett Packard** from the list of manufacturers. Double-click on the network service **HP JetAdmin**.

> *NOTE: You are not allowed to install HP JetAdmin (NetWare Support) and HP JetAdmin on the same machine; you are also not allowed to install either more than once on a single machine.*

Click on **OK** and restart the computer when prompted. An icon representing the HP JetAdmin application appears in the Control Panel.

Network Neighborhood displays an HP Network Printers server icon.

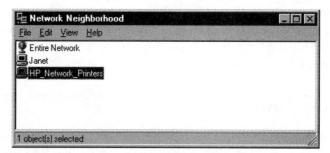

To run HP JetAdmin:

1.   Double-click on the HP JetAdmin icon in the Control Panel. Printers can be added and configured in the utility.

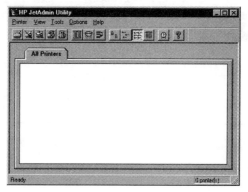

   NOTE: The IPX/SPX protocol must be installed to use the HP JetAdmin Utility.

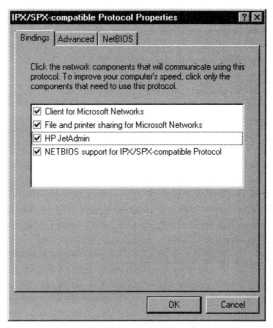

The HP JetAdmin utility provides an online Windows-based troubleshooter through Help which will walk a user through making changes to Windows settings.

Windows 95 Print Queues

Each defined printer on a Windows 95 workstation has a print queue that contains a list of documents waiting for service by the printer. To access this queue, open the desired printer in the Printers folder.

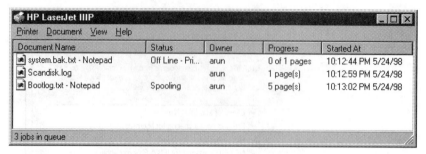

NOTE: The open print queue window accepts new jobs through drag and drop.

To change the order in which queued print jobs print, drag and drop the print job to the position desired. Jobs that are currently printing cannot be reordered; they only can be deleted. To delete a print job, highlight the desired job and either open the **Documents** menu and run **Cancel Printing**, or right-click the document and select **Cancel Printing**. Jobs can be paused in the same fashion.

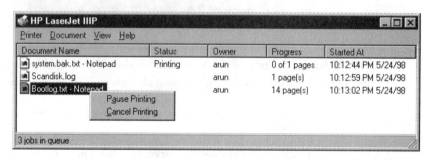

PRINTER TROUBLESHOOTING

This section describes various troubleshooting methods for printer problems. The following topics are discussed:

- Troubleshooting Font Problems
- Troubleshooting Windows Printing Problems
- Troubleshooting Local Printer Problems

Troubleshooting Font Problems

If you receive distorted fonts in a printed document, you may want to try the following troubleshooting methods:

1. View the document in the Print Preview view. If there is no distortion visible, then try changing to a different font and/or font size.

2. Check the resolution on the **Graphics** tab of Printer Properties. If you are using a non-TrueType font, you will get the best results using 300 dpi for the resolution.

3. Try printing the text from another application. If the printout still shows distortion, remove and reinstall the font.

4. If you are trying to print a large graphic, you may need to check the printer's memory.

If your text overlaps when printing, you may want to check the resolution. If the fonts print out clipped, then you may want to check the printable region configured for the printer. This selection is available by clicking on **Unprintable Area** on the Printer Properties' **Paper** tab.

Troubleshooting Windows Printing Problems

If you run into problems where you cannot print from a Windows application, you may need to change your bi-directional printing settings. You may have to experiment with different settings until you find a combination that works for your system. Bi-directional printing relies on the 1284 IEEE specification. If the printer cable you are using does not support this specification, then you cannot use bi-directional printing.

If you have problems printing legible documents or graphics in Windows 95, you may try one of two options:

- Use the Generic/Text Only printer driver.

   You can install the Generic/Text Only printer driver by running **Start/ Settings/Printers**. Then launch the Add Printer Wizard. Click on **Next** to pass the introduction screen. Install a local printer and click on **Next**. Click on **Generic** from the list of manufacturers and **Generic/Text Only** from the list of printers. Click on **Next**. Verify the port and click on **Next**. Accept the default name of the printer. Click on **Next**. Let the Wizard print a test page to confirm everything prints clearly. Click on **Finish**.

- Update your driver.

   Sometimes drivers are updated and stored on the company's Web site for users to download. Download the file (usually a self-extracting file). Double-click on the *.EXE file to extract it. Then use the Add Printer Wizard to install the new driver by clicking on **Have Disk** instead of choosing the actual printer. You can also change the driver by clicking on the **Details** tab's **New Driver** button. It will take you through the same process as the Add Printer Wizard.

Another problem you might encounter is a user complaining that since he chose to print a document some minutes ago, he has been trying to access the document to save and exit the application, but nothing is working. This may be due to the printer's spool settings. By clicking on **Spool Settings** in the **Details** tab, you can set the printer to print after the first page has been spooled. Using this option allows the user to gain access to the application while printing continues in the background. However, the amount of disk space used will be somewhat greater and the total time it takes to print the document will be longer.

Troubleshooting Local Printer Problems

If you continue to have problems with a local printer printing properly, you can try to print to the LPT1.DOS port. To do so, open the Printers folder from either My Computer or **Start/Settings**. Right-click to display the properties for the printer that is not working correctly. Click on the **Details** tab. Click on the **Add Port** button to add the LPT1.DOS port. Click on the **Other** option and select **Local Port**. Click on **OK**. Type LPT1.DOS as the new port name and click on **OK**. Printing may take longer than printing to the regular local port.

If you are receiving garbled images or text when trying to print, start the computer in safe mode first. Try to reprint. If the problem persists, disable EMF spooling by clicking on **Spool Settings** in the **Details** tab. Change EMF to RAW. Next, try to print with a printer using a PostScript driver. If the document prints intact, then there is a problem with the UNIDRV.DLL file. Also, be sure that you are printing one job at a time.

SCENARIOS

Scenario 1

One of your users has called Support for printing problems. He has been trying to print a detailed document filled with graphics for the past 30 minutes. The text and graphics are printing unclear. What are some troubleshooting methods you should implement?

....

....

Scenario 2

One of the users in your company has called in complaining that she cannot move on to a different task in the same application once she starts a print job. She has to wait for the entire document to go to the printer before she can open another file. What can you do to fix the problem?

....

....

Scenario 3

You have recently purchased a new printer that is attached to a Windows 95 print server. The necessary print drivers have been copied from the manufacturer's installation disk. The printer is shared by ten additional Windows 95 computers on a peer-to-peer network. What will happen when the first print job is sent to the new printer from each computer?

....

....

Scenario 4

Tom hurt his ankle playing basketball and must stay home for a week. During that week, Tom must finish a proposal and turn it in for printing and processing. It is important that the document be formatted for the printer at the office. How can Tom prepare the document for the HP LaserJet 5P printer at the office while he is at home?

....

....

SUMMARY

In this chapter, you learned how to install and configure printers for use from a Windows 95 client. This included:

- Using the Printers folder.

- Installation and removal of printer drivers.

- Resource sharing of printers.

- Discussion of the configurations set through the property pages of a printer.

- Setup of Point and Print printing.

- Creation, reordering, and deletion of Windows 95 print queues.

- Purpose and use of minidrivers and universal drivers.

- Access of a printer via a NetWare network.

- Installation and use of HP JetAdmin.

- Troubleshooting local printing problems, as well as Windows printing problems.

In the next chapter you will see how a Windows 95 computer can be connected to a remote computer.

POST-TEST QUESTIONS

The answers to these questions are in Appendix A at the end of this manual.

1. How can you ensure spool print jobs will finish faster–starting printing after the last page is spooled or starting printing after the first page is spooled?

   ....

   ....

2. Which type of spool data format can be used in conjunction with a spool setting for faster output?

   ....

   ....

3. What can you do to troubleshoot print problems that produce unclear graphics?

   ....

   ....

4. You want to install and use the HP JetAdmin utility. Which protocol must you install?

   ....

   ....

5. Why would you use Point and Print printing?

    ....

    ....

6. Describe the difference between the universal printer driver and the minidriver.

    ....

    ....

CHAPTER 16

Remote Access

OBJECTIVES

At the completion of this chapter, you will be able to:

- Install and configure a new modem.
- Describe the features of Microsoft's Unimodem V.
- Install and configure Microsoft's Internet Explorer.
- Install and configure Internet Mail.
- Discuss the purpose of the Messaging API.
- Distinguish between the three components of MAPI.
- Discuss the purpose of the Telephony API.
- List functions provided by TAPI.
- Describe the two TAPI interfaces.
- List MAPI service providers included within Microsoft Exchange.
- Configure the Microsoft Exchange client.
- Briefly relate the steps required to set up a new Microsoft Mail post office.
- List the steps necessary for sharing a fax modem to other network users.
- Describe how to access a shared fax modem.
- Configure remote access clients.
- Configure remote access servers.
- Troubleshoot modem problems.
- Troubleshoot remote access problems.

PRE-TEST QUESTIONS

The answers to these questions are in Appendix A at the end of this manual.

1. Where can you view port, IRQ address, and interrupt information for a modem?

   ....

   ....

2. Even if you have Internet Explorer set up on your system, how can you reinstall and reconfigure it?

....

....

3. List a couple of troubleshooting methods for when a user tries to use his dial-up connection, but the call does not go through.

....

....

INTRODUCTION

This chapter begins with a discussion of how to install and configure a new modem in the Windows 95 operating environment. The Add New Hardware Wizard walks users through the installation of a new modem. As you will see, Windows 95's Plug and Play capabilities enable users to add a new modem and install the drivers. The properties sheets available for a selected modem will also be discussed. Next, the chapter briefly discusses Microsoft's Unimodem V.

The chapter then introduces the Internet environment in Windows 95. You will learn to install and configure both Internet Explorer and Internet Mail.

Next, the chapter discusses MAPI, TAPI, and Microsoft Exchange. You will also learn how to configure the Microsoft Exchange client as well as setting up a new Microsoft Mail post office.

This chapter also introduces Windows 95's new Dial-Up Networking utility. This allows users to create new dial-up connections as remote clients or remote servers. The chapter concludes with a discussion of troubleshooting modem and remote access problems.

CONFIGURING A NEW MODEM

This section discusses the installation and configuration of a new modem using the Add New Hardware Wizard. Properties sheets available for a given modem will also be covered. The following topics are discussed in this section:

- Adding a New Standard Modem
- Adding a New Specific Modem
- Modem Properties
- General Modems Properties
- Properties Option
- Logging Modem Errors
- Dialing Properties
- Unimodem V

Windows 95 can automatically detect and install modems by using the Modems control panel or the Add New Hardware control panel. Modem properties can be customized to reflect a user's specific requirements when installed.

Adding a New Standard Modem

You can add a new modem to your system using one of two methods. The first is to use the Modems utility and the other is to use the Add New Hardware utility. Both launch the Add New Hardware Wizard. To launch the Wizard using the Modems utility, launch the utility and click on the **Add** button. The Wizard launches, displaying its introductory screen. The Wizard is covered in detail below.

> *NOTE:*   *Internal legacy modems which are not Plug and Play must first have their COM port configured by using the Add New Hardware option in the Control Panel.*

To add a modem using the Add New Hardware utility, first launch the utility. Click on **Next** to proceed past the informational screen. The prompt "Do you wish Windows to search for your new hardware?" appears. Select **No** to specify a search for a modem and click on **Next**. The following screen appears:

Select Modem and click on **Next**. The following screen appears:

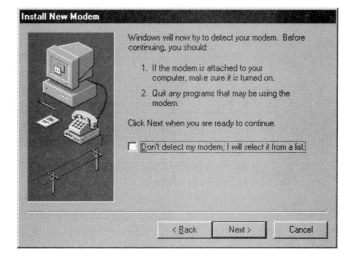

Click on **Next** unless you have an installation diskette or CD-ROM from the modem manufacturer. To install a modem that requires a manufacturer's diskette or CD-ROM, check the **Don't detect my modem; I will select it from a list** checkbox and click on **Next**. This diskette or CD-ROM may contain device drivers that are more recent than or not contained in the Windows 95 files. Installing a modem using a manufacturer's diskette is covered a little later.

The following screen appears as Windows looks for the modem:

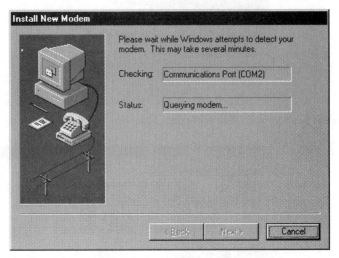

If a modem is found, the Verify Modem dialog appears. Standard Modem is selected if Windows can't match your modem type with device drivers already in the system. This may be fine. However, some advanced features of your modem, such as volume control and flow control, may not be available.

If you would rather install your modem's device drivers and have the manufacturer's diskette or CD-ROM, or if you want to install a modem from the Windows list, click on **Change**.

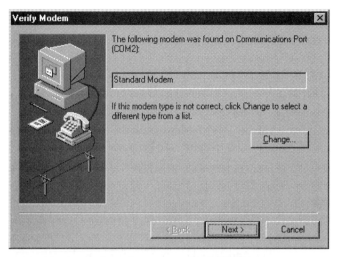

If the modem cannot be located on the system, the following screen appears:

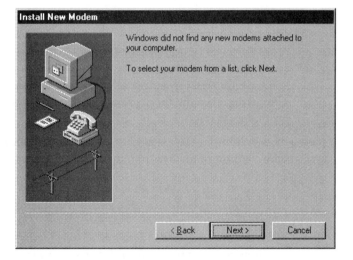

There are several reasons why the modem may not be detected:

- The modem may not be connected properly to the computer.

    If it is an external modem, check the connection to the computer. Turn the modem off and on; then retry the installation.

- The COM port may be assigned to another device.

    Use the Device Manager in the System control panel or MSD to determine which COM ports are being used.

- The modem is already installed.

    The Install Wizard will not find modems which are currently in the Installed Modems list.

- The COM port may not be configured properly.

    The Add New Hardware control panel can be used to detect and install the COM port.

- The COM port's IRQ setting is in conflict with an IRQ setting of another device.

    IRQ conflicts are displayed on the **Resources** tab of the specific COM port's properties dialog. Display the COM port properties dialog by expanding and selecting the particular COM port in Device Manager. Click on **Properties**, then display the **Resources** tab. If another device is in conflict with this port, it is listed in the Conflicting device list.

To choose a modem from a list, click on **Next**. Windows will allow you to continue with the installation by selecting a modem from the list of modems.

> NOTE: *Be careful. If a modem is installed this way, the modem may not work properly. Any modem can be added to Windows regardless of whether there is actually a valid modem or COM port selected. The modem will appear in the Device Manager modem listing even though it may not be functional at all. To ensure that a modem is working properly, use the **Diagnostics** tab in the Modems control panel. Modem troubleshooting is covered at the end of this chapter.*

Click on **Next** to continue the installation. The following screen appears:

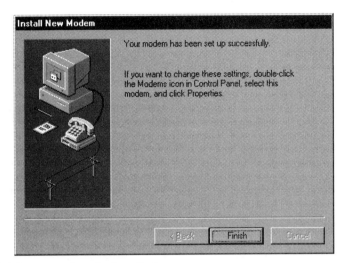

Click on **Finish** to complete the installation.

Adding a New Specific Modem

The following screen appears when you select the **Don't detect my modem; I will select it from a list** checkbox and click on **Next**. It will also be displayed if you click on **Change** to select a specific modem from the Windows list which is different from the modem Windows detected:

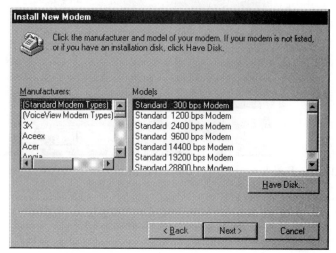

Select a modem from the list and click on **Next** or click on **Have Disk** to install the drivers from a diskette or CD-ROM. Click on **Browse** to change the path, if necessary. Click on **OK** to continue.

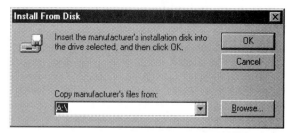

You may be requested to select your modem's specific type of from a listing. If so, select it and click on **Next**.

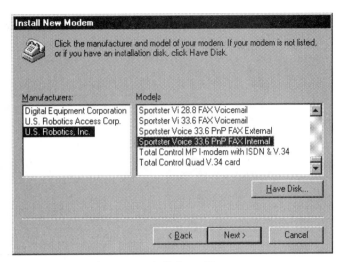

Select the correct COM or LPT port and click on **Next**.

NOTE: *COM ports 1 and 3 use the same IRQ, so do not try to use COM1 if COM3 has another device, such as a mouse, attached to it. COM 2 and COM4 also share the same IRQ setting. Some modems have conflicts when assigned to COM4. Try to use COM4 as a last resort.*

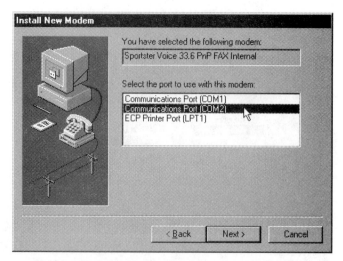

A screen appears, verifying that the modem has been successfully installed. Click on
Finish to complete the installation.

Modem Properties

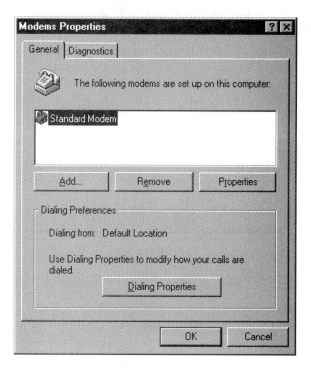

Once you launch the Modems utility, two properties sheets are available: General and Diagnostics. Let's take a look at the General properties sheet for now. The **Diagnostics** tab will be discussed at the end of this chapter.

General Modems Properties

The **General** tab contains a listing of the modems currently installed on the computer. This properties sheet also displays four options: **Add**, **Remove**, **Properties**, and **Dialing Properties**. Modems can be added here by clicking on the **Add** button. This launches the Add New Hardware Wizard, which was discussed previously in this chapter. You can also delete a modem by selecting it and clicking on the **Remove** button.

Let's look at the other two options on this properties sheet: Properties and Dialing Propeties.

Properties Option

Additional modem configurations, such as port settings, speaker volume, and maximum connection speed are displayed by clicking on **Properties**. The Properties dialog appears for the selected modem. This Properties dialog contains two tabs: **General** and **Connection**.

General Tab

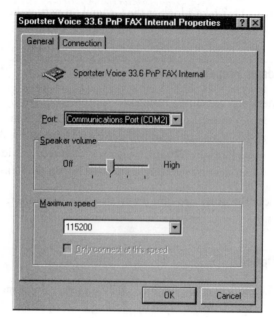

Available General properties are:

Port	A drop-down list that contains available ports.
Speaker volume	This option controls the volume of telephone sounds, such as dial tone.
Maximum speed	This option determines the highest speed at which the modem can connect.

Connection Tab

Modem connection configurations are set up on the **Connection** tab. Some modems do not support all of these features. If a feature is not available, it is displayed in gray.

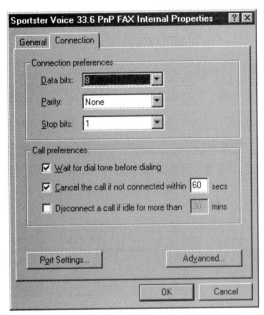

The **Connection** tab allows the following properties to be configured along with two additional options: **Port Settings** and **Advanced**.

Connection preferences

> Configures the settings of the modem to which you are connecting. These settings are usually set up by the application making the connection.

Wait for dial tone

> In certain locations and on certain phone systems, a dial tone may not be recognized by the modem. In these situations, the dial tone should be disabled.

Cancel the call if not connected

> Sets the number of seconds before the modem will timeout and cancel the call. For example, this time increment may need to be increased when making an international call.

Disconnect a call if idle

> Sets the number of minutes before an idle connection is disconnected.

Port Settings

> Clicking on **Port Settings** allows you to configure specific port-related transfer and receive settings if "Use FIFO buffers" is enabled. The following dialog displays when you click on **Port Settings**.

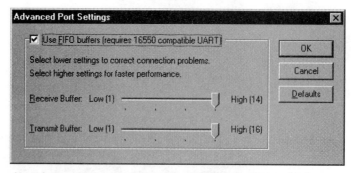

Clicking on the **Advanced** button of the **Connection** tab of a modem's properties sheet offers connection configurations, such as use error control and modulation type. A modem may not support all of these features.

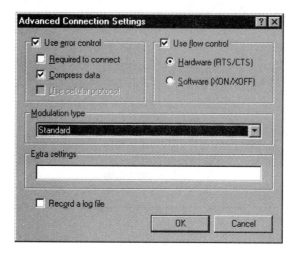

You can set the following Advanced Configuration properties:

Use error control

This option can provide a more stable connection, especially when communicating over noisy phone lines. However, setting this option can cause connection problems. If you are having trouble connecting, disable this setting and try to reconnect.

Required to connect

This option requires error control to be used for all connections.

Compress data

This option compresses data so that it can be sent faster over the phone line. Enabling this setting can cause connection problems. If you are having trouble connecting, disable this setting and try to reconnect. This setting may also cause problems when trying to send compressed files.

Use cellular protocol

This option specifies that a special protocol for cellular calls should be used. This option may cause problems with non-cellular calls when enabled. You may need to disable this option when making non-cellular calls.

Use flow control

This option is used by external modems to control the flow of data from the modem to the computer. Unless a modem has RTS and CTS cables, software (XON/XOFF) flow control should be selected.

Modulation type

This option enables a modem to better communicate with the modem with which it is trying to connect. Both computers must be set to the same modulation type to exchange data successfully.

Extra Settings   Additional modem settings can be stored here. These settings are sent to the modem after all other configuration settings and override all previous settings.

Record a log file   If this box is checked, a file named MODEMLOG.TXT is created in the Windows directory. This file contains diagnostic information regarding the commands that are issued and the modem's response. Let's look more closely at MODEMLOG.TXT.

Logging Modem Errors

Capturing a log of the communications session may be helpful in diagnosing modem problems. You can turn on the logging process by selecting the **Properties** option on the **General** tab of a modem's properties sheet. Then select the **Connection** tab and click on the **Advanced** button. Click on the **Record a log file** checkbox to start the logging process during communications. The results will be written to the file MODEMLOG.TXT located in the Windows directory. The MODEMLOG.TXT file can be viewed with any text editor.

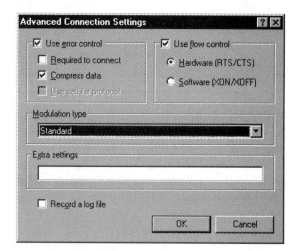

Dialing Properties

Dialing properties are set by clicking on the **Dialing Properties** button on the **General** tab of a modem's properties sheet. This properties sheet contains information necessary to make international calls and specifies calling card rules to use.

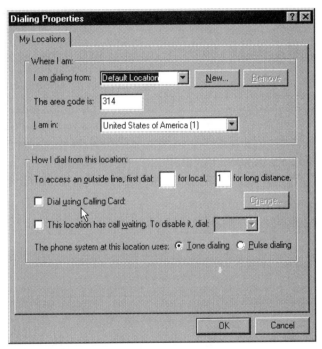

You can set the following Dialog Properties:

I am dialing from	This field specifies a name for your location. Click on **New** to add a new location.
The area code is	This field contains the area code.

I am in	This field identifies the country where you are located and its international code. Use the drop-down list to look up other countries.
To access outside line, first dial	If the phone line for this location normally requires a number to be dialed first, it should be entered here. There is a box for local and one for long distance.
Disable call waiting	You can select to disable call waiting when a particular number is dialed. Call waiting can disrupt modem communications.
Tone dialing or Pulse dialing	This option indicates whether the phone lines you are calling from use tone or pulse dialing.
Dial using Calling Card	This option allows you to provide calling card information.

To set up calling card information, click on the **Dial using Calling Card** checkbox. The Change Calling Card dialog appears:

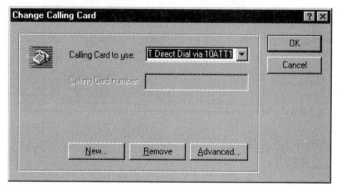

Select the calling card to use from the list of calling cards. If the one you want to use is not in the list, click on **New**, type a name for the calling card, and click on **OK**.

Click on **Advanced** to set up the dial string for calls being made within the same area code, long distance calls, and international calls.

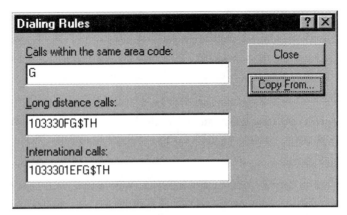

Type in the information necessary to place the call. There are several codes which are used to define the dialing rules. These codes are listed by clicking on the question mark. The cursor then becomes a question mark. Once you click in the desired field, a popup dialog appears listing all of the specifications for configuring the calls within the same area code, long distance calls, and international calls.

Unimodem V

The Microsoft Unimodem V modem drivers add enhanced features to Microsoft's universal modem driver. Features include:

- Support for data/fax/voice modems
- Wave playback
- Recording to and from the telephone line
- Wave playback and recording to and from the telephone handset
- Caller ID
- Call forwarding
- Speakerphone support

- Unique/distinctive ringing

To install the Unimodem V drivers, run the self-extracting executable UNIMODV.EXE, and specify the destination directory. Access the directory you specified, right-click on the UNIMODV.INF file, and run **Install**. Once installation is complete, restart your computer.

Launch the System utility and select the **Device Manager** tab. Double-click on the Modem icon, select your modem, and click on **Remove**. Click on **Refresh** to update the display.

If your modem is a plug and play device, Windows 95 will detect the modem and reinstall it using the new Unimodem V drivers. If the modem is not plug and play-compatible, launch the Modems utility and click on **Add** to use the Add New Hardware Wizard. This will allow the system to detect your modem and install the drivers.

> *NOTE:*   *If you ever choose to remove the Unimodem V drivers from your computer, you may have to reinstall Windows 95.*

Exercise 16-1:
Adding and Configuring a New Modem

This exercise will teach you how to install a new modem and configure certain properties. You do not need to have an actual modem, nor its drivers.

1. Launch the Modems utility.
2. Verify that you are on the **General** tab and click on **Add**.
3. Click on the **Don't detect my modem; I will select it from a list** checkbox.
4. Click on **Next**.
5. Select (Standard Modem Types) from the list of manufacturers.
6. Select Standard 28800 bps Modem from the list of models.
7. Click on **Next**.
8. Select COM2 for the port.
9. Click on **Next**.
10. Click on **Cancel** if you are prompted to enter location information.
11. Select the Standard 28800 bps Modem from the list of installed modems and click on **Properties**.
12. Click on the **Connection** tab.

13. Click on **Advanced**.

14. Click on the **Record a log file** checkbox.

15. Click on **OK**.

16. Click on **OK** to close the Properties dialog.

17. Click on **Dialing Properties**.

18. Enter the area code as 555.

19. Click on **OK**.

20. Click on **Close** to close the Modems Properties dialog.

21. Close the Control Panel.

USING DIAL-UP NETWORKING

This section describes the ease of using Dial-Up Networking to allow users to create connections to Internet Service Providers (ISPs) or remote servers. The installation and configuration of Internet Explorer will also be discussed. The following topics are discussed within this section:

- Dial-Up Networking

- Installing Dial-Up Networking

- Creating a New Dial-Up Connection

- Dial-Up Networking File Menu

- Dial-Up Networking Edit and View Menus

- Dial-Up Networking Connections Menu

- Configuring a Remote Access Client

- PPTP/VPN

- SLIP Connection Protocol

- Windows 95 As a Remote Server

- Configuring a Dial-Up Server Type
- Accessing a Remote Windows NT Server

Even if you use dial-up connections in your home environment, you may want to consider securing the files and information located on your computer.

Dial-Up Networking

Dial-Up Networking enables users to create dial-up connections to remote servers such as ISPs or perhaps a server on a network at work. Windows 95 provides the Dial-Up Networking utility to make creating these connections easy. Again, the interface is that of a wizard. As you have probably guessed by this time in the course, the wizard interface is Windows 95's answer to allow users of all experience levels to perform hardware or administrative tasks on their system.

Dial-Up Networking gives mobile users the opportunity to work as if they were connected directly to the remote network. Once a network connection has been established using Dial-Up Networking, you will be able to access resources just as you would from a local network connection. Keep in mind, however, that the speed of a dial-up connection will be much slower than a direct network connection. Word processing and spreadsheet applications can still be accessed remotely, but will function much more slowly.

The Windows 95 Dial-Up Networking subsystem allows mobile Windows 95 users to designate their computer as a dial-up client or server. From a remote site, you can use Dial-Up Networking to connect the dial-up client to a Windows 95 dial-up server or other remote access servers, such as:

- Shiva NetModem
- Shiva LanRover
- Novell NetWare Connect
- Windows NT Workstation 3.1, 3.5.x, or 4.x
- Windows NT Server 3.1, 3.5.x, or 4.x
- Windows for Workgroups 3.11
- UNIX server running PPP (Point-to-Point Protocol), SLIP (Serial Line Internet Protocol), or CSLIP (SLIP with IP header compression)

Let's consider the following example. You may have a dial-up connection set up to connect to an ISP. The ISP allows you to log in to the server and access the Internet or access files on its server. Sometimes, an ISP will provide utility files on their server that their users can access. Personal Web pages are stored and run off this remote server.

However, Windows 95 also allows you to connect to other computers remotely, through the use of dial-up networking. You can configure a Windows 95 client to act as either a Dial-Up Networking client or a server. You must have Dial-Up Networking installed prior to any configuration. If you are using the OSR version of Windows 95 or higher, Dial-Up Networking can be installed automatically, or after installation using the **Windows Setup** tab of the Add/Remove Programs utility. If using other versions of Windows 95, you must install Dial-Up Networking from the Microsoft Plus! pack.

Installing Dial-Up Networking

To install Dial-Up Networking from the Add/Remove Programs utility, launch Add/ Remove Programs from the Control Panel. Click on the **Windows Setup** tab. Select **Communications**. Click on **Details**. Select **Dial-Up Networking**. Click on **OK**. Click on **OK** to close the Add/Remove Programs Properties dialog.

You must also install the appropriate Windows 95 network protocols such as TCP/IP, IPX/SPX, and NetBEUI. To be able to communicate across the network, you must have the same protocol installed on the client and the server. If you have installed network protocols prior to installing Dial-Up Networking, these protocols will be automatically bound to the Microsoft Dial-Up Adapter. The Dial-Up Adapter is automatically configured once installation of Dial-Up Networking is complete.

Dial-Up Networking utilizes the Windows 95 communication architecture. It:

- Initializes the modem.
- Determines device status.
- Dials the phone number using TAPI and the Unimodem driver.

NOTE: *NetBEUI and IPX/SPX-compatible protocols are automatically installed and bound to the Dial-Up adapter upon installation of the adapter.*

Dial-Up Networking also supports share-level and user-level security.

Installing the Dial-Up Adapter

If you should need to manually install the Dial-Up Adapter, launch the Network utility. Click on **Add**. Select **Adapter**. Select Microsoft from the list of manufacturers and Dial-Up Adapter from the list of network adapters. Click on **OK**. Click on **OK** to close the Network dialog. You will need to restart your computer for changes to take effect.

Creating a New Dial-Up Connection

Next, you will need to use the Make New Connection Wizard to create a client connection to the remote access server. The Make New Connection Wizard can be launched from within the Dial-Up Networking selection in My Computer, Windows Explorer, or **Start/Programs/Accessories/Dial-Up Networking**.

To create a new Dial-Up Networking connection, Windows 95 supplies the Make New Connection Wizard. Start this wizard by opening the Make New Connection object in the Dial-Up Networking folder. The wizard asks the user for dial-up server and modem information.

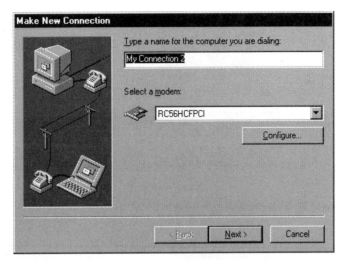

Clicking on **Configure** reveals the properties sheets for the modem. As you can see, the modem's property dialog has an additional properties sheet from those discussed earlier in the chapter. This properties sheet is only available when creating the Dial-Up connection. It is not available through the **Properties** option in the Modems utility, **General** tab.

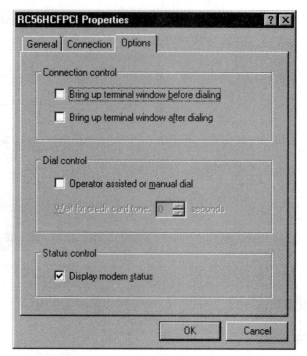

This dialog allows you to set connection controls such as displaying the terminal window before or after dialing. Administrators may want the use of the terminal window so that they can manually enter commands to communicate directly with the modem themselves. The terminal window then displays the responses received from the modem for interpretation by the administrator as to whether or not the modem is communicating properly. You can have operator assisted or manual dial control. There is also a selection for enabling a credit card dial tone.

The last option available on this properties sheet is status control, which allows you to display modem status. This displays messages showing the communication between the system and the modem.

Next, the Wizard asks the user for information about the telephone number and the country code.

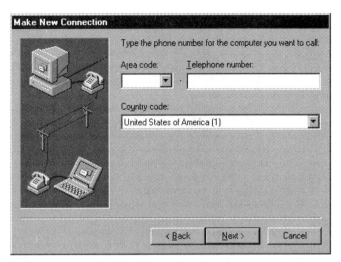

Click on **Next** to display the following dialog. You can click on **Finish** to complete the new dial-up connection configuration. If at a later time, you need to edit the connection, run **File/Properties** from the menu of the Dial-Up Networking utility or right-click on the connection icon and select **Properties**.

Finally, the Wizard creates the new connection. The new Dial-Up Networking connection appears in the Dial-Up Networking folder. In the graphic below, the connection is named My Connection 2.

Dial-Up Networking File Menu

If you select an existing dial-up connection icon in the Dial-Up Networking window, the **File** menu allows you to select from the following choices: **Connect**, **Create Shortcut**, **Delete**, **Rename**, **Properties**, and **Close**. **Connect** allows you to begin the dial-up connection. This option is the same as double-clicking on a dial-up connection, and clicking on **Connect**. **Properties** displays the available properties sheets for the connection.

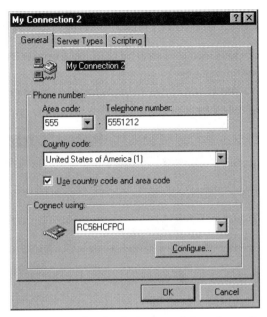

All of the properties sheets except for the Scripting tab have been discussed previously. The **Scripting** tab allows you to provide a script file to be used with the connection. The rest of the **File** menu options are self-explanatory.

Dial-Up Networking Edit and View Menus

These menu commands are the exact duplicate of those found in the Windows Explorer. These commands were defined earlier in the course.

Dial-Up Networking Connections Menu

The **Connections** menu offers three options: **Connect, Make New Connection**, and **Settings**. **Connect** allows you to display the Connect To dialog to begin the connection. **Make New Connection** launches the Wizard to create a new connection. The **Settings** command displays the following dialog:

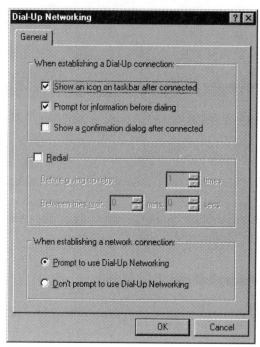

When establishing a dial-up connection, you can enable three additional options:

- Show an icon on taskbar after connected

- Prompt for information before dialing

- Show a confirmation dialog after connected

You can also set options for when you establish a network connection. You can prompt to use Dial-Up Networking or not prompt to use Dial-Up Networking. Basically, this means that if you launch Internet Explorer and there is no dial-up connection established, you will be prompted with the Connect To dialog to establish a new connection. Then Internet Explorer will open.

You can also set redial options through the **Connections/Settings** option of Dial-Up Networking. You can specify the amount of time to wait before trying to redial a connection phone number.

NOTE: *The Status box on the Dial-Up Server properties sheet lists any active connections to your computer.*

Configuring a Remote Access Client

To configure a Windows 95 remote access client, you must first create a dial-up connection using the Dial-Up Networking utility. Once the connection has been set up, you must configure the server type. To do so, right-click on your new connection icon. Select **Properties**. Clicking on the **Server Types** tab will display types of remote servers to which the Windows 95 client can connect.

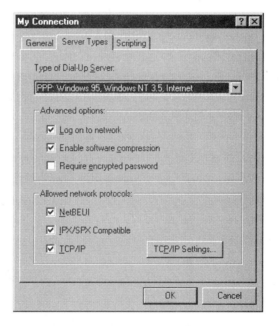

The most common are:

- NRN:NetWare Connect

- PPP:Windows 95, Windows NT 3.5 or 4.0, Internet

- SLIP:UNIX Connection

- Windows for Workgroups and Windows NT 3.1

- CSLIP:UNIX Connection with IP header compression

On the **Server Types** tab, you can also enable software compression and require an encrypted password. Windows 95 only supports software compression when connected to a computer that also provides software compression. Password encryption is a useful selection to use if you will enable users to log on to a remote access server, such as one on Windows NT. This provides better security for logon.

As you select the server type, the supported network protocols for that server type will be displayed at the bottom of the dialog. If the server type supports TCP/IP, you can click on **TCP/IP Settings** to configure TCP/IP information.

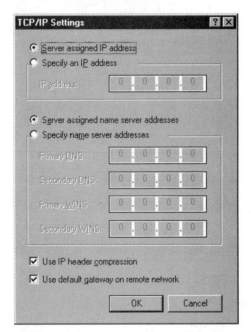

The **Server assigned IP address** option should be used if the remote server has IP addressing available through a DHCP server. If not, then you should specify the IP address to be used for the local computer.

If the **Server assigned name server addresses** option is selected, the dial-up connection will accept DNS and WINS server addresses from a PPP server. If there are no DNS or WINS addresses available from the PPP server, those addresses specified in the Network utility for these settings will be used.

If the PPP server does not provide DNS and WINS addresses, you can specify Primary DNS, Secondary DNS, Primary WINS, and Secondary WINS addresses. You can also enable **Use IP header compression**, which allows data transfers to be optimized.

Lastly, if you enable **Use default gateway on remote network**, all IP address traffic is routed to the default gateway address on the network.

PPTP/VPN

Point-To-Point Tunneling Protocol (PPTP) is provided as an add-on to Windows 95. The key advantage of PPTP is that it uses public-switched telephone networks to provide a secure Virtual Private Network (VPN). Through the use of an Internet Service Provider (ISP), mobile users can *tunnel* through the Internet and establish a secure session with their corporate network. Because PPTP provides security over public telephone lines, it eliminates the need for expensive leased lines.

The only computer equipment required are the client computers, a network access server, and the PPTP server.

A VPN can also be established by using PPTP on a LAN. If a VPN is configured on a LAN, an additional network access server is not required.

SLIP Connection Protocol

SLIP is a connection protocol that is only supported as a client in Windows 95. It is primarily used for connecting to older UNIX remote access servers. To install SLIP, launch the Add/Remove Programs utility. Display the **Windows Setup** tab. Click on **Have Disk**. Browse to the appropriate path. For Windows 95 versions older than OSR, the path to installation files is:

\ADMIN\APPTOOLS\DSCRIPT\RNAPLUS.INF

For OSR versions, the path is:

\WIN95\SERVPACK.95\ADMIN\COMPONTS\DSCRIPT
\NETSETUP\RNAPLUS.INF

Click on the Dial-Up Scripting Tool selection.

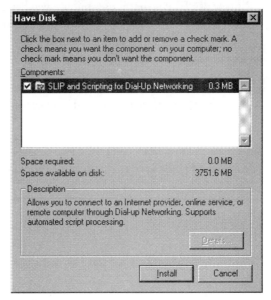

Click on **Install**. Click on **OK** to close the Add/Remove Programs Properties dialog.

On the Server Types dialog, you can also enable software compression and require an encrypted password. Windows 95 only supports software compression when connected to a computer that also provides software compression. Password encryption is a useful selection to use if you will enable users to log on to a remote access server, such as one on Windows NT. This provides better security for logon.

The **Configure** button on a connection's Properties dialog displays three tabs: **General**, **Connection**, and **Options**. The **General** tab displays:

- The name of the modem used for connection.

- The port the modem uses.

- Speaker volume settings.

- Maximum speed options for connection with a checkbox to require connection at the selected speed.

Now you are ready to connect to a remote access server. To do so, double-click on your new connection icon. Click on **Connect**. The modem will attempt to dial in to the remote server.

Windows 95 As a Remote Server

A Windows 95 machine can be configured to act as a remote access server. This can be done using Dial-Up Networking. The remote access server can share its file and print resources through dial-up networking to only one client at a time. You must first install Dial-Up Server if you are using a Windows 95 version older than OSR. To install Dial-Up Server, you must use the Microsoft Plus! Pack. If you are using the OSR version, it is installed with Dial-Up Networking.

Configuring a Dial-Up Server Type

To enable a Windows 95 machine to serve as a remote access server, open Dial-Up Networking from My Computer, Windows Explorer or **Start/Programs/Accessories/Dial-Up Networking**. Display the **Connections** menu. Select **Dial-Up Server**.

Dial-Up Server Security

This window will look different depending on share-level or user-level security. User-level security displays the following dialog for Dial-Up Server:

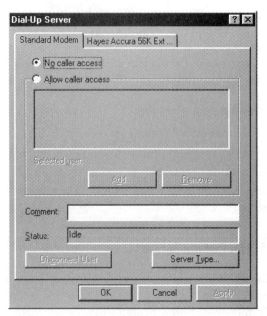

Once you enable the **Allow caller access** selection, you can add users from your domain
who will access the remote server.

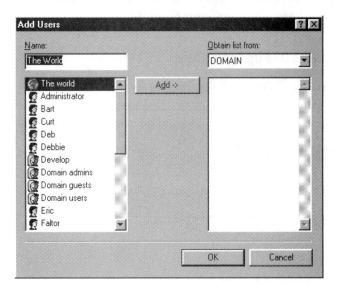

Share-level security displays the following dialog:

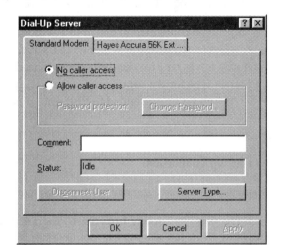

To add a password for logon to the remote access server, click on the option for **Allow caller access**. Then, click on **Change Password** to display the following dialog:

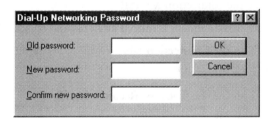

Selecting the **Allow caller access** option enables the Windows 95 machine to be configured as a remote access server. To disable remote access server functionality, select **No caller access**. You can either disable dial-up server support on each computer, or create a system-wide policy in System Policy Editor.

Windows 95 Clients Accessing a Remote Windows NT Server

Windows 95 can also be configured to dial in to a Windows NT remote server. A dial-up connection must be created with the Windows NT server's phone number. There is no need to configure a server type for the connection. Dial-Up Networking sets the proper protocols and server type for the connection automatically. However, the Windows NT Server's server type should be configured to PPP, since it is the recommended protocol.

Exercise 16-2:
Creating a New Dial-Up Connection

This exercise demonstrates creating and configuring a new dial-up connection.

1. Launch Dial-Up Networking from **Start/Programs/Accessories/Dial-Up Networking**. You can also use My Computer or Windows Explorer to launch the utility.

2. Double-click on **Make New Connection**.

3. Name the connection My ISP.

4. Verify that a modem is indeed available and click on **Configure**.

5. Click on the **Connection** tab.

6. Click on **Advanced**.

7. Click on the checkbox for **Record a log file**.

8. Click on **OK**.

9. Click on the **Options** tab.

10. Enable the **Bring up terminal window before dialing** option.

11. Verify that **Display modem status** is selected. If it is not, enable the option.

12. Click on **OK**.

13. Click on **Next**.

14. Enter the area code as 555 and the telephone number as 555-1212.

15. Verify that the country is selected as United States of America. If it is not, please change it. Click on **Next**.

16. Click on **Finish**.

17. If the Microsoft Dial-Up Adapter has not been installed previously, you will be prompted to do so. Click on **OK** to start the installation of the adapter.

18. Select your new connection named My ISP and run **Connections/Settings** from the menu.

19. Click on the checkbox for **Redial**.

20. Enable the connection redial three times before giving up.

21. Click on **OK**.

22. Close the Dial-Up Networking window.

ACCESSING THE INTERNET

This section discusses the installation procedures for the Internet Explorer browser and Internet Mail. Internet Mail is one of the clients users can use to retrieve e-mail. We will also discuss how to maintain security of local resources from hackers on the Internet. The following topics are discussed within this section:

- Installing Internet Explorer
- Using the Internet Connection Wizard
- Internet Mail Setup
- Securing Resources While Connected to the Internet

Installing Internet Explorer

Internet Explorer is the browser that shipped with Windows 95. It is Microsoft's browser version for the Windows 95 operating system. At the time this book went to print, Internet Explorer 4.01 had been available for a few months. Internet Explorer allows users to access the World Wide Web.

To install Internet Explorer 3.02, double-click on the setup icon on the desktop. This will launch the setup program. After accepting the licensing agreement, you must select which Internet components you would like to install.

Optional Components

In addition to Installing Microsoft Internet Explorer 3.01 on your computer, you may also elect to install any of the optional components by checking the appropriate box.

OK

Cancel

Component	Size
☑ Internet Mail	1960 KB
☑ Internet News	1960 KB
☑ NetMeeting (Windows 95 only)	4980 KB
☑ ActiveMovie	635 KB
☑ HTML Layout Control	2048 KB

These components consist of: Internet Mail, Internet News, NetMeeting, ActiveMovie, and HTML Layout Control. You may install any or all of the components listed. Normally, Internet Explorer is installed into the C:\WINDOWS directory by default. You may specify a different location if you choose. The setup program will then begin to install the components you selected. Once installation is complete, you must restart your computer for settings to take effect.

You will notice that the icon for Internet Explorer has been added to the desktop environment.

The Internet

Using the Internet Connection Wizard

Now that setup has installed the files for Internet Explorer, you must use the Internet Connection Wizard to set up a connection to the Internet. This might be based on a new connection method or an existing connection method.

Setup Options

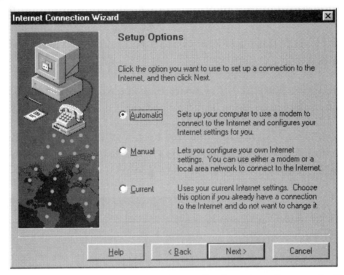

There are three options to set up a connection to the Internet: **Automatic**, **Manual**, and **Current**.

Automatic   This selection will set up a connection to use the modem. Internet settings will also be configured for you. This selection should be used for novice users. It is also the quickest way to set up a new connection.

Manual   This selection is for advanced users. It allows you to set your own Internet settings via the modem or a local area network connection.

Current   This selection can be chosen if you would like to use existing connection information. It will use all current Internet settings, assuming a connection is already set up.

If you select **Automatic**, you will need to first select the modem to use for connection. The Wizard will then ask you for location information such as area code and the first three digits of your phone number. The wizard will then dial in to the Microsoft Referral List Server to download a list of preferred Internet Service Providers available in the selected calling region.

If you select **Current**, the Connect To dialog will open automatically to begin connection to the Internet. As soon as the connection is made, Internet Explorer will launch itself.

If you select **Manual**, you will need to choose the method by which you will connect to the Internet. You can either connect through a modem line or over a local area network (LAN). The steps involved will be discussed shortly.

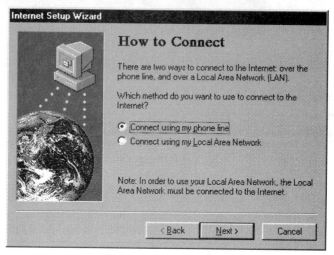

Once this is selected, you must now decide whether you want to receive and send e-mail using Windows Messaging. Windows Messaging is the default Windows tool. If you decide to use a tool other than Windows Messaging, you must install and set up the software yourself outside of this Internet Setup Wizard. Windows will now install the drivers and files needed to create the connection itself.

Service Provider Information

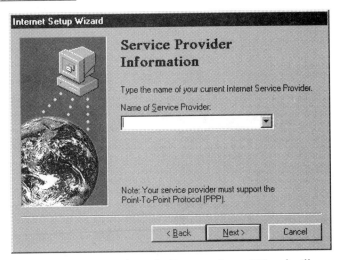

If you selected a connection by modem, the Internet Setup Wizard will set up a Dial-Up Networking connection for you. The Service Provider Information dialog requires you to either select an existing connection or create a new one. If you have more than one Dial-Up Networking connection created, you may select which one you want to associate with Internet-related applications. For example, if you double-click on Internet Explorer prior to launching the Dial-Up Networking connection icon, Windows will open the Connect To dialog. Once the connection has been established, Internet Explorer will open. Internet Explorer will open even if you cancel out of the Connect To dialog. You will receive a message that Internet Explorer cannot connect to the selected home site. If you click on **OK**, Internet Explorer will display C:\WINDOWS\SYSTEM\BLANK.HTM.

Phone Number

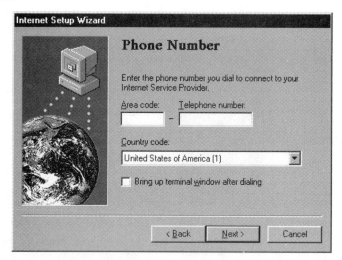

Once you select the Internet Service Provider, you must enter the area code and phone number for your ISP. To change the country from which you will be dialing, display the country code options. This will provide the connection with information for dialing access codes for the selected country. You may also select to open up the terminal window after dialing. This option is also available in the Dial-Up Networking window in Connections/Dial-Up Server dialog.

User Name and Password

You must also provide username and password information to connect to the selected Internet Service Provider.

IP Address and DNS Server Address

The Internet Connection Wizard will next ask you to configure network protocol and server information. You can either assign an IP address already assigned for your system or allow the Internet Service Provider to provide one dynamically. Not all Internet Service Providers provide a static IP Address for their users.

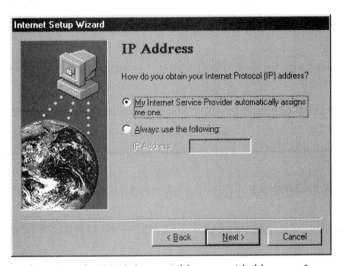

You will also need to enter the DNS Server Address provided by your Internet Service Provider. They may also give you an alternate DNS Server address. This information is often available on the Internet Service Provider's Web page.

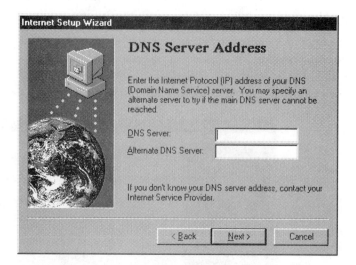

Internet Mail Setup

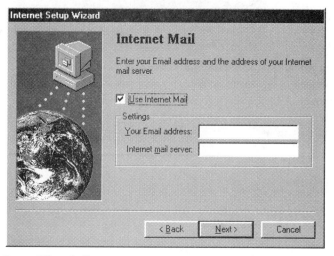

The Internet Setup Wizard allows you to set up Internet Mail. You must specify an e-mail address, as well as the Internet mail server for that address. To view electronic mail, launch Internet Explorer. Run **Go/Read Mail**. The location of the Internet Mail option may be different in versions prior to IE 3.02.

Windows Messaging Profile

Windows Messaging will try to detect any previously defined profiles. If Microsoft Exchange settings have been identified at any time, it will display this profile as a default option. You may create a new profile by clicking on **New**. Type in a new profile name and click on **OK**.

Finally, the Internet Setup Wizard will copy any remaining files needed and installation is complete.

Securing Network Resources While Connected to the Internet

You should consider implementing security measures for your resources when connecting to the Internet. Without the proper security, hackers can access resources on your computer or even on network servers. This could be extremely dangerous even if you are at a company where private documents are stored on a hidden network drive. Hidden does not mean inaccessible. It just means that it does not show up when browsing resources.

To provide security when you are directly connected to the Internet, you should disable File and print sharing services on Windows 95 systems. To unbind the file and printer sharing service, select the TCP/IP protcol from the **Configuration** tab and click on **Properties**. Select the **Bindings** tab. Uncheck the box for **File and printer sharing for Microsoft Networks**. Disabling this binding keeps hackers from accessing local resources.

If you have Windows 95 stations that need access to the Internet, but also to a LAN, you might consider installing a proxy server. A proxy server acts as an intermediary between an intranet and the Internet. To identify the proxy for your computer, open the Internet utility. Click on the **Connection** tab. Check the **Connect Through a Proxy Server** checkbox. Click on **Settings** to enter the address of the proxy server.

Exercise 16-3:
Installing Internet Explorer

This exercise is designed to familiarize you with the setup wizard of Internet Explorer. You must have completed Exercise 16-2 prior to doing this exercise.

1. Open **Start/Programs/Accessories/Internet Tools/Internet Setup Wizard**.

2. Click on **Next** past the introductory screen.

3. Verify that you are connecting using the phone line, and click on **Next**.

4. If you have file and printer sharing services installed on your system, you will receive a message stating that you may want to disable this service so that others cannot access your resources while connected to the Internet. Click on **Yes**.

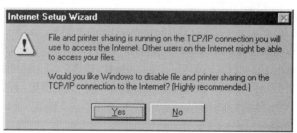

5. Click on the option for **I already have an account with a different service provider**.

6. Click on **No** for Internet Mail.

7. Accept the default modem selection and click on **Next**.

8. Select My ISP as the service provider from the drop-down list.

9. Click on **Next**.

10. Click on the checkbox for **Bring up terminal window after dialing**.

11. Enter the user name as jsmith and the password as summer.

12. Click on **Next**.

13. Keep the default and click on **Next**.

14. Do not specify any DNS Server addresses. Click on **Next**.

15. Click on **Yes** to continue.

16. Click on **Finish**.

SETTING INTERNET EXPLORER PROPERTIES

This section discusses the configuration and settings available in the Internet utility. This utility was discussed briefly earlier in the course. However, now we will take a close look at each property page available in the Internet utility. The following topics are discussed within this section:

- Internet Properties
- General Internet Properties
- Internet Connection Properties
- Navigation Internet Properties
- Programs Internet Properties
- Advanced Internet Properties

We will discuss the **Security** tab of the Internet utility in the next section.

Internet Properties

The Internet utility is used to set properties for Microsoft's Internet Explorer. These properties can also be displayed by opening **View/Options** from the menu within Internet Explorer. These properties range from setting the default Web page to be displayed upon opening Internet Explorer to selecting the security levels for users accessing the World Wide Web from your local workstation.

Let's take a closer look at each of these properties sheets and the functions of each available option.

General Internet Properties

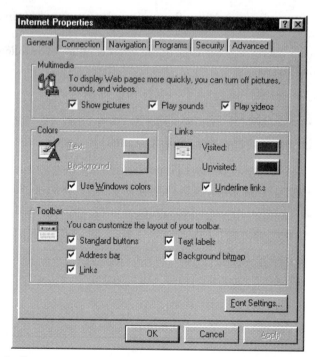

The **General** tab allows you to set properties related to multimedia devices, colors, links, and the toolbar.

Multimedia	The **Show pictures** option can be cleared to not display graphic pictures, thus allowing Web pages to be displayed quickly. **Play sounds** can be selected if you want to hear audio clips on Web pages. Audio clips sometimes slow down the opening of a Web page. Clear this option if you want your Web pages to be uploaded quickly. If enabled, the **Play videos** option allows animated and video clips to be displayed when viewing Web pages.
Colors	The Colors property allows users to select the color of the text and background they want to see when viewing Web pages. If you want to use default colors, you can select the **Use Windows colors** option.
Links	This option can be used to select the color of links available on a Web page, as well as the color for those links you have visited previously. If you wish to have links display an underline, you can select the **Underline links** option.

Toolbar

This property allows users to select the toolbar buttons they wish to have available on the browser's toolbar. Options include: **Standard buttons, Address bar, Links, Text labels,** and **Background bitmap.**

The Standard buttons include **Back, Forward, Stop, Refresh, Home, Search, Favorites, Print, Font,** and **Mail.**

The Address bar is the field where Web addresses are displayed. To view the Web sites viewed in the past, you can click on the drop-down arrow for the addresses. These entries are known commonly as History. There is a history folder that is created in the Microsoft Internet Explorer directory that holds the number of Web sites visited. We will discuss how to set this value in a moment.

Links by default include the following Web sites: Best of the Web (http://home.microsoft.com/best.best.asp), Today's links (http://home.microsoft.com/links/links.asp), Web gallery (http://www.microsoft.com/gallery/default.asp), Product news (http://www.microsoft.com/ie), and Microsoft (http://www.microsoft.com).

You can also specify the style of font that you would like to use for your browser by clicking on the **Font Settings** button. The following dialog is displayed:

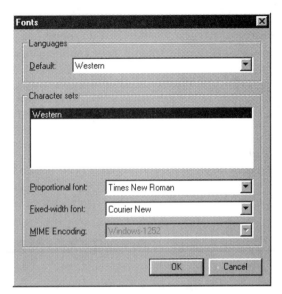

The Proportional font setting contains all of the installed fonts on your system. The Fixed-width font contains those fonts associated with the selected proportional font. In this case, we have selected Times New Roman as the proportional font, which supplies us with only one choice for fixed-width font as Courier New. MIME Encoding is set to Windows-1252 by default. Users are not able to change this setting.

Internet Connection Properties

This property page enables the user to select the dialing method for connecting to the Internet by clicking the checkbox for **Connect to the Internet as needed**. Users must then select the dial-up networking connection. If there are multiple dial-up connections created (i.e., one for each Internet Service Provider), the user must specify which they would like to use for connection to the Internet.

Clicking on **Add** launches the Make New Connection Wizard. **Properties** displays the three properties sheets available for a dial-up connection: **General, Server Types,** and **Scripting.** Two additional settings may be configured for Dialing.

Disconnect if idle for _____ minutes

> You can enable the system to disconnect from the Internet if idle for more than a specified amount of minutes.

Perform security check before dialing

> This option lets you specify whether you would like Internet Explorer to do a security check for password information on your system before dialing to the remote server.

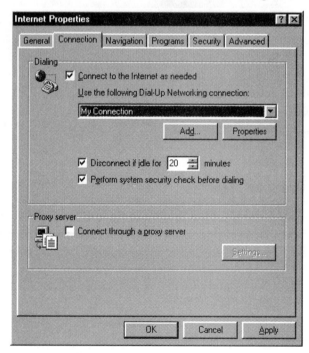

Users can also select to connect to the Internet via a proxy server. To enable this option, click on the checkbox for **Connect through a proxy server** and click on **Settings.** The following dialog is displayed:

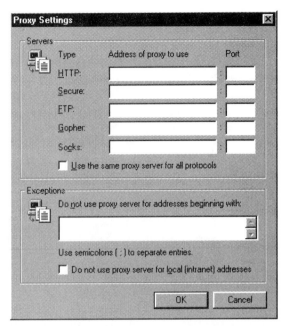

Administrators must enter the necessary information relating to the proxy server being used. This information includes HTTP, Secure, FTP, Gopher, and Socks addresses, as well as the ports that each will use. Specified addresses for proxy servers may be excluded by entering them in the Exceptions section of the dialog. If you have multiple proxy servers that you wish to exclude, you must use a semicolon to separate each address.

Navigation Internet Properties

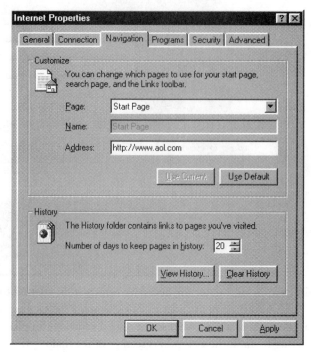

The **Navigation** tab allows users to specify the http address for Internet Explorer's Start Page, Search, and Links 1 through 5. These are the settings that are available as the Links option within Internet Explorer. We mentioned that on the **General** tab, these are Best of the Web, Today's Links, Web Gallery, Product News, and Microsoft by default. The **Navigation** tab enables you to change those default addresses and sites. If at any time you want to revert to the default sites and addresses, you can click on **Use Default**.

History information can also be configured on this property page. You can select the number of days you wish to keep the history current. History items are listed in the Address bar of Internet Explorer. They can be viewed simply by clicking on the drop-down arrow on the Address bar. This allows users to quickly access those sites in the current history quickly and without having to retype the entire address. If you wish to view history items from outside of Internet Explorer, you can click on **View History**. This opens a dialog listing all history items including the name of the Web page, the Internet address pertaining to that page, the date and time the page was last visited, and the date that the history item will expire. As you can see, this example shows that the item was visited on May 29, 1998. In the above dialog, the **Number of days to keep pages in history** is set to 20 days. Therefore, the expiration date for that history item is June 18, 1998. After June 18, 1998, that history item will no longer be available.

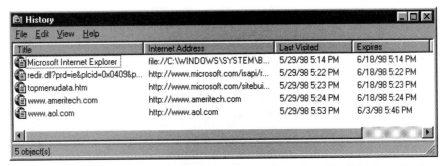

The History dialog also has menu options similar to those found in Windows Explorer. The popup menu enables users to open the history item, which launches Internet Explorer and opens the selected Web page. You can also delete a selected history item by selecting **Delete History Item**.

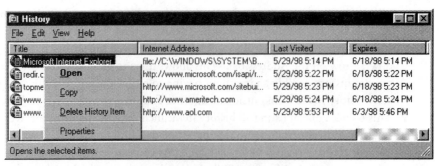

You can also view an item's properties by clicking on **Properties**. This property page
simply lists the title of the Web page, the Internet address to the Web site, the time the
page was last visited, the time the history item will expire, and the last time the page was
updated. The upper entry of the Web site specifies the title page on the displayed
Internet address. For example, www.ameritech.com has a Web page within this site,
www.ameritech.com/paging. In this case, the upper entry would list
www.ameritech.com/paging and the Internet address would list www.ameritech.com.

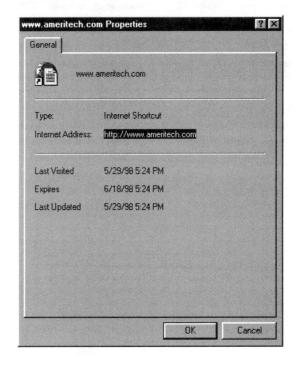

To remove the history entries entirely, you can click on **Clear History** from the
Navigation tab of the Internet utility or **View/Options** within Internet Explorer. This
clears the history entries in the address bar of Internet Explorer.

Programs Internet Properties

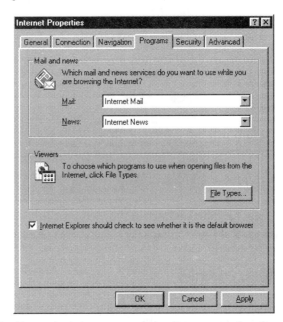

The **Programs** tab allows administrators to set up Internet mail and news servers for
users. If you are using a different mail client other than Internet mail (such as Windows
Messaging), you can specify it from the **Mail** setting. The same holds true for the news
server.

File Types displays the same options as those discussed earlier in the course for Windows
Explorer. Administrators can configure the applications to be used when opening files
from the Internet.

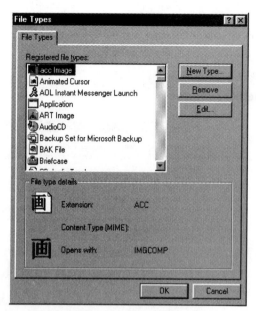

If your system has different internet browsers installed, you can specify that a check be performed to see if Internet Explorer should be set to the default browser.

Advanced Internet Properties

The **Advanced** tab enables you to configure warnings that are passed over the Internet and to your system, storage of temporary Internet files, and additional settings.

Show friendly URLs	This option allows the complete Web address to be displayed on the status bar of Internet Explorer.
Highlight links when clicked	This option enables focus to be displayed when clicking on a link in Internet Explorer.
Use smooth scrolling	This option sets a predefined speed to be used for the cursor when scrolling through pages on the Internet.
Use style sheets	This option enables Internet Explorer to display Web pages using the HTML style.

Enable Java JIT compiler

This option enables Java programs to be executed using the Java virtual machine. If you do not enable this option, you will not be able to view Java programs that may be available on a Web site.

Enable Java logging

This option can be enabled to keep a log of all Java activity while on the Internet.

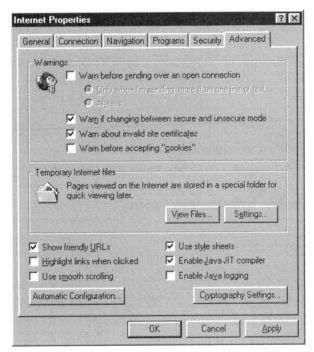

Warnings

Warn before sending over an open connection

If checked, this option displays a dialog warning users before unsecure information is about to be sent over the Internet. You can specify this type of warning for **Only when I'm sending more than one line of text** or **Always**.

Warn if changing between secure and unsecure mode

This option, if checked, will allow Internet Explorer to warn you when switching between secure and unsecure Web sites. This type of option is a valuable choice to use if you are sending personal information such as credit card numbers via the Internet.

Warn about invalid site certificates

This option enables you to receive a warning if the URL in a site certificate is invalid.

Warn before accepting "cookies"

A *cookie* is a small text file that the server (for an Internet Web site) writes to the user's hard disk without the user's permission if this option is not enabled. A cookie contains data enabling one Web page to pass information to another Web page. In some cases, cookies are useful for users who tend to shop on the Internet since the text file will store information about the user. However, in other cases, this is not such an advantage. Many times, these cookies are used by other Web sites as a way of contacting you via e-mail. Many marketing firms use these cookies to monitor users' habits and preferences on the Internet. If you wish to receive a warning before your system accepts a *cookie*, you should check this option.

Temporary Internet Files

If you click on the **View Files** button, a dialog will open listing all files contained within the temporary Internet directory. These files are located in the \WINDOWS\TEMPORARY INTERNET FILES directory. The menu options in this dialog are similar to those available in Windows Explorer. The pop-up menu enables you to open the temporary file with its associated application. In our example, if **Open** was selected for the home.gif file, Internet Explorer would open to display the graphic file. You can also delete the file by selecting **Delete Local Copy**.

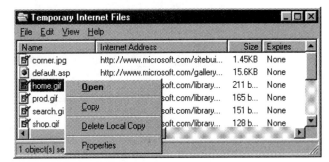

You can also view the temporary Internet file's properties by selecting **Properties**:

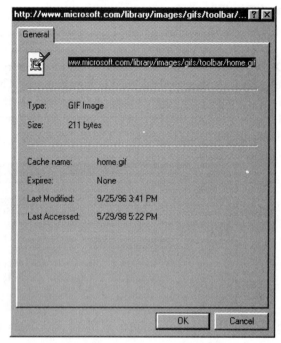

This property page's title bar displays the complete Web address for the selected temporary Internet file. The property page also displays the type and size of the file. The cache name is listed, which is the temporary Internet file's name. There is no expiration date for a temporary Internet file. You can also view the last modified and last accessed dates.

You can also configure settings for Temporary Internet Files by clicking on **Settings** from the **Advanced** tab of the Internet utility:

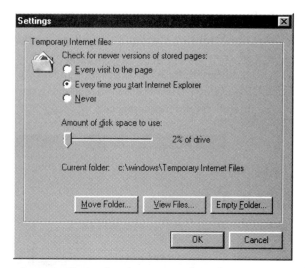

As each temporary Internet file is a local copy stored on the system, it enables the Web page to be loaded quickly the next time the user accesses the page. You can select Internet Explorer to check for newer versions of stored pages **Every visit to the page**, **Every time you start Internet Explorer**, or **Never**. These options can be configured depending on a user's preferences and needs. You can also specify the amount of hard disk space that should be used for storing these temporary Internet files.

You can move the folder from the \WINDOWS\TEMPORARY INTERNET FILES location to another location by clicking on **Move Folder**. Files can be viewed by clicking on **View Files**. The same dialog is displayed as the **View Files** option available on the **Advanced** tab. If you want to empty the folder, you can click on **Empty Folder**. This deletes all local copies of temporary Internet files.

Automatic Configuration

If you click on the **Automatic Configuration** button on the **Advanced** tab, you can configure Internet Explorer using information that is stored on the Internet at a particular URL address. **Refresh** can be used to update the settings immediately upon entering the URL address. If this option is not selected, settings will not be updated until the next time Internet Explorer is launched.

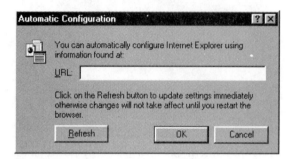

Cryptography Settings

Administrators can set cryptography settings for any of the three types of security protocols available on this dialog:

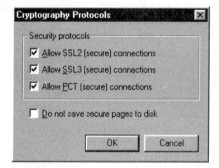

- Allow SSL2 (secure) connections
- Allow SSL3 (secure) connections
- Allow PCT (secure) connections

You should enable the **Do not save secure pages to disk** option if you do not wish for this information to be saved to your hard disk.

SECURITY FOR THE INTERNET

This section describes the various types of settings that can be configured to provide security for accessing the Internet. These configurations include setting restrictions for users to certain types of Internet content using a content advisory password. The following topics are covered in this section:

- Security Internet Properties
- Content Advisor
- Certificates
- Active Content

Security Internet Properties

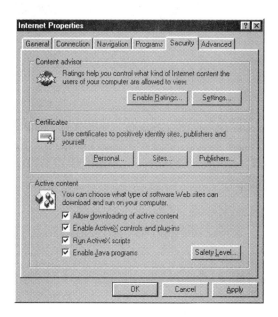

The **Security** tab enables the administrator to configure security settings for the user while he or she is connected to the Internet. In an office environment, it is not appropriate for some Internet content to be viewed. Administrators can use the Content advisor to set appropriate restrictions for connections to the Internet for users while at work. In many organizations, viewing such controversial content is cause enough to be discharged from employment.

Content Advisor

Enable Ratings can be used to set a password for the Content Advisor. The Content Advisor is the user who can set restrictions to certain Internet content. Clicking on this option for the first time displays the following dialog.

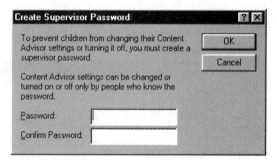

Once a password is set, the option no longer says **Enable Ratings**. It will then say **Disable Ratings**. If you click on **Settings** for the first time or without having enabled ratings, you must specify a supervisor password first. The same dialog as that shown above is displayed.

Once a supervisor password has been created, the following three property pages will be displayed: Ratings, General, and Advanced.

Ratings Restrictions

The **Ratings** tab displays the various categories available for setting security restrictions. They include: Language, Nudity, Sex, and Violence.

Language	This setting allows you to set restrictions to display information on the Internet containing only inoffensive slang and no profanity.
Nudity	This setting allows no nudity.

Sex	This setting prohibits animated clips of sexual and romantic activities.
Violence	This setting restricts any violent acts of natural or accidental incidences.

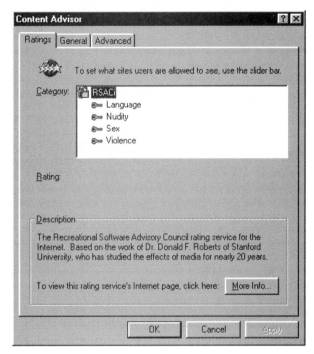

As a restriction is selected, a scroll bar is displayed in the Rating section of the dialog. Administrators and users can change the level simply by using the scroll bar. To view detailed information about a rating service, click on **More Info**. This connects you to the corresponding web page in Internet Explorer.

General Restrictions

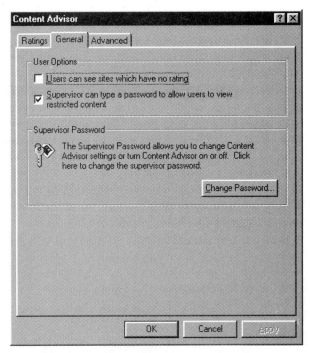

The **General** tab allows users to view sites that have no ratings imposed on them, or to allow a supervisor to enter a password to allow users to view restricted content. The **Supervisor can type…content** option can be enabled if ratings have been configured, but you do not need to impose the ratings for the particular user on the system at a given time.

This property page also allows the Content Advisor to change the current password.

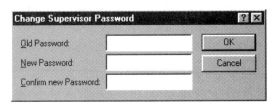

Advanced Restrictions

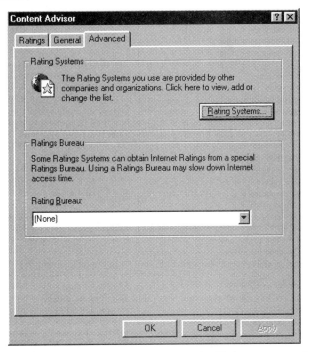

The **Advanced** tab enables administrators to view and add the current rating systems provided by other companies and organizations on the Internet. To view the listing, click on **Rating Systems**.

Each rating system consists of a *.RAT file format. To add a rating system, click on **Add**. You must then browse to locate the *.RAT file you want to impose. To remove a rating system, select the *.RAT file and click on **Remove**.

Certificates

Generally, there are two types of certificates used for the Internet: Personal and Sites. Let's take a close look at each type of certificate.

Personal

Personal certificates are created when a user has sent personal information to a client authentication server to request access to a Web site. That certificate is then used to identify the user. Depending on the sites a user visits, there could be any number of certificates listed in this dialog.

Sites

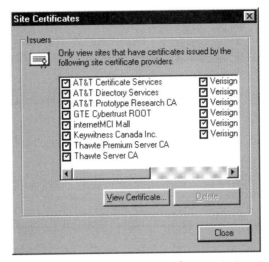

Site certificates are a bit different than personal certificates. A site certificate is used by organizations and companies to provide secure information to Internet Explorer about that Web site. These certificates are generally valid for a specified period of time only. This type of security is very important to an organization. For companies doing business over the Internet, especially those involving sales, it is important to provide a secure environment to their customers. Using site certificates enables their Web site to be designated as a safe and secure environment. Also, by holding a site certificate, it keeps other Web sites from attaining the prestige and identity of a secure Web site.

To view a certificate, simply click on **View Certificate:**

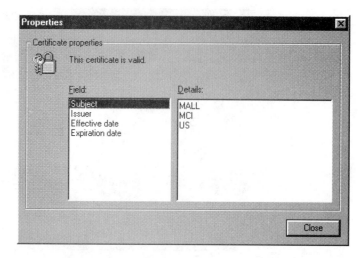

Publishers

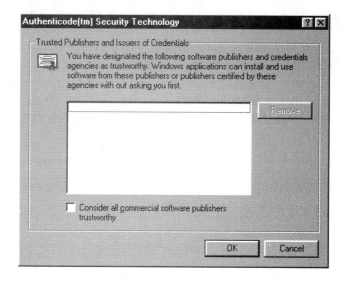

This list of publishers allows you to permit individual and commercial software publishers to install software on your system without attaining your permission first. You can also list credential agencies in this list. A credential agency is an agency that attests to the identity of the software publishers. This allows you to know that they are indeed reputable companies. If you do list a credential agency in this list, any software publisher registered with the agency will be permitted to install software on your system without permission. Therefore, it is important to check out the companies listed with a credential agency.

Active Content

The Active Content portion of the **Security** tab allows you to set configurations for the following options:

- Allow downloading of active content

  This option allows Internet Explorer to download any active content, which includes multimedia files and animations from the Internet.

- Enable ActiveX controls and plug-ins

  This option allows Internet Explorer to show active content on a Web page that may be constructed from an ActiveX control or plug-in.

- Run ActiveX scripts

  This option allows Internet Explorer to run ActiveX scripts automatically from a Web page.

- Enable Java programs

  This option allows Internet Explorer to run Java programs automatically as they come across on a Web page.

You can also specify the safety level you wish to use by clicking on the **Safety Level** button on the **Security** tab of the Internet utility or **View/Options** in Internet Explorer.

There are three safety levels:

- High

  A high security level is recommended for users of beginner experience level or the average user surfing the Internet. This security level protects users from all security problems.

- Medium

  A medium security level is recommended for use by expert users and developers. This level of security enables users to be notified of all security issues broached on the Internet.

- None

  This security level is not recommended as it does not protect you from security issues on the Internet. It can potentially damage your system, as it is very possible to download a virus with any software from the Internet. Unless you are absolutely sure that the Web sites you visit have a site certificate, you should not use this level of security.

MESSAGING

This section will introduce MAPI, the Messaging API utility. The following topic is discussed within this section:

- MAPI

Electronic messaging applications make use of Windows 95's MAPI support to provide communications and scheduling.

MAPI

The MAPI (Messaging API) standard supports different messaging systems through the provision of API functions and an OLE interface. The MAPI architecture defines and supports messaging clients, such as Microsoft Exchange or Lotus cc:Mail. MAPI utilizes the following components:

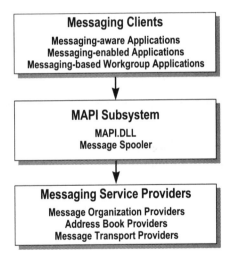

- Messaging Clients

    Messaging-aware applications, such as Microsoft Word, utilize messaging service providers as an optional feature.

    Messaging-enabled applications, such as Lotus cc:Mail and the Microsoft Exchange client, require messaging capability to provide full functionality for the application.

    Messaging-based workgroup applications, such as Microsoft Schedule+, require the full messaging capabilities provided by MAPI.

- MAPI Subsystem

    The MAPI subsystem provides services to integrate messaging clients with messaging service providers. Services include the MAPI dynamic-link library and message spooling.

- Messaging Service Providers

    Message organization providers furnish storage and recovery services for the messaging system.

    Address book providers furnish lists for addressing and distributing messages.

    Messaging transport providers furnish message conveyance between messaging clients.

TELEPHONY

This section will introduce TAPI, the Telephony API utility. The following topic is discussed within this section:

- TAPI

As more users need remote access to either networks at work or for Internet access, TAPI comes into play.

TAPI

TAPI (Telephony API) services support communication applications with modem support. TAPI-aware applications utilize Windows 95 communications services through the Telephony API. TAPI is written to accommodate future telephony features and new telephone networks.

The Windows 95 implementation of TAPI provides a standard for communications applications to access telephony functions. These functions integrate support for data, fax, and voice calls. TAPI directs all signaling between the Windows 95 computer and the telephone network.

Functions provided by TAPI include:

- Dialing the modem.

- Answering inbound calls.

- Hanging up after call completion.

- Hold, transfer, conference, and call park as provided by PBX and ISDN networks.

TAPI consists of two interfaces:

- A Win32 TAPI API that can be used by developers to write TAPI-aware applications.

- A service provider interface (SPI) that TAPI-aware service providers use to establish the connections to specific telephone networks.

Due to TAPI management of requests from communications applications, Win32-based applications can make outgoing calls while other Win32-based applications are waiting for incoming calls.

MICROSOFT EXCHANGE

This section will introduce the Microsoft Exchange client that installs with Windows 95. This client would normally be used within a network environment. Other communication services that are included in Windows 95 will also be discussed. The following are topics discussed within this section:

- Microsoft Exchange Client
- Configuring Microsoft Exchange Client

- Internet Mail

- Internet Mail Properties

- Local Postoffice Administration

- Microsoft Fax

- Sharing a Fax Modem

- Accessing a Shared Fax Modem

Electronic messaging, specifically electronic mail, has become a critical part of doing business. Also, Windows 95 allows a user to set up his or her machine as a fax client.

Microsoft Exchange Client

The Microsoft Exchange client is included with Windows 95. Exchange is a message-enabled messaging client that retrieves messages from several types of messaging service providers, including Microsoft Mail, The Microsoft Network, Microsoft Fax, and other MAPI-compliant service providers.

Upon installation of the Microsoft Exchange client, several MAPI service providers are available:

- Microsoft Fax services

- Microsoft Network services

- Internet Mail

- Internet Mail Properties

- CompuServe Mail services

- MAPI Personal Address Book services

- MAPI Personal Folder services

- Microsoft Exchange Server services

- Microsoft Mail Postoffice services

The Exchange client keeps individual profiles for each user. This feature enables more than one user to share the same computer and still send and receive mail.

NOTE: You must exit and restart Microsoft Exchange to switch between profiles.

The Exchange client uses a universal inbox/outbox known as a Personal Folder File (.pst). This file is used to send messages to and receive messages from the service providers. Because of its location in the Exchange subdirectory, the Personal Folder File can be easily backed up. The Personal Folder File can be stored on a network drive to ensure that roving users can access their mail from anywhere on the network.

Configuring the Microsoft Exchange Client

To start the Microsoft Exchange client from the desktop, open the Inbox object. You can enable Exchange to automatically download mail for all service providers upon opening the Inbox. To add a service provider, open the Mail and Fax object within the Control Panel.

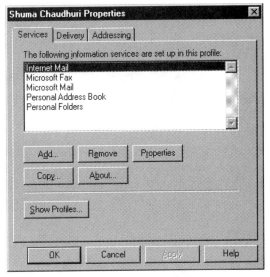

Verify that you are on the **Services** tab and click on **Add** to add a new service provider.

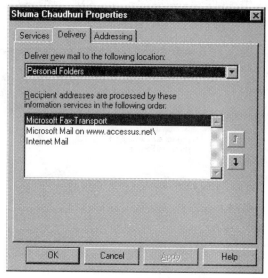

The **Delivery** tab of this property sheet contains the following:

The **Delivery** tab allows you to select where you want your new mail delivered. By default, all mail is delivered to the Personal Folders item. The box below this option displays all the information services that process incoming mail from recipient addresses.

The **Addressing** tab contains address list options. If you have more than one address book created, you can specify in which order you want names to be checked when sending out a new e-mail.

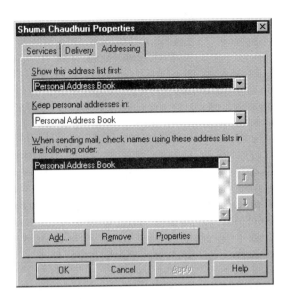

Internet Mail

The Internet is becoming an increasingly important means of communication. In addition, the integration of Exchange with Windows 95 has made the Internet even more accessible. Let's spend some time discussing how to configure Microsoft Exchange to send and receive Internet mail.

To configure Exchange for Internet mail, access the Mail and Fax utility. When the MS Exchange Settings Properties dialog appears, click on **Add** to access the Add Service to Profile dialog.

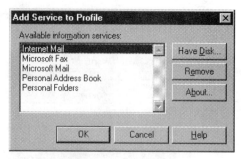

Select **Internet Mail** and click on **OK**.

When the Internet Mail service has been added, you will be presented with the Internet Mail dialog. This dialog is used to configure the Internet mail service. To change the setting in this dialog at a later time, access the Mail and Fax utility, select Internet Mail from the **Services** tab, and click on **Properties**.

Internet Mail Properties

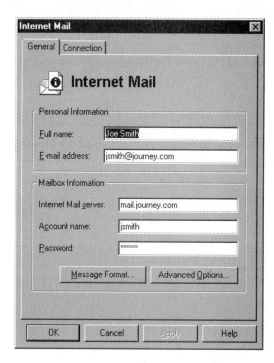

General Tab

You will need to supply the following information:

- Full name

    This name will appear in the e-mail header. This defaults to the name that was used during the Windows 95 installation.

- E-mail address

    Enter the user's Internet mail address.

- Internet Mail server

    Enter the name of the Internet mail server. If different servers are used for incoming (POP3) and outgoing (SMTP) mail, enter the name of the POP3 server in this field. Click on the **Advanced Options** button to enter the name of the SMTP server.

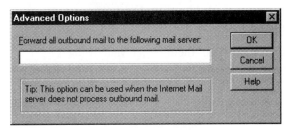

- Account name

    Enter the POP3 e-mail account name.

- Password

    Type the password for the POP3 e-mail account.

- Message Format

    The message format dialog is used to set up the character set and message format to be used in e-mail messages.

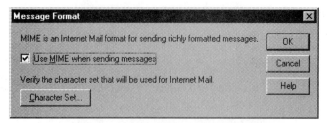

To change the character set, click on **Character Set...**

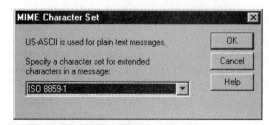

Connection Tab

The **Connection** tab of the Internet Mail dialog is used to specify information about the type of connection that will be used to send and receive e-mail.

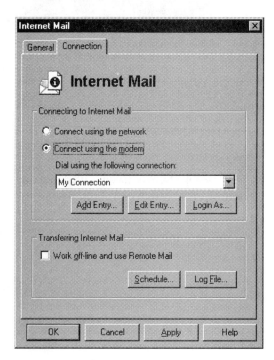

- Connect using the network

  Select this button if you will be accessing the mail server via a LAN connection.

- Connect using the modem

  Select this button if you will be using a dial-up connection to access the mail server. In order to use this feature, Dial-Up Networking must be installed on the computer. Click on **Add Entry** to create a new connection. This launches the Make New Connection Wizard. Click on **Edit Entry** to display General, Server Types, and Scripting properties sheets for the selected dial-up connection. **Login As** allows you to set a new login and password for the dial-up connection.

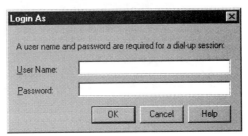

- Work off-line and use Remote Mail

  Check this option if you want to use the Remote Mail feature of Microsoft Exchange. The **Schedule** button is used to set up mail delivery schedules. It also enables you to schedule the frequency of automatic dial-up to send and receive e-mail from a dial-up connection.

The **Log File** button provides a way to record e-mail events in a log file.
This feature can be very helpful when troubleshooting e-mail problems.
You can select from No Logging, Basic, and Troubleshooting as the levels of
logging you wish to use.

Local Postoffice Administration

The Microsoft Mail postoffice that ships with Windows 95 is a scaled-down version of
the Microsoft Mail Server. It allows one computer to act as the postoffice, while allowing
other users in the workgroup to send and receive mail. The Windows 95 version contains
only the basic administration tools, provides no access to Microsoft Mail gateways, and
does not permit mail exchange with users from other postoffices.

From the Control Panel, open the Microsoft Mail Postoffice utility. The user is asked
whether to administer an existing Workgroup Postoffice or to Create a new Workgroup
Postoffice.

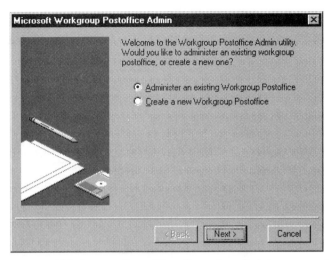

Selecting **Create a new Workgroup Postoffice** allows the administrator to designate a new postoffice location.

When selecting the location for the workgroup postoffice, it is recommended that you place the postoffice on a computer that will always be accessible. In addition, the computer should have at least 8 MB of memory. You should also have 2 MB of free disk space with room to grow as the number of users and messages increases. If you will have more than 20 users, you should consider placing the postoffice on a dedicated computer.

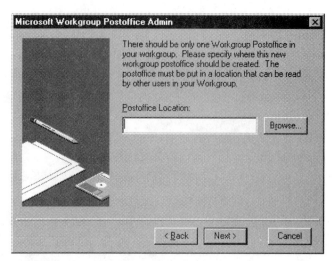

The administrator will be prompted to confirm the creation of the new postoffice.

After creation of the new postoffice, the administrator must enter account details:

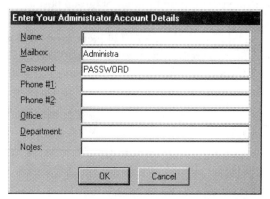

After entering administrator details, an informational dialog box appears.

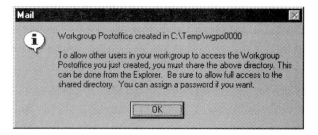

Messages are temporarily stored in the workgroup postoffice until the user retrieves them. If the message is addressed to more than one recipient, only one copy of the message is stored. The message will have a counter that is decremented each time the message is retrieved. When the counter reaches 0 the message is deleted.

Microsoft Fax

Open the Mail and Fax utility. Select Microsoft Fax and click on **Properties**.

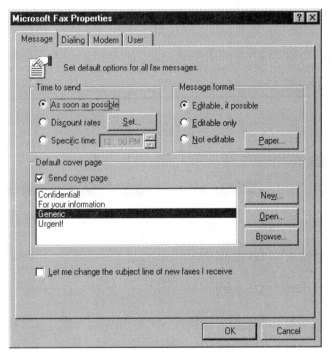

There are four properties sheets available for configuring the fax modem: Message, Dialing, Modem, and User.

Message Properties

The **Message Properties** tab allows you to set the time to send a fax. You can select from as soon as possible, discount rates, or at a specific time that you set. Discount rates can be used for users whose telephone companies provide discount telephone rates if the call is made at a particular time of day. You can specify the time settings by clicking on the **Set** button next to this option.

You can also specify the message format of your fax: Editable, if possible; Editable only; or Not editable. Enabling the **Editable** option allows those users receiving the fax to receive the editable format only if they are using Microsoft Fax. If they are not using Microsoft Fax, they will receive a bitmap image. If you select **Editable only**, users using Microsoft Fax will be able to edit the fax directly. If users are not using Microsoft Fax for this option, they will not receive the fax at all. **Not editable** sends the fax as a bitmap image only.

You can also select the type of cover page you would like to send. If you have a pre-made cover page, you can set it from this properties sheet.

Dialing Properties

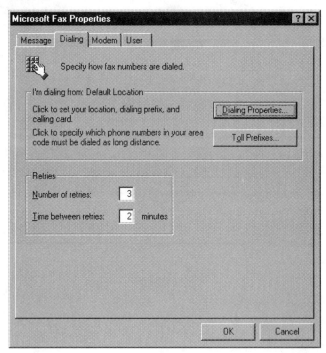

The **Dialing Properties** option available on this properties sheet is the same as that which was discussed earlier in this chapter. **Toll Prefixes** enables you to select from the available toll prefixes in the dialog below.

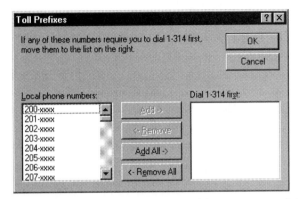

You can also set the number of times that you would like to try to send the fax if the line is busy, as well as the time between tries.

Modem Properties

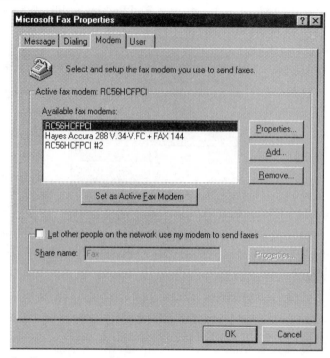

The **Modem** tab allows you to configure additional properties for a selected modem, add a new modem, or remove an existing modem. Clicking on **Properties** displays the following options for the selected modem:

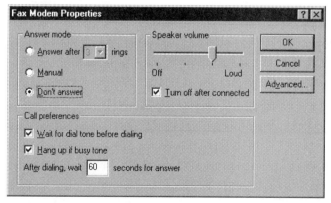

You can set the answer mode for the modem to answer after a specified number of rings, manual answer mode, or to not answer at all. You can also specify the speaker volume of the modem's communication signal. You can also set call preferences such as:

- Wait for dial tone before dialing.

- Hang up if a busy tone.

- After dialing, wait ____ seconds to answer.

Clicking on the **Advanced** button displays the following settings:

The Advanced dialog allows you to set the following modem settings:

- Disable high-speed transmission

    This option should be used if you do not want the fax modem to answer transmissions sent at 9600 bps or higher.

- Disable error correction mode

    This option will not send uneditable images or formats using the error correction mode.

- Enable MR compression

    This option allows you to enable compression or no compression for Microsoft Fax.

- Use Class 2 if available

  If this option is selected, you will not be able to receive editable faxes or use error correction mode. You should enable this option if your modem is a Class 1 or Class 2 device, but you are unable to send faxes successfully.

- Reject pages received with errors

  You can set the tolerance level of whether you want pages with errors to be received or not. You can select from high, medium, low, and very low. The lower the tolerance, the more garbage you may receive.

User Properties

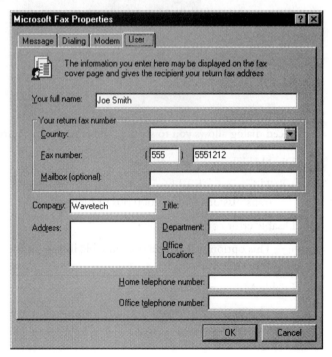

The **User** tab allows you to change any information that may be displayed on the fax cover page, if you have selected to use one.

Sharing a Fax Modem

Microsoft Fax allows users to share their local fax modems to others on the network. To enable fax sharing, launch the Inbox and open the **Tools/Microsoft Fax Tools/Options** to access the Microsoft Fax properties sheet, which was discussed previously. Select the **Modem** tab of this properties sheet.

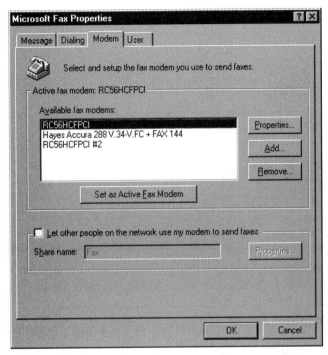

Check the **Let other people on the network use my modem to send faxes** checkbox. You can click on the **Properties** button to add permitted users, depending on the type of access control that is implemented on the system. The fax modem is shared across the network in the same fashion as other resources utilizing user-level or share-level security. Our example demonstrates user-level security:

A folder with the name of NetFax will be created in the root directory of the drive selected. The fax modem is shared across the network in the same fashion as other resources utilizing user-level or share-level security.

Accessing a Shared Fax Modem

To access a shared fax modem on the network, launch the Inbox and open the **Tools/ Microsoft Fax Tools/Options**. The Microsoft Fax properties sheet appears again. Click on the **Modem** tab. Add a new fax modem by clicking on the **Add** button. Select **Network fax server** from the options presented and click on **OK**.

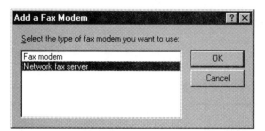

The user is prompted for the shared network fax directory:

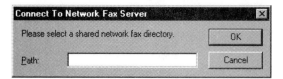

After adding the network fax server, highlight it on the available fax modems table and select the **Set as Active Fax Modem** option. The fax server is now available for use.

Application developers are encouraged to add a **Send to Fax** item to the application's **File** menu. However, many applications do not have that option. To send a fax from an application that does not have a **Send to Fax** menu item, run **Print** and select Microsoft Fax as your printer.

TROUBLESHOOTING REMOTE ACCESS PROBLEMS

This section describes some troubleshooting procedures for modem and remote access problems. The following topics are discussed within this section:

- Modem Problems
- Modem Diagnostic Tools
- The MODEMLOG.TXT File
- Dial-Up Networking Problems

Keep in mind that Windows 95 has troubleshooting utilities available through the Help utility.

Modem Problems

Windows online help should be the first resource for troubleshooting modem problems. Online modem help can be accessed by clicking on **Help** from the **Diagnostics** page of the Modems Properties dialog or by selecting **Help** from the Control Panel menu and clicking on **Help Topics**. Open the Troubleshooting listing, select **If you have trouble using your modem**, and click on **Display**.

Modem Diagnostic Tool

The primary troubleshooting tool for modems is located on the **Diagnostics** tab of the Modems Properties dialog.

To check a particular port for modem information, select the Port and click on **More Info.**

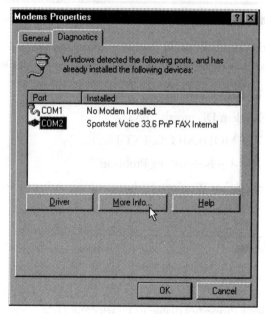

A Please Wait dialog appears which says "Communicating with modem. This may take a few minutes." Once the modem information is found, it is displayed on the screen. The response area provides a lot of valuable troubleshooting information. For instance, the actual modem currently connected to the COM port is listed. This is the only way to verify the actual modem type of the modem that is connected to the port. This is particularly useful if the modem was installed as a Standard Modem. The COM port's IRQ and I/O addresses are displayed. These settings should be consistent with the COM port or modem adapter settings.

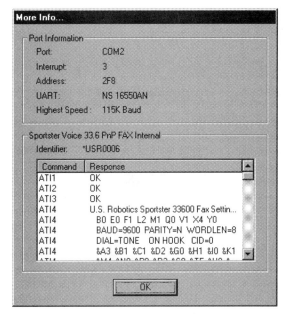

If the modem is not valid, the following error dialog appears:

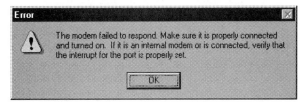

Note that a modem can be malfunctioning or not properly connected even though the Device Manager and the **General** tab of the Modems Properties page indicate that the modem is functioning.

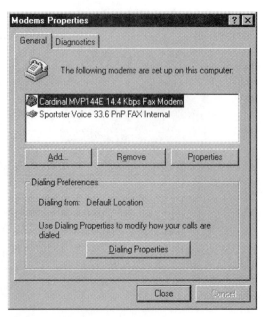

The Device Manager not only displays the modem, it also indicates that the modem is working properly, as shown in the following graphic:

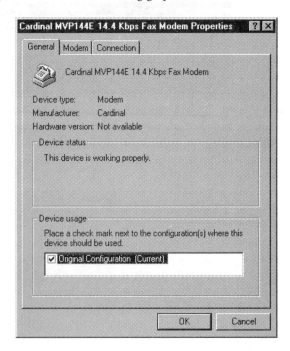

The MODEMLOG.TXT File

If the checkbox **Record a log file** is checked on the Advanced Connection Settings dialog of the **Connection** tab in the modem's property page and a connection is attempted, the MODEMLOG.TXT file is created in the Windows directory. This file provides important information regarding the modem. This sample file was created by attempting to make a connection using Dial-Up Networking. In this case, the phone line was not connected to the modem. The problem is reported through the line "Interpreted response: No Dialtone." Of course, Dial-Up Networking also gave an error message indicating that there was no dial tone, but there is no guarantee that every software application will do the same.

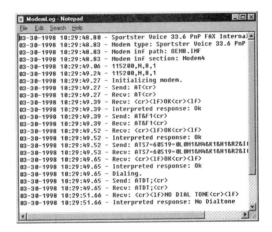

Dial-Up Networking Problems

When a user trying to connect to a Windows 95 remote access server receives a message stating that the username is not valid, check the list of users allowed to access the remote access server. To do so, open the Dial-Up Networking window from My Computer or Windows Explorer. Run **Connections/Dial-Up Server**. Click on the **Add** button to view the list of permitted users. Verify that the user is listed. If not, you must add the user.

When a user tries to use a Dial-Up Networking connection, but has trouble connecting, there could be several causes.

- If the modem is dialing, but no connection is made

  Check the connection information, particularly the area code and phone number. If the number is long distance, verify that the appropriate access codes and call billing options are set.

- If the user is using an internal modem and the problem persists

  Try installing the modem with a generic driver instead of the modem-specific driver.

- If the user is using an external modem

  Check to see that the phone line is connected properly to the jack and the modem. Verify that the modem is connected to the computer.

- If the user gets disconnected

  Verify that call waiting is disabled. Call waiting can sometimes cause modem lines to disconnect.

You can also check to see if the modem is using a valid COM port. To do so, display the device in the **Device Manager** tab of the System utility. Check the IRQ settings for the COM port to verify that it is indeed a free IRQ address. If the COM port is on a predefined IRQ address, assign a new IRQ.

If you receive a message stating that the server is not answering incoming calls, disable the **Allow caller cccess** option in **Connections/Dial-Up Server** for Dial-Up Networking. If you are using an internal modem, restart the computer to clear the COM port's buffer. If you have an external modem, switch the modem off and on. Once the computer restarts, reset the Dial-Up Server configuration to "Allow caller access."

If the remote access server uses share-level security and a user forgets the password, you will need to reconfigure a password. Run **Connections/Dial-Up Server** from the Dial-Up Networking computer in My Computer or Windows Explorer. Disable the **Allow caller access** option. Restart the computer. Then delete the RNA.PWL, which is located in C:\WINDOWS. Enable **Allow caller access** for the dial-up server. Enter a new password. Password synchronization is not available for Dial-Up Networking.

SCENARIOS

Scenario 1

One of your salespeople complains that he often has trouble checking his e-mail through a dial-up connection when traveling. The salesperson's laptop is running Windows 95 and has a PCMCIA modem. What tool can you use to diagnose the problem?

....

....

Scenario 2

You are configuring a network for a group of software consultants. Each consultant has a computer, but the budget would only allow for one of them to contain a fax modem. All of the consultants need to send faxes. How can you configure this?

....

....

Scenario 3

You have just had Caller ID enabled on your telephone service. Your Plug and Play modem is enabled for voice. You install Unimodem V and reboot your computer. However, you cannot get Caller ID or the voice portion of the modem to work. What should you do?

....

....

Scenario 4

Your office has a small peer-to-peer Windows 95 network. Your marketing representative needs to connect to the Internet. What should she do to ensure that no one can access the confidential information on her computer?

....

....

Scenario 5

You are configuring a Windows 95 computer as a remote access server. It is part of a Windows NT network and will share resources using user-level security. You would like the passwords to be encrypted as they go across the wire. Which connection protocol will you use?

....

....

Scenario 6

One of the salespeople in your company frequently dials in to a Windows NT remote access server in order to access the customer's database. She often calls from customer sites and periodically gets disconnected before she can finish her transaction. What should she do?

....

....

SUMMARY

In this chapter, you saw how to configure Windows 95 for various types of remote connectivity. This included:

- Configuring remote access clients.
- Configuring remote access servers.
- Installing Internet Explorer and configuring Internet Mail.
- Configuring a Microsoft Exchange client.
- Sharing and accessing a fax modem.
- Troubleshooting methods for modem problems.
- Troubleshooting methods for remote access problems.

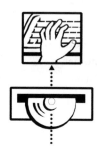

Stop now and complete the Chapter 16 NEXTSim simulation exercise on the Interactive Learning CD-ROM.

POST-TEST QUESTIONS

The answers to these questions are in Appendix A at the end of this manual.

1. List some reasons why a modem may not be detected while using the Add New Hardware Wizard.

    ....

    ....

2. How can you configure a modem to display the terminal window after dialing?

    ....

    ....

3. How can you set up a log file for the modem?

    ....

    ....

4. If you select **Editable only** in the Message properties sheet of Microsoft Fax properties, will users be able to edit the fax copy?

    ....

    ....

5. How can you secure local resources from computer hackers on the Internet?

....

....

6. How is a fax modem shared to network users?

....

....

CHAPTER 17

Ongoing Maintenance

OBJECTIVES

At the completion of this chapter, you will be able to:

- Enable remote administration.
- Install the Microsoft Registry Service.
- Use NetWatcher to administer a remote computer's shared resources.
- Use System Monitor to monitor a remote computer's system performance.
- Use the Registry Editor to connect to and disconnect from a remote registry.
- Use the System Policy Editor to access remote registry policies.

PRE-TEST QUESTIONS

The answers to these questions are in Appendix A at the end of this manual.

1. What service do you need to access remote registries?

    ....

    ....

2. What is another method to launch NetWatcher or System Monitor besides using the **Start** menu?

    ....

    ....

3. What service must you install prior to using NetWatcher?

    ....

    ....

INTRODUCTION

The course concludes with a discussion of remote administration. Windows 95 provides several tools that allow an administrator to manage properly configured computers on a network. The administrator can manage the file system, share or restrict directories, and make changes to the registry. In addition, there are several important tools that can be used to troubleshoot performance problems. This chapter discusses each of these.

REMOTE ADMINISTRATION

This section discusses remote administration which allows administrators to administer remote computers. It will look at how NetWatcher, System Monitor, Registry Editor, and System Policy Editor can be used to connect to remote computers and administer those computers later in the chapter. The following topics are discussed within this section:

- Introduction to Remote Administration
- Enabling Remote Administration
- Microsoft Registry Service

Introduction to Remote Administration

You can administer a Windows 95 computer from another Windows 95 client as long as the network has a Windows NT or NetWare authenticator. The authentication is necessary in order for the remote administration tools to provide administrative privileges to the remote machine. Remote administration is useful for connecting to a remote machine when factors exist where the administrator cannot get to the remote machine's location.

Windows 95 has several utilities to allow for remote workstation administration. These include:

- The NetWatcher (NETWATCH.EXE)

    The NetWatcher allows for management of shared resources on a remote computer. Connections to a shared resource can be monitored, created, and deleted using this utility.

- The System Monitor (SYSMON.EXE)

    Troubleshooting performance problems on a remote computer is the primary function of the System Monitor.

- The Registry Editor (REGEDIT.EXE)

    The Registry Editor can connect to and modify registries on remote computers.

- The System Policy Editor (POLEDIT.EXE)

    In addition to the capabilities previously discussed, the System Policy Editor can edit registries in realtime for remote computers.

Through the use of these utilities, the system administrator has the ability to identify and solve many problems encountered by users without having to physically touch the computer.

Enabling Remote Administration

For remote administration to be enabled, you must complete the following steps on both the machine you plan to administer and the machine from which you are going to do the administration:

1. Verify that remote administration is enabled. To enable remote administration, display the Passwords utility, **Remote Administraton** tab.

2. Verify that user-level security is selected and that a domain name has been entered. If you enable user-level security through the Passwords utility, remote administration is enabled automatically and the Domain Admins group is given administrative rights.

3. Verify that a common Microsoft protocol is running on both the remote machine and the administrator's machine.

4. Restart your computer.

Once remote administration is enabled, two shared directories are created: ADMIN$ and IPC$. ADMIN$ is a share that provides administrators with access to file systems on the remote computer. IPC$ provides an interprocess communication (IPC) channel between the administrative computer and the remote computer.

Adding the Remote Administrator

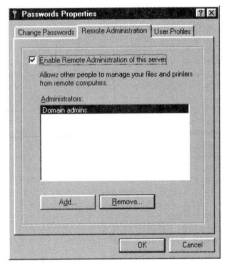

You must add the user who is going to perform remote administration from the list of users. To do so, click on the **Add** button in the above picture.

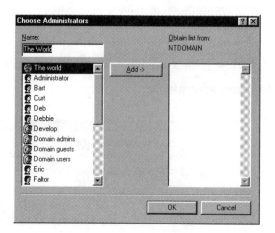

Microsoft Registry Service

Microsoft Registry Service must be installed if you will be accessing the remote computer's Registry or using System Monitor. This service is not a requirement for Net Watcher .

To install Microsoft Remote Registry services, launch the Network utility. Verify that you are on the **Configuration** tab and click on **Add**. Select **Service** and click on **Add**. Then click on **Have Disk**. When the Install From Disk dialog box appears, type the path to the ADMIN\NETTOOLS\REMOTREG directory on the Windows 95 CD. Click on **OK**. Click on **OK** in the Install From Disk dialog box. In the Select Network Service dialog box, select **Microsoft Remote Registry**, and click on **OK**. If you are prompted to specify the location of additional files, specify the path to the Windows 95 installation files.

USING NETWATCHER

This section discusses the installation and use of the NetWatcher remote administration utility. The following topics are discussed within this section:

- NetWatcher
- Installing NetWatcher
- Using NetWatcher

NetWatcher

Net Watcher allows you to view, access, and create shared resources on the remote computer. Out of all the remote administration tools such as System Monitor, System Policy Editor, and Registry Editor, this is the only tool that does not require Windows NT or NetWare authentication. The File and Printer Sharing Service for Microsoft Networks must be installed only if you will be using the Net Watcher tool to browse and manage shared resources located on the remote computer. Installing this service allows the Windows 95 client to become a peer server. Installation of the File and printer sharing service was discussed earlier in the course.

Installing NetWatcher

To install NetWatcher, launch the Add/Remove Programs utility. Select the **Windows Setup** tab. Select the **Accessories** component and click on the **Details** button. Select NetWatcher and click on **OK**. If prompted, provide the path to the Windows 95 installation files.

You can have NetWatcher installed during a custom Setup or you can add it later through Add/Remove Programs. After NetWatcher has been installed, you can launch it from **Start/Programs/Accessories/System Tools**. You can also launch NetWatcher from the **Start/Run** dialog by typing the following and pressing *ENTER*:

```
netwatch
```

Using NetWatcher

Once NetWatcher opens, you will be able to view any connections presently visible. To connect to a server, display **Administer/Select Server**.

You can either type the name of the server you wish to administer, which would be the remote Windows 95 machine, or you can browse the network to find it.

Once connected to the remote server, you can access, view, and create shared resources. The available menus are **Administer, View,** and **Help.**

The **Administer** menu allows you to connect to a remote server, add shared folders and stop sharing folders. You can also view the properties of shared folders and disconnect a selected user who is connected to the remote machine.

The **View** menu offers you three methods of viewing the remote shares: By Connections, By Shared Folders, and By Open Files. The **Help** menu is the standard help that is offered in all Microsoft applications. It contains **Help** and **About** information.

Adding a New Share

To add a new share on the remote computer, run **Administer/Add Shared Folder.** You may either enter the path you wish to share or browse for the path. If browse is selected, the following dialog appears:

The administrator can verify that the share has been created successfully, as the share will appear in the Shared Folders view.

Stopping a Current Share

To stop a current share on the remote machine, run **Administer/Stop Sharing Folder.** You will receive the following confirmation dialog:

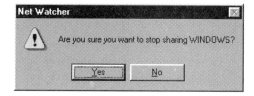

The share will then disappear from the Shared Folders view.

Modifying Shared Folder Properties

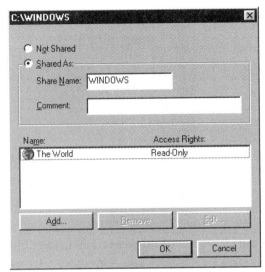

You can also view and modify a shared folder's properties. The properties dialog allows the administrator to add access for new users or remove current users from the share. You can also edit user access by clicking on **Edit**. The Change Access Rights dialog displayed below allows the administrator to give three types of access: Read-Only, Full Access, and Custom Access. Custom Access provides a more extensive list of restrictions or access that may be given to users for the selected share. These permissions are: Read Files, Write to Files, Create Files and Folders, Delete Files, Change File Attributes, List Files, and Change Access Control.

It is not a bad idea to refresh the connections to shared folders from time to time. The **Refresh** command is available in the **View** menu. **Refresh** is helpful for times when the administrative machine may not register changes that occur on the remote machine.

USING SYSTEM MONITOR

This section discusses the installation and use of the System Monitor as a remote administration utility. The following topics are discussed within this section:

- System Monitor
- Installing System Monitor
- Connecting To a Remote Server
- Monitoring Processes
- Using System Monitor To Identify Problems

System Monitor

System Monitor enables the administrator to monitor the file system, IPX/SPX compatible protocol, kernel, and memory manager. The administrator can also monitor processes for clients. This is dependent on which client is installed on the remote machine when using System Monitor. For this utility, you must have Microsoft Remote Registry Service installed. You also need to have a Windows NT server running as an authenticator to provide administrative privileges on the Windows 95 administrative server. The File and printer sharing service needs to be installed so that the machines are servers instead of client machines.

Installing System Monitor

To install System Monitor, launch the Add/Remove Programs utility. Select the **Windows Setup** tab. Click on **Accessories** from the list of components. Then, click on the **Details** button. Scroll down the list of components until you find System Monitor. Select the component and click on **OK**. Click on **OK** to close the Add/Remove Programs Properties dialog.

To launch System Monitor, run **Start/Programs/Accessories/System Tools/System Monitor** or open the **Start/Run** dialog. Type the following and press *ENTER*:

```
sysmon
```

Connecting To a Remote Server

To connect to a remote server, run **File/Connect**. You will need to enter the name of the computer to which you want to connect. Once connected to the remote server, you can add, remove, or edit items to monitor. These are all available through the **Edit** menu.

Monitoring Processes

The **Edit/Add Item** selection displays the following items that you may add for monitoring processes:

File System Counters

The file system counters that are available in System Monitor are as follows:

Bytes read/second	This item monitors the number of bytes being read on the file system of the remote computer.
Bytes written/second	This item monitors the number of bytes being written on the file system of the remote computer.
Dirty data	This item monitors the number of pending bytes waiting to be written to the file system. Since this number is constantly changing on the remote computer, there may be a discrepancy in what is being reported on System Monitor and what the actual value is on the remote system at a given moment.
Reads/second	This item monitors the number of read operations on the file system of the remote computer.
Writes/second	This item monitors the number of write operations on the file system of the remote computer.

IPX/SPX Compatible Protocol

The following items can be tracked for the IPX/SPX-compatible protocol:

IPX packets lost/second	This item monitors the number of IPX packets lost when communicating across a network using the IPX/SPX protocol.
IPX packets received/second	This item monitors the number of IPX packets received when communicating across a network using the IPX/SPX protocol.

IPX packets sent/second	This item monitors the number of IPX packets sent when communicating across a network using the IPX/SPX protocol.
Open sockets	This item monitors the number of free sockets available at a given time.
Routing table entries	This item monitors the number of routes that the IPX network is utilizing on the remote computer.
SAP table entries	This item monitors the number of service advertisements sent by SAP.
SPX packets received/second	This item monitors the number of SPX packets received per second on an SPX network.
SPX packets sent/second	This item monitors the number of SPX packets sent per second on an SPX network.

Kernel

The following items can be monitored for kernel usage on System Monitor:

Processor Usage (%)	This item monitors the percentage of available processor time being used on the remote machine.
Threads	This item monitors the current number of threads.
Virtual Machines	This item monitors the current number of virtual machines being used on the remote machine.

Memory Manager

The following items can be monitored for Memory Manager:

Allocated memory	This item monitors the total number of bytes allocated for application memory as well as swap memory. A changing value represents cache memory which is resizing itself.
Discards	This item monitors the number of swap pages being discarded
Disk cache size	This item monitors the current disk cache size in bytes.
Free memory	This item monitors the amount of RAM available. If free memory is zero, memory is still available for allocation depending on the size of the hard drive containing the swap file.
Instance faults	This item monitors the number of instance faults per second.
Locked memory	This item monitors the amount of memory that is locked.
Maximum disk cache size	This item displays the maximum size for a disk cache. This value is determined at system startup.
Minimum disk cache size	This item displays the minimum size for a disk cache. This value is determined at system startup.
Other memory	This item monitors the amount of allocated memory not stored in the swap file.
Page Faults	This item monitors the number of page faults per second.
Page-ins	This item monitors the number of pages swapped into memory per second.
Page-outs	This item monitors the number of pages swapped out of memory and written to the disk per second.

Swapfile defective	This item monitors the number of defective bytes on the swapfile.
Swapfile in use	This item monitors the number of bytes being used in the swapfile.
Swapfile size	This item monitors the number of bytes in the swapfile.
Swappable memory	This item monitors the number of bytes used in the swapfile.

Microsoft Client for NetWare Networks

You can also select client/server items depending on which client is installed on the remote computer. The following items can be monitored for the Microsoft Client for NetWare Networks:

Burst Packets Dropped	This item monitors the number of burst packets lost over network communication.
Burst Receive Gap Time	This item monitors the gap time of incoming packet traffic per microsecond.
Burst Send Gap Time	This item monitors the gap time of outgoing packet traffic per microsecond.
Bytes in Cache	This item monitors the current amount of data bytes in cache.
Bytes Read Per Second	This item monitors bytes read per second from the redirector.
Bytes Written Per Second	This item monitors the bytes written per second from the redirector.
Dirty Bytes In Cache	This item monitors the amount of dirty data bytes cached by the redirector and waiting to be written.

NCP Packets Dropped	This item monitors the number of NCP packets dropped in traffic.
Requests Pending	This item monitors the number of requests pending response from the server.

Microsoft Network Client

The following items can be monitored for the Microsoft Network Client:

Bytes read/second	This item monitors bytes read per second from the redirector.
Bytes written/second	This item monitors the bytes written per second from the redirector.
Number of nets	This item monitors the number of current operating networks.
Open files	This item monitors how many files are open on the network.
Resources	This item monitors the current number of resources on a network.
Sessions	This item monitors the current number of sessions on a network.
Transactions/second	This item monitors the number of SMB transactions processed by the redirector per second.

Microsoft Network Server

System Monitor offers the following items to be monitored for the Microsoft Network Server:

Buffers	This item monitors how many buffers are used by the system.
Bytes Read/sec	This item monitors how many bytes are read from the disk per second.
Bytes Written/sec	This item monitors how many bytes are written to the disk per second.
Bytes/sec	This item monitors how many bytes are read from and written to the disk per second.
Memory	This item monitors how much memory a server uses.

| NBs | This item monitors the number of network buffers across a server. NB stands for network buffer. |
| Server Threads | This item monitors the number of threads used on a server. |

Using System Monitor to Identify Problems

System Monitor is a great tool to use when you have users complaining of system problems such as slowness in system performance.

For example, if an application is not freeing memory, the kernel's threads counter will continue to increase. If System Monitor does show that the application is not freeing the memory, you might need to close and restart the application from time to time.

If a user complains of slow performance, you can begin to troubleshoot the problem using System Monitor. Set System Monitor to monitor the kernel's processor usage and the memory manager's page faults and locked memory items. If the value for processor usage is high when the system is supposed to be idle, check to see which application may be using the processor.

If the value for page faults is high, you can safely assume that the application requires more memory than is available on the system.

If the locked memory item shows a high portion of allocated memory being locked up, you should assume that the user has an application running which locks memory unnecessarily.

If you see that the memory manager's discards and page-outs show high activity, your performance problems might be caused by not having enough RAM. In this case, the memory manager must swap a lot of information in and out of memory. To fix this problem, you should add more memory to your system.

CONNECTING TO REMOTE REGISTRIES

This section discusses how to connect to remote registries using the Registry Editor and the System Policy Editor. There is a slight difference between the types of registry entries to be configured with the two tools which we will discuss shortly. The following topics are discussed within this section:

- Registry Editor
- Accessing Remote Registries With System Policy Editor
- Using Remote Administration Tools from Network Neighborhood

Lastly, in this section, we discuss another method for accessing the remote administration tools discussed in this chapter.

Registry Editor

The Registry Editor, REGEDIT.EXE, can be used to connect to remote registries. It is recommended that administrators use the System Policy Editor to access remote registries as a habit. However, if you must access the registry entries for a remote computer, you can do so using REGEDIT.EXE.

System Policy Editor only displays registry entries related to policies. To display all the registry entries of the remote computer, you can connect using Registry Editor on the administrative machine.

You will then see your local registry listed at the top, and the remote registry listed beneath. Any changes you make to the remote computer's registry are automatically enabled. Therefore, it is important that you know what you are doing in the Registry. If you are not comfortable with the Registry environment, it is strongly recommended that you use the System Policy Editor to access the remote registry.

If you do decide to continue using REGEDIT to make changes to the remote registry, you should make a copy of the USER.DAT and SYSTEM.DAT files in case you need to restore the registry. These files were discussed earlier in the course.

After registry modifications have been made, you should disconnect from the remote registry. You can do so by clicking on **Registry/Disconnect Remote Registry**. A dialog will be displayed listing any or all remote computer connections. You must select the computer you wish to disconnect from and click on **OK**. Doing so saves changes to the remote computer's registry. Depending on the nature of the changes, the remote computer may have to be restarted before they will take effect.

Accessing Remote Registries With System Policy Editor

System Policy Editor with remote administration enables connection to a remote machine. The administrator can then define or update user and system policies for the remote user. The administrator can also connect to the registry of the remote computer. Before you can use the System Policy Editor to modify a remote computer, the Microsoft Remote Registry Service must be installed. This was discussed earlier in this chapter.

It is important to realize that any changes made in the System Policy Editor will be saved to the registry of the remote computer. To connect to a remote computer in System Policy Editor, click on **File/Connect**. You will then see that the title bar of System Policy Editor displays the connection to the remote computer. You can then change or define policy settings for users that connect to the remote machine.

Using Remote Administration Tools from Network Neighborhood

You can launch NetWatcher and System Monitor through Network Neighborhood. You must first select the server that you want to administer remotely through Network Neighborhood. To do so, double-click on Network Neighborhood on the desktop. Right-click on the remote server you want to administer. Display **Properties**. Click on the **Tools** tab. There are buttons for each of the administrative tools in the Properties dialog.

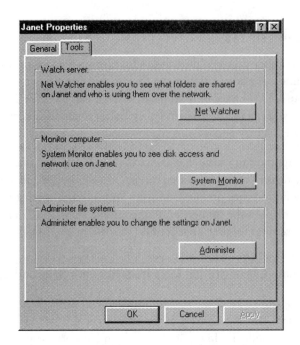

SCENARIOS

Scenario 1

You have enabled remote administration on the JDoe computer and on your computer at home. John Doe called you at home to complain that he is having memory problems. You suspect it is a problem caused by one of the applications he runs. Upon questioning John further, you determine that he has changed several computer settings. He has changed his swapfile settings to no swapfile and his access control to share level. What must he change so that you can monitor the memory usage on his system?

....

....

Scenario 2

You are administering a peer-to-peer network for an automobile repair shop. All of the computers are running Windows 95 and are set up so that you can administer them remotely. One of the technicians is on vacation. He called you from Cancun to let you know that he had just remembered that he left his Customers folder shared out to the World with full permission. He would like you to restrict the permission to read-only. How can you do that?

....

....

Scenario 3

You are trying to determine which Windows 95 computers in your network are most in need of an upgrade. Fifteen users have requested memory upgrades, but the company can only afford to upgrade five computers. You want to monitor memory usage under normal circumstances. How can you watch memory usage without the users being aware that their usage is being watched?

....

....

Scenario 4

One of the users is complaining of sluggish performance when switching between applications. How can you determine whether a processor upgrade or a memory upgrade would be more beneficial?

....

....

SUMMARY

In this chapter, we focused on administering remote computers using various administration tools, as well as the following concepts:

- Enabling remote administration
- Installation of the Microsoft Registry service
- Installation and usage of NetWatcher
- Installation and usage of System Monitor
- Accessing remote registries using the Registry Editor and System Policy Editor
- Troubleshooting file system problems with System Monitor

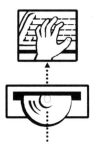

Stop now and complete the Chapter 17 NEXTSim simulation exercise on the Interactive Learning CD-ROM.

POST-TEST QUESTIONS

The answers to these questions are in Appendix A at the end of this manual.

1. What are two methods that can be used to access remote registries?

    ....

    ....

2. For which of the remote administration tools must you install the Microsoft Registry service?

    ....

    ....

3. Which counter should you monitor in System Monitor if you suspect that an application is not freeing memory once it is finished?

    ....

    ....

4. What type of processes can you monitor in System Monitor?

    ....

    ....

5. What two hidden shares are created once remote administration is enabled?

    ....

    ....

6. When enabling remote administration, which user should you add to be a permitted user accessing the remote computer?

    ....

    ....

SELF STUDY

Appendix A—Answers to Pre-Test and Post-Test Questions

CHAPTER 1

Pre-Test Answers

1. The user only needs to open the document; all associated applications are loaded.
2. 600 KB
3. Novell NetWare and Microsoft networks (such as NT Server domains)
4. Windows NT

Post-Test Answers

1. Windows 3.0
2. Windows NT 3.x
3. 255 characters
4. Windows Explorer
5. Intuitive user interface, built-in networking support, Plug and Play device installation, system policies, roving user support, and built-in backup agents

CHAPTER 2

Pre-Test Answers

1. 80386DX
2. MS-DOS 3.2 or above, Windows 3.x, and Windows for Workgroups 3.x
3. C:\WINDOWS\COMMAND
4. Enter BOOTMULTI=1 under the [OPTIONS] section in the MSDOS.SYS file.
5. If you have installed Windows 95 as an upgrade to Windows 3.x or Windows for Workgroups, you can uninstall Windows 95 using the Add/Remove Programs utility.

Scenario Solutions

Scenario 1

Back up the data. Install MS-DOS, reformatting the drive as FAT. Install Windows 95. Restore the data.

Scenario 2

Launch Setup from within Windows for Workgroups. Install Windows 95 into the \WINDOWS directory.

Scenario 3

Back up the data. Repartition the drive so that there is an HPFS partition and a FAT partition. Restore the data to the HPFS partition. Install MS-DOS on the FAT partition. Boot to DOS and install Windows 95 on the FAT partition. When prompted, disable the OS/2 Boot Manager. After Windows 95 is installed, run OS/2 Fdisk from the OS/2 boot disk to enable the OS/2 Boot Manager.

Scenario 4

You need to reinstall the application while running Windows NT Workstation.

Scenario 5

Create an NTFS partition on the drive. Employees will not be able to see it when the system is booted to Windows 95. Do not provide the employees with a logon to Windows NT.

Scenario 6

Use NETSETUP.EXE to create a shared directory containing the installation files. Create an MSBATCH.INF file, specifying all of the parameters so that the user will only be prompted for the serial number. Create a login script that maps a drive to the shared installation directory and launches SETUP.EXE using the MSBATCH.INF file.

Scenario 7

The files containing the compressed older operating system have been deleted. Look in MSDOS.SYS for the path to the files. Use Explorer to navigate to the correct path and show hidden files. Locate W95UNDO.DAT, W95UNDO.INI, and SUHDLOG.DAT. If any of them are missing, you will not be able to revert to the previous operating system.

Scenario 8

Edit the MSDOS.SYS file to include the line:

```
BOOTGUI = 0
```

Scenario 9

You will have to reinstall Windows 95.

Post-Test Answers

1. MS-DOS 3.2

   80386DX Processor

   4 MB Memory

2. C:\WINDOWS\HARDWARE.TXT

3. Windows 3.1: 20 to 30 MB

   Windows for Workgroups 3.11: 10 to 20 MB

   MS-DOS: 30 to 60 MB

4. Setup information and PC detection, configuration questions, copying component files, and restart and final configuration

5. A non-Plug and Play system

6. Install Windows in a separate directory and add the following to MSDOS.SYS:

   ```
   BootMulti=1
   ```

   The advantage to a dual-boot system is that it allows you to retain an operating system that might be needed to run certain software.

7. It is used to install installation source files from a network server.

8. Press *F8* when **Starting Windows 95...** appears.

9. DETCRASH.LOG

CHAPTER 3

Pre-Test Answers

1. Bootstrap

2. It launches the application that is associated with the file extension.

3. Press *SHIFT* while deleting the item.

Post-Test Answers

1. Bootstrap with system BIOS in control

   MS-DOS drivers and TSRs load for compatibility

   Virtual Device Drivers (VxD) are initialized in real mode

   The protected mode operating system takes control and loads the remaining VxDs

2. Programs, Documents, Settings, Find, Help, Run, and Shut Down

3. All logical drives, Control Panel, Printers, and Dial-Up Networking

4. Networks and attached servers

5. Open the Recycle Bin, locate the object, and drag the object to the desktop or select the file in the Recycle Bin and run **File/Restore**.

CHAPTER 4

Pre-Test Answers

1. Files, applications, printers, directories

2. Drag an application and drop it onto the **Start** button.

3. In the local computer policy, check **Remote Update** and select Manual. Set the path to where the policy will be located.

4. Network and System

Scenario Solutions

Scenario 1

User profiles are not enabled. Jill and Tom are sharing the same desktop settings. To prevent the problem in the future, enable user profiles so that Jill and Tom can customize their settings.

Scenario 2

Create a default user policy that enables Hide All Desktop Items, Custom Start Menu, Custom Startup Folder, and Only Run Allowed Windows Applications. Put only the Shutdown command in the **Start** menu. Add only a shortcut to CASHREG.EXE to Only Run Allowed Windows Applications. Put CASHREG.EXE in the Custom Startup Folder.

Create a user policy for your logon so that you can manage the system.

Scenario 3

Create a policy for him. Enable the **Disable Registry Editing Tools** option.

Post-Test Answers

1. Create a desktop shortcut to the database file.

2. Click on **Start/Settings/Taskbar**. Click on the **Show Clock** option.

3. Set the **Include desktop icons and Network Neighborhood contents in user settings** option in the Passwords utility, **User Profiles** tab.

4. CONFIG.POL is the default file, name that Windows recognizes to look for xisting policy settings.

5. For a user, settings are stored in HKEY_LOCAL_USER. For a system, settings are stored in HKEY_LOCAL_MACHINE.

6. Control Panel, Desktop, Network, Shell, and System

7. The checked state means that the policy will be implemented when the user logs on. Checked also changes the state of the policy in the registry. The cleared state means that the policy will not be implemented. Registry entries are removed for this policy when the user logs on. The grayed state means that you do not want the user's local policy to be changed. Windows 95 does not process this entry when the user logs on. There are no changes made to the registry for the grayed state.

CHAPTER 5

Pre-Test Answers

1. Accessibility Options utility

2. Multimedia utility

3. Launch the Network utility and view the installed components on the **Configuration** tab.

4. Right-click on the desktop and select **Properties**

5. Legacy

Scenario Solutions

Scenario 1

Use the Keyboard utility's **Language** tab to add the Spanish language to the system.

Scenario 2

Copy the current hardware profile to create a portable hardware profile. Display the **Device Manager** tab in the System utility. Expand the Network listing to select the network adapter that the portable computer uses. Click on **Properties** and enable the **Disable in this hardware profile** option.

Post-Test Answers

1. Change Passwords, Remote Administration, and User Profiles

2. Open the Mouse utility and select the **Motion** tab. Enable the **Show pointer trails** option.

3. Number, Currency, Time, and Date property pages

4. The Device Manager will display a yellow exclamation point for any disabled devices.

5. *Cold* docking and *Hot* docking

6. Plug and Play BIOS, Plug and Play hardware devices, and Plug and Play operating system

7. **Device Manager** tab

CHAPTER 6

Pre-Test Answers

1. The MBR identifies the bootable partition, the operating system for each partition by its system indicator, the starting location and size of each partition, and contains a signature of 55AAh, which indicates a valid MBR.

2. FAT

3. If your system crashes, it will be easier to restore the most current information.

4. Dblspace.000 and Readthis

Scenario Solutions

Scenario 1

None of the Windows 95 tools can help in this situation. The data on drives compressed with DriveSpace cannot be accessed under Windows NT. Your best solution is to buy an additional hard drive.

Scenario 2

The compression ratio is an estimated ratio. The file you are copying cannot be compressed to fit in the estimated available space.

Scenario 3

Use FDISK to repartition the drive into four 1-GB FAT partitions. Install Windows 95.

Scenario 4

Set up System Agent on his local computer. Select Low Disk Space Notification to monitor disk space each evening. You must instruct him to leave his computer on each night.

Scenario 5

You need to check to see if your administrator is backing up to a network drive. If he is doing so, then you will need to reschedule backups during off-hours to minimize network resources being utilized.

Scenario 6

You will have to back up to a network drive. Microsoft Backup does not support SCSI tape drives.

Post-Test Answers

1. FDISK
2. This prevents users from accessing file sets and causing corruption.
3. Run **Tools/Redetect Tape Drive** from the menu of the Backup utility.
4. System Agent allows you to schedule disk maintenance utilities such as Disk Defragmenter and ScanDisk for routine performance.
5. Changes should be made to the **Troubleshooting** tab when trying to resolve problems resulting from applications that may not be compatible with the Windows 95 operating environment and system
6. The **Hard Disk** tab can be used to optimize system performance depending on the typical role of the machine. The **CD-ROM** tab can be used for to optimize system performance when a CD-ROM is accessed. The **Troubleshooting** tab can be used to resolve problems that occur from non-compatible applications for the Windows 95 operating environment.
7. You should consider the size of data files that will most often be stored on the drive.
8. DriveSpace creates compressed drives of up to 512 MB, while DriveSpace3 provides compression for drives up to 2 GB in size.

CHAPTER 7

Pre-Test Answers

1. Expand the Network Neighborhood entry in Windows Explorer to view network servers and resources.

2. File menu

3. Right-click on the resource you wish to explore, and select **Explore**.

4. Filenames can be up to 255 characters long. Filenames can include spaces and certain punctuation.

Post-Test Answers

1. Run **Start/Programs/Windows Explorer** or open the **Start/Run** dialog, type the following

    ```
    explorer
    ```

    and press *ENTER*.

2. Right-click on the desired disk to be formatted, and select **Format**.

3. The filename is changed to an 8-character file name. The two characters of the filename are displayed as ~1.

CHAPTER 8

Pre-Test Answers

1. A process is the memory address assigned when a 32-bit application is launched and loaded into memory. A process cannot execute any commands and does not use any processor time. An application can have more than one process. A 32-bit application requires each process to have at least one thread. The thread of the process is responsible for executing its code. A process must have at least one thread, but can have many more.

2. Cooperative processing depends on applications *sharing* processor time. With preemptive processing, the operating system remains in control, providing system resources where necessary.

3. Virtual memory aids the system in running multiple programs at the same time.

Post-Test Answers

1. Windows 95 can then run without a memory paging file

2. In the initial 640-KB block.

3. Preemptive multitasking

4. Yes

5. Compressed

6. *CONTROL+ALT+DELETE*

CHAPTER 9

Pre-Test Answers

1. Thunking

2. 16-bit Windows applications

3. Identify the program as running in MS-DOS mode.

4. A dialog box listing all active applications, options to end a task and shut the system down, and the option to cancel the dialog box.

Scenario Solutions

Scenario 1

Change its properties so that it runs in MS-DOS mode.

Scenario 2

The default PIF is probably loading EMM386.EXE with the **/noems** switch. To run the program, create a special PIF and load EMM386.EXE without the **/noems** switch.

Post-Test Answers

1. System and MS-DOS

2. Win16, Win32, and MS-DOS

3. The application can violate system integrity by performing a prohibited command or the application can lock up by failing to respond to messages sent to it from the operating system.

4. START MYFINA~1.DOC

5. Press *CONTROL+ALT+DELETE*

CHAPTER 10

Pre-Test Answers

1. Seven:

> HKEY_LOCAL_USER
>
> HKEY_LOCAL_MACHINE
>
> HKEY_USERS
>
> HKEY_CLASSES_ROOT
>
> HKEY_CURRENT_USER
>
> HKEY_CURRENT_CONFIG
>
> HKEY_DYN_DATA

2. REGEDIT.EXE

Post-Test Answers

1. \WINDOWS; USER.DAT and SYSTEM.DAT
2. REGEDIT.EXE can be used to import a REG file
3. HKEY_LOCAL_MACHINE
4. USER.DA0 and SYSTEM.DA0

CHAPTER 11

Pre-Test Answers

1. Client, Adapter, Protocol, and Service
2. 15 characters
3. NWLink and TCP/IP

Scenario Solutions

Scenario 1

You need to add the Client for Microsoft Networks, a network adapter driver, and the NetBEUI protocol.

Scenario 2

Since there is no requirement for routing or accessing NetWare or UNIX computers, NetBEUI will be your best choice.

Scenario 3

You need to set the frame type to the same frame type used by the servers.

Scenario 4

Number of subnets

```
4 = 100
```

You will need three bits for the subnet mask.

Number of hosts

```
26 = 11010
```

You will need five bits for the host addresses.

This network can be set up using a single Class C address.

Subnet mask

```
11111111.11111111.11111111.11100000
255.255.255.224
```

Network addresses

```
00100000 = 3201000000 = 64
01100000 = 9610000000 = 128
```

Address Ranges

Minimum	Maximum	Min. (decimal)	Max. (decimal)	Broadcast
00100001	00111110	33	62	63
01000001	01011110	65	94	95
01100001	01111110	97	126	127
10000001	10011110	129	158	159

Scenario 5

Check to make sure that the WINS server settings are configured correctly.

Post-Test Answers

1. Microsoft Client for NetWare Networks and Microsoft Client for Microsoft Networks

2. Microsoft NetBEUI, TCP/IP and IPX/SPX-compatible protocols

3. WINIPCFG

CHAPTER 12

Pre-Test Answers

1. A persistent share is one that is reestablished each time you log on.

2. File and printer

3. Servers to which you are currently attached

4. UNC (Universal Naming Convention) of *server**share_name*

Scenario Solutions

Scenario 1

You need to add Client for Microsoft for Networks, NetBEUI protocol, and the File and printer sharing Service for Microsoft Networks.

Scenario 2

They should store their passwords in the password list.

Scenario 3

He should enable password protection on his screen saver and synchronize the password with the Windows password.

Scenario 4

Use either Find Computer or type the UNC of the computer in the Run dialog.

Scenario 5

Set one computer's Browse Master to either Automatic or Enabled.

Post-Test Answers

1. Read only, Full, and Depends on Password

2. Disabled, Enabled, and Automatic

3. Share the folder. Provide one password for read-only access and a different one for full access. Give the full access password to the managers. Give the read-only password to the other employees.

4. He pressed Cancel on the logon dialog and is logged on as *nobody.*

CHAPTER 13

Pre-Test Answers

1. Yes

2. In the user's home directory on the Windows NT server

3. Select the user's account in User Manager for Domains and enable the **User Cannot Change Password** option.

Scenario Solutions

Scenario 1

You will need to create the users in the Accounting domain.

Scenario 2

Install the network adapter driver, the TCP/IP protocol, and the Client for Microsoft Networks. Modify the Client for Microsoft Networks properties so that the **Log on to Windows NT domain** is checked. Set the domain to SALES.

Scenario 3

You need to configure a trust relationship so that SALES trusts MARKETING.

Scenario 4

Add Sam to the TECHSUPPORT group. Grant Sam read-only access to the STATUS share.

Scenario 5

You will have to disable **User Cannot Change Password**.

Scenario 6

Add a group policy for TELEMKT to CONFIG.POL. Add a user policy for SAM to CONFIG.POL. Set the appropriate restrictions in each.

Post-Test Answers

1. As a domain controller

2. The only way to give him access is to go to the office and change his password using User Manager.

3. Create a logon script that runs the virus scanner, SCANDISK, and a program that sends the results to the server. Select all users in User Manager and set the path to the new logon script. When you believe that all computers are clean, select all users and disable the logon script.

CHAPTER 14

Pre-Test Answers

1. WINDOWS_PASSTHRU

2. SYS:MAIL*UserID*

3. SYSCON

4. Users, groups, file servers, print servers, and other logical and physical entities on the network

Scenario Solutions

Scenario 1

Install Windows 95. Install Microsoft Client for NetWare. Install IPX/SPX. Use SYSCON to create a user account for Ralph on each NetWare server in the network. Set his preferred server to be the one you wish to validate him.

Scenario 2

Include it in Trustee Directory Assignments

Scenario 3

You can't. File and printer sharing for NetWare Networks only works with user-level security.

Scenario 4

You need to remove File and printer sharing for NetWare Networks.

Scenario 5

The servers are not running bindery emulation.

Post-Test Answers

1. Yes, both clients can be installed and running on the same machine. File and print sharing services cannot be installed for both Microsoft and NetWare. Only one can be installed and running on a machine.

2. SYS:PUBLIC

3. Peer servers can be used for additional storage space for the network, additional printer support for users, and central administration of peer servers through System Policies and NetWatcher utilities.

4. NET.CFG

5. On the **General** tab of the property pages for Client for NetWare Networks

6. Preferred server

7. SAP advertising should be used for a network containing more than 1500 systems.

8. Display the Advanced property sheet for File and printer sharing for NetWare Networks and select Enabled: Preferred Master.

CHAPTER 15

Pre-Test Answers

1. Any user account with Supervisor privileges

2. Use the Add Printer Wizard or install a shared printer using Network Neighborhood.

3. It allows you to control the setup and configuration of Hewlett-Packard printers that are connected to an HP JetDirect print server.

4. Right-click on the selected printer that you wish to enable defer printing and select **Pause Printing** for a local printer or **Work Offline** for a network printer.

Scenario Solutions

Scenario 1

You could install the Generic/Text Only printer driver and allow the wizard to print a test page to confirm everything prints clearly. You might also want to check the settings for resolution.

Scenario 2

Set the printer to print after the first page has been spooled.

Scenario 3

The necessary files will automatically be downloaded when the printer is added via the Add Printer Wizard.

Scenario 4

Set the printer to **Work Offline**. He can create the document and preview how it will print. When he returns to work, he will just need to turn off the **Work Offline** option and print the document.

Post-Test Answers

1. Start printing after the first page is spooled

2. EMF

3. Use the Generic/Text Only printer driver or update your driver.

4. IPX/SPX

5. Allows the Windows 95 user to install printer drivers for a remote printer from a network source

6. The Universal Printer Driver is provided by Windows 95 while the minidriver is provided by the manufacturer of the printer.

CHAPTER 16

Pre-Test Answers

1. The **Diagnostics** tab of a Modems properties sheet

2. Run **Start/Programs/Accessories/Internet Tools/Get on the Internet**.

3. Check the connection information, install the modem using a generic driver, check to see that the phone line is connected properly to the jack and the modem, and verify that call waiting is disabled.

Scenario Solutions

Scenario 1

Turn on **Record a Log File** in the Advanced Connection Settings dialog of the Modems properties sheet. When he comes into town, copy his MODEMLOG.TXT file from his Windows directory and examine it.

Scenario 2

Use Microsoft Fax to share the modem.

Scenario 3

Display the **Devices** tab in System utility. Remove the modem. Click on **Refresh**.

Scenario 4

Turn off **File and Printer Sharing**.

Scenario 5

The only connection protocol that allows password encryption is PPP.

Scenario 6

She should configure her modem to disable call waiting when she dials out.

Post-Test Answers

1. The modem may not be connected properly to the computer, the COM port may be being used by another device, the modem is already installed, the COM port may not be configured properly, or the COM port's IRQ setting is in conflict with an IRQ setting of another device

2. Right-click on the selected dial-up connection and select **Properties**. Click on **Configure** and click on the **Options** tab. Enable the **Bring up terminal window after dialing**.

3. Launch the Modems utility. Select the modem for which you wish to record a log file and click on **Properties**. Click on the **Connection** tab. Click on **Advanced** and enable the option for **Record a log file**.

4. No

5. Unbind the file and printer sharing service for the TCP/IP protocol

6. Open the Inbox's **Tools/Microsoft Fax Tools/Options** dialog. Select the **Modem** tab. Check the option for **Let other people on the network use my modem to send faxes**. To add permitted users, click on **Properties** and select the users.

CHAPTER 17

Pre-Test Answers

1. Microsoft Registry Service

2. Use the **Start/Run** dialog or use the properties sheet for the server in Network Neighborhood.

3. File and printer sharing services for the client

Scenario Solutions

Scenario 1

He must change his access control to user-level security.

Scenario 2

Use Net Watcher to connect to his computer and change the access permissions on his computer.

Scenario 3

Connect to the computer you wish to monitor using System Monitor. Add counters for Allocated Memory, Free Memory, and Swap File.

Scenario 4

Use System Monitor. Set counters to monitor the % Processor Usage, Allocated Memory, and Free Memory.

Post-Test Answers

1. Registry Editor and System Policy Editor

2. For accessing remote registries and to use the System Monitor

3. Kernel's threads

4. File system, IPX/SPX-compatible protocol, kernel, and memory manager

5. ADMIN$ and IPC$

6. Usually an administrator account, but it should be the user who will be administering the remote computer

SELF STUDY

Appendix B—Custom Setup

SAMPLE BSETUP.INF FILE

```
[BatchSetup]
Version=1.0a
SaveDate=08/01/95

[Setup]
Express=1
InstallDir="C:\WINDOWS"
EBD=0
ChangeDir=0
OptionalComponents=1
Network=1
System=0
CCP=0
CleanBoot=0
Display=0
PenWinWarning=0
InstallType=3
DevicePath=1
TimeZone="Central"
Uninstall=0
VRC=0
NoPrompt2Boot=1

[NameAndOrg]
Name="Scott Schaffer"
```

```
Org="Wave Technologies International, Inc."
Display=0


[Network]
ComputerName="Scott'sNEC"
Workgroup="Development"
Description="Scott's NEC Versa Laptop"
Display=0
Clients=VREDIR, NWREDIR
Protocols=NETBEUI, NWLINK, MSTCP
Services=VSERVER
IgnoreDetectedNetCards=0
Security=domain
PassThroughAgent="Wonderland"


[NWLINK]
FrameType=4
NetBIOS=0


[MSTCP]
DHCP=1
DNS=0
WINS=DHCP


[NWREDIR]
FirstNetDrive=F:
PreferredServer=STL_NW3
ProcessLoginScript=1
```

```
[VREDIR]
LogonDomain="Wonderland"
ValidatedLogon=1



[OptionalComponents]
"Accessibility Options"=0
"Briefcase"=1
"Calculator"=1
"Character Map"=0
"Clipboard Viewer"=0
"Desktop Wallpaper"=0
"Document Templates"=1
"Games"=0
"Mouse Pointers"=0
"Net Watcher"=0
"Object Packager"=1
"Online User's Guide"=0
"Paint"=1
"Quick View"=0
"System Monitor"=0
"System Resource Meter"=0
"Windows 95 Tour"=0
"WordPad"=1
"Dial-Up Networking"=0
"Direct Cable Connection"=0
"HyperTerminal"=1
"Phone Dialer"=1
"Backup"=0
"Defrag"=1
```

```
"Disk compression tools"=1

"Microsoft Exchange"=0

"Microsoft Mail Services"=0

"Microsoft Fax Services"=0

"Microsoft Fax Viewer"=0

"Central European language support"=0

"Cyrillic language support"=0

"Greek Language support"=0

"Audio Compression"=1

"CD Player"=1


"Jungle Sound Scheme"=0

"Media Player"=1

"Musica Sound Scheme"=0

"Robotz Sound Scheme"=0

"Sample Sounds"=0

"Sound Recorder"=1

"Utopia Sound Scheme"=0

"Video Compression"=1

"Volume Control"=1

"Additional Screen Savers"=0

"Flying Windows"=1

"The Microsoft Network"=0
```

Server-Based Setup Options for Custom Scripts

Option	Setup script parameter
Setup Options: Automated Install Setup Mode Create an Emergency Boot Disk Install Verification Enable Pen Windows Warning	**[Setup]** Express=[0 | 1] InstallType=[0 | 1 | 2 | 3] EBD=[0 | 1] Verify=[0 | 1] PenWinWarning=[0 | 1]
Installation Location: Install Directory Server based Setup	**[Setup]** InstallDir= *directory_path* [Network]
Name and Organization: Display name and organization page Name Organization	**[NameAndOrg]** Display=[0 | 1] Name=*Name* Organization=*Organization*

Network Options:
Display network screens during
    custom setup
Clients to Install
Hard Disk Boot
    (for shared installations)
Remoteboot (RPL) Setup
Workstation Setup
Display Workstation Setup
	[Network]
	Display=[0 | 1]
	
	Clients=*network_client_list*
	
	HDBoot=[0 | 1]
	RPLSetup=[0 | 1]
	WorkstationSetup=[0 | 1]
	DisplayWorkstationSetup=[0 | 1]

Client for Microsoft Networks: Validated Logon Logon Domain	**[Vredir]** ValidatedLogon=[0 | 1] LogonDomain=*domain_name*
Client for NetWare Networks: Preferred Server First Network Drive Search Mode	**[Nwredir]** PreferredServer=*servername* FirstNetDrive=*drive_letter* SearchMode=[0 - 7]
Protocols: Protocols to Install	**[Network]** Protocols=*protocol_list*

Option	Setup script parameter
IPX/SPX-compatible protocol: Frame Type NetBIOS support	**[Nwlink]** FrameType=[0 | 1 | 2 | 3 | 4] NetBIOS=[0 | 1]
Microsoft TCP/IP: DHCP IP Address Subnet Mask WINS Primary WINS Secondary WINS Scope ID Enable DNS Hostname Domain DNS Server search order Domain search order LMHOST Path Gateways	**[Mstcp]** DHCP=[0 | 1] IPAddress=*IP_address* SubnetMask=*IP_address* WINS=[0 | 1] PrimaryWINS=*IP_address* SecondaryWINS=*IP_address* ScopeID=*scope ID_string* DNS=[0 | 1] Hostname=*hostname_string* Domain=*domain_string* DNSServers=*list_of_DNS_servers* DomainOrder=*list_of_domains* LMHostPath=*path_to_LMHOSTS_file* Gateways=*list_of_IP_addresses*
Network adapters: Network adapters to install	Netcards=*list_of_network_adapters*
Services: Services to install	Services=*list_of_services*
File and Printer Sharing for NetWare Networks: SAP Browsing Browse Master	**[Nwserver]** SAPBrowse=[0 | 1] BrowseMaster=[0 | 1]
File and Printer Sharing for Microsoft Networks: LMAnnounce Browse Master	**[VServer]** Announce=[0 | 1] BrowseMaster=[0 | 1]

Option	Setup script parameter
Identification: Computer Name Workgroup Description Access Control Security Type Pass-through Agent	**[Network]** ComputerName=*name_string* Workgroup=*workgroup_string* Description=*description_string* [Network] UserSecurity=[share | domain | msserver | nwserver] PassThroughAgent=*server_or_domain*
System Components: Power Management Locale Machine Pen Windows Tablet Keyboard Monitor Display Mouse	**[System]** Power=*Inf_section_name* Locale=*Inf_section_name* Machine=*Inf_section_name* PenWindows=*Inf_section_name* Tablet=*Inf_section_name* Keyboard=*Inf_section_name* Monitor=*Inf_section_name* Display=*Inf_section_name* Mouse=*Inf_section_name*
Most Recently Used Paths: UNC name for path to Windows 95 source files	**[InstallLocationsMRU]** *install_path*

SELF STUDY

Appendix C—Microsoft Plus!

Microsoft Plus!

The Microsoft Plus! product is an enhancement product for the Windows 95 environment. It includes new Desktop themes allowing users to further customize their desktop environment, as well as additional visual enhancements.

For administrators, this package includes the System Agent, DriveSpace 3, and Dial-Up Networking Server tools.

Installing Microsoft Plus!

You can install Microsoft Plus! in one of three ways:

- Once the CD has been inserted, the screen below is displayed. Click on **Install Plus!** to begin installation.

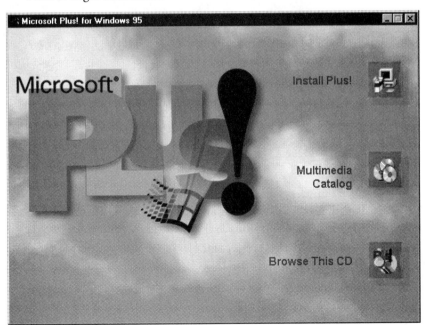

- Open the **Start/Run** dialog. Browse to the CD-ROM drive and locate the setup file. Select SETUP.EXE and click on **OK**.

- Launch Windows Explorer. Expand the CD-ROM and launch the SETUP.EXE file from the Contents pane.

Click on **Continue** to continue past the inroductory screen. You will then be asked for information on the name and organization of the user. Click on **OK** when you have finished typing in this information. To confirm that the information is correct, click on **OK**. Next, you must enter the CD key for the Microsoft Plus! product. Click on **OK** once you have finished entering that information. Click on **OK** again to confirm the complete Microsoft product information.

By default, the setup program installs Microsoft Plus! into the \PROGRAM FILES\PLUS! directory. You can change the location by clicking on **Change Folder**. Click on **OK** if you choose to install into the default location.

Types of Installation

Now, you can select one of two types of installation: Typical or Custom. Typical installation installs the most common components of Microsoft Plus! such as Desktop themes, 3D Pinball, and Visual Enhancements.

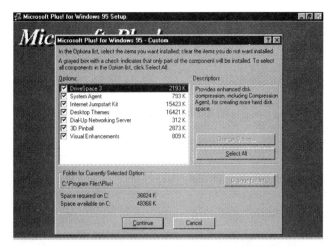

To install components such as System Agent, Dial-Up Networking Server, and DriveSpace 3, you must select the **Custom** installation. **Custom** installation enables you to select from all of the available components which include:

- DriveSpace 3

- System Agent

- Internet Jumpstart Kit

- Desktop Themes

- Dial-Up Networking Server

- 3D Pinball

- Visual Enhancements

The setup program will then install the files necessary for the selected components. If you select the **Typical** installation or choose to install the Desktop Themes component through a **Custom** installation, you will be prompted to select your new desktop theme.

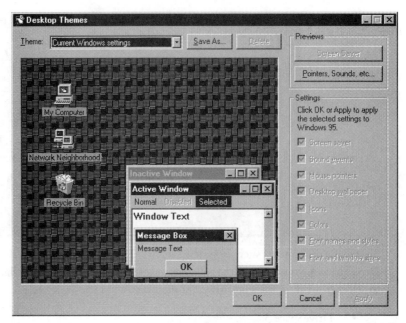

From this dialog, you can specify which Windows 95 components you would like the new desktop theme to use. You can select from the following:

- Screen saver

- Sound events

- Mouse pointers

- Desktop wallpaper

- Icons

- Colors

- Font names and styles

- Font and window sizes

Once the installation has completed, you must restart your computer for the last settings to take place on the system.

Microsoft Plus! Environment

Once you have installed Microsoft Plus! there are several new additions to your Windows 95 environment. The Display utility allows you to change your Desktop themes.

The System Agent and DriveSpace 3 system tools can be launched from **Start/Programs/ Accessories/System Tools**. System Agent also has a Taskbar icon which can be used to open the utility. These utilities have been discussed in the course in greater detail.

Dial-Up Networking Server can be accessed through the Dial-Up Networking utility's **Connections** menu.

Removing Microsoft Plus!

To remove Microsoft Plus! from your computer system, you must use the setup program. If you choose to use the Add/Remove Programs utility to remove Microsoft Plus!, the setup program will launch.

You must click on **Remove All** to remove all components of Microsoft Plus! This will uninstall all components and the \PROGRAM FILES\PLUS directory.

SELF STUDY

Glossary

Accessories	Microsoft Windows or Windows NT applets.
Address mask	A bit mask used to select bits from an Internet (TCP/IP) address for subnet addressing. The mask is 32 bits long and selects the network portion of the Internet address and two or more bits of the local portion. It is sometimes called subnet mask.
Address space	A block of addresses that a process can assign to a particular block of data. The memory allocated from an address space must be backed by physical memory.
Alias	This is the MS-DOS filename associated with a long filename in Windows 95 or Windows NT.

American National Standards Institute (ANSI)

A group of committees formed to establish voluntary commercial and government standards. The committee responsible for computing, data processing, and information technology is ANSI-X3, formerly named USASI (United States of America Standards Institute). ANSI is a member of the International Standards Organization (ISO).

American Standard Code for Information Interchange (ASCII)

The American Standard Code for Information Interchange (ASCII) character set is used to translate a byte into a character or number. Devised in 1968, ASCII is used for the purpose of standardizing the transmission of data to achieve hardware and software compatibility.

ASCII has 128 characters and uses seven of the eight bits to form these characters. The eighth bit is used for error checking.

IBM developed the Extended Character Set, which contains 256 characters. In this character set, the eighth bit is used for special symbols, such as bullet points, fractions, and copyright or trademark symbols.

Architecture	The specific design and construction of a computer. Architecture usually refers to the hardware makeup of the central processing unit and the size of the byte or set of bytes it processes, such as 8-bit, 16-bit, or 32-bit architecture.
Attribute	A characteristic describing or distinguishing a piece of hardware or software, such as security attributes or database field character types.

AUTOEXEC.BAT

The DOS environment is set up and configured by loading device drivers. This is done through the system configuration files AUTOEXEC.BAT and CONFIG.SYS. When DOS is booted, these files are executed.

AUTOEXEC.BAT is a text batch file that must be located at the root directory of the boot drive. The AUTOEXEC.BAT file is executed by COMMAND.COM after the CONFIG.SYS file, and is used to customize the environment and automatically start applications.

It is a good idea to make a backup of this file prior to installing a new application. Many applications will make changes to this file during their installation. It is wise to make note of the changes in case of system errors or problems. Applications that alter this file typically make a backup copy. Refer to the application's documentation for details.

Changes to the AUTOEXEC.BAT file will not take effect until the system is rebooted.

Mistakes in the AUTOEXEC.BAT file may cause system startup errors. You can bypass the execution of AUTOEXEC.BAT by pressing the F5 key when you see the "Starting DOS" message.

AUTOEXEC.BAT is still supported with Windows 95 to provide backward compatibility with DOS.

Background application

An application that is running but does not have focus and cannot receive user input.

Background Printing

A feature that allows a computer to print in the background while other applications execute in the foreground.

Background process

A process that is not the focus of user input.

Background task

An active process that is not receiving interactive user input.

Backup

1. Pertaining to a system, device, file, or facility that can be used to recover data in the event of a malfunction or loss of data.

2. To copy information, usually onto diskette or tape, for safekeeping.

Backup Domain Controller (BDC)

Windows NT Server having a backup copy of domain security information. The BDC can validate logon and security access.

Base memory address

The bit where a block of allocated memory begins.

Basic Input/Output System (BIOS)

Software or firmware embedded in chips on the circuit board which determines compatibility. Examples of these are IBM, Compaq, AMI, Award, and Phoenix.

Batch	A method of computer job processing where input is collected and run through the processing programs all at once, and outputs are produced in the form of files and reports. Batch is the opposite of interactive job processing, in which an operator at a terminal interacts with the processing program directly during data entry. Most personal computers employ interactive processing. Mainframes use batch processing.
Batch program	A text file that contains operating system commands. When you run a batch program, the operating system carries out the commands in the file as if you had typed them at the command prompt.
Baud	1. Abbreviation for Baudot, which gets its name from J. M. Emile Baudot (1845-1903), who invented the code. The Baudot code is a special set of binary characters using five bits per character to form 32 combinations. The number of combinations was increased to 62 through the use of two special shift characters. The Baudot code was mainly used to handle telex messages by common communications carriers such as Western Union. The main disadvantage of the Baudot code is its lack of an error-checking bit.
	2. Used commonly to refer to transfer rates on dial-up lines.
Baud rate	The data transmission speed setting of a serial device. Typical rates include 300, 1200, and 2400. Higher speeds, 9600, 19200, 38400, and 57600 baud, are achieved through data compression. Sometimes refered to simply as baud.
Bindery	In NetWare 3, the bindery stores information about users, groups, file servers, print servers, and other logical and physical entities on the network. Network information, such as passwords, account balances, and trustee assignments, are also kept in the bindery.
	The bindery files, NET$OBJ.SYS, NET$PROP.SYS, and NET$VAL.SYS, are stored in the SYSTEM directory on the SYS volume. The files are system files and do not appear in a normal directory search.
	BINDFIX is a utility that rebuilds the bindery files, purges deleted users and groups, and then removes their mail directories and trustee rights. The original bindery files are copied to NET$OBJ.OLD, NET$PROP.OLD, and NET$VAL.OLD.
	BINDFIX runs without other parameters. One should be logged in as SUPERVISOR and have SYS:SYSTEM as the default directory before running the utility. Ensure there is no other activity on the system before running BINDFIX.
	BINDREST is a utility used to restore the original bindery files should BINDFIX fail for any reason. BINDREST runs without additional parameters.

Bindery context	A server's bindery services is enabled in this container object.
Bindery emulation	A process by which NetWare v4.x emulates bindery functions to support legacy clients.
Bindery objects	An object placed in the Directory tree by an upgrade or migration utility is represented by this leaf object. NDS cannot identify the object, and it provides backward compatibility with bindery-oriented utilities.
Binding and unbinding	Binding assigns a communication protocol to network boards and LAN drivers. Unbinding removes the protocol. Each network board needs at least one communication protocol bound to its LAN driver, to process packets. Multiple protocols can be bound to the same LAN driver and board. You can also bind the same protocol stack to more than one LAN driver on the server. Workstations with different protocols can be cabled on the same scheme.
Bits per second (bps)	Usually the number of bits (binary digits) which can be transmitted or transferred each second.
Block	The smallest amount of disk space that can be allocated at one time from a disk partition or volume. Block size is determined by disk size, operating system, and file system type.
Boot	To start or restart your computer, loading the operating system from a disk drive.
Briefcase	A specialized folder that allows synchronization of various files across multiple systems.
Broadcast	1. A transmission of a message intended for general reception rather than for a specific station. 2. In LAN technology, a transmission method used in bus topology networks that sends all messages to all stations even though the messages are addressed to specific stations. 3. A NetWare console command that transmits a message to all network nodes or list of nodes.
Browser	1. This client program (software) is used to look at various Internet resources and retrieve information. 2. Windows service that collects and organizes shared network resources in a hierarchical manner.
Browsing	1. Allows you to find objects in the NetWare Directory, which is arranged in hierarchical order. 2. Viewing and retrieving data from the Internet. 3. Viewing available network resources in hierarchical order.

Byte	Short for "binary digit eight." A unit of information consisting of usually eight bits. A file's size is measured in bytes or potential storage capacity is measured in bytes, but when dealing with very large numbers, the terms kilobyte, megabyte, or gigabyte are used.
Bytes per second (Bps)	Usually the number of bytes which can be transmitted or transferred each second.
Cache	An area of computer memory set aside for frequently used data to speed operations. Some caches are general purpose, while others are for specific operations. A disk cache is an area of system memory reserved for caching disk reads and writes. A CPU cache is a dedicated, high-speed memory array used to cache pending instructions.
Cache memory	This is a dedicated area of RAM memory used for temporary storage of data. It provides faster access and typically improves overall performance. This is a function of most operating systems and many applications. The specific content of the cache memory is operating system and application specific.
Client	1. A client is a workstation that requests services of another computer (server).
	2. The portion of a client/server application providing the end-user interface (front-end).
com	This is an extension for Internet addresses representing commercial enterprises. For example, galeds@msen.com.
COM port	A connection on the computer where the cable for a serial device is attached. The serial device could be a printer, network interface card, modem, or other device. COM ports are often called serial ports. COM ports are numbered, and generally COM1 through COM4 are supported on most personal computers. It is possible to have more or less than four COM ports.
Command	Any executable statements.
Command prompt	A displayed symbol, such as C:>, that informs the user that a DOS system is idle. It represents that the command-line interface is ready to receive input.
COMMAND.COM	The program that interprets and runs DOS commands.
Communication protocols	Rules used by a program or operating system to communicate between two or more points. It allows information to be packaged, sent, and delivered.
Communications rate	Also called the transfer rate or the transmission rate. The communications rate cannot exceed the maximum rate that both devices can handle.

Compact Disc Read-Only Memory (CD-ROM)

A read-only optical disc commonly used to distribute applications software or archive data.

Complete trust model

In Microsoft Windows NT's complete trust model, each domain can act as both a master domain and a resource domain. In most cases, each domain is managed separately, with access to other domains granted through two-way trust relationships.

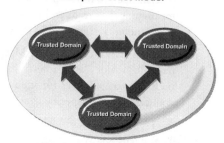

The complete trust model is a mix of independence and interdependence–independent in that each domain has its own users and groups. Each domain sets its own access, rights, and permission policies. Each domain administrator is responsible for his or her domain, and must be trusted to manage that domain properly.

The model is interdependent because unless there is a need to share resources between domains, there would be no reason for setting up a complete trust model. Domain administrators must work together to provide resource access while insuring that security is not compromised.

This model is most appropriate to organizations that do not have a central MIS department available to manage master domains. It often fits well into organizations made up of somewhat independent departments or divisions. Companies must be ready, however, to accept the potential risks inherent in a non-centralized management structure.

CONFIG.SYS

The DOS environment is set up and configured by loading device drivers. This is done through two system configuration files: AUTOEXEC.BAT and CONFIG.SYS. When DOS is booted, these two files are executed.

CONFIG.SYS is a text file. It must be located at the root directory of the boot drive. The CONFIG.SYS is called by the IO.SYS file, and contains commands to configure hardware and load device drivers.

It is always a good idea to make a backup of this file prior to installing a new application. Many applications will automatically make changes to this file during the installation process. It is wise to make note of these changes in case of system errors. Applications that alter this file typically make a backup copy. Refer to the application's documentation for details.

Changes to the CONFIG.SYS file will not take effect until the system is rebooted.

Mistakes in the CONFIG.SYS file may cause system startup errors. You can bypass the execution of CONFIG.SYS by pressing the F5 key when you see the "Starting DOS" message. Using F8 instead of F5 will allow you to selectively bypass commands in the CONFIG.SYS file. This can help isolate problem lines within the configuration file.

CONFIG.SYS is still supported with Windows 95 to provide backward compatibility.

Container object

1. The type of object in NetWare's NDS used to organize other objects on the network into "groups," such as work groups, departments, or divisions. A container object will "contain" other objects.

2. Visual Basic object defining a set of objects as a group.

Control Panel

1. On a Macintosh, the Control Panel is a system software utility stored in the Control Panels folder (found in the System Folder). Panels are used to configure various services such as AppleTalk and user preferences such as desktop patterns and wallpaper.

2. Windows-family utility containing management tools.

Conventional memory

The first 640 KB of memory in a PC is called conventional or base memory. It is used to load the DOS command processor, device drivers, and Terminate and Stay Resident (TSR) programs. It is also used by DOS applications.

Conventional Memory

640 KB

DOS Applications

Device Driver
Device Driver
DOS Kernel

0 KB

Cooperative multitasking	A multitasking method where an application must release the processor before the next application may be given processor time.
Data communication	The transfer of data from one device to another via direct cabling: telecommunication links involving modems, a telephone network, or other connection methods. Transfer of information between functional units by means of data transmission according to a protocol.
Data compression	This refers to the technique that eliminates gaps and redundancies in data files. It is beneficial for users, since smaller files take less time to transmit through a network.
Default	One of a set of operating conditions that is automatically used when a device such as a printer or computer is turned on or reset. Pertaining to an attribute, value, or option when none is explicitly specified.
Default drive	This is the drive the workstation is currently using. It is identified by a drive prompt, such as A:> or F:>.
Default profile	User profile called when a user account does not have an assigned profile or the user's personal profile is not available from the server.
DELETED.SAV	A hidden directory in NetWare v3.x, v4.x, and Portable NetWare containing files from deleted directories. DELETED.SAV is automatically created in each volume.
Desktop	Most Graphical User Interfaces (GUIs) refer to the work area on the computer screen as the desktop. All window items appear and are moved around on this desktop area.
Device	Any computer peripheral or hardware component (such as printer, mouse, monitor, or disk drive) capable of receiving and/or sending data, generally through the use of a device driver.
Device driver	Hardware-specific software that acts as an interface between the operating system and the hardware attached to a computer. Device drivers allow applications to communicate with hardware in a controlled and orderly fashion. A device driver is installed when the system is initialized, either by the operating system or through an installable device driver. Some examples of installable device drivers are mouse, graphical/video monitor, communications port, printer, and network interface card.
Dial-up connection	This is a connection between computers which has been established over standard telephone lines.
Directory	1. Part of a structure for organizing files on a disk. A directory can contain files and subdirectories. The structure of directories and subdirectories on a disk is called a directory tree. The top-level directory in a directory tree is the root directory.

2. In NetWare, the highest organizational level is the file server. Each server's main directory is called a VOLUME, and subdirectories are called directories.

Directory and file permissions

These permissions, assigned to users and groups, set user access level.

Directory path

Information including the server name, volume name, and name of each directory connected to the file system directory you need to access.

Directory permissions

Access permissions assigned to users or groups.

Directory rights

Rights that specify what a trustee can do with a directory in the file system.

Directory services

Information about every resource on the network is maintained by these built-in NetWare 4 services.

Directory structure

Most computers use a tree or filing system to organize volumes, directories, files, and data on their hard disks.

Disk fragmentation

A phenomenon that occurs during normal system usage. As files are copied to, moved, and deleted from a disk drive, the disk blocks used to store data become fragmented (split to different areas of the disk). Fragmented files require more time to retrieve and can result in a condition known as "disk thrashing"–a significant amount of head movement required to read or write all the blocks of a file. Disk optimization utilities such as Norton Speed Disk #Should we list Windows 95's Disk Defragmenter?can be used to place files into contiguous disk blocks, which allows data to be efficiently stored and retrieved.

Disk Operating System (DOS)

The software programs that control the operation of the computer and the movement of information throughout the computer system.

DOS is the medium by which the user communicates with the computer system and manipulates data.

Display adapter

The circuitry used to drive a video display monitor. Some computers include the video adapter circuitry on the system board while others require an expansion card. There are two formats with which data may be sent from the adapter to the display: analog or digital.

Document-centric design

A technique used by Windows 95 that allows users to focus on documents instead of their associated applications.

Domain

1. A logical grouping for file servers within a network, managed as an integrated whole.

2. Used in NetWare DOMAIN as a console command that will create a protected operating system domain for running untested NLMs in Ring 3. This prevents a module from interferring with the core operating system.

3. In the Internet, a domain is a part of the naming hierarchy. The domain name is a sequence of names (separated by periods) that identify host sites. For example: galenp@mail.msen.com

Domain controller
Server within a domain and storage point for domain-wide security information.

Domain name
A unique domain name designates a location on the Internet. Domain Names always have two or more parts separated by periods. The leftmost part is the most specific, and the part on the right is the most general. A given machine may have more than one Domain Name, but a given Domain Name points to only one machine.

Domain Name System (DNS)
The Domain Name System (DNS) is a hierarchical, distributed method of organizing system and network names on the Internet. DNS administratively groups hosts (systems) into a hierarchy of authority that allows addressing and other information to be widely distributed and maintained. A big advantage of DNS is that using it eliminates dependence on a centrally maintained file that maps host names to addresses.

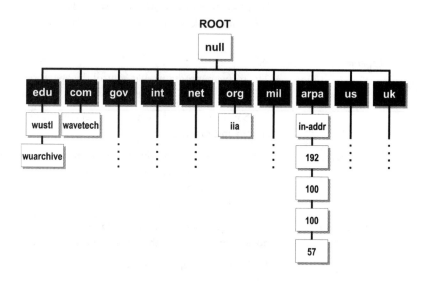

The diagram above shows the hierarchical organization of domain names. The bottom level of the tree structure contains the names of companies or even machines within a company. For example, consider wuarchive.wustl.edu. The bottom of the tree is wuarchive. This is the name of a particular piece of equipment within the wustl domain, which is under the edu domain.

The name of a particular domain is read from the bottom of the tree up to the root. The root is unnamed and is represented with just a period. For example, wavetech.com is a particular domain. If we were to give the fully qualified domain name (FQDN), we would include the unnamed root, so it would be written as "wavetech.com". The final period at the end of the name specifies the root of the tree. The root must always be specified for the host equipment. To make it easy, most software will convert a domain name to an FQDN for the user, by appending any missing domain names all the way to the root.

The top of the tree lists the top-level-domains. These are reserved names. Every domain will have a top-level domain by type or country.

Some of the types are com (commercial), edu (educational), gov (governmental), mil (military), net (network provider), org (non-profit organization), and int (international).

The two-letter country, top-level-domains identify the country of a particular Internet site. Most of the countries have formed a similar structure for categorizing site types under the country domains. There is a two-letter country domain for every country. Examples include uk (United Kingdom), za (South Africa), us (United States), de (Germany), fr (France), hk (Hong Kong), jp (Japan), br (Brazil), and mx (Mexico).

When a domain name is registered with the InterNIC, it is added to the tree under a particular top-level-domain. The company registering the name is given control over the sub-domain they've registered. Because control of the sub-domains is given over to the individual registries, they must provide a DNS Server for their own domains. The DNS Server provides the domain name to TCP/IP address resolution. When an Internet user refers to a particular host on the Internet by name, there must be a mapping made between the name entered and the TCP/IP address required for creation of the data packets.

DOS prompt   The character or characters that appear at the beginning of the DOS command line. This indicates that the computer is ready to receive input.

Dot pitch	On color monitors, the dot pitch is the mask through which the electron beam is focused for each set of red, green, and blue phosphors. The dot pitch is the spacing between the holes. The smaller the spacing, the more dots and phosphors; therefore, a finer (i.e., smaller) dot pitch provides a sharper image.
Dots per inch (dpi)	A measurement (dpi) of the resolution of a video display monitor, printer or other output device.
Download	A process where a file is transferred from a host computer to a user's computer. Download is the opposite of upload.
Downloading	Downloading is the transfer of a file from a remote computer to the user's computer.
Drive mapping	A letter assigned to a directory path on a network drive. To locate a file, users follow a path that includes the drive letter and any subdirectories leading to the file.
Driver	Software used to allow the operating system to communicate with an add-on hardware device such as a disk controller or display adapter.
Dynamic-link library (DLL)	
	A module that is linked at load time or run time.
edu	The Internet address suffix that identifies educational institutions. For example, xxx@stanford.edu.
Electronic Mail (e-mail)	Electronic mail (e-mail) is the most popular Internet application and the driving force behind the Internet's rapid growth. While controlling another computer remotely or transferring files from one computer to another may be useful, neither is as exciting as being able to communicate with millions of Internet users around the globe. Many users join the Internet just for e-mail access.
	Fortunately, it is possible to exchange e-mail with people who are not directly part of the Internet. For example, by using gateways to other public e-mail networks, Internet e-mail can reach users with commercial service provider accounts such as CompuServe, BITNET, America Online, Prodigy, and the Microsoft Network. E-mail can also reach users who work at companies that get their mail access from corporate network providers such as, MCImail, Applelink, and uuNet.

E-mail is popular because it works very quickly. While traditional mail can take a day or two to cross town or weeks to reach an international destination, e-mail can travel from sender to receiver within hours (sometimes minutes), despite the distance between them. If the network is extremely busy, or if an administrator configures a user's system to send e-mail once a day (as opposed to every few minutes), the e-mail may take a little longer to arrive. In general, however, e-mail moves around the world at a rapid pace. It is possible for a person in the U.S. to send a message to West Africa, receive a response, and send another message, all in the space of an hour.

E-mail is also very flexible. Users can attach different types of files to their e-mail messages. Marketing departments can embed audio and video clips within text messages, co-workers can transfer spreadsheets or project updates, families can share pictures and birthday messages.

Electronic mail address	Designation given to an individual or domain that directs messages or other information over computers in general to a specific person or destination.
Error control	An arrangement that combines error detection and error correction.
Error log	A data set or file in a product or system where error information is stored for later access.
Ethernet	Ethernet is a Carrier Sense, Multiple Access with Collision Detection (CSMA/CD) specification.

Ethernet was originally developed by Xerox, Intel, and Digital Equipment Corporation in the late 1970s, with specifications first released in 1980. The standard defines the cabling, connectors, and other characteristics for the transmission of data, voice, and video over local area networks at 10 Mbps. Recent improvements have increased the speed to 100 Mbps.

There are four types of Ethernet frames defined: 802.2, 802.3, Ethernet_SNAP, and Ethernet II. These are similar but incompatible.

The types of Ethernet cables are Thin Ethernet (Thinnet), Thick Ethernet (Thicknet), Twisted Pair, and Fiber Optic.

Extension	1. The period and up to three characters at the end of a DOS format filename. The File Allocation Table (FAT) file system is used by DOS and some other operating systems. Many applications use the extension to designate a particular type of information or data contained in the file.

2. A system software utility that adds functionality to the operating system.

File

A sequence of bytes stored on a secondary storage medium such as a floppy disk or hard disk. Generally, a computer file contains either a program or data.

Program files contain instructions or commands which are to be executed by the computer. Data files which contain only ASCII characters are text files, while files containing binary data, i.e., data other than ASCII characters, are called binary files. Bytes that comprise a file are not necessarily stored on contiguous disk blocks and may be scattered across a disk due to fragmentation.

Macintosh files generally consist of a Data Fork (the file contents) and a Resource Fork (a pointer to the application that created the file).

File Allocation Table (FAT)

The File Allocation Table (FAT) system is the file system used by DOS machines. Some other operating systems also support the FAT system.

In order to organize your disk, DOS divides it into two parts. The first part is a small system area that DOS uses to keep track of key information about the disk. This system area uses approximately 2% of a floppy diskette, and approximately several tenths of a percent of a hard disk. The second part is the data storage area, which represents the bulk of the disk area.

The system area is divided into three parts called the boot record, FAT, and root directory.

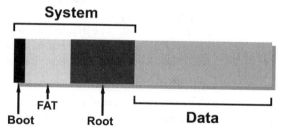

The boot record holds a very short program that performs the job of beginning the loading of the operating system into the computer's memory.

The next part of the system portion of a disk is called the File Allocation Table (FAT). The operating system divides the disk storage area into logical units called clusters. The FAT contains an entry for each data cluster on the disk. A file's FAT entry points to the first cluster for the file. Each cluster points to the next cluster assigned to the file. The final cluster contains a delimiter of FFF (hex) which signals the end of the file.

File caching

This improves file access time by using the RAM memory to store recently accessed files.

File compression	More data can be stored on server hard disks by compressing files that are not being used. NetWare and Windows NT support identifying files and directories to be compressed. With DOS, Windows, and Windows 95, disk partitions are identified for compression.
File format	The arrangement of information in a file. There are many standard and non-standard file formats used on various computing platforms. The use of standard formats for information such as vector graphics, bitmapped graphics, audio, word processing and spreadsheets, allows information to be accessed by applications from multiple vendors.
File rights	Rights which specify what a trustee can do with a file.
File sharing	1. The ability for more than one person to use the same file at the same time. 2. The process of making a file or directory available for network client access.
File transfer	The process of copying a file from one computer to another over a network. FTP is a popular program used to copy files over the Internet.
File Transfer Protocol (FTP)	The File Transfer Protocol (FTP) is a part of the TCP/IP suite that is used to transfer files between any two computers, provided they support FTP. The two computers do not have to be running the same operating system. In general, people use FTP to move files from one account or machine to another, or to perform what is called an "anonymous FTP." For example, if storage space on a particular machine is low, the user can free up storage space by using FTP to move the files to a machine with more space. Another reason to move a file to a different account is to print a file to a particular printer. If the file is on a machine that cannot access the desired printer, it must be moved to a machine that does have access. Whatever the reason for the transfer, FTP requires the user to know the proper login name and the password for both computers to move files between them. While an anonymous FTP also moves from one computer to another, it has two main differences. An anonymous FTP session usually involves gathering files that a user does not have. Anonymous FTP does not require the user to know a login name and password to access the remote computer.

The Internet has many anonymous FTP sites. Each site consists of an FTP server, a large number of files, and guest login names such as "anonymous" or "FTP." This allows any user to visit these systems and copy files from the FTP site to their personal computer. With the appropriate authority, users can copy files from their system to an anonymous FTP site.

Despite the variety of FTP servers and clients on the Internet and the different operating systems they use, FTP servers and clients generally support the same basic commands. This standard command set allows users to accomplish tasks such as looking at a list of files in the current directory of the remote system, regardless of the operating system in use. Other common commands allow users to change directories, get specific file information, copy files to a local machine, and change parameters.

Graphical Web browsers transform the traditional character-based, command-line FTP interface into a point-and-click environment. The only way a user may know that they are in the middle of an FTP session is that the Universal Resources Locator (URL) box in the browser will change from an address that begins with "http://..." to "ftp://...".

Firewall	A firewall is used as a security measure between a company's local area network (LAN) and the Internet. The firewall prevents users from accessing certain address Web sites. A firewall also helps to prevent hackers from accessing internal resources on the network.
Floppy disk	A magnetically sensitive flexible disk used as a secondary storage medium. The two most common sizes are the 3-1/2-inch disk which is fully enclosed in a rigid plastic casing and the 5-1/4-inch floppy disk.
Floppy drive	A device which stores data externally on small portable devices called "floppies." Floppies come in different sizes and hold different amounts of data. The two most common sizes are the 5-1/4 inch and the 3-1/2 inch.
Font	In typography, a complete set of characters of one particular size, style, and weight, including punctuation marks, symbols, and numbers. The term font is often confused with typeface, which refers to a particular style of character, or type family to which the font belongs.
Foreground process	A process that can receive user input.
Foreground task	A task that is able to receive interactive input from a user.
Frame relay	Commonly referred to as "bandwidth on demand." Unlike other transmission protocols or processes, frame relay offers users significant benefits over other transmission services, such as T1, by eliminating the processing overhead associated with packets of data moving between packet-forwarding devices.

Gateway	Gateways are the primary linkage between mixed environments such as PC-based LANs and host environments such as SNA.
	Gateways generally operate at all seven layers of the OSI Reference Model. They may provide full content conversion between two environments, such as ASCII to EBCDIC, as well as other application and presentation layer conversions.

Gateway Functionality

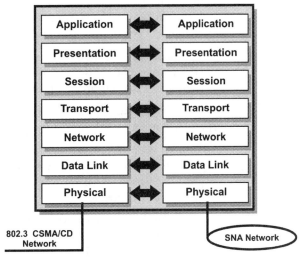

Other types of gateways include fax gateways, which allow users to send and receive faxes from their workstations. These may also be integrated with mail service gateways, which allow communications between users of different mail systems.

Global group	A group definition allowing permission assignments to local machines or other domains through local group membership of the global group.
Gopher	A hierarchical, menu-based information service developed at the University of Minnesota. It provides access to information collections across the Internet by taking file directories and turning them into easily navigable menus. Gopher also makes file transfer convenient.
	Gopher functions as a client server that connects the user to the menu item(s) selected from the gopher server menu. The user must have a Gopher Client program.
	Although Gopher spread rapidly across the globe in only a couple of years, it is being largely supplanted by Hypertext, also known as WWW (World Wide Web). There are thousands of Gopher Servers on the Internet and they will remain for a while.

gov

A governmental organization is identified by this Internet address suffix, for example, whitehouse.gov.

Graphical User Interface (GUI)

A program that executes commands given by the user to the computer. A GUI uses graphic representations of commands and/or a menu format to display commands that the user may execute with a mouse or similar device.

The graphical user interface makes using a computer easier, especially for the beginner. Mosaic is a Graphical User Interface for the Internet. Microsoft Windows, OS/2, and the Macintosh operating system are examples of graphical user interfaces for personal computers.

Graphics mode

The mode enabling applications to display graphics in addition to text. GUI-based applications always run in a graphics mode. DOS applications can run either in graphics or text mode.

Group

A collection of users. All members get, as implicit rights, any rights assigned to a group.

Hacker

A hacker is a person who is an expert at solving problems with computers. The term is often confused with cracker, which is the name given to a person who illegally attempts to access computer systems or has destructive intentions.

Hard disk

A peripheral mass-storage device which uses sealed, rotating, non-flexible, magnetically coated disks to store data and program files. Hard disk types include SCSI, IDE, and EIDE.

Hard disk controller

The board that communicates with and controls the hard (fixed) disk drive.

Hardware

All electronic components of a computer system, including peripherals, circuit boards, and input and output devices. Hardware is the physical equipment, as opposed to software consisting of programs, data procedures, rules, and associated documentation.

Header

A header contains identifying information.

Electronic mail message headers contain the message originator's name and address, receiver, subject, date, etc.

A packet header carries the source and destination addresses along with other information.

Hidden file

A file that is not visible in a directory listing.

High Performance File System (HPFS)

This is the native file system for OS/2.

HIMEM.SYS	An extended memory manager. It coordinates the use of the computer's extended memory. This prevents two applications from using the same block of memory at the same time.
Home directory	On Local Area Networks, a directory which belongs to a single user for storage of data. Normally, the user is the only person with access to this directory. On most networks, the Supervisor or Administrator can also access any user's home directory.
Home page	A document coded in HTML (Hypertext Markup Language) that acts as a top-level document for an Internet site or a topic. A home page contains hypertext links to related documents.
Host	A computer that is remotely accessible and provides information or services for users on a network. It is quite common to have one host machine provide several services, such as WWW and USENET. A host computer on the Internet can be accessed by using an application program such as electronic mail, telnet, or FTP. A host computer may also be a bulletin board.
Hostname	The name given to a computer that identifies it as an Internet or other site.

HyperText Markup Language (HTML)

Standard Generalized Markup Language (SGML) is a worldwide method of representing document formatting. It is also a broad language that is used to define particular markup languages for particular purposes.

The language that the Web uses is a specific application of SGML called HyperText Markup Language (HTML). As HTML has evolved, it has moved away from the SGML conventions. With newer versions of HTML, there has been some effort to rebuild the relationship between the two languages. Because of the worldwide investment in SGML, future versions of HTML will most likely comply with SGML even more closely.

HyperText Markup Language (HTML) is the standard language that the Web uses for creating and recognizing hypermedia documents. Web documents are most often written in HTML and normally have an .html or .htm extension.

Languages such as HTML follow the SGML format and allow document creators to separate document content from document presentation. As a markup language, HTML is more concerned with the structure of a document than with the appearance.

HTML documents are standard 7-bit ASCII files with formatting codes that contain information about layout (document titles, paragraphs, breaks, lists) and hyperlinks. Although most browsers will display any document that is written in plain text, by creating documents using HTML, writers can include links to other files, graphics, and various types of media.

HTML specifies a document's logical organization. While a formatting language, such as Rich Text Format (RTF), indicates typeface, font size, and style of the text in a document, HTML uses tags to mark the headings, normal paragraphs, and lists (and whether or not they are numbered).

While the HTML standard supports simple hypermedia document creation and layout, it is not capable of supporting some of the complex layout techniques found in traditional document publishing. As the Web and HTML gain additional momentum and are used by more people for more purposes, it will most likely gain some of the functionality used in desktop publishing.

HTML has been added to most major Internet browsers. Examples include Netscape Navigator and Microsoft Internet Explorer.

HTML is an evolving language. Different Web browsers recognize slightly different HTML tags. Some Web document creators attempt to get around formatting limitations in HTML by using graphics and browser-specific HTML tags. The creators do this in an attempt to make their documents look a certain way in a particular browser. Though approximately 80% of all users view Web documents with Netscape or Microsoft browsers, browser-specific documents look bad or can be inaccessible with the other browser.

Even with comprehensive capabilities, HTML is still an easy-to-use language, and is simple enough to type directly into a word processing application without the use of an HTML editor.

HyperText Transfer Protocol (HTTP)

HTTP is a set of directions for Web servers that tells them how to respond to various events initiated by users. HTTP is the most important protocol used in the World Wide Web (WWW).

The simplest example is clicking on a link to another part of the same file. The server receives the information that the link has been activated, and sends back the designated part of the file for display.

An HTTP client program is required on one end, and an HTTP server program on the other.

Icon

A graphical picture used to represent an application, folder, file, disk drive, or printer.

Initialization files   Files with the extension .INI that contain information that define your setup and various other parameters which are needed by a program. This is used extensively in Microsoft Windows and OS/2 for storing environmental or other device information.

Integrated Services Digital Network (ISDN)

A special kind of telecommunications network designed to handle more than just data. Using existing telephone lines and computer networks, integrated networks can handle video, text, voice, data, facsimile images, graphics, etc.

Internet address   A 32-bit value written or displayed in numbers that specify a particular network and node on that network.

Internet Service Provider (ISP)

Internet Service Providers are companies that provide an Internet connection for educational institutions, individuals, companies, and organizations.

Internetwork Packet Exchange (IPX)

IPX is used with SPX as the resident protocol in NetWare. A router with IPX routing can interconnect local area networks (LANs) so that Novell NetWare clients and servers can communicate.

In v3.x of NetWare, IPX is the name of the command-line utility used to see the versions and options of IPX.COM. This was used prior to the introduction of ODI drivers.

InterNIC   The Internet Network Information Center (InterNIC) was developed in 1993 by General Atomics, AT&T, and NSI to provide information services to Internet users. It offers a reference desk that provides networking information, referrals to other resources, and associate users with their local NICs. It also provides coordination to share information and activities with U.S. and international organizations; and education services to train midlevel and campus NICs, and end users to promote Internet use.

Interrupt Request Lines (IRQ)

Interrupt Request Lines are normally referred to as IRQ lines, and each line requires a separate IRQ number. Many PC add-in boards and devices require a unique dedicated IRQ line. Some IRQs are assigned to system devices.

The original IBM PC was an 8-bit system with eight available IRQ lines numbered 0 through 7. These lines support the system timer, keyboard, COM and LPT ports, and the floppy disk controller.

With the 16-bit IBM AT came eight additional IRQ lines which "cascade" through IRQ2. These IRQ lines support the Real Time Clock, hard disk controller, math coprocessor, and other devices. Examples of devices that use these IRQ lines are VGA and network adapters, CD-ROM drives, and SCSI controllers.

Some COM ports share IRQ lines. All odd-numbered COM ports (COM1, COM3, etc.) share IRQ 4, while all even numbered COM ports share IRQ 3.

Intranet

An intranet is a private Internet, usually within a company, for facilitating information sharing. It looks and acts just like the public Internet.

IP address

Each host in the network is assigned a unique IP address for each network connection (installed network adapter). The IP address is used to identify packet source and destination hosts.

An IP address is a 32-bit address, written as four octets (bytes) separated by periods, for example, 195.143.67.2.

This way of representing an IP address is also known as dotted decimal notation. Each address will also have an associated subnet mask, dividing the address into its network prefix and host suffix. For example, you might have the following defined as a subnet mask: 255.255.255.0. The subnet mask is used to identify the network and host portions of the address.

The network portion identifies where the host is located, and the host portion identifies the device connected to that network.

When dealing with a network the size of the Internet, address assignments must be carefully coordinated. With millions of hosts operating on thousands of networks, the potential for duplicate addresses is significant. The job of coordinating Internet IP addresses is given to the Network Information Center.

An assigned address is only required if your network is connected to the Internet. If connected to the Internet, your network address will be assigned through the Internetwork Network Information Center, or InterNIC.

To get an Internet address, contact the InterNIC at InterNIC Registration Services, c/o Network Solutions, Inc., 505 Huntmar Park Drive, Herndon, Virginia 22070, (800) 444-4345, or at hostmaster@internic.net.

An organization is assigned a network address. The organization can further divide this into its own subnets and assign the host addresses.

	Rather than going to the InterNIC, it is more likely that an organization will work through a local provider for address assignment. The organization will then subdivide the address, if necessary, and assign host addresses.
Kernel	A set of essential operating routines used by the operating system (usually hidden from the user) to perform important system tasks such as managing the system memory or controlling disk operations.
Kernel mode	Lower-level Windows NT or Windows 95 operating system functions.
Keyboard	The device which allows the user to input data into the computer or to execute commands. Most keyboards resemble a typewriter. The standard is a 101-key keyboard.
Legacy	Older, non-plug and play hardware in use.
LMHOSTS	The LMHOSTS file lists the IP address and NetBIOS name for each network machine with which the local machine may need communication.
Local Area Network (LAN)	A Local Area Network (LAN) is a group of computers running specialized communications software, and joined through an external data path.

A LAN will cover a small geographic area, usually no larger than a single building. The computers have a direct high-speed connection between all workstations and servers, and share hardware resources and data files. A LAN has centralized management of resources and network security.

PC-based networks can trace their heritage back to what are now often referred to as legacy systems. These systems were mainframe and minicomputer hosts accessed through dumb terminals.

There are a number of similarities between LANs and these legacy systems, such as centralized storage and backup, access security, and central management of resources. There are, however, a number of differences.

Traditional host systems are characterized by centralized processing, dumb terminals, custom applications, high expansion costs and management overhead. LANs are characterized by distributed processing, intelligent workstations (PCs), and off-the-shelf applications. LANs are modular, inexpensive to expand, and have more moderate management costs.

Local printer	A printer directly connected to one of the ports on the computer. The opposite is one connected through a network, which would be a remote printer.

Login	The act of entering into a computer system, usually requiring a password.
	LOGIN is also the NetWare command-line utility whose execution will log a user into the network. The login process includes a defined set of commands called the login script.
Logon scripts	DOS or NT batch file or executable that may run when a user logs onto a computer system. Login scripts can be used to map drives and search drives to directories, display messages, set environment variables, and execute programs or menus.
LPT port	The LPT port is also known as a parallel port. It is a connection on the computer, usually LPT1, where the cable for a parallel printer is connected. Generally, LPT1 through LPT3 can exist on a personal computer. Special equipment can be added to extend this capability.
MAIL directory	NetWare directory that provides electronic mail boxes. The MAIL directory is automatically created in the SYS volume when the network is installed and contains a subdirectory for each user. The subdirectory serves as a mailbox with the user ID as an address.
	In NetWare v3.x or lower, the subdirectory also contains user login scripts and PRINTCON definition files.
	Mail programs compatible with NetWare use the SYS:MAIL directory.
Mandatory Profile	A server-based profile defined for the user by the domain administrator. Users cannot store changes made to a mandatory profile.
MAP	A NetWare command-line utility and login script command. It is used for creating, viewing, or changing drive mappings or search drive mappings. It may also be used to map a false Root directory. Drive mappings are not saved from session to session. They are installed during execution of a login script or at the command prompt.
Mapping	1. Mapping is the transferring of data between a disk and a computer's RAM.
	2. Attaching to a server-based directory using the local drive ID.
Memory	A hardware component of a computer system that can store information and applications for later retrieval. Types of memory are RAM (Random Access Memory), ROM (Read Only Memory), conventional, expanded, and extended memory.
Memory manager	The section of an operating system that allocates both physical memory and virtual memory.
Messaging API (MAPI)	One of the primary ways that people use the computer to communicate with each other. This is accomplished by sending messages and documents to each other via an electronic mail system.

Most companies are using at least one type of electronic mail system. Unfortunately, many companies are not using a single unified mail system for all their employees and other companies need interconnectivity with users who work for different companies.

Traditionally, corporations have installed gateways to get around this problem. However, gateways are highly specialized and can only be used to connect a particular pair of mail systems. Corporations often need a number of gateways to handle the different combinations of mail systems used by their employees and other contacts.

To resolve this problem, an API was developed which allowed for connectivity between various mail service providers and mail-aware/mail-enabled client applications. The result was the Messaging API, otherwise known as MAPI.

MAPI has a layered architecture that allows various client applications to communicate with multiple messaging systems. The main components are the client application, the MAPI subsystem, the MAP spooler, service providers, and the messaging system.

The client application is a front-end application that makes MAPI calls.

The MAPI subsystem, also known as the messaging subsystem, handles the client application's calls and provides standard user interface objects, such as dialog boxes and forms.

The MAPI spooler is responsible for forwarding the message to the appropriate transport service provider.

Service providers are responsible for translating MAPI methods to a format the messaging system can understand.

The messaging system is a back-end application that is responsible for routing messages over the network or across phone lines. Messaging systems currently available include Microsoft Mail, cc:Mail, IBM PROFS, X.400, and Novell MHS.

Migration

1. The conversion of NetWare servers from NetWare 2, NetWare 3, or from another operating system, to NetWare 4. Operating system migration is different from data migration, which is the moving of files to near-line or off-line storage devices.

2. Transfer of users, groups, directories, and files from a NetWare Server to a Windows NT Server.

3. Transfer of users, groups, and application data from one application to another.

Modem	Modem is an abbreviation for modulator/demodulator. A modem is a peripheral device that permits a personal computer, microcomputer, or mainframe to receive and transmit data in digital format across voice-oriented communications links such as telephone lines.
MS-DOS	MS-DOS is Microsoft's version of the DOS operating system.
Multicast	A special form of broadcast where copies of the packet are delivered to only a subset of all possible destinations.
Multiprocessing	The ability to execute more than one thread simultaneously.
Multitasking	A mode of operation that provides for the concurrent performance or interleaved execution of two or more tasks.

Musical Instrument Digital Interface (MIDI)

The Musical Instrument Digital Interface is a standard communications protocol for the connection of a computer to a musical synthesizer. MIDI enables musicians to compose complex music on a piano-style keyboard and then capture that information using a computer which can be used to automatically write the score.

Name resolution	The process of mapping a node name into the corresponding network address.
NDIS	The modular network driver interface standard, developed by Microsoft and 3COM. It has become an industry standard.
NDS Object Types	The NetWare Directory Services (NDS) is a database containing all network information, such as users, printers, and servers. It is important to divorce the concept of individual printers, servers, and users being on a particular server. NDS maintains these objects globally for the whole network, not on a server basis.

In the NetWare Directory Services (NDS) database, each object represents a defined item. Each object contains properties and their values for identification purposes. For example, a user is an object with a property called name; the value is the actual name itself.

Some object properties, such as name, are mandatory; while other properties, such as phone number, are optional.

The three types of objects are [ROOT], Container, and Leaf.

All objects make up the directory tree. This is a logical organization for the NDS.

At the top of each directory tree is the [ROOT] object, which is created at the time of installation. Only one [ROOT] should be created for each LAN/WAN, due to the inability of [ROOT] objects to communicate with each other. When referring to the root, it is to place brackets around the object name ("[ROOT]"). Because the [ROOT] contains all objects, it can be considered a Container object.

Container objects are objects which hold (or "contain") other objects, and are used to build the NDS and align it with an organization's work flow or structure.

NDS Object Types

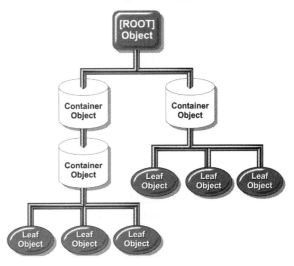

Net

Net is an Internet domain designated for networks that include network service centers, network information centers, and others items. An example is nyser.net or concentric.net.

NET.CFG

NET.CFG is a NetWare shell configuration file that can be created with a text editor and used to customize the parameters a workstation is given through the NetWare shell or DOS Requester. It is used for managing its interactions with the network, including data transmission packet handling, print jobs, and network drives.

NetBIOS

Standard programming interface for the development of distributed applications.

NetBIOS Extended User Interface (NetBEUI)

This is a non-routable transport protocol written to the NetBIOS interface.

NetBIOS Names

Microsoft networks, including workgroups and NT Server domains, always use NetBIOS names to identify workstations and servers. Machines recognize each other through unique machine names. Shared resources, files and printers, are accessed using NetBIOS names. For example, resources are identified by their Universal Naming Convention (UNC) name that uses the format \\server\share_name.

In a UNC name, *server* is the NetBIOS name of the machine where the resource is physically located, and *share_name* is the name uniquely identifying the resource.

Microsoft NetBIOS names may contain up to 15 characters and are used to identify entities to NetBIOS. These entities include computers, domain names, workgroup names, and users.

In an internetwork TCP/IP environment, it is necessary to support resolution between NetBIOS names and IP addresses. Microsoft provides two methods of supporting this name resolution: LMHOSTS and Windows Internet Naming Service (WINS).

LMHOSTS name resolution is based on a locally stored ASCII text file.

WINS Name resolution is based on WINS servers.

When designing your network, you will need to select the most appropriate method for your organizational requirements.

NetWare Client for DOS and MS Windows
Software that connects DOS and MS Windows workstations to NetWare networks and allows their users to share network resources.

NetWare Directory database
The database (commonly referred to as the Directory) that organizes NetWare Directory Services objects in a hierarchical tree setup called the Directory tree.

NetWare Directory Services (NDS)
The NetWare Directory Services (NDS) is a database containing all network information, such as users, printers, and servers. It is important to divorce the concept of individual printers, servers, and users being on a particular server. NDS maintains these objects globally for the whole network, not on a server basis.

Each server on the network "looks" to the global NDS for information on objects. Therefore, all servers and clients have access to the same information. When a network administrator makes any changes to the NDS, it is made once, and all servers "see" the new information.

This is sometimes referred to as the Directory Tree.

Network
A group of computers and other devices connected together so they can communicate with each other.

Network adapter
The card that allows a computer to interface with the network. Also known as a Network Interface Card (NIC).

Network address
1. A network number which uniquely identifies a network cable segment. It may be referred to as the IPX external network number.

2. A network address can also be the network portion of an IP address. For a Class A network, the network address is the first byte of the IP address. For a Class B network, the network address is the first two bytes of the IP address. For a Class C network, the network address is the first three bytes of the IP address. In each case, the remainder is the host address.

Network drive

The common name for a logical drive.

Network Interface Card (NIC)

Workstations communicate with each other and the network server via this circuit board which is installed in each computer. It can also be referred to as an NIC, LAN card, or network card.

Network Monitor

An SMS utility that functions as a "sniffer" and is used to capture, transmit, and display network packets.

Network printer

A printer shared by multiple computers over a network.

NETx.COM

NETx.COM is a NetWare shell file. The x represents the station's version of DOS. NET3.COM is used for DOS v3.x, NET5.COM for DOS v5.x. Novell has also released a "universal" version of this program called NETX.COM. (In this case, the X is the character "X," not representative of a number.) This version of the program works with DOS versions 3.x through 6.x. The file is automatically executed when the filename is included in the AUTOEXEC.BAT file. Novell's VLM files replace this program.

New Technology File System (NTFS)

This is the native file system for Windows NT.

Node

A device at a physical location that performs a control function and influences the flow of data in a network. Node can also refer to the points of connection in the links of a network. Any single computer connected to a network.

Non-preemptive Multitasking

Windows handles the multitasking of 16-bit applications nonpreemptively. There is one thread of execution to be shared between all 16-bit applications. An application will control the thread until the application either terminates or returns control to the operating system. Unless the application was terminated, the contents of the registers will be saved and another application will take control of the thread of execution. The contents of the registers will be restored to the values held when the controlling application was last suspended.

It is up to an application to return control to the operating system. This means that the application developer needs to divide the application into minuscule tasks or scatter PeekMessage calls throughout the application.

Dividing the application into minuscule tasks can sometimes be difficult. Some tasks, particularly those that involve nested loops, are difficult to subdivide. Writing code to handle multitasking in this manner is unnatural and unnecessarily complicated.

The PeekMessage function offers control to the operating system, which can then give control to another application. There can be a long delay between the user action and the desired response depending on the placement of PeekMessage calls. For example, if a spreadsheet application performs a complicated recalculation without calling PeekMessage, a user who clicks on a background window may not receive a response for an extended period of time.

Non-preemptive multitasking involves switching between applications, also known as tasks. It often seems that tasks are running simultaneously, but it only appears that way to the user. Each application is offering control to the operating system often enough that the user cannot distinguish the time lapse between the task from which the user is expecting response and the task that actually has control of the thread.

Problems with the non-preemptive multitasking approach are evident when the following situations occur:

One problem arises when an application has a long task to perform. For example, a user chooses to reformat a large document. If the application was written so the reformat command completes before giving control back to the operating system, the user cannot access any other 16-bit application until the operation is complete. If the user is running Windows v3.x, the user cannot access any part of the operating system.

Another problem is with application bugs. Often, a bug in an application causes a loop to be executed continuously. If there is no PeekMessage in the loop and the loop's exit condition can never be met, the operating system will never regain control of the thread of execution and the computer will appear to have "hung" or stopped.

The altering of data can be another problem. For example, a user could be running both a word processing program and a presentation program. This particular presentation program allows the user to edit word processing files. The user has opened a file with the word processing program and changed some text but not saved it. The user then runs the presentation program and notices that the text has not been changed. Next, the user opens the word processing file in the presentation program to change the text, but the file is not saved. Each version of the text is slightly different. When the user switches back to the word processing program and saves the changes, the changes made in the presentation program are lost.

Non-Windows application

An application designed to run with DOS, but not specifically with Microsoft Windows. The application may not be able to take full advantage of all Windows features, such as memory management.

Null modem

A device that connects two DTE devices directly by emulating the physical connections of a DCE device.

Online access

Refers to direct interaction with a host computer through local or long-distance telecommunications links.

Octet

A set of 8 bits or one byte.

Operating System

The software program that controls all system hardware and provides the user interface.

org

Org is an Internet domain that identifies nonprofit organizations. An example is ddn.internic.org.

Paging File

Dedicated hard disk space used to emulate RAM for virtual memory.

Parallel Ports

In a parallel interface, eight bits of data are sent at the same time, in parallel, on eight separate wires. Therefore, parallel transmissions are faster than serial transmissions.

Parallel ports, also called LPT ports, were originally used to connect line printers and terminals. Most systems have at least one parallel port, which is called LPT1.

There are two parallel standards: Bi-Tronics and Centronics (IEEE 1284). Centronics cables support a higher data rate. The Centronics connector is a 25-pin D-shell connector and is considered the standard.

Printers generally use parallel communications, as do some early notebook PC network adapters. Devices are available which allow the connection of SCSI devices to a parallel port.

Parent directory

This is the term for the directory immediately above any subdirectory. For example, SALES would be the parent of the SALES/NEW.

Password

A word or set of letters and numbers allowing access to a facility, computer, or network. A password may be accompanied by some other unique identifier before the user is allowed to login.

Path

1. In hierarchical data structures, such as operating system directories, the path is the chain from a root directory (as in MS-DOS) or volume (as in NetWare) to a specific subdirectory or file.

2. In data communications, the path is the transmission route from sending node to receiving node.

Pathname	The pathname is information that uniquely designates an item on a server. Pathnames have the form "volume/folder/.../name," where the volume is the storage device (typically a hard disk) on which the file resides, and "folder/.../" designates the series of nested folders (or, in the DOS and UNIX worlds, directories) containing the file.
	Because pathnames use the slash (/) to separate the labels they contain, it is a good idea not to use slashes in the names of HTML files even when, as on Macs, it is legal to do so. A URL will typically include a pathname.
PC Card (PCMCIA)	PCMCIA is a bus definition which defines a hardware interface that supports very small peripherals, such as credit-card-sized modems, network interface cards, hard drives, and memory cards.
PCONSOLE	An abbreviation for Print CONSOLE. A NetWare menu utility used to define queue and print server configurations, and to provide print queue and print server information and control.
Peer	A Windows Socket application that functions as both a server and a client.
Peer-to-peer	Communication in which two communications systems communicate as equal partners sharing the processing and control of the exchange, as opposed to host-terminal communication in which the host does most of the processing and controls the exchange.
Persistent connection	A network connection that is restored each time the workstation or user logs on to the network.
PING	This utility is used to test the presence of other computers on the network. You can use IP addresses or NetBIOS names if you have a WINS server running or have made the appropriate entry in the LMHOSTS file.
Pitch	In printing, pitch refers to the number of characters per horizontal inch and is related to the character point size. Some fonts use a fixed pitch, where the spacing is the same for each character. Many fonts use a variable or proportional pitch, where each character has a different width. Overall, controlling the pitch makes for a better document appearance.
Pixel	A pixel (sometimes called a pel) is an individual picture element. This is the smallest single element that can be displayed on the screen. Screen resolution is given in horizontal and vertical pixel counts. The more pixels, the greater the resolution.
Point-to-Point Protocol (PPP)	
	The successor to the SLIP protocol, PPP allows a computer to use a regular telephone line and a modem to make IP connections. PPP can also carry other routable protocols such as IPX.

Port	1. A memory address that identifies the physical circuit used to transfer information between a microprocessor and a peripheral.
	2. On the Internet, "port" often refers to a number that is part of a URL, appearing after a colon (:), immediately after the domain name. Every service on an Internet server "listens" on a particular port number on that server. Most services have standard port numbers. Web servers normally listen on port 80. Services can also listen on non-standard ports, in which case the port number must be specified in a URL when accessing the server. You might see a URL of the form: gopher:// peg.cwis.uci.edu:7000/ which shows a gopher server running on a non-standard port (the standard gopher port is 70).
	3. Port also refers to translating a piece of software from one type of computer system to another, for example, translating a Windows program that will run on a Macintosh.
Postoffice	Microsoft Mail message store element.
PostScript	PostScript is a registered trademark of Adobe Corporation and is the accepted language standard for high resolution printing on laser printers. PostScript is a language used to tell the printer how to print a character on the page. PostScript uses vector information to define graphics. Some printers, such as Apple LaserWriter printers, are true PostScript printers. Some printers use PostScript emulation, either at the system or in the printer.
Power On Self Test (POST)	
	When you first start a PC, it will go through a Power On Self Test (POST). The various parts of the computer are checked in a particular order. If errors are detected, they are reported to the user.
	The first part tested is the basic system. This includes the microprocessor, bus, and system memory. The extended system is checked next (the system timer, and, if installed, the ROM BASIC interpreter).
	The third group tested is related to the video display. The video signals and display-adapter memory are tested. If there is more than one display adapter installed, only the primary adapter is tested.
	The memory is tested next. All addressable memory (conventional and extended) is tested through a write/read test.
	The keyboard interface is tested, and the keyboard checked for malfunctioning (stuck) keys.
	Finally, the system will then determine if any disk drives (floppy and/or hard disks) are installed. If so, they are then tested.

POST errors are reported as audio beeps and numeric error codes. While many manufacturer's codes are similar, you will want to refer to documentation for your particular system to identify any error messages.

Power Supply	A PC's power supply is a device that takes the AC (alternating current) electric current from the wall and converts it into the DC (direct current) current required by the computer.
	The power supply outputs four discreet voltages: +5 VDC, -5 VDC, +12 VDC, and -12 VDC. Spikes are smoothed out with capacitors connected across the power supply leads.
	For a list of power supply manufacturers and their home pages, see www.yahoo.com/Business_and_Economy/Companies/Computers/ Hardware/Components/Power_Supplies.
Preemptive multitasking	A multitasking method where the operating system allocates processor time to tasks according to their relative priority.
Print queue	A network directory which stores print jobs. The print server takes the print job out of the queue and sends it when the printer is ready. It can hold as many print jobs as disk space allows.
Print server	A network computer, either dedicated or non-dedicated, used to handle the printing needs of workstations.
Print Spooler	A program that allows background printing so that a computer may be used for other processing tasks while a print job is in progress.
Printer	A printer is a peripheral hardware device that produces printed material.
Printer Control Language (PCL)	
	Hewlett Packard developed PCL for its own LaserJet printers. PCL instructs the printer on how to construct the output on a page. A large number of other manufacturers also support the HP PCL language.
Printer driver	A program which translates the file that is printed into the language the printer understands. A printer cannot be used unless the correct driver is installed.
Printer fonts	Fonts which are built into the printer. They may also be downloadable soft fonts.
Printer languages	In addition to simple control characters, more advanced printers (such as laser printers) support a command and control language, which allows for even greater application support. PCL (Hewlett-Packard) and PostScript (Adobe) are two primary, de facto industry standards for printer languages.
Printer Port	A communications port located on the rear panel of a computer-designed for the connection of a printer.

Process	Once a 32-bit application is launched, it is loaded into memory. It receives a block of memory addresses. A process cannot execute any commands and does not use any processor time.
Program Information File (PIF)	A file used by Microsoft Windows and Windows NT to provide parameters necessary for running non-Windows applications.
Property sheet	A grouping of an object's properties that can be viewed or changed.
Protocol	1. A set of strict rules (usually developed by a standards committee) that govern the exchange of information between computer devices. Also, a set of semantic and syntactic rules that determine the behavior of hardware and software in achieving communication.
	2. PROTOCOL is also a NetWare v3.x console command that displays the protocols registered on a file server, along with the names of their frame types and protocol identification numbers as included by the LAN driver when it is installed.
Proxy	1. Proxy is the mechanism whereby one system "fronts for" another system in responding to protocol requests. Proxy systems are used in network management to avoid implementing full protocol stacks in simple devices, such as modems.
	A copy of an out-of-process component's interfaces. Its role is to marshal method and property calls across process boundaries.
PUBLIC	A NetWare directory that contains files in general use, such as utilities and overlay, and other files used for running menu utilities. Public files are available to all users and are placed in PUBLIC.
Random Access Memory (RAM)	RAM is the computer's storage area to write, store, and retrieve information and program instructions so they can be used by the central processing unit. The contents of RAM are not permanent.
RCONSOLE	An abbreviation for Remote CONSOLE. It is a NetWare v3.x, v4.x, and Portable NetWare menu utility that allows a workstation to be used as a virtual file server console.
Remote access	The ability of a computer to access an offsite or distant computer using telephone lines or a network.
Remote Management	Use of a remote console by a network supervisor or by a remote console operator to perform file server tasks.

Resolution	In monitors, this refers to the sharpness of the displayed image or text on a monitor and is a direct function of the number of pixels in the display area. Resolution is the number of pixels across one line of the monitor by the number of lines down the screen (for example, 800x480). The greater the pixel count, the higher the resolution and the clearer the screen image.
Resources	Objects an application needs, such as icons, cursors, and regions.
Restore	To bring back computer data or files that have been lost through tampering or other corruption or through hardware malfunction. Files should be backed up frequently to protect against such loss.
Root directory	The first-level directory of a disk, created when the user first formats a disk and then is able to create files and subdirectories in it.
Router	1. A connection between two networks that specifies message paths and may perform other functions, such as data compression. 2. In early versions of NetWare, the term bridge was sometimes used interchangeably with the term router.
Screensaver	A system utility used to prevent monitor damage by powering the video monitor down or displaying a moving graphic.
Serial Port	In a serial interface bits of information are sent in a series, one at a time. Data bits are typically surrounded by starting and ending flags which provide synchronization. Serial ports are also called communications (COM) ports and referenced by number; COM1 is serial port 1. Most systems come with two COM ports. The standard serial port connector is a 9-pin D-shell connector, but some systems still have older 25-pin D-shell connectors. Adapters are available to convert between the two standard connectors. With either connector, only nine connector pins are soldered to nine wires inside the cable. Most serial cables are no longer than 50 feet. Use of longer cables can result in transmission errors. Modems, serial printers, and serial mice use serial communications. A new bus type, the Universal Serial Bus (USB), will become more prevalent in the future. The concept behind the USB is to consolidate all desktop peripherals into a single high-speed (12 Mbps) access route. The USB allows up to 64 devices to be daisy-chained together. The single USB connector type will support many devices, including some that in the past used the serial, parallel, keyboard, mouse, or game ports.

The USB will usher in a new set of hardware peripherals and accessories, including products such as digital cameras and virtual-reality gloves.

More information about USB can be found at the Universal Bus Implementers Forum Home Page: www.usb.org

Server

A computer or a software package that provides services to client software running on other computers on a network. Possible services include file sharing, printer sharing, or communications services.

Service Advertising Protocol (SAP)

The protocol used by NetWare service providers such as file server, print server, etc., to notify network elements of services provided on the network.

SETPASS

An abbreviation for SET PASSword. It is a NetWare command-line utility used to create or change a user's password to the file server. The password can have up to 127 characters.

Share name

The name give to a shared resource. The universal naming convention references machine name and share name.

Shortcut

A technique that allows a Windows 95 or Windows NT user to create a link to a file or program in an alternative location.

Simple Mail Transfer Protocol (SMTP)

The Internet standard protocol for transferring electronic mail messages between computers.

Simple Network Management Protocol (SNMP)

The Simple Network Management Protocol (SNMP) is one of the most comprehensive tools available for TCP/IP network management. It operates through conversations between SNMP agents and management systems. Through these conversations, the SNMP management systems can collect statistics from and modify configuration parameters on agents.

The agents are any component running the SNMP agent service and are capable of being managed remotely. Agents can include minicomputers, mainframes, workstations, servers, bridges, routers, gateways, terminal servers, and wiring hubs.

Management stations are typically more powerful workstations. Common implementations are Windows NT or UNIX stations running a product such as HP OpenView, IBM Systemview/6000, or Cabletron Spectrum. The software provides a graphic representation of the network, allowing you to move through network hierarchy to the individual device level.

There are three basic commands used in SNMP conversations: GET, SET, and TRAP.

The GET command is used by the management station to retrieve a specific parameter value from an SNMP agent. If a combination of parameters is grouped together on an agent, GET-NEXT retrieves the next item in a group. For example, a management system's graphic representation of a hub includes the state of all status lights. This information is gathered through GET and GET-NEXT.

The management system uses SET to change a selected parameter on an SNMP agent. For example, SET would be used by the management system to disable a failing port on a hub.

SNMP agents send TRAP packets to the management system in response to extraordinary events, such as a line failure on a hub. When the hub status light goes red on the management systems representation, it is in response to a TRAP.

An SNMP management station generates GET and SET commands. Agents are able to respond to SET and GET and to generate TRAP commands.

SLIP
An Internet protocol used to run IP over serial lines such as telephone circuits or RS-232 cables interconnecting two systems. SLIP is now being replaced by PPP.

Small Computer Systems Interface (SCSI)
A high-speed interface bus used for disk drives, scanners, printers, CD-ROM drives, digital cameras, and other devices. Available in several versions including SCSI-I, SCSI-II (Fast SCSI), Wide (16-bit data path) or UltraWide.

Socket
The destination of an IPX packet is represented by this part of an IPX internetwork address in a network node. Some sockets are reserved by Novell for specific applications; all NCP request packets are delivered to socket 451h. By registering those numbers with Novell, third-party developers can reserve socket numbers for specific purposes.

SPOOL
NetWare v3.x console command used to list, create, or change spooler assignments.

Spooler
System software used to provide background printing.

SPX
SPX is abbreviated for Sequenced Packet eXchange. It is the Novell protocol used as the resident protocol in NetWare, along with IPX.

Start menu
The pop-up menu containing Windows 95 functions that is accessed by pressing the Start button on the Taskbar.

Startup disk
The system boot drive. May be a floppy disk, hard disk, CD-ROM, or other drive.

Subdirectory
This is a directory that lies below another in the file system structure. For example, in SALES/NEW, NEW is a subdirectory of SALES.

Subnet	The primary reason to divide a network into subnets is network performance and available bandwidth. Without separate networks, each transmission would be broadcast across the entire internetwork, waiting for the destination system to respond. As the network grows, this causes increases in traffic until it exceeds the available bandwidth.

Subnets

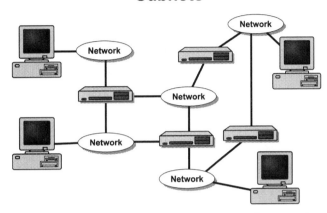

Routers divide, as well as provide communications between the networks. Packets bound for a destination within the local network are kept local. Only packets bound for other networks are broadcast across the network, moving from router to router. Overall traffic levels are reduced.

Subnet mask	A filter which separates subnetted addresses into network and local entities. Local systems have subnet masks so they can restrict the broadcast to be received on the local network only.
Subnetting	When a complex network is recognized as a single address from outside of the network.
Super VGA	Super VGA is also known as VGA Plus, Extended VGA, and abbreviated SVGA. It provides analog output by varying the intensity of the three primary colors. SVGA provides higher resolutions than VGA.
Suspend	An action that causes an active program to become temporarily inactive. In effect, the suspended program is waiting for the user to reactivate it.
Swap file	A file that contains temporary data moved out of main storage to the swap file on disk. A swap file is sometimes known as a paging file.
Swapping	A process that interchanges the contents of an area of main storage with the contents of an area of auxiliary storage. Swapping is sometimes known as paging.

SYSCON	An abbreviation for SYStem CONfiguration. It is a NetWare menu utility used to control network accounting and information.
SYSTEM	A directory automatically created in NetWare's SYS volume when a network is installed. SYSTEM contains NetWare utilities that are used only by network supervisors and must not be deleted,.
SYSTEM.INI	An initialization file used by Microsoft Windows. It contains hardware- and setup-specific information used for the operation of Windows. It includes printer driver references and other device driver information.
T1	A leased-line connection capable of carrying data at 1,544,000 bps. At maximum theoretical capacity, a T1 line could move a megabyte in less than 10 seconds. That is still not fast enough for full-screen, full-motion video, for which you need at least 10,000,000 bps. T1 is the fastest speed commonly used to connect networks to the Internet.
Task	In a multiprogramming or multiprocessing environment, one or more sequences of instructions created by a control program as an element of work to be accomplished by a computer.
Taskbar	The Windows 95 user interface element that shows the running applications and open windows.
Threads	Each process must have at least one thread. Threads are responsible for executing code.
Transmission Control Protcol (TCP)	The reliable connection-oriented protocol used by DARPA (Defense Advanced Research Projects Agency) for their internetworking research. TCP uses a three-way handshake with a clock-based sequence number selection to synchronize connecting entities and to minimize the chance of erroneous connections due to delayed messages. TCP is usually used with IP (Internet Protocol), the combination being known as TCP/IP.
Transmission Control Protocol/Internet Protocol (TCP/IP)	Originally designed for WANs (Wide Area Networks), TCP/IP was developed in the 1970's to link the research center of the U.S. Government's Defense Advanced Research Projects Agency. TCP/IP is a protocol that enables communication between the same or different types of computers on a network. TCP/IP can be carried over a wide range of communication channels. The Transmission Control Protocol is connection-oriented and monitors the correct transfer of data between computers. The Internet Protocol is stream-oriented and breaks data into packets.
Transmission rate	The transmission rate is stated in baud or bps. If the connection cannot be made at the selected transmission rate, most modems and communications software will automatically attempt to connect at a slower speed.

Trust relationships	Trust relationships are only significant in a multiple domain environment. A trust relationship is a one-way logical relationship established between two Windows NT Server domains. Once established, the domains are referred to as the trusted domain and the trusting domain.
	The trusted domain can be assigned rights and permissions in the trusting domain. In other words, the trusting domain says, "I trust you to access my resources." This is a One-Way Trust Relationship.
	The trusted domain does not automatically receive rights or permissions in the trusting domain. These must be explicitly assigned. The trust relationship makes it possible for these assignments to be made.
	You can also have Two-Way Trust Relationships, which is a mutual trust between domains. This is established as two one-way trusts, one in each direction.
Trusting domain	The domain granting security rights and permissions to another (trusted) domain.
Two-way trust	A trust relationship where there is mutual trust between two domains.
Uniform Resource Locator (URL)	
	A URL is the pathname of a document on the Internet. URLs can be absolute or relative. An absolute URL consists of a prefix denoting a "method" (http for Web sites, gopher for gophers, and so forth). The prefix is followed by a colon and two slashes (://), and an address. The address consists of a domain name followed by a slash and a pathname (or 'username@domain name' for mailto). The last part is an optional anchor which is preceded by a #. The # symbol points to a place within the Web page.
Uninterruptible Power Supply (UPS)	
	If power loss, surges or drops (brownouts) are a significant concern, an Uninterruptible Power Supply (UPS) may be your best option. With a UPS, line voltage is fed into a battery keeping it constantly charged. The computer is, in turn, powered from the battery. Because the computer is already running from the battery, there is no switching time if power is lost. UPS systems supply protection against power events more effectively than most other devices. Uninterruptible Power Supplies are considered essential for network servers. If normal power is lost or interrupted, the UPS allows time to safely shut down the file server. Many UPSs can alert network users to warn when the system is going down.
	When selecting a UPS, examine the software and hardware available for the UPS. Options and features vary greatly.

Universal Naming Convention (UNC)

A file-naming convention that uses the //*machine_name*/*share_name* format.

Upload

A process where a user copies a file "up" to a host computer. Opposite of download.

User Datagram Protocol (UDP)

A transport protocol in the Internet suite of protocols. UDP, like TCP, uses IP for delivery. However, unlike TCP, UDP provides for exchange of datagrams without acknowledgements or guaranteed delivery.

User login script

This login script sets environment specifics for a user. It is optional, but most often used for items that cannot be included in a system or profile login script. If used, it will run after container and profile login scripts.

User Manager

A Windows NT user and group administration utility.

User Manager for Domains

User Manager for Domains is a utility installed on all NT Server systems. On additional servers it is operationally identical to the Windows NT Workstation version of the utility, User Manager. The utility is also installed as part of the NT Server remote management tools.

When User Manager for Domains is started, the current domain users and groups are displayed. Domain Administrators and Account Operators can view and modify users and groups by selecting the appropriate account and running Properties from the User menu, or by double-clicking on the account. Administrators can manage any account.

Additional menu selections let you create and manage accounts, select the sort order for account names, manage domain policies, and establish trust relationships.

User name

The name by which a login ID is known within the context of a database.

User profile

Environment configuration settings applied when a user logs on to a Windows 95 workstation in either a peer-to-peer network or a mixed networking environment including a Windows NT workstation or Windows NT Server domain. Either a user profile, a roving profile, or a mandatory profile is applied for the user. Each user is given either a personal or a mandatory profile.

Utility

The capability of a system, program, or device to perform the functions for which it is designed.

Video card

The hardware board that contains the electronic circuitry to drive a video display monitor.

Video Graphics Array (VGA)

VGA uses a DAC chip and sends analog signals at varying intensities to alter the three primary colors. By varying the intensity, a seemingly infinite number of color variations can be produced and displayed on the monitor.

Virtual machine

The Windows technique used to execute an application. Virtual machines include a virtual address space, processor registers, and privileges.

Virtual memory

Some operating systems have the ability to increase the apparent physical system memory through virtual memory. Virtual Memory is a file on the hard disk that emulates physical Random Access Memory (RAM). This file is called a swap file.

With virtual memory, a portion of the program and data is kept in RAM at all times, with the remainder stored on the disk. This is normally referred to as "swapping" the information to the disk. When an attempt is made to access code or data on the disk, it is swapped back into RAM, and if necessary, other code or data will be swapped out to make room available. The swapping process is controlled by the VMM (Virtual Memory Manager).

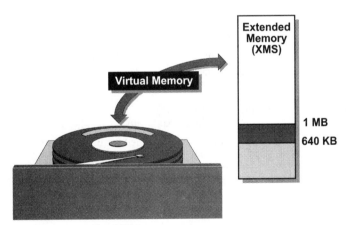

Hard Disk

Except for a loss of performance when swapping occurs, virtual memory is transparent to the user and application.

Virtual memory gives you more memory, providing the ability to launch more concurrent applications and work with larger data files. The system's capabilities are increased, but at a small performance decrease. Adding more physical memory will still provide better system performance.

Web browser   A Web browser is a client program that serves as the interface between the user and the resources of the World Wide Web.

What You See is What You Get (WYSIWYG)
                             WYSIWYG is a word processing term which means that what is seen on the computer screen will correspond to what prints out on paper. This includes typeface, layout, and size.

Wide Area Networks (WANs)
                             Wide Area Networks (WANs) expand the basic LAN model by linking Local Area Networks (LANs), and allowing them to communicate with each other. By traditional definition, a LAN becomes a WAN when it crosses a public right-of-way, requiring a public carrier for data transmission. More current usage of the term usually includes any situation where a network expands beyond one location/building. A WAN is characterized by low- to high-speed communication links, and usually covers a wide geographic area. The remote links may be operational LANs or only groups of workstations. With the exception of a WAN's wider area of operation, the benefits and features of LANs and WANs are the same.

Wildcard characters   Characters that have special meaning when used in pattern-matching strings. They can represent one character or any number of characters or exclude certain characters.

WIN.INI file   An initialization file used by Microsoft Windows. The file contains settings used to customize the Windows environment. Windows applications will sometimes store initialization information in the WIN.INI file.

Windows Internet Naming Service (WINS)
                             A Windows NT utility that translates a NetBIOS name into an IP address. It is designed for use in a routed network.

Workgroup   A defined set of Windows for Workgroups, Windows 95, or NT stations that are able to communicate and share file and print resources.

World Wide Web (WWW)

The World Wide Web (WWW) is a recent and fast-growing addition to the Internet.

In 1991, Tim Berners-Lee developed the World Wide Web for the European Council for Nuclear Research (CERN). It was designed as a means of communicating research and ideas between members of the high-energy physics community.

Browsers are the client tools that allow users to view the contents of the Web. The Web at that time had no easily accessible viewing capabilities. The browsers were text-only, line-mode tools that offered no graphical capabilities and few navigation links.

Early in 1993, a team at the National Center for Supercomputing Applications (NCSA) at the University of Illinois at Champaign-Urbana developed an Internet browsing program called Mosaic. The NCSA had no way to disseminate or market the program.

Later that year, a former NCSA graduate student (Tim Krauskopf) offered the University of Illinois a business plan and was given the rights to license Mosaic. The company is called Spyglass. Another company, with the help of former NCSA programmers, created its own Internet browser company and wanted to call it Mosaic Communications, but the NCSA would not allow this. The company was renamed Netscape, and their graphical Web browser, was named Netscape Navigator. Netscape markets their browsers and servers directly to consumers, while Spyglass markets Mosaic to component suppliers such as AT&T, IBM, and Microsoft.

Because the Mosaic project initiated the graphical browser implementation, the term Mosaic is sometimes still used to describe any graphical Web browser.

The Web unifies many of the existing network tools with hypertext (also called hyperlinks). HyperText gives users the ability to explore paths of information in non-linear ways. Instead of reading through files in a pre-planned sequential arrangement, users can move from item to item in any order they choose.

Some hyperlinks lead to ftp sites, newsgroups, gopher sites, and other Web sites which house additional graphical Web documents. To navigate these Web sites and find links, search engines are available. While current engines can only identify sites that meet the user's criteria, second generation search engines will use artificial intelligence to report to users on information that exactly meets their needs.

The graphical interfaces make the Internet much more appealing, powerful, and simple. Besides being more intuitive than text-based tools, graphical browsers offer full hypermedia support. As recently as 1994, few trade journals mentioned the Web.

Today, Web addresses (URLs) are included in television, radio, magazine, and movie advertisements, and on billboards. By 1995, Web traffic was doubling every four months, and was growing more than twice as fast as general Internet traffic. Entire businesses now reside on the Web and millions of people use it as a communications and educational resources.

– ACRONYMS –

-A-

AAL	ATM Adaptation Layer
Abend	Abnormal end
ABR	Automatic Baud Rate Detection
ACDI	Asynchronous Communications Device Interface
ACE	Access Control Entry
ACF/VTAM	Advanced Communications Function/Virtual Telecommunications Access Method
ACK	Acknowledgement
ACL	Access Control List
ACSE	Association Control Service Element
AD	Administrative Domain
ADB	Apple Desktop Bus
ADMD	Administration Management Domain
ADSP	AppleTalk Data Stream Protocol
AEP	AppleTalk Echo Protocol
AFP	AppleTalk Filing Protocol
AIFF	Audio Interchange File Format
ANI	Automatic Number Identification
ANSI	American National Standards Institute
AOW	Asia and Oceania Workshop
APA	All Points Addressable
API	Application Program Interface
APPC	Advanced Program-to-Program Communications
ARA	AppleTalk Remote Access
ARP	Address Resolution Protocol
ARPA	Advanced Research Project Agency
ARPANET	Advanced Research Projects Agency Network
ARQ	Automatic Request for Retransmission

ASCII	American Standard Code for Information Interchange
ASMP	Asymmetric Multiprocessing
ASN.1	Abstract Syntax Notation One
ASP	AppleTalk Session Protocol
ATM	Asynchronous Transfer Mode
ATP	AppleTalk Transaction Protocol
AUI	Attachment Unit Interface
AUP	Acceptable Use Policy
AWG	American Wire Gauge
-B-	
BBS	Bulletin Board System
bcp	Bulk Copy Program
BDC	Backup Domain Controller
BER	Basic Encoding Rules
BIOS	Basic Input/Output System
BISDN	Broadband ISDN
bit	Binary Digits
BITNET	Because It's Time Network
BNC	British Naval Connector
BOC	Bell Operating Company
Bps	Bytes per second
bps	Bits per second
BRI	Basic Rate Interface
BSC	Binary Synchronous Communications
BSD	Berkeley Software Distribution
BTAM	Basic Telecommunications Access Method
-C-	
CAP	Competitive Access Provider
CATV	Community Antenna Television
CBR	Constant Bit Rate
CBT	Computer-Based Training
CCITT	International Consultative Committee for Telegraphy and Telephony

CCL	Common Command Language
CCR	Commitment, Concurrency, and Recovery
CCTV	Closed-Circuit Television
CD-ROM	Compact Disc Read-only Memory
CERN	European Laboratory for Particle Physics
CERT	Computer Emergency Response Team
CGA	Color Graphics Adapter
CGI	Common Gateway Interface
CICS	Customer Information Control System
CIR	Commited Information Rate
CISC	Complex Instruction Set Computer
CIX	Commercial Internet Exchange
CLNP	ConnectionLess Network Protocol
CLTP	ConnectionLless Transport Protocol
CMIP	Common Management Information Protocol
CMOS	Complementary Metal Oxide Semiconductor
CMOT	CMIP Over TCP
CN	Common Name
CO	Central Office
Codec	Coder-decoder
CONP	Connection Oriented Network Protocol
COS	Corporation for Open Systems
COSINE	Cooperation for Open Systems Interconnection Networking in Europe
CPE	Customer Premise Equipment
CPI	Common Programming Interface
cps	Characters per second
CPU	Central Processing Unit
CRC	Cyclic Redundancy Check
CREN	Corporation for Research and Educational Networking
CRT	Cathode Ray Tube
CSMA	Carrier Sense Multiple Access
CSMA/CA	Carrier Sense Multiple Access with Collision Avoidance

CSMA/CD	Carrier Sense Multiple Access with Collision Detection
CSNET	Computer Science Network
CSU	Customer Service Unit
CU	Control Unit
-D-	
DAC	Digital to Analog Converter
DACS	Digital Access Cross Connects
DARPA	Defense Advanced Research Projects Agency
DAV	Digital Audio Video
DB2	IBM Data Base 2
DBCS	Double Byte Character String
DBMS	Database Management System
DBO	Database Owner
DBOO	Database Object Owner
DCA	Defense Communications Agency
DCE	Distributed Computing Environment
DCE	Data Communications Equipment
DD	Double Density
DDE	Dynamic Data Exchange
DDL	Data Definition Language
DDM	Distributed Data Management Architecture
DDN	Defense Data Network
DDP	Datagram Delivery Protocol
DES	Data Encryption Standard
DET	Directory Entry Table
DFT	Distributed Function Terminals
DID	Direct Inward Dial
DIMM	Dual, In-line Memory Module
DISA	Defense Information Systems Agency
DIX	Digital, Intel, Xerox
DLC	Data Link Control
DLCI	Data Link Connection Identifier

DLL	Dynamic- link library
DMA	Direct Memory Access
DMI	Digital Multiplexed Interface
DML	Data Manipulation Language
DNS	Domain Name System
DOS	Disk Operating System
dpi	Dots per inch
DQDB	Distributed Queue Dual Bus
DRAM	Dynamic Random Access Memory
DS	Data set
DS	Double-Sided
DS1	Digital Signaling Level 1
DS2	Digital Signaling Level 2
DS3	Digital Signaling Level 3
DSA	Directory System Agent
DSDD	Double-Sided, Double-Density
DSE	Data Service Equipment
DSHD	Double-Sided, High-Density
DSP	Digital Signal Processor
DSU	Data Service Unit
DTE	Data Terminal Equipment
DTR	Data Terminal Ready
DUA	Directory User Agent
DXF	Drawing interchange Format
DXI	Data Exchange Interface
-E-	
E-mail	Electronic mail
EARN	European Academic and Research Network
EBCDIC	Extended Binary-Coded Decimal Interchange Code
ECF	Enhanced Connectivity Facilities
EDI	Electronic Data Interchange
EEHLLAPI	Entry Emulator High-Level Language Application Program Interface

EFF	Electronic Frontier Foundation
EGA	Enhanced Graphics Adapter
EGP	Exterior Gateway Protocol
EIDE	Enhanced IDE
EMS	Expanded Memory
EPS or EPSF	Encapsulated PostScript File
ER Model	Entity/Relationship Model
ES-IS	End System-Intermediate System
ESDI	Enhanced Industry Standard Architecture
ESF	Extended Super Frame
EUnet	European UNIX Network
EUUG	European UNIX Users Group
EWOS	European Workshop for Open Systems
-F-	
FAQ	Frequently Asked Questions
FARNET	Federation of American Research NETworks
FAT	File Allocation Table
FCB	File Control Block
FCC	Federal Communications Commission
FCS	Frame Check Sequence
FDDI	Fiber Distributed Data Interface
FEP	Front End Processor
FFAPI	File Format API
FIPS	Federal Information Processing Standard
FM	Frequency Modulation
FNC	Federal Networking Council
FPU	Floating Point Unit
FRICC	Federal Research Internet Coordinating Committee
FT1	Fractional T1
FT3	Fractional T3
FTAM	File Transfer, Access, and Management
FTP	File Transfer Protocol

FYI	For Your Information
-G-	
GDI	Graphics Device Interface
GIF	Graphics Interchange Format
GOSIP	Government OSI Profile
GUI	Graphical User Interface
-H-	
HAL	Hardware Abstraction Layer
HCSS	High Capacity Storage System
HD	High-Density
HDLC	High-level Data Link Control
HDX	Half-duplex
HFS	Hierarchical File System
HLLAPI	High-Level Language Application Program Interface
HMA	High Memory Area
HPFS	High Performance File System
HTML	Hypertext Markup Language
HTTP	Hypertext Transfer Protocol
Hz	Hertz
-I-	
IAB	Internet Activities Board
ICMP	Internet Control Message Protocol
IDE	Integrated Drive Electronics
IEEE	Institute of Electrical and Electronics Engineers
IESG	Internet Engineering Steering Group
IETF	Internet Engineering Task Force
IFS	Installable File System
IGP	Interior Gateway Protocol
IGRP	Internet Gateway Routing Protocol
IIS	Internet Information Server
IMHO	In My Humble Opinion
INTAP	Interoperability Technology Association for Information Processing

IONL	Internal Organization of the Network Layer
IP	Internet Protocol
IPX	Internetwork Packet Exchange
IPXODI	Internetwork Packet Exchange Open Data-Link Interface
IRC	Internet Relay Chat
IRQ	Interrupt Request Lines
IRTF	Internet Research Task Force
IS-IS	Intermediate System-Intermediate System
ISAPI	Microsoft Internet Server Application Programming Interface
ISDN	Integrated Services Digital Network
ISO	International Standards Organization
ISODE	ISO Development Environment
ISP	Internet Service Provider
IXC	Inter-exchange Carrier
-J-	
JANET	Joint Academic Network
JPEG	Joint Photographic Experts Group
JUNET	Japan UNIX Network
-K-	
KB	Kilobyte
Kb	Kilobit
KBps	Kilobytes per second
Kbps	Kilobits per second
-L-	
L2PDU	Layer Two Protocol Data Unit
L3PDU	Layer Three Protocol Data Unit
LAN	Local Area Network
LAPB	Link Access Protocol Balanced
LAPD	Link Access Protocol Device
LAPS	LAN Adapter and Protocol Support
LATA	Local Access and Transport Area
LCD	Liquid Crystal Diode

LDT	Local Descriptor Table
LEC	Local Exchange Carriers
LEN	Low Entry Networking
LLAP	LocalTalk Link Access Protocol
LMI	Local Management Interface
lpi	Lines per inch
LSL	Link Support Layer
LU	Logical Unit
-M-	
MAC	Media Access Control Sublayer
MAN	Metropolitan Area Network
MAP	Manufacturing Automation Protocol
MAPI	Messaging API
MAU	Multi-Station Attachment Unit
MB	Megabyte
Mb	Megabit
MBps	Megabytes per second
Mbps	Megabits per second
MCGA	Multi-Color Gate Array
MDI	Multiple Document Interface
MHS	Message Handling System
MHz	Megahertz
MIB	Management Information Base
MIDI	Musical Instrument Digital Interface
MILNET	Military Network
MIME	Multipurpose Internet Mail Extensions
MIPS	Million Instructions Per Second
MLID	Multiple Link Interface Driver
MOO	Mud, Object Oriented
MPEG	Moving Pictures Experts Group
ms	Milliseconds
MTA	Message Transfer Agent

MTU	Maximum Transmission Unit
MUD	Multi-User Dungeon or Dimension
MVS	Multiple Virtual Storage
MVS-CICS	Multiple Virtual Storage-Customer Information Control System
MVS/TSO	Multiple Virtual Storage/Time-Sharing Option
-N-	
NAK	Negative AcKnowledgment
NBP	Name Binding Protocol
NCC	NetWare Control Center
NCP	NetWare Core Protocol
NCP	Network Control Point
NCSA	National Center for Supercomputing Applications
NDS	NetWare Directory Services
NetBEUI	NetBIOS Extended User Interface
NetWare DA	NetWare Desk Accessory
NFS	Network File System
NIC	Network Information Center
NIC	Network Interface Card
NIST	National Institute of Standards and Technology
NLM	NetWare Loadable Module
NLQ	Near Letter Quality
NLSP	NetWare Link Services Protocol
NMS	Network Management Station
NNS	NetWare Name Service
NNTP	Network News Transfer Protocol
NOC	Network Operations Center
NREN	National Research and Education Network
NSAP	Network Service Access Point
NSEPro	Network Support Encyclopedia Professional Volume
NSEPro	Network Support Encyclopedia Professional Edition
NSF	National Science Foundation
NSFnet	National Science Foundation Network

NT	Windows NT
NT1	Network Termination 1
NT2	Network Termination 2
NTAS	Windows NT Advanced Server
NTFS	New Technology File System
NTP	Network Time Protocol
NWADMIN	Network Administrator
-O-	
OBS	Optical Bypass Switch
ODI	Open Datalink Interface
OIW	Workshop for Implementors of OSI
OLE	Object Linking and Embedding
ONC	Open Network Computing
OOP	Object-oriented programming
OPAC	Online Public Access Catalog
OSI	Open Systems Interconnection
OSPF	Open Shortest Path First
-P-	
PAD	Packet Assembler/Disassembler
PAP	Printer Access Protocol
PBX	Private Branch Exchange
PCI	Peripheral Component Interconnect
PCI	Protocol Control Information
PCL	Printer Control Language
PCM	Pulse code modulation
PCMCIA	Personal Computer Memory Card International Association
PDC	Primary Domain Controller
PDF	Printer Definition Files
PDN	Packet Data Network
PDS	Processor-Direct Slot
PDU	Protocol Data Unit
PID	Process Identification Number

PIF	Program Information File
Ping	Packet internet groper
PMMU	Paged Memory Management Unit
POP	Point of Presence
POP	Post Office Protocol
POSI	Promoting Conference for OSI
POST	Power On Self Test
POTS	Plain Old Telephone Service
ppm	pages per minute
PPP	Point-to-Point Protocol
PPTP	Point-to-Point Tunneling Protocol
PRAM	Parameter RAM
PRI	Primary Rate Interface
PRMD	Private Management Domain
PROFS	Professional Office System
PSN	Packet Switch Node
PU	Physical Unit
PUC	Public Utility Commission
PVC	Permanent Virtual Circuit
-Q-	
QMF	Query Manager Facility
-R-	
RAID	Redundant Array of Independent Disks
RAM	Random Access Memory
RARE	Reseaux Associes pour la Recherche Europeenne
RARP	Reverse Address Resolution Protocol
RAS	Remote Access Service
RAS	Remote Access Server
RBOC	Regional Bell Operating Company
REM	REMARK
RFC	Request For Comments
RFS	Remote File System

RIP	Raster Image Processor
RIP	Router Information Protocol
RIPE	Reseaux IP Europeenne
RISC	Reduced Instruction Set Computer
ROM	Read-Only Memory
ROSE	Remote Operations Service Element
RPC	Remote Procedure Call
RTF	Rich Text Format
RTMP	Routing Table Maintenance Protocol
RTSE	Reliable Transfer Service Element
-S-	
SAA	Systems Application Architecture
SAP	Service Access Point
SAP	Service Advertising Protocol
SAPI	Service Access Point Identifier
SAPS	Service Access Point Stations
SAR	Segmentation and Reassembly protocol
SCSI	Small Computer Systems Interface
SDH	Synchronous Digital Hierarchy
SDI	Storage Device Interface
SDLC	Synchronous Data Link Control
SDN	Software Defined Network
SDU	SMDS Data Unit
SFT	System Fault Tolerance
SGML	Standard Generalized Markup Language
SGMP	Simple Gateway Management Protocol
SID	Security Identifier
SIMM	Single, In-line Memory Module
SIP	SMDS Interface Protocol
SLIP	Serial Line IP
SMDS	Switched Multimegabit Data Service
SMI	Structure of Management Information

SMP	Symmetric Multiprocessing
SMS	Storage Management Services
SMTP	Simple Mail Transfer Protocol
SNA	System Network Architecture
SNMP	Simple Network Management Protocol
SONET	Synchronous Optical Network
SPAG	Standards Promotion and Application Group
SPE	Synchronous Payload Envelope
SPX	Sequenced Packet Exchange
SQL	Structured Query Language
SRAM	Static RAM
SRPI	Server Requester Programming Interface
SS7	Signaling System 7
SSL	Secure Sockets Layer
STDM	Statistical Time Division Multiplexing
STM	Synchronous Transport Module
STS	Synchronous Transport Signal
SVC	Switched Virtual Circuit
Sysop	Systems Operator
-T-	
TA	Terminal Adapter
TAC	Terminal Access Controller
TCP	Transmission Control Protcol
TCP/IP	Transmission Control Protocol/ Internet Protocol
TDM	Time-Division Multiplexor
TE1	Terminal Equipment Type 1
TE2	Terminal Equipment Type 2
Telex	Teleprinter Exchange
TIFF	Tagged Image File Format
TLI	Transport Layer Interface
TNX	Teletypewriter Exchange Service
TP0	OSI Transport Protocol Class 0

TP4	OSI Transport Protocol Class 4
TSA	Target Server Agent
TSR	Terminate and Stay Resident program
TTF	TrueType fonts
TTL	Time to Live
TTS	Transaction Tracking System
TWX	Teletypewriter Exchange Service
-U-	
UA	User Agent
UDP	User Datagram Protocol
UMA	Upper Memory Area
UMBs	Upper Memory Blocks
UNC	Universal Naming Convention
UPS	Uninterruptible Power Supply
URL	Uniform Resource Locator
UUCP	UNIX-to-UNIX Copy Program
-V-	
VBR	Variable Bit Rate
VCI	Virtual Connection Identifier
VDM	Virtual DOS Machine
Veronica	Very Easy Rodent Oriented Net-wide Index to Computerized Archives
VGA	Video Graphics Array
VLM	Virtual Loadable Module
VLSI	Very Large-Scale Integration
VM/CMS	Virtual Machine/Conversational Monitor System
VMM	Virtual Memory Manager
VNET	Virtual Network
VPI	Virtual Path Identifier
VPN	Virtual Private Network
VRAM	Video RAM
VRC	Vertical Redundancy Check
VRML	Virtual Reality Modeling Language

VSE/CICS	Virtual Storage Extended-Customer Information Control System
VT	Virtual Terminal
-W-	
WAIS	Wide Area Information Servers
WAN	Wide Area Network
WATS	Wide Area Telephone Service
WWW	World Wide Web
WYSIWYG	What You See is What You Get
-X-	
XDR	External Data Representation
XMS	Extended Memory
XNS	Xerox Network System
-Z-	
ZIP	Zone Information Protocol

S E L F S T U D Y

Index